BRIAN STAFFORD

THE
GREAT
WINDSHIPS

How Sailing Ships Made the Modern World

To order additional copies of this book, contact:
Xlibris
AU TFN: 1 800 844 927 (Toll Free inside Australia)
AU Local: 02 8310 8187 (+61 2 8310 8187 from outside Australia)
www.xlibris.com.au

ISBN:	Softcover	978-1-6698-8816-1
	Hardcover	978-1-6698-8814-7
	EBook	978-1-6698-8815-4

Library of Congress Control Number: 2022907694

Rev. date: 03/23/2023

CONTENTS

Foreword..XV

Chapter 1   How A Sailing Ship Works...1

Introduction..1
The Limitations on a Sailing Ship 1
Getting There and Back: Ocean Gyres 2
The Trade Winds 3
The Prevailing Westerlies 3
Currents..3
The First Voyages to the East 4
The Importance of the Tide...5
'Weatherliness'...5
    Measuring Weatherliness 5
Sailing into the Wind 6
    Tacking..6
    Wearing...6
The Rules of the Road 7
Hull Length and Speed..7
The Three-Masted Ship...8
The Fully Rigged Ship 8
The Masts 10
The Sails 10
'Standing' Rigging...11
'Running' Rigging..11
Crewing 11
Manoeuvring a Big Sailing Ship 12
Measuring Ship Size the Traditional Way 12
The Moorsom System..13
Wood, a Strategic Material 13
    In Europe 13
    In the Americas 14
The Transition to Iron and Steel...15

Chapter 2   From Caravel To Windjammer 16

    Achievements 16

    Environmental Efficiency 16

    Prehistory 17

    Mediterranean Beginnings 17

    The Open-Ocean Barrier 18

    Two Eras 19

    Galleys and Galleasses 19

    The Caravel 21

    The Carrack 23

    The Iberians versus Northern Europe: The Emergence of the Galleon 25

    The 'Race Built' Galleon 26

    The East Indiamen 28

    England versus the Netherlands 29

    The Dutch 'Fluyts' 29

    British East Indiamen 30

    Prototype Liners 32

    The 'Country Trade' 33

    EIC Denouement 34

    The French East Indiamen 34

    The Frigate 35

    A Many-Faceted Revolution 37

    The Abolition of the Slave Trade 37

    The Western Ocean Packets (the Liner Services) 37

    The Emergence of America as a Merchant Marine Power 38

    The Effects of the Peace 39

    The Clippers 40

        The Setting 40

    The Attributes 41

        Full Body 41

        Minimum 'Deadrise' 42

        Waterline Length 42

        Sharp Entry 42

        Concave Bow 43

        Champagne Glass Stern 43

        Straight Run and Minimal Sheer 43

    The End of the Clipper Era 44

    The Decline of the United States as a Merchant Maritime Power 44

    The Advent of Steam and Steel 44

    The Windjammers 45

Chapter 3   The Age of Exploration 47

    Introduction 47

    The Age of 'Discovery' 48

The Immensity of the Earth 48

Why Europe? 49

China and Zheng He 49

The European Era 52

The Politics of Expansion 53

Portugal 54

Bartholomeu Dias 55

Christopher Columbus 58

The Treaty of Tordesillas 61

Non-trade Goods: The Columbian Exchange 62

Vasco da Gama 63

Pedro Álvares Cabral 65

Ferdinand Magellan 66

Sir Francis Drake 70

Chapter 4   The Age of Exploitation 74

Introduction 74

Portugal 74

The 'Wharf between Two Seas' 75

The Rise of England and the Netherlands 76

Spain 76

The Spanish Armadas 77

England 80

The Joint-Stock Company 81

The Muscovy and Levant Companies 82

The British East India Company (EIC) 84

The Tea Trade 84

England versus the Netherlands 85

Marine Manpower 85

Porcelain: An Accidental Treasure 86

England's Balance of Payments Problem 86

The Decline of Portugal 87

The Jewel in the Crown 88

The Wind System Constraint 88

The English East Indiamen 88

The 'Shipping Interest' 89

Indolent Passages 89

Indian Influence on British Shipbuilding 90

The End of the Indiamen 90

Securing the Colony 91

The Importance of the 'Country Trade' 93

The Denouement 93

The Dutch East India Company (VOC) 94

Formation of the VOC 94

Fine Spice Monopoly 95

Financial Superiority 95

The Dutch East Indiamen (Fluyts) 96

Getting to the Spice Islands 96

Rise to Trading Power 97

Decline 98

A Similar Fate 98

The Spanish Empire 99

The Portuguese Empire 100

The Age of New Ideas 100

Chapter 5   **The Slave Trade** 102

Introduction 102

The West Indian and American Slave Trade 102

The Novel Products 103

Westward Movement 103

The 'Triangular Trade' 104

Beginnings 104

The First Leg 105

The Infamous 'Middle Passage' 105

The Third Leg 107

Feeding the Slaves: Another 'Triangular' Trade 107

The Impact of Banning the Trade 108

America's Involvement 108

The Role of Cotton 110

Alabama Fever 111

The 'Cotton Packets' 111

'Hard-Driving' 112

Chapter 6   **The Opium Clippers** 113

The Need for Speed 113

Cutters: The Predecessors 113

Schooners, Brigs, and Luggers 114

Britain's Manpower Problem 114

The Anglo-American War and the Baltimore Clippers 115

The Basis of the Opium Trade 116

The Risks of the Trade 116

Britain's Trade Deficit 118

The Opium Wars 120

The Opium Clipper Fleet 121

The Prominent Opium Runners 123

Jardine Matheson & Co. 123

Dent & Co. 125

Russell & Company 125

The Denouement...127

Influence on Clipper Design 128

Chapter 7   The Western Ocean Packets 129

Introduction...129

The 'Liner' Service 130

The Beginnings 130

Impact of Competition...132

Nathaniel Palmer and the Dramatic Line 133

The Eastward and Westward Courses 135

The Packet Captains and Crew 135

Feeder Services...136

The Erie Canal...136

Casualties...138

Famine Creates Emigrant Back-Freight..138

Liberal Revolutions in Europe..140

Emigrant Numbers 141

Abysmal Conditions...141

Regulation Fails 141

Fire Hazard..142

Repeal of the Corn Laws..142

Steam and Steel Spoil the Party...143

The End for the Western Ocean Packets 143

Influence on Clipper Design 144

Chapter 8   The Rise of the Clipper Ships 145

Introduction...145

The Agents of Change..146

A Transatlantic Trade Boom 147

The Designers and the Builders..147

The Fastest Sailing Ships..148

The Transition from Packet to Clipper 151

The Flat-Bottom Revolution 152

John W. Griffiths..152

Profitability..153

The Navigation Acts and the Tea Trade...154

The Californian Gold Rush 155

Designer Response..156

Samuel Hartt Pook..156

Donald McKay...158

The Largest Clipper..159

The Limit of Wooden Construction...160

Matthew Maury, Scientific Sailor 161

Eleanor Creesy, Maury, and Flying Cloud 162

The Quest for Speed 163

The Australian Gold Rush 164

Extending the Boom 165

'Great Circle' Routes 165

The Dominance of the American Wooden Clipper 165

Clipper Building Boom 167

Chapter 9   The Decline of the Clipper Ships 169

The Glut and Depression 169

A Last Hurrah 170

Crossing the United States and the Suez Canal 171

A Sad End: The Guano and Coolie Trades 172

Vale Clipper Americana 174

The Rise of the English Tea Clippers 176

Iron and Steel Replace Wood 177

Problems with Iron and Steel Construction 179

The Great Tea Race 180

America versus Great Britain 182

Brevity and Romance 184

Chapter 10 Steam and Steel—Creative Destruction 185

The Steam Revolution—a Simple Process 185

'Creative Destruction' 186

The Development of the Marine Steam Engine 187

A Symbiotic Relationship—for a Time 188

Steel and Sail 189

The Impact of Explosive Shells 189

Corrosion 190

Biofouling 190

The Rise of Iron and Steel 191

Advances in Boiler Pressure 191

The 'Triple Expansion' Marine Steam Engine 193

Steam Turbines 194

The Transition to Metal Construction 194

The Inevitable Symbiosis—Steam and Steel 195

Marine Diesel Power 197

A Secondary Symbiosis—Steel and Sail 197

Chapter 11 The Windjammers—A New Era 198

American Dominance 198

America Abandons the Sea 199

The Big Schooners 200

From Wood to Iron and Steel...202

Sailing Ships: From Wood through Iron to Steel...204

Sail versus Steam...205

The Crossover...207

Great Britain Reasserts Itself—the Age of Steel and Sail.....................................208

Double the Carrying Capacity...208

Dedicated Freighters..210

Creative Ferment...210

America's Mercantile Decline..211

The Limits of Steam Navigation..212

The 'White Gold Rush'—Chilean Nitrate Deposits..212

Copper Ore..213

The Dangers of the Nitrate and Coal Trades...213

Early British Dominance...213

Other Markets..214

The Windjammer Rigs..214

Chapter 12 The Windjammers—Zenith and Decline......................................216

The Seven Five-Masters...216

Their Place in History..217

The Rise of the Four-Masted Barque...218

Europe's Dominance...224

Glasgow Windjammer Central..224

Impact of French Subsidies..226

The Golden Age of the Windjammer...227

The Flying 'P' Line..228

Great Britain's Dominance...229

The New Kids on the Block..229

  Germany..229

  France...231

The Decline of the Nitrate Trade..233

Gustav Erikson..234

The Twilight of the Windjammers...235

Chapter 13 The Future..238

Celebration..238

A Revival of Merchant Sail?...238

What Really Led to the Demise of Sail?..241

Conclusion...243

Selected Bibliography..245

Index...249

LIST OF ILLUSTRATIONS

The Great Four-masted Barque Windjammer *Moshulu* xvii

Global Ocean Gyres 2

The Sail Plan of a Fully-rigged Ship 9

Seventeenth-century Galleass 20

Caravela Lateena 21

The Gokstadskipet: Strong, Seaworthy, and Beautiful 22

Replica of Magellan's Carrack *Victoria*, the First Ship to Sail Around the World 24

The Great Spanish Freighters: A Replica of the Spanish Galleon *Andalusia* 25

Drake's *Golden Hind*: A Race-built Galleon 27

Instruments of Power: a Fleet of British East Indiamen at Sea 31

A New Generation: the Blackwall Frigate *Kent* 36

Donald McKay's Magnificent Medium Clipper *Flying Cloud* 41

The Biggest Sailing Ship Ever Built: The Windjammer *Preussen II* 45

Zheng He and his Flagship 50

Voyages of the Yongle Emperor's Great Admiral Zheng He 51

Prince Henry the Navigator 54

João I (King John I of Portugal) 54

Bartholomeu Dias (1450–1500) 56

Christopher Columbus (1451-1506) 58

Vasco da Gama (1469-1504) 63

Ferdinand Magellan (1480-1521) 67

The First Vessel to Sail Around the World: Replica of Magellan's Ship *Victoria* 69

Sir Francis Drake (c.1540-1596) 71

The Second (and First English) Ship to Circumnavigate the World: Sir Francis Drake's *Golden Hind* 72

King Philip II of Spain (1527-1598) 78

A Replica of the Spanish Galleon *Andalusia* 79

Queen Elizabeth I of England (1533-1603) 80

Robert Clive (1725-1774) 91

Replica of the Ill-fated VOC Flagship *Batavia* 97

The Infamous Triangular Trade 105

Stowage of the British Slave Ship *Brookes* under the Regulated Slave Trade 1788 106

The Later American Slave Ship *Wanderer* 109

Pride of Baltimore II – a Replica of the Original Baltimore Clipper Ship 115

An East Indian Proa or Prahu 117

A Malay Lorcha 117

Small Fast Ships: the Barque Opium Runner *Sylph* 118

The 'Clipper-brig' Opium Runner *Lanrick* 122

William Jardine (1784-1843) 124

James Matheson (1796-1878) 124

Sir Francis Baring (1740-1810) 125

Samuel Russell (1789-1862) 126

Warren Delano (1809-1898) 127

Superior—An Early (1822) Black Ball Line Packet 131

The Later (1851) and Largest Black Ball Line Packet Ship *Great Western* 133

Nathaniel Palmer (1799-1877) 134

A Vital Artery—the Erie Canal 137

Famished Children, West Cork 1847 139

Irish Immigrants Embarking for America 139

Emigration to the USA: 1820-1880 140

Sovereign of the Seas—The Fastest Ever Merchant Sailing Ship 149

Donald McKay's Transatlantic Record Holder *Lightning* 150

The Mighty Clipper *James Baines* 151

John W. Griffiths (1809-1882) 152

San Francisco in 1851 During the Gold Rush 155

Samuel Hartt Pook (1827-1901) 157

Clipper Ship Designer Extraordinaire: Donald McKay (1810-1880) 158

Donald McKay's Biggest Clipper: *Great Republic* 159

Matthew Maury (1806-1873) 161

Donald McKay's Beautiful Clipper: *Flying Cloud* 163

American Clipper Construction: 1845-1857 (GRT OM) 167

James Baines (1822-1889) 171

The Infamous Islas Chinchas 173

The Big but Ill-fated British Wooden Clipper *Schomberg*... 175

Taeping and *Ariel* Battle it out in the Great Tea Race (1866) 180

A Beautiful End to the Line: *Cutty Sark*... 181

American vs. British Clipper Tonnages Built: 1845-1870 (GRT) 182

The First Practical Steamboat: *Charlotte Dundas*.. 187

Cutaway View of a Triple-expansion Steam Engine 193

All Vessels Constructed in Great Britain by Material: 1850-1908 (000's net tons).............. 195

Glasgow About 1860 196

Ship Construction in the USA; Sail and Steam: 1850-1915 (Gross Tons) 198

American Imports and Exports; US Ships vs. Foreign Ships: 1840-1915 ($M) 199

The Seven-masted Schooner *Thomas W. Lawson*.. 201

Steamship Construction in Great Britain by Material: 1850–1908 (000's net tons) 203

Sailing Ship Construction by Material in Great Britain: 1850-1908 (000's net tons) 204

World Trade: Sail vs. Steam/Motor Vessels: 1820-1914 (net tons M)................................. 205

Great Britain; Sailing vs. Steamships Built and First Registered: 1850-1914 (000's net tons)............... 206

Great Britain; Sailing vs. Steamships Built and First Registered: 1850-1914 (000's net tons 10-year m.a.) 207

A Typical Windjammer: the *Chile* Trading in the South Pacific... 209

The *Preussen II*—the Largest Sailing Ship Ever Built.. 217

The Seven Five-masted Windjammers 218

Four-masted Vessels Built 1874–1931 219

Selected Great Four-masted Barque Windjammer Merchant Sailing Ships 220

The *Falls of Clyde*... 221

The Great *Herzogin Cecile*... 222

The Long-lived *Pamir* 223

Windjammer Construction by Location: 1874-1914 (GRT) 225

Carl Ferdinand Laeisz (1853-1900)... 228

Antoine-Dominique Bordes (1815-1883)... 232

The Giant Windjammer *France* 233

Gustav Erikson (1872-1947).. 234

Norsepower Rotor Sails Fitted to the Tanker *Maersk Pelican* 239

The *Ceiba*—A Modern Approach to Traditional Merchant Sail 240

The *Ultramax 2030* 65K DWT Bulk Carrier 242

FOREWORD

Imagine it is 1938. You are standing on Point Spencer at the mouth of the Spencer Gulf on the southern coast of Australia. The weather is fine, with a strong breeze fetching up from the south. Over the horizon, a tiny white rectangle appears, a tall obelisk of pale canvas, a panoply of sails emerging tier by tier. Below the sails, you see a small dark rectangle. Slowly, it reveals itself to be the sturdy riveted steel hull of a big four-masted barque.

The vessel is the great 'windjammer' *Moshulu*, operated by the Finnish sailor and shipowner, Gustaf Erikson. She has sailed all the way from London to load almost 5,000 tons of grain from the wheat fields of South Australia at Port Lincoln, further up the gulf. In ten days' time, she will make the ninety-one-day return voyage to Great Britain.

From her deck to the top of her mainmast, *Moshulu* measures 185 feet, equal to thirteen London double-decker buses stacked one on top of another. She is six cricket pitches long. Empty, she displaces (weighs) 1,700 tons, but her hold, which makes up most of the ship, can accommodate 5,300 tons of cargo, a ratio of over 3:1.

On board *Moshulu* on this particular voyage is apprentice seaman Eric Newby. He will later immortalise the barque in his 1956 book *The Last Grain Race*.

Moshulu's trip to Australia covered over 13,000 nautical miles (around 21,000 kilometres) of wild, open, and trackless ocean. Except for the creaking of spars and the rush of water away from her brave bow, her journey from London has been silent. She has used only wind and ocean currents, the muscle and sinew of hardy souls that man her, and the seamanship of her master and mate.

Once her hull is packed with jute sacks of golden grain, she will retrace her path to the mouth of the gulf before facing the Roaring Forties. The 'ocean highway' that brought her here will push her further south on a 'great circle' path down to the fearsome fifty-plus latitudes. There she will sail much of the more than 15,000-nautical-mile track home.

On the way, she must round Cape Horn—the only milestone of her homeward journey—and traverse the fearsome maelstrom between South America and Antarctica. Cape Horn is a choke point pressured by the perpetual westerly winds that characterise the very south of the globe. An enormous volume of water is forced into a space only 400 miles wide, causing mountainous seas driven by the unabating wind. Sometimes, the situation is exacerbated by turbulent cyclones bulleting down off the Andes. Once through this dreadful gateway to another ocean, *Moshulu* will enjoy a relatively easy run for the remaining 5,000 miles of her voyage north up the Atlantic.

By the time she docks in Liverpool, she will have travelled over 28,000 nautical miles, considerably more than the circumference of the globe. She will also have brought back enough food to sustain thousands of people for many months. Other than the provisions for her crew and minor maintenance stores, she will have consumed nothing.

Certainly no non-renewable resources.

—⁓⁓—

Built by William Hamilton & Co. in Glasgow in 1904 for the nitrate trade, *Moshulu* entered the great age of merchant sail in its twilight years. Her original name was *Kurt* after the principal of Siemers & Co., a Hamburg shipping company.

Kurt just happened to be in a United States port when it entered the First World War in April 1917. She was commandeered and given the American Indian name *Moshulu*, reputedly by the wife of Woodrow Wilson, the US president at the time. After the war, she was bought for a song and carried timber from the US west coast to Australia. By 1935, having passed through many hands, she had been acquired by Gustav Erikson, and it was under his flag that she made this voyage to Australia. A native of the Åland Islands off Sweden, Erikson had crewed or managed sailing ships all his life. He loved sail and was determined to keep the great windjammers working.

In 1940, *Moshulu* was seized by the German government. But her sailing days were over, and she would be used mainly as a storage hulk until she was rescued by an American dining chain and rerigged.

Today, she is a floating restaurant at Penn's Landing in the US state of Philadelphia.

With no space required for engines or fuel, the barque is an example of perhaps the most efficient transport device ever conceived by humans. She is the result of centuries of continuous development, from the fragile caravels that first ventured out through the Straits of Gibraltar to the great windjammers that no distance or sea condition on earth could daunt.

Countless sailing ships have been turned into museums, youth hostels, training vessels, and restaurants over the years. No national celebration is complete without a parade of tall ships. Modern society finds romance in these vessels and reveres them. Unconsciously, perhaps, we pay homage to their gallant history and the contribution they made to the modern age. Form has followed function to create an object of beauty and environmental efficiency. This book is an attempt to trace their development— and how world history moulded that process over half a millennium.

The Great Four-masted Barque Windjammer *Moshulu*

Source: From an original oil painting by Robert Carter OAM, Moshulu in the South East Trades

They mark our passage as a race of men,
Earth will not see such ships as these again.

—John Masefield

1
CHAPTER

How A Sailing Ship Works

Introduction

To better understand the following chapters in this book, a basic explanation of some concepts integral to sailing ship operation and development might be helpful—for example, how they are measured, navigated, and rigged; their strengths and limitations; and a little about the defining form, what's known as the 'fully rigged' ship. If the reader is more interested in the story of the great windships, then this chapter can be ignored or perhaps returned to later.

Most historians believe that hand paddling—possibly while lying or sitting on a log—was the first means we adopted to move across the water. Our relationship with wood and water has evolved over millennia, to the point where it might be said to have entered our DNA. In time, iron, then steel (and later aluminium and various forms of advanced plastic) surpassed the use of wood. Wood has largely disappeared from the merchant marine, though our affinity with the material remains in the construction and restoration of wooden vessels for recreational and craft purposes.

The Limitations on a Sailing Ship

The greater part of the history of ships has been written by 'square-rigged' vessels—those with 'square' sails set at right angles to the hull. They moved directly *before* the wind (i.e. with the wind blowing from behind) or up to around right angles *across* it. When they were blown directly before the wind, the sails on the foremast would be somewhat blanketed by those on the mainmast.

The *fastest* way for any vessel to sail is in fact on a broad 'reach'. Here, the broadest area of sail on all masts and stays is presented to the wind. The triangular fore-and-aft sails (rigged along the centre line of the hull) can also be pushed. As well, they provide power from the pressure differential between the two surfaces of the sail. The effectiveness of fore-and-aft sails is increased the more the wind comes on to the side of the vessel, reducing the extent to which they are blanketed by the square sails.

The ship will 'heel' (lean over) the further the wind comes 'abeam' (towards the side of the ship) where it can exert pressure on a larger sail area.

The classic form of the sailing ship is the three-masted 'fully rigged' ship with a large wardrobe of both square and fore-and-aft sails. It is the square sails, however, that do the heavy lifting.

Getting There and Back: Ocean Gyres

The Italian explorer Christopher Columbus noted that large bodies of water generally have circular ocean currents and accompanying wind systems. They are caused by several forces but are mainly due to the 'Coriolis effect', which is a product of the earth's rotation. Columbus realised that it was possible to use this combination of wind and currents to return to the point at which the voyage began in a ship that only moved effectively before the wind. These systems are called ocean 'gyres', and they move in a clockwise direction in the northern hemisphere and an anticlockwise direction in the southern. They are separated by what's known as the 'tropical zone'.

When Columbus left Spain, he sailed south-west to pick up the southern side of the North Atlantic gyre, which eventually took him to the West Indies. He used the other side of the gyre to come home, carried north by the powerful Gulf Stream, and east by the permanent westerlies that make up the top of the same gyre.

Similarly, when the Portuguese explorer Bartolomeu Dias set out for the East Indies, he sailed south until he picked up the counter-rotating South Atlantic gyre, which swept him across the Atlantic almost to the coast of South America before taking him south. He was then able to pick up the permanent westerlies of the bottom of the gyre to take him east towards the Cape of Good Hope. He used the wind and current (the Benguela) of the eastern side of the gyre to come home.

Global Ocean Gyres

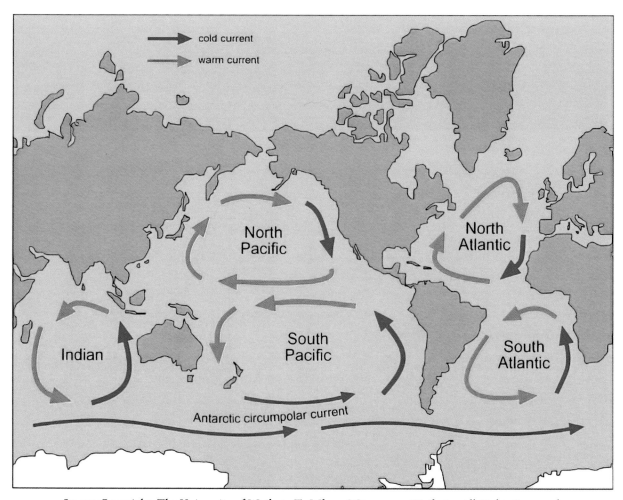

Source Copyright: The University of Waikato Te Whare Wānanga o Waikato. All Rights Reserved.

The Trade Winds

Ocean gyres do not extend into the earth's tropical zone. Here the sailor must depend on what became known as 'trade winds'. These seasonal systems exist on each side of the tropical 'dead' zone, also known as the 'horse' latitudes. (If ships carrying horses were delayed in these 'doldrums', they would run out of fresh water and have to throw the beasts overboard.)

The south-west monsoon trade winds blow from May to September and were used by Arab traders long before the arrival of Europeans. Once they had rounded the Cape of Good Hope, early European explorers would sail north up the east coast of Africa and through the Mozambique Channel between the African coast and the island of Madagascar. Once through the channel, they could catch the south-west 'trades' as they came to be known, blowing them in a north-easterly direction towards India.

After an interval of light airs either side of and during October, the monsoon winds then conveniently reverse and, from November to March, blow from the north-east, driving the vessels back towards Africa. This is an oversimplification. Monsoon winds were convenient but also notoriously unreliable. They always arrive, but the time of their arrival and departure can vary considerably from year to year.

The Prevailing Westerlies

In the areas of the globe between thirty degrees and sixty degrees north and south of the equator, winds tend to blow from the west. The phenomenon is related to the 'intertropical convergence' where hot air in tropical regions rises and moves towards the poles. Due to the Coriolis effect caused by the counterclockwise rotation of the earth, these air movements become westerly winds.

Westerlies have proved especially beneficial to global navigation in the southern hemisphere, where they blow continuously around the globe, unimpeded by land. They create what is known as the 'Antarctic circumpolar current', providing a highway that sailing ships could move in and out of, depending on their destination. The Antarctic circumpolar current also enables what are known as 'great circle' routes.

Because the earth is a flattened sphere, the further south a ship ventures, the shorter the voyage will be between two points at lower latitudes. There are dangers, however. The winds become stronger the further south you go. There is also the ever-present risk of colliding with icebergs. Imagine, if you can, a pitch-black night with freezing rain bucketing down and a howling gale whipping up huge seas. A big windjammer is rolling and bowling along at fifteen knots with nothing but the sharp eyes of the lookout and the quick action of the steersman between it and disaster. To a 'landlubber', this is a nightmarish scenario, but the clippers and the windjammers endured it on every voyage along what became known as the 'clipper' route.

Currents

Ocean currents were exploited by early navigators wherever they were favourable. When unfavourable, they were avoided. But even favourable currents could be a hazard. If a sailing ship riding the north-flowing current up the west coast of South America was deprived of wind opposite its destination, it could be carried miles past. The only option may be sailing a giant circle to escape the current to where it can sail south again and rejoin the current below its destination, hoping for better fortune on the second approach.

Ships returning from India would ride the warm Agulhas current down the east coast of Africa. It forms the south-flowing westerly side of the Indian Ocean gyre. The cold Benguela current, on the other hand, forms the eastern side of the South Atlantic gyre up the other side of Africa. It is a pair to the cold Humboldt current which flows up the west coast of South America and makes up the easterly side of the Pacific Ocean gyre. This current was used by the windjammers engaged in the nitrate and guano trades.

The 'Gulf Stream' is one of the world's most powerful currents. It forms the westerly and northern sides of the North Atlantic gyre. It was very useful to the first navigators visiting South America because it took them back to Europe. It also has a benign influence on the weather of the United Kingdom. It splits at its easterly extremity with some of its warm water moving down the easterly side of the gyre and some flowing north up the western side of the British Isles. The Western Ocean packets would use the system when delivering cotton from America into the port of Liverpool. ('Packet' ships were vessels that originally carried royal and other mail 'packets' between England, Ireland, and the continent and later to America, from where they evolved to carry cargo.)

The First Voyages to the East

The earliest regular forays to the east were made in Portuguese carracks, or 'naus'. These were slow, solidly built freighters with copious hulls that sailed in annual armadas of from five to fifteen vessels. Their departure date was determined by the monsoon winds in the faraway Indian Ocean. Vessels left Portugal from February to April riding the South Atlantic gyre to arrive off the Cape of Good Hope around June or July. They would then proceed up the east coast of Africa, avoiding the vicious south-flowing Agulhas current, through the Mozambique Channel to Mombasa or Malindi, where they would take onboard provisions. From there, south-west monsoon winds would push the fleet across the Indian Ocean to ports on the west coast of India.

On the return journey, the ships would depart India under the influence of the north-east monsoon in January and have a somewhat shorter route home. Once through the Mozambique Channel, they could avail themselves of the south-flowing Agulhas current and, having rounded the Cape of Good Hope, use the cold north-flowing Benguela current—the other side of the South Atlantic Gyre—to carry them north around the hump of West Africa.

The fleet would typically arrive back in Lisbon between June and August, after the critical departure time of the next fleet. Faster ships, probably caravels (slim-hulled vessels with a mainly fore-and-aft rig) would be sent ahead to deliver news of the success or failure of the previous year's fleet and any relevant intelligence on market and political conditions in the east.

Under the Treaty of Tordesillas of 1496, sanctioned by Pope Julius II, the Portuguese acquired the right to explore the eastern half of the world. They were extremely successful navigators and, for a century, made the absolute most of it. Their knowledge and expertise, sometimes accidentally acquired, allowed them to travel past India and the Spice Islands, and on to China, Korea, and Japan.

Making the return voyages successfully was a complex business, and the Portuguese confided detailed information on how to do it to their so-called rutters. These carefully compiled navigational instructions showed the way to immense riches in Oriental merchandise trading. As intellectual property, the rutters were almost priceless—the equivalent to atomic secrets in the twentieth century. The northern Europeans, especially the Dutch and the English, stole these secrets. The theft would enable them to eventually dominate the eastern oceans.

The Importance of the Tide

There's an old saying we inherited from the early days of sailing ships—'Time and tide wait for no man'. Sailing ships were carried out of port on an ebbing (outgoing) tide, hoping that it would convey them clear of land and into an offshore breeze. If there was no wind, the ship would have to drop anchor 'in the offing' to resist the flowing (incoming) tide that would otherwise carry them back to land. They would then have to hope for an offshore breeze to carry them on their way. It was not uncommon for ships to spend days awaiting a favourable wind.

Similarly, they would try to enter port on a flowing tide, although an onshore breeze might enable them to 'stem the tide'. Sailing ships wasted a lot of time entering and leaving port, but the introduction of steam engines mounted in powerful tugs helped the process. Steamboats made sailing ships more efficient, especially in the days before they could confront the oceanic conditions in which sailing vessels revelled.

'Weatherliness'

Ships were 'blown' around the globe before prevailing winds and carried along on favourable currents, but they could not generally make progress *into* the wind. They were limited by the 'square' nature of the rig where the sails are rectangular and set on 'yards' (horizontal beams) that are mounted at right angles to the centre line of the ship. Those yards could be swung around to some extent to enable the vessel to sail across, instead of directly before, the wind. To be able to make up to windward (a characteristic known as 'weatherliness'), the yards had to be swung so the 'weather' ends of the yards (that half of the yards on the windward side) 'pointed' as far forward as possible towards the direction of the wind. This would allow the bow, in turn, to point as close as possible to the wind. There was, however, a limitation to the yards' travel in this direction: the 'lee shrouds', the fixed lines supporting the mast on the other ('leeward') side of the ship.

Measuring Weatherliness

Typically, a ship could be helmed up to within eighty or ninety degrees of the wind, but at this point of sailing, it is simply 'reaching' across the wind. In other words, it is not making any progress to windward. It would be losing ground because there is a second aspect to weatherliness known as 'leeway'. Wind blowing at any angle other than directly behind a vessel is, as well as propelling it forward, also pushing it to some extent sideways.

For a vessel sailing at around eighty degrees of the eye of the wind, to make progress into the direction of the wind would have to be being pushed sideways by less than ten degrees. It is the combination of these two characteristics—the ability to 'point' up into the wind combined with the extent to which it makes leeway—that constitutes 'weatherliness'. If a vessel could 'make up' to within, say, seventy degrees of the wind and lose only ten degrees to leeway, it would be making ten degrees to windward.

Sailing into the Wind

A square-rigged ship is designed to sail predominantly before the wind, but there will inevitably be circumstances when it will need to try to make progress to windward, adopting a zigzag course. Or it may need to change the orientation of the ship to the wind for other reasons, such as wind changes or weather conditions. Two manoeuvres are available: 'tacking' or 'wearing' ship.

Tacking

'Tacking' is the zigzag course a sailing vessel adopts to make progress into the wind. If a square-rigged ship succeeds in making up to 80 degrees of the wind, then tacking will take the bow through 160 degrees to settle at the same angle on the other tack. This achievement can be compared to fore-and-aft rigs that were used on small boats at the time and are the standard rig on modern yachts. They can sail easily at 45 degrees to the wind swing through only 90 degrees in a tack and lose less to leeway due to the despatch with which the manoeuvre can be performed. (But fore-and-aft rigs lose their advantage downwind and for this reason have traditionally been supplemented by 'spinnakers' or large-reaching sails which are 'gybed' downwind.)

For a square-rigged vessel, the most expeditious way (and the one that loses the least to leeway) is tacking, when the bow of the vessel is taken through the 'eye' (direction) of the wind until it presents on the other side of the ship. To tack the ship, enough speed must be gained to carry the bows through the eye of the wind when it will be receiving no power from the sails. Failure to do so would put the ship 'in irons', i.e. pointing directly into the wind but unable to get the sails to fill on the other (or either) tack. The ship would then be pushed backwards, losing the ground it had been trying to make up to windward.

There were various strategies an officer in charge could employ to avoid this situation (such as maximising speed immediately prior to the manoeuvre), but they may not be available to him due to ship design (e.g. bluff bows) or to wind and sea conditions such as light airs, adverse tide, and heavy seas. Conversely, some well-designed vessels (such as crack Royal Navy frigates) were known, in the right conditions, to be able to tack successfully in their own length.

Wearing

The alternative to tacking is a manoeuvre known as 'wearing', whereby the stern (as opposed to the bow) of the ship is taken through the eye of the wind. To achieve this, the bow must be allowed to 'fall off' the breeze until the stern presents to the wind. Then assisted by some of the sails, the bow of the ship travels through 200 degrees (if it is making 80 degrees to the wind) before it again presents to the wind, but on the other side of the ship.

The disadvantage in 'wearing ship' is the distance from windward lost during the manoeuvre. For some of the time, the ship would be moving before the wind (in the opposite direction to which it is trying to make progress), and the distance travelled to complete the manoeuvre could be up to four times the vessel's length. The larger square sails had to be 'feathered' to avoid them preventing the stern from passing through the eye of the wind. However, wearing ship was generally a less-fraught manoeuvre than tacking and was easier on the rigging.

The Rules of the Road

The International Regulations for the Prevention of Collisions at Sea make up a hefty volume, but for our purposes, it is sufficient to provide a general overview. A ship has two sides: a 'port' or left-hand side (identified by a red light) and a 'starboard' or right-hand side (identified by a green light). Additionally, when underway, a ship can have a 'weather' side, the side from which the wind is coming, and a 'leeward' side, which is sheltered from the wind. Wind from directly in front of a ship is called a headwind, and from directly behind, a following wind.

If a ship is sailing with the wind over the starboard side, it is said to be on the 'starboard tack'. If the wind is coming over the port side of the ship, it is said to be on the 'port tack'. If two sailing ships are approaching each other on opposite tacks, the ship with the wind over the starboard side has the right to 'stand on', that is, keep its course and not alter its speed. If two ships are approaching each other on the same tack (say, with both having the wind on their starboard side) and there is a danger of collision, it is the ship 'hardest' on the wind (sailing closest to the direction of the wind) that has the right to 'stand on'.

A sailing ship has no brakes, and while it can try to reduce sail to slow down, that takes time. Thus, it is more vulnerable to collision than a powered ship, which can put its propellers astern and slow down considerably. Since the days of steam power, therefore, it has been generally accepted that a ship under power gives way to a vessel under sail. This rule of navigation did not, however, prevent many collisions, especially in confined waters such as the English Channel. Many a sailing ship, including the largest ever built, came to grief because of the failure of steamer captains (especially cross-channel ferries) steering at right angles to big ocean-going sailing ships, to accurately estimate their speed.

Hull Length and Speed

The French were among the first to realise that there was a relationship between the waterline length of a vessel and speed and that there was a theoretical limit to the speed of a displacement hull through the water. Put simply, the longer the hull, the faster it could be made to go. As a displacement hull moves through the water, it creates two waves: one at the bow and one at the stern. There is a natural law that states that the speed of a series of waves in knots (nautical miles per hour) equals 1.34 times the square root of their wavelength (the distance between the two waves in feet). The waves created by a displacement hull occur at each end of its waterline length. The longer the distance between them, the faster that hull can be made to go. Longer hulls could be made to go faster, but a large sailing vessel would rarely reach its maximum. For example, a hull two hundred feet long would have a maximum hull speed of $1.34 \times 14.142 = 19$ knots, the equivalent of 35 kilometres per hour. The great wooden medium clippers of the mid-nineteenth century would come closest sailing ships have ever come to attaining their maximum hull speed, but it would only be achieved by being driven hard and in exceptional sea and wind conditions.

The Three-Masted Ship

With its two square-rigged masts and one fore-and-aft-rigged mast on the stern, the three-masted ship of the type developed in Europe in the fifteenth century was one of the most significant technological advances in the history of humanity. Coupled with the knowledge of wind and current systems, a sailing ship could now take navigators to anywhere on the almost three-quarters of the globe covered by saltwater. Not only could the vessel carry trade goods and all the fresh water and food required to sustain its crew on its outward voyage, it could also store enough cargo on its return journey to more than adequately reward its promoters. The only fuel it required was sustenance for the crew. All else—wind, current, and the earth's magnetism—were provided free by the natural world.

As the volume of cross-Mediterranean trade grew, so, necessarily, did the size and configuration of the ships employed to carry it. The Arab dhow, used so extensively on the Nile River, was well-suited to sailing with the wind on the beam (side) of the vessel but less successful when the wind was astern. A square sail is the most efficient and stable in this situation. As the size of ships increased, any concomitant increase in the size of a single square sail placed undue stress on the keel of the vessel. Given that the mast was 'stayed' (supported) by ropes tied to the gunwales (sides) of the vessel, too big a mast could cause the planking to open up with disastrous consequences. At some point, it was decided to divide the sail area between two or, better still, three masts.

There was another advantage in having three masts. Besides spreading the pressure applied to the keel, three masts increased manoeuvrability. Leverage could be applied to either end of the vessel, and it would pivot around the mast in the middle. A further advantage was that two types of sail—square and fore-and-aft sails—could be carried on a single vessel. The square sail gave the vessel speed and stability before the wind and was safer than an all-lateen (fore-and-aft sails) rig on that point of sailing. The fore-and-aft sails, meanwhile, enabled the ship to sail both across and into the wind.

Sailing across the wind required another adaptation. The 'boom' on which the square sail was carried had to be able to pivot around the mast rather than be fixed at right angles to the ship's longitudinal axis. Unlike the fore-and-aft 'lateen' sail, the boom carrying the square sail was attached forward of the mast. As the ships and the sails got bigger, it was also advantageous to divide these square sails into sections (mainsail, topsail, upper topsail, and so forth) to provide flexibility in a variety of wind conditions. This transformation would eventually be applied to the lateen sails when they would be transformed into headsails, staysails (mounted between the masts), and a jigger, or spanker sail, on the after mast.

The Fully Rigged Ship

The 'fully rigged' ship is a progression from the race-built galleon whereby the lateen sails on the after masts were swapped from the stern of the ship on a galleon to the bow. Multiple fore-and-aft triangular sails were rigged on a more elaborate bowsprit that, on the galleon, had carried one or two small square 'sprit' sails. These square sails were then added to the mizzen mast, sometimes with the lateen sail still in place. This lateen sail would eventually morph into the 'jigger' sail, which is just the after part of the original lateen sail with its lower edge fixed to a boom. The bowsprit in time became more substantial as the number of headsails increased. New standing rigging structures (in the form of the 'martingale' and the 'dolphin striker') were required to brace against the bowsprit to withstand the increased upward force placed upon it by the forestays. The martingale is an iron rod fixed from the end of the bowsprit to a point on the ship's bow near the waterline. The dolphin striker is a rod fixed at right angles to the underneath of the bowsprit through the end of which the martingale is run in such a way that the bowsprit functions as a beam.

The Sail Plan of a Fully-rigged Ship

1: flying jib, 2: outer jib, 3: inner jib, 4: jib, 5: fore skysail, 6: fore royal, 7: fore topgallant sail, 8: fore upper topsail, 9: fore lower topsail, 10: foresail, 11: main royal staysail, 12: main topgallant staysail, 13: main topmast staysail, 14: main skysail, 15: main royal, 16: main topgallant sail, 17: main upper topsail, 18: main lower topsail, 19: mainsail, 20: mizzen skysail, 21: mizzen royal, 22: mizzen topgallant sail, 23: mizzen upper topsail, 24: mizzen lower topsail, 25: crossjack, 26: spanker or jigger. Source: Author research

As opposed to the independently stayed masts in a lateen rig, on a fully rigged ship, the whole standing rigging (wires or ropes that don't move during the normal operation of the ship) are highly interdependent. The diagonal bracing of the mast, from deck level immediately behind the foremast, for example, to the crosstrees on the mainmast behind it, also opened up opportunities to rig more fore-and-aft sails. This innovation would enhance the ship's manoeuvrability, its ability to make to windward, and its speed when the wind was on or aft of the beam. (Wind on the beam of a ship is coming at right angles to the ship's direction. Anywhere aft of the beam, but not directly behind the ship, are the fastest points of sailing.)

The process was a gradual one. For example, illustrations of some of the later galleons show square sails on the mizzen mast, above the attachment point for the lateen sail. An illustration of a replica Dutch East Indiaman in Amsterdam shows the mizzen mast fully rigged with square sails with no lateen sail at all.

Fully developed, the fully rigged ship would dominate the latter part of the age of sail. Variations would occur subsequently in the form of the 'barque' (square-rigged on the two forward masts and fore-and-aft rigged on the mizzen) and 'barquentines' where the square sails were replaced by fore-and-aft, or 'schooner' sails, on the mainmast as well. These were responses to the needs of particular trades and the fact that, in times of rising labour costs, the ships needed fewer hands to man them. Generally speaking, the terms *brig* and *brigantine* are roughly the same principles applied to a (smaller) two-masted ship. The brig is square-rigged on both masts whereas the brigantine is square-rigged on the foremast and fore-and-aft rigged on the mainmast. (The term *brig* is said to have originated to describe the small, fast, and agile ships preferred by pirates, or 'brigands'.)

The complete fully rigged ship did not emerge until around the middle of the eighteenth century and was pushed along by England's bid for naval supremacy over its age-old rival, France. The French inherited a talent for naval design from their corsair days and, uninhibited by petty rules to prevent smuggling (as in England), were constantly building ships that were superior to British designs. When captured, they were often incorporated into the English fleet. The French, however, needed more than sheer speed to prevail, and the French navy could never equal the speed and accuracy of the English gunners.

The Masts

Vertically, each mast on a fully rigged ship was made up of several sections: the lower mast, the topmast, the topgallant mast, and (possibly) a royal mast. The mainmast, in the middle of the three, was the tallest and set the largest sails. The foremast was the next highest and the mizzen mast was the shortest.

All three masts generally 'crossed' (carried) four square 'yards' (horizontal beams) to which were attached (from bottom to top) a mainsail, a topsail, a topgallant sail, and a royal sail. The mizzen also carried a fore-and-aft sail called a 'spanker' (or jigger) on its trailing edge. The mizzen would generally not carry a mainsail (the lowest and largest sail) on its lower yard (called a cross-jack) because it would have been partly blanketed by the spanker. The yard, instead, was used to control the bottom edge of the mizzen topsail.

The Sails

As vessels and the standard sails got larger, it was customary to split the sails above the mainsail into two to make for easier handling. It also meant you needed less crew. Thus, instead of a topsail, there would be a lower and upper topsail and a lower and upper topgallant sail. Above the topgallant sails was the royal and, as masts got higher and more extreme rigs were introduced (as on clipper ships), possibly a skysail and, above that even, a moonraker.

There were generally three 'head' sails—fore-and-aft sails mounted forward (in front of) the foremast. From the outermost, they were the flying jib, then the outer jib, and then the inner jib. If there were four headsails, the innermost would be the fore topmast staysail. As demands for weatherliness increased, so more fore-and-aft sails were added between the masts. These were rigged on the stays supporting the masts (hence, 'staysails') and named according to their location. Those forward of the mainmast were called (from top to bottom) main royal staysail, main topgallant staysail, and main topmast staysail. Those between the main and the mizzen masts were the mizzen royal staysail, the mizzen topgallant staysail, and the mizzen topmast staysail. A standard fully rigged ship carried thirty sails in all: eighteen square and twelve fore-and-aft. This standard wardrobe could be supplemented by 'stunsails' that were rigged on extensions to the yards when conditions were favourable.

'Standing' Rigging

The rigging on a sailing ship can either be 'standing' or 'running'. Standing rigging is permanently fixed 'lines' (hemp rope and, later, steel wire) that support the masts. They're called 'stays'. They support the mast on each side and in front, with the side stays set slightly aft. Here they pull against the forestays, stabilising the mast. The stays on the side of the ship also provided the line ladders whereby the crew climbed the masts to handle the sails. These were called 'ratlines', with steps woven horizontally into the stays to make a ladder.

In the days of natural fibre line (hemp rope) standing rigging, multiple purchase pulleys were located at the bottom of each stay so that the stretch in the stays could be taken up to ensure the masts remained rigidly perpendicular. Hundreds of thousands of these pulleys were manufactured each year to keep the navy and the merchant marine operating, not to mention the thousands of miles of rope and acres of canvas.

'Running' Rigging

The running rigging is made up of all the lines that move to control the sails. Each square sail has a line attached to its bottom corners (the clews) and also one attached to each end of the yard on which it is hung. The lines attached to the bottom corner of each square sail are called sheets and are used to hold down the bottom of the sail as it catches the wind.

The lines attached to the end of each yard are called braces and are used to alter the angle of the yard to the wind. In addition to the sheets and braces, there are the halyards (literally 'haul yards') which are used to haul up the yards on which sails are set or (in the case of staysails) haul up the sails themselves.

Crewing

A fully rigged ship has over 250 separate pieces of rigging, and a common sailor (ordinary seaman) had to know them all and be able to react immediately to commands. Any ignorance or hesitation could spell disaster. 'Able' seamen were sailors with more than two years' experience who were 'well acquainted at their duty'. All seamen were expected to be able to steer the ship, that is, take their 'trick' at the wheel and to act diligently as lookouts.

The crew was generally divided into two 'watches' (called either the port or starboard), for periods on duty, which could be four hours or six hours depending on the time of the day. In emergencies, at the command 'all hands on deck', or simply 'all hands', everyone 'stood to' to help work the ship. The second in command after the captain, the 'first mate', oversaw the starboard watch while the second mate (third in charge) directed the port watch. These procedures were common on ships for centuries, but it was the custom on steamships, in the latter days of sail, to man a ship with three watches. To do so placed a heavy financial burden on sailing ships and influenced their demise.

Manoeuvring a Big Sailing Ship

The massive square sails of the windjammers provided the primary propelling force when travelling before the wind. The fore-and-aft sails supplied vital extra power when the wind was abeam or slightly ahead of the beam. The fore-and-aft sails also provided manoeuvrability. Those on the bowsprit supplied valuable assistance when the helmsman wished to bear (steer) away to leeward from, say, a beam reach (wind on the side of the ship) to square to the wind (wind over the stern). The jigger-mast sails at the stern balanced the headsails, helping to maintain a steady course by also pushing the stern of the ship away and the bow towards the wind.

To help change direction on these massive ships that only had a relatively small rudder mounted right on the stern of the hull, the officer of the watch would upset this balance of forces. He would do so by freeing the sheets on one or other of these two sets of sails. If a ship was sailing hard on the wind (pointing as close into the wind as possible) and the aim was to turn away from the wind, the spanker, which has been pushing the bow into the wind, is eased to allow the bow to fall away from the direction of the wind. The headsails would also be eased to take advantage of sailing 'freer'.

Conversely, sheeting the spanker in towards the centre line of the vessel will cause the bow to come 'up' towards the direction of the wind. The headsails would then be sheeted in also to take advantage of the new wind direction. Windjammers were, like any square-rigged ship, limited in their ability to make to windward by the extent to which their giant yards could be braced up to windward. As ever, movement in this direction was limited by the stays that supported the masts.

Measuring Ship Size the Traditional Way

There are several ways to measure the size of a ship. One is 'displacement', which is simply the weight of the vessel—the weight of water it 'displaces'. Although it is a size guide, different types of ships can have widely different displacements. A battleship, for example, would have a high displacement for its overall size. 'Tonnage' (gross or net, but generally, gross) has been the traditional means of determining the internal space and, hence, the cargo-carrying capacity of a merchant ship for revenue levying purposes. Under the builder's old measurement, a commercial cargo vessel was measured officially and 'registered' for the purpose, hence the term *gross 'register' tons*, or GRT.

A *tun* (in English) or *tonelada* (in Spanish and Portuguese) was originally a cask of wine that held 954 litres, or 252 gallons. It weighed 1,016 kilograms or 2,240 pounds—the origin of the imperial ton—and was subsequently used to determine mass, not volume. In the early days of trade between the Iberian Peninsula and England, much of the cargo was wine, and ships paid port dues according to how many standard casks (or tuns) they could carry. It is therefore a measure of the internal space available to carry cargo.

Originally, the cubic capacity or number of 'tuns' a ship could carry was arrived at by multiplying (simply put) the length by the beam (breadth) and the depth of the ship. Depth, for some reason, was not measured but assumed to be half of the beam. This custom was subject to abuses that affected the stability and seaworthiness of vessels. Builders strove to minimise the breadth measurement at deck level, thereby minimising the depth measurement as well and maximising carrying capacity for a given 'tonnage' measurement. Ships were built with excessive 'tumblehome'—the extent to which a ship's maximum breadth ('beam') exceeds its breadth at deck level.

Once such a ship was rolled on to its side by a strong wind (said to be on its 'beam ends'), there was little to prevent it from turning upside down. Many ships would be lost because their design was distorted in an attempt to minimise port levies. These levies, being one of the state's chief sources of income, were high and a considerable expense for shippers. The system would gradually be reformed, but the process wouldn't be completed until the nineteenth century with the advent of the Moorsom system.

The Moorsom System

The traditional method of calculating the tonnage of cargo vessels was unfair to steamships whose engines and machinery occupied a substantial part of their internal volume. It was reformed in Great Britain in 1849 by the adoption of what is known as the Moorsom system, which became law in 1854. Admiral Moorsom was charged with designing a system that was proportional to the earning capacity of the ship, whether for cargo or passengers. The total internal volume was measured in cubic feet and divided by 100 to produce to produce what was called gross register tonnage. From this figure was deducted the space taken up by fuel and machinery and other non-revenue-producing items. The result was 'net register tonnage' on which government revenue was then levied. This system was in use until 1982.

Wood, a Strategic Material

In Europe

When Portugal triggered the Age of Discovery, it was already running short of oak forests to provide the vast amounts of wood required to build caravels, carracks, and (later) galleons. As well as the shortage of wood, European oak was unsuitable for ships travelling to the tropics, a problem that had never been encountered until the voyages of discovery. Oak has no resistance to teredo worms, otherwise known as the termites of the sea. They would eat their way into the underwater planking, fatally weakening it. Until the adoption of copper sheathing in the latter years of the eighteenth century, they were the bane of all ships built of temperate zone wood.

Exploring the west coast of Africa and the north Atlantic island groups, Portugal was fortunate to discover a hitherto untapped supply of shipbuilding timbers. It was then able to exploit these forests to build its trading fleet. (One of those islands, Madeira, means 'wood' in Portuguese.) Nevertheless, not long after Vasco da Gama made it to India, Portugal was building teak and mahogany ships in India because of the resistance of these tropical woods to teredo worm.

With its much larger land mass, Spain had a better supply of the ubiquitous European oak, but it nonetheless had to place restrictions on the size of ships in order to conserve its forests. England had, for some time, been mindful of the limited supply of mature oak trees, and Henry VIII forbade their use for anything other than shipbuilding. Mature trees are vital, not only to provide the large, strong, one-piece timbers necessary for the hull's rigidity, but the branches were also precious to provide the enormously strong 'grown knees' that connected the sides of the ship to the decks. This pivotal role of large hardwood trees would continue into the nineteenth century and would only disappear with the ability to cast iron for ships' keels and scantlings.

In England's case, it was able to expand its trading and naval fleet by plundering the vast teak and mahogany resources of the Indian subcontinent. For the trade conducted between Asian countries, the big bonus accruing to the various East India companies, it soon became superfluous to send these timbers home. Instead, they had their ships built in India, using local lumber and the highly skilled woodworking labour force. Always short of seamen, they also began crewing them with locals as well. Known as lascars, they hailed from the Indian subcontinent, Southeast Asia, and the Arab world—in practice any native east of the Cape of Good Hope. Whereas European crews were susceptible to tropical disease and inclined to flee once they reached India, the lascars were skilled, more amenable than British tars, and most importantly, cheaper. The practice was so popular that by 1860 (under the Navigation Acts), the proportion of lascars in a crew reaching England was limited to 75 per cent.

In the Americas

Early American settlers were forced to take to the sea because they didn't have much choice. In New Hampshire, Connecticut, Rhode Island, Vermont, Maine, and Massachusetts, the soils were poor. Not only that, these new 'empire' states were also susceptible to bad weather. The early inhabitants were forced to make at least part of their living from the sea. But they were lucky in two ways. While the soils weren't good, New England is one of the most heavily forested regions in the United States, extensively covered with mature old growth trees—fine shipbuilding timbers such as white pine, oak, maple, beech, birch, hickory, and ash.

The second piece of good luck was having abundant fishing grounds close by, on the Grand Banks. Poor soils obliged the early settlers to combine these two resources to become expert boatbuilders. They were also efficient, with craft skills passed from father to son.

Cattle failed to thrive in the West Indies due to tropical diseases, and the shallow seas did not support a large school fishery. There was thus a ready market to feed the expanding slave labour force there. Besides boatbuilding and fishing, the New Englanders went further and, unfettered by petty regulation, built fast ships, becoming a force in the international slave trade.

Up until the latter part of the eighteenth century, sailing ship development was slow and incremental. The situation changed when the Americans became involved. America had an ideal background and the resources to supply the transatlantic packet lines which exploded on to the scene following the Anglo-American War of 1812–1814. It was also lucky to have a group of very talented merchant ship designers. As such, America, at the beginning of the nineteenth century, possessed all the strategic elements on which to build a large merchant fleet. It would use these assets to become the foremost merchant maritime force in the world by the middle of the nineteenth century.

American ship designers and builders would take wood to the limit of its capabilities, but eventually, the resource became increasingly scarce. Having made its fortune on the sea, the United States turned its back on saltwater in favour of its ever-expanding Western frontier.

The Transition to Iron and Steel

In Europe, the adoption of iron and later steel in ship construction was prompted not only by the shortage of wood but by something far more sinister: the development of explosive shells. Explosive cannonballs had been around for centuries, but they had a fuse that had to be lit before the ball was fired. If the gunner got it wrong, the ball could explode inside the cannon with disastrous consequences.

Making such a projectile explode on impact changed everything.

Long (as opposed to spherical) projectiles, called shells, with impact-detonating heads, replaced cannonballs. Another development was to replace the smooth bore of a cannon with a grooved, or 'rifled', barrel. When projectiles were fired from a rifled barrel, they spun rather than tumbling over and over, making their trajectory more predictable and accurate—and their impact deadlier.

The logical solution was to build a vessel out of iron, or at least make it iron-clad. However, when the first hulls were made completely of iron, they faced two problems. One was rust, and the other was marine fouling, with the latter the most serious. These problems were eventually overcome in warships, opening the way for the maritime arms race that culminated in the First World War.

The new technology, with its promise of superior strength and lower maintenance, was also applied to merchant ships, both steamers and sailers. The first iron-framed, and then iron-clad, sailing ships were the British tea clippers. They were followed by the great windjammers, which were mainly built out of steel. Here, the superior strength of steel construction opened up the way to build bigger sailing ships at precisely the time they were needed. They would serve as freighters bringing bulk raw materials from distant ports that weren't easily accessible to steamers.

The miracle of steel construction would prolong the life of sailing ships by half a century.

2
CHAPTER

From Caravel To Windjammer

Achievements

The great windships were extraordinarily efficient. Their hulls could carry far more cargo than any form of land-based transport, and they managed to get from A to B with minimal cost to nature. They opened up the world and for centuries carried its trade and facilitated the movement of its people. They were the original engines, so to speak, of globalisation. They revealed the great centres of civilization to each other, created immense wealth, and spread knowledge. They also fashioned the building blocks of the sciences of oceanography and meteorology.

These achievements were possible because of their affinity with the natural world. In an age of relatively primitive technology, they were, and probably still are, the most efficient 'solar pump' ever devised. The sun drives the global wind systems, and a sailing ship harnesses that solar energy. Unlike other attempts to harness solar power that are dependent on the sun shining, the wind systems of the world blow day and night, endlessly.

However, all achievements aside, these sailing ships were also employed in some of humanity's most infamous trades, of which slavery and opium trafficking are two prominent examples.

Environmental Efficiency

Other than food and water, living space for the crew, and some basic ship's stores, the hull of a windship was free to carry cargo, not sacrificed to machinery or the fuel to drive it. Even when their popularity began to wane, it would be this trait that would enable sailing ships to cling on as revised rigs employing less labour and younger and younger crews extended their economic lives. It is interesting to note that the first steamship to cross the Atlantic could not carry any cargo—its entire hold was devoted to machinery and fuel. It was this sacrifice of space, together with a sailing ship's ability to go practically anywhere on earth where there is water, that would keep them in business for a century after the rise of steam power.

Yet in less than 100 years, just as they had achieved their most efficient and romantic forms—the fully rigged clipper and, later, the giant four-masted windjammer—they disappeared from the world's oceans, victims of the disrupting technologies of steam and steel, and another of humanity's developing preoccupations: time. The time value of money, that obsession of American capitalists and preoccupation of economists, drove a need for a level of certainty about the future and the perceived necessity to do things as soon as possible.

Steam-driven ships could stick to schedules.

The great windships could not.

Prehistory

Humanity harnessed the wind to move across water long before it used it to grind cereals and pump water. It would subsequently master hydraulic power in the form of water wheels to drive machinery, to drain swamps, and to produce, among other things, flour and paper. Still, other than to quench our thirst and grow our food, the most enduring use of water for human purposes has been transport. Progress across the land was arduous and required considerable exertion by either humans or draught animals or both. A draught horse that could move a ton on land could haul sixty tons on a canal. Without water transport, the ancient Egyptians would not have been able to move the massive blocks of stone to build their temples and tombs. They also used sails, but confined to the narrow channel of the Nile, rowing was also necessary.

Mediterranean Beginnings

Progress across the sea, using the winds, currents, and tides, required increased skill but was infinitely easier and more efficient than travelling by land. Sails were used in conjunction with oars, and the Egyptians began making voyages to Crete as early as the third millennium BCE. The Greek historian Herodotus tells us that in 600 BCE, the king of Egypt despatched a fleet from a Red Sea port that returned via the Mediterranean more than two years later, having apparently circumnavigated the African continent.

The Cretans, and more so the Phoenicians, were avid sailors, reliably criss-crossing the Mediterranean on trading voyages. To avoid the fickle nature of the wind in that enclosed sea and to increase speed and manoeuvrability, warships remained oar- and sail-driven. But rowing ports made them vulnerable to being swamped from a side-on sea. Moreover, rowers, and the food needed to sustain them, took up valuable cargo space. Trading ship design increasingly eschewed oars and began to rely on sail alone.

All this development was taking place in relatively benign waters. Julius Caesar observed that ships in the higher latitudes tended to have more 'freeboard', making them more seaworthy offshore, and utilised sail exclusively. They also employed the 'clinker' system of overlapping planks (as opposed to the 'carvel' method of edge-on planking used in the Mediterranean), which made the hull more robust and more rigid. These vessels benefited from, and could withstand, the more cyclonic sea conditions of the high latitudes. In contrast, the fluky winds typical of the prolonged high-pressure systems of the Mediterranean had discouraged reliance on sail alone.

The Open-Ocean Barrier

Bluewater (open-ocean) sailing required the superior seaworthiness of high-sided vessels. It also needed a quantum leap in technical skill and a strong incentive. Technical skill, too, was required to build strong, capacious ships that could withstand the ocean's wrath and carry sufficient food and water to endure months at sea, with no opportunity of replenishment.

Open-ocean sailing also required a new approach to rigging. Single sails were used to push the vessel in the direction of the wind. To gain flexibility, allowing the spar carrying the sail to rotate around the mast, permitted the ship to sail across the wind. Employing additional masts with fore and aft, or 'lateen' sails, assisted this process, even allowing a vessel to some extent to sail 'into the wind', the process known as 'weatherliness'. They also improved manoeuvrability.

Going faster, however, meant increasing the size of the sail or, for safety's sake, increasing the number of masts and the number of sails on each mast. Doing so provided flexibility to vary the amount of sail carried to match the prevailing wind conditions. The development of the three-masted ship was the most significant advance in sailing technology (and possibly technology in general) ever made. It would serve mariners for centuries to come and carry humanity along the way to modernity.

Next came the developments that allowed seafarers to find their way on a trackless ocean, out of sight of land. Mariners developed mathematical knowledge and method, used the earth's magnetism, and closely observed the natural world.

Lastly, open-ocean sailing required immense human courage (and incentive) for mariners to sail blithely over the horizon and to proceed for thousands of miles across empty ocean. They did so with the hope that the forces that bore them forward could also be exploited to bring them back. And it all had to happen before storm, tempest, or starvation overtook their small vessels.

The wind and the ocean currents were free. The one limitation was their ability to sustain the crew. Carrying enough food and water, and still leave space for trade goods, limited the range of the early sailing ships. Had the Americas not stood in Columbus's way and, instead, a vast ocean between Europe and China (which he had set out to reach), he and his crew would have died of starvation and thirst.

The longest voyage made in the Age of Discovery was from Cape Horn to the Philippines. Ferdinand Magellan and his crew almost starved, eating rats, leather, and sawdust to stay alive, before making landfall. These two voyages were a revelation. Courage, venturing, greed, and necessity proved the world was larger than early ocean-going sailors believed—they now had a better idea of what they were dealing with.

The oceans cover over 70 per cent of the world's surface, and they insert themselves between the immense land masses within which other civilisations had developed. Crossing them would prove to be the source of tremendous wealth, riches beyond the most febrile dreams of the first adventurers.

Mineral wealth was, however, unevenly distributed with most of it in countries that lay beyond the pale of developing mid-millennium civilisations. As well, the extent of the Euro–Asian land mass was so great, and communications from one side to the other so poor that mighty civilisations could exist in the middle (e.g. India) and at the other end (e.g. China) and very little be known about them.

The great windships opened up these centres of civilisation and stimulated the trade that was so mutually beneficial.

Two Eras

The age of the great windships can be divided roughly into two eras. The first stretched from the fifteenth century through to the end of the eighteenth century. Shipbuilding stalled for centuries until the stimulus of the Age of Discovery jump-started it again. What followed was a period of almost continuous development and the steady accretion of knowledge of the sea and how to utilise it to create wealth and power. It was also the era of the rise of the sailing ship as the almost exclusive means of communication between continents and civilisations.

The second era was much shorter, barely 100 years, and stretched from the turn of the nineteenth century to the turn of the twentieth. It was the great age of merchant sail, an era when the sailing ship reached its full maturity.

The Enlightenment and the Industrial Revolution fostered an age of rapid progress in the development of the sailing ship, both in its design and operation. Finally, after centuries of wooden construction, it changed the material used to build them and the method of their construction. The Industrial Revolution would also bring about their demise.

Nevertheless, sail as a method of ocean transport was the handmaiden of an extraordinary age.

Galleys and Galleasses

The combination of steam and steel would sound the knell for the wooden sailing ship, but it was the combination of wood and wind that pushed civilisation forward for millennia. Those early paddlers would have no doubt realised that it was easier to make progress if the wind was blowing in the same direction. Although it is impossible to know now, they may well have sought to assist their passage before the wind by holding or propping up a sheet of bark or woven material to increase their resistance. The earliest sails were made of woven reeds, bamboo, and possibly bark slats. When stitched together horizontally, they had the additional advantage of being able to be rolled, reducing resistance as required.

Paddles were introduced to increase the effort that could be exerted by the human body. The development of the rowlock allowed a longer paddle shaft and the ability, via the fulcrum it provided, to apply more upper-body muscle power to the increased leverage.

Oars, and oar–sail combinations, have provided an ongoing means of propulsion since well before the Christian era. In time, large numbers of rowers in banks propelling 'galleys' became the primary means of conducting trade and hostilities on water. The use of these vessels extended over more than three millennia, and they were still widely used well after the development of sailing ships. They provided offensive advantages in protected waters where variable winds and currents limited the manoeuvrability and dependability of craft relying entirely on sails.

Sails were used to supplement human muscle when the wind was favourable but were rigged on a boom at right angles to the hull and easily furled when it was not. The wind's direction didn't limit them, and they could be rowed forward at considerable speed over a short distance to ram an enemy. They could then move in reverse to extricate themselves. So potent were galleys as a means of waging war that they featured extensively up until at least the sixteenth century. Galleys formed part of the Spanish armadas, the largest offensive fleets of the time. There were four galleys and four galleasses (rowed ships assisted by sails) in the Spanish armada brought against England in 1588.

The Mediterranean Sea figures largely in the development of modern Western civilisation, partly because of its navigability. It has a limited continental shelf and a steep decline into its deepest parts, facilitating tidal current flows. Water enters the Mediterranean at the Strait of Gibraltar and follows along the northern coast of Africa until it reaches the toe of the Italian peninsula where it splits. One flow continues eastward until it is turned north by the coast of Asia Minor and then westward by the coast of Turkey flowing through the Greek Archipelago, up the Adriatic, and down the east coast of Italy.

The second flow follows the west coast of Italy north until it is turned west by its northern coast. It then follows along the French coast until it is set south by the Spanish coast to arrive once again at the Strait of Gibraltar.

At the sea's widest parts, there are 'mesoscale' gyres that were used by its earliest navigators. (A gyre, it will be remembered, is an extensive system of circulating ocean currents, especially those associated with large wind systems.) The assistance they would have received from these coastal water flows explains why early navigators in the Mediterranean did not often proceed far out of sight of land, 'coast-hopping' instead. With patience, they would have almost always have been carried to their destination, no matter where they set off.

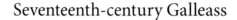

Seventeenth-century Galleass

Source: Author research

The Mediterranean was, however, the birthplace of the first craft utilising sail power, although there is a suggestion that the 'dhow', featuring a single fore and aft (or 'lateen') sail, may well have been developed by the Arabs in the Red Sea. The first record of the dhow was making passages along the Nile. It features a fore-and-aft sail mounted on a long, angled boom attached to the after-side of the mast. The sacred river's current would have carried the craft north, assisted by the sail and oars, and the fore-and-aft rig and oars would have enabled it to return south against the current. Given the size of the blocks of stone used in pyramid building, they must have been substantial vessels and loaded and manned very skilfully. Modern attempts to replicate the process have met with mixed results.

The Caravel

The development of the three-masted ship was a major prerequisite of the Age of Discovery. It was also the most significant advance ever made in the development of the sailing ship and one of mankind's greatest innovations. Open-ocean sailing required that the vessel be able to make the most of the wind regardless of its direction. Around the middle of the fifteenth century and under the auspices of Prince Henry the Navigator, the Portuguese developed the 'caravel' (in Portuguese 'caravela') to explore and trade down the west coast of Africa.

Caravela Lateena

Source: Author research

There were several configurations. Early caravels had two or three masts, all rigged with fore-and-aft sails. To distinguish them from later versions, they were known as *caravela lateena* after the lateen (or Latin) fore-and-aft sails they carried. Despite their 'weatherliness', caravels carried a lot of sail outside the confines of the ship when sailing downwind and could be unstable, inclined to roll excessively. To overcome this problem, the largest and foremost mast would eventually be rigged with a large square sail and a third fore-and-aft mast added.

Their ability to sail across or into the wind and their relatively high length-to-beam ratio made caravels quite fast. They were also flexible and suitable for exploring close inshore. It has been said that the most serious enemy of a sailing ship is land. Being caught on what is known as a 'lee shore'—where the wind changes to blow from the sea towards the land—is a serious predicament. Caravels, with their ability to make their way up to windward, were able to fight their way out to sea.

Caravel hulls were clad by the method known in English as 'carvel' planking. The term may have been a contraction of *caravel*. Further north in Scandinavia, England, and the Low Countries, ships had been built using the 'clinker' method of overlapping planks for centuries, having first been observed by Julius Caesar. The clinker method features planks that are fixed to the frames of the boat and each other through the overlap and made for a strong and rigid hull, well-suited to the rougher, more northerly sea conditions.

The Gokstadskipet: Strong, Seaworthy, and Beautiful

Source: Wikimedia Commons

Viking longships, which were not decked, are testimony to the hull strength that could be obtained by this method of construction. For all its advantages, the clinker method obviously required more material but permitted lighter frames. During the fifteenth century, the carvel method of fixing each plank to the frames independently and sealing the gap between spread to northern shipbuilders. Requiring less material, it was cheaper and resulted in a smoother hull surface, but it did require heavier frames than the clinker method.

There are drawings showing caravels stepping four masts, with a small after mast mounted on the very stern. This arrangement would have increased the vessel's manoeuvrability in tight situations, but the stern-most sail would not have been carried in the open sea. The caravel also had a shallow keel, enabling it to navigate in shallow and shoaling conditions, such as up rivers. Their disadvantage lay in their relatively long, narrow hulls which, unfortunately, also limited their cargo capacity. Their length-to-beam ratio was around 3.5:1.

To try to get the best of both worlds, the Portuguese developed the *caravela redonda*, or 'round' caravel, where the sides of the ship were curved outwards to improve cargo-carrying capacity. This characteristic is known as 'tumblehome', the extent to which the overall beam of the vessel exceeds its beam at deck level.

Round caravels were, however, small ships and somewhat fragile, rarely exceeding 200 gross tons. Their ability to travel vast distances across the open ocean was inhibited by their capacity to carry sufficient food and water. Often, they were used as store ships that were never intended to complete the voyage. When the stores were exhausted, they would be sunk, abandoned, or burnt. They were used extensively by both the Portuguese and the Spanish for exploration, especially along coastlines, but when it came to the heavy lifting of regular trade, a bigger, more commodious vessel was needed. Nevertheless, two of Columbus's ships were caravels but rigged as carracks, that is to say, with one mast square-rigged to improve their downwind performance and stability.

The Carrack

The *carrack* (in Spanish) or *nau* (in Portuguese) followed the caravel, although the two coexisted for decades, and fleets were often made up of both types. They were much bigger and more stoutly constructed vessels. Navigators had now learnt to exploit the wind systems and gyres of the great oceans, which meant sailing most of a voyage before the wind.

Carracks generally had three masts, with the mainmast being very strong. They carried up to six sails: a bowsprit (or 'sprit') sail; two square-rigged masts, each with two sails; and a lateen sail on the mizzen (after mast). They were beamier (wider) in relation to their length, having a ratio of about 3:1.

Carracks, too, had pronounced tumblehome, but their distinguishing characteristic was their prominent fore and after 'castles': superstructures intended for the defence of the ship. Boarders in the lower waist (middle) of the ship were at the mercy of defenders positioned up in the fore and aftercastles. But the castles presented resistance to the wind and affected stability. They also affected the extent to which the ship made 'leeway'. Any vessel sailing other than directly before the wind will be pushed sideways to the extent that its profile offers resistance to the wind. The large castles were inefficient because they wasted the driving force provided by the wind and increased the distance the ship had to travel between any two points. Perhaps the most famous carrack in history was Magellan's *Victoria*, the first ship to circumnavigate the world. It wasn't his flagship (that was *Trinidad*), but it was the one remaining ship that Juan Elcano succeeded in bringing home to Spain.

Replica of Magellan's Carrack *Victoria*, the First Ship to Sail Around the World

Source: Courtesy of Fundacion Nao Victoria

The carrack was the first oceanic freighter. Their hulls were multi-decked and voluminous and therefore better suited for trading and to carrying adequate stores for longer voyages. They also got progressively bigger, rapidly doubling and tripling in size. The first carracks to embark on the 'India Run' (the *Carreira da India*) were only about 100 tons and carried around fifty men. In stages, they grew to be the largest ships of their time, often measuring over 1,000 tons. Their multiple decks also provided plenty of room for armament, which made the Portuguese ships so superior to those of the Arab traders who frequented the East Indies.

The largest vessel to make the run was the *Madre de Dios*, a massive vessel of seven decks, a capacity of 1,600 tons, and a crew of around 600. She amply demonstrated, however, the folly of putting, if not all, then a very large number, of eggs in one basket. In 1592, off the Azores, west of Lisbon, she was intercepted and taken by the English privateer Sir John Burroughs. The value of her captured cargo was estimated to have been equal to the entire English treasury of the time. The disaster prompted a return to much more reasonably sized ships.

The Iberians versus Northern Europe: The Emergence of the Galleon

The carracks were the traditional workhorses of the Portuguese and Spanish fleets. Later, enlarged and with their waist filled in, their sail plan was revised to make them more powerful and flexible. They plied the routes to and from the East and West Indies for over a century.

The Spanish subsequently came up with a new design based on the ships used by French corsairs along the Atlantic coast of Europe: the 'galleon'. It had a narrower beam, and the high forecastle of the carrack was lowered to increase sail area and make the ship more manoeuvrable. The multiple decks were braced to increase the overall strength and rigidity of the hull. This extra strength meant the hull could be built longer. The increased length-to-beam ratio also made for faster sailing.

Another distinguishing characteristic of the galleon was a snout, or beak, protruding from the stem. Presumably, this facilitated the handling of the bowsprit sail, or 'spritsail' as it became known. At this stage, the spritsail was still also square, i.e. mounted on a yard at right angles to the bowsprit. The galleon utilised the longer hull to rig generally four masts. The two foremost masts were mostly square-rigged, with the two after masts carrying fore-and-aft lateen sails.

The strongly reinforced decks had the added advantage of serving as robust gun platforms for larger cannons, which could now be carried lower in the hull to increase stability. The galleon was thus faster, a better sailer, and capable of being heavily weaponised—in effect, a floating fortress.

The age of the battleship had arrived.

The Great Spanish Freighters: A Replica of the Spanish Galleon *Andalusia*

Source: Courtesy of Fundacion Nao Victoria

Numbering just seventeen vessels in 1550, Spain's galleon fleet soon grew in both number and vessel size. To further guard against the depredations of the privateers, it also introduced the convoy system. Having a number of these floating fortresses sailing together made them less vulnerable to the speedy French and English corsairs. A disadvantage of travelling together was that they were all subjected to the same extreme weather events, potentially magnifying losses. Spain's first treasure convoy to leave the Americas, comprised of some thirty ships, was all but wiped out by a single storm.

Another disadvantage was that the convoy was limited in speed to that of the slowest ship—easily overtaken by nimble privateers. Nevertheless, the bounty these vessels succeeded in landing in Spain, both from the Americas and the Philippines (the 'Manila galleons') made Spain the richest and most powerful country in Europe and the first global superpower.

The galleon form was gradually improved, but the basic concept would last for nearly two centuries. It would eventually be surpassed by the emergence of English and Dutch East Indiamen, which, over time, eschewed the high aftercastle for a more uniform profile. The galleon was also the forerunner of the heavily weaponised 'ship-of-the-line'.

The 'Race Built' Galleon

Despite their seeming impregnability, pesky English privateers proved very successful at raiding Spanish and Portuguese galleons. Spain's determination to invade England; overthrow its Protestant monarch, Elizabeth I; and return it to the Holy Roman Empire would have other very practical outcomes. It would prevent England from preying on Spanish shipping and stop Elizabeth from meddling in European affairs by supporting the Dutch in their war against Spain.

Over time, King Phillip II constructed no fewer than four armadas for the purpose. Instead of cargo, the galleons' vast holds were filled with soldiers, stores, and armaments for military conquest. Considerably smaller in wealth and population, England badly needed an answer to the Spanish galleon, which had become the largest and most fearsome craft of the era. England's maritime heroes of the age, Sir John Hawkins and Sir Francis Drake, found it, not by going even bigger but by going smaller.

Enter the 'race-built' galleon.

Drake's *Golden Hind*: A Race-built Galleon

Source: Drawing by Ray Aker Courtesy of Point Reyes National Seashore

A 'razee' is a sailing ship that has been cut down, with the rig, and sometimes the number of decks reduced often as the ship aged and was less capable of fulfilling its original purpose. Hawkins's ships, however, were purpose-built galleons that, following the French corsair design, had been 'shaved' of pronounced fore and aftercastles, and their length increased in relation to their beam.

The result was a faster, sleeker, more manoeuvrable, and lower-profile ship that presented less of a target to the Spanish gunners.

The English would improve on the powerful French design to make the normally ponderous galleon an attack as well as a defensive vessel. The distribution of armament was also altered with cannons mounted in the bow and the stern allowing the ship to attack head-on, minimising the outline it presented to the enemy. It would then bear away to bring the big amidships guns to bear in a 'broadside'. Following the broadside, the ship would gybe away to bring the stern cannon on to the target, again minimising its profile as the vessel departed. (A 'gybe' is achieved by steering the ship so that the wind changes from one aft quarter to the other.)

Defensively, the race-built galleon had a low-profile rudder entirely below the waterline, thereby reducing the possibility of it being shot away, leaving the ship unmanageable. It was also equipped with smaller bore long-range cannon that could inflict damage without closing on a more heavily armed enemy. If forced to close on a Spanish galleon, they sought to get near enough to be at an angle below that which the enemy could depress its cannon. The English galleon, however, could depress its guns sufficiently to hole the enemy below the waterline.

As domination of the sea became synonymous with national might, the race-built galleon would show the way forward as ship designers looked increasingly to sailing qualities rather than floating fortresses. By 1573, Sir John Hawkins was in charge of what was emerging as a permanent English navy. *Foresight* and *Dreadnought* were the first two race-built galleons constructed under his supervision. They had forty-one guns and were reputed to be able to run circles around the clumsier Spanish competition. These ships were pointing towards the more uniform profile of the fully rigged ship and the frigates that would dominate the merchant marine through the eighteenth and nineteenth centuries.

The East Indiamen

Strictly speaking, an East Indiaman was not a type of ship but any vessel voyaging from any European country to the East Indies. Originally, the East Indiamen were carracks, galleons, and (from the Dutch) 'fluyts'. Gradually, however, over the course of two and a half centuries, they evolved into larger, more competent vessels. Nevertheless, the pace of development was slow, and there was very little in the way of genuine innovation. When the East Indiamen were finally sold off in the first half of the nineteenth century, they were still using the same principles and procedures as merchant ships were over 200 years earlier. Their design and development had essentially stagnated.

What made them special was the immensely lucrative nature of the trade they conducted. That trade—supplying Europe with exotic spices, condiments, and medicaments—drove ocean-going commerce and became the vehicle for the development and expansion of the European merchant navies for two centuries.

Portugal was the first along the route, and at the outset, their ships were carracks accompanied by caravels. Some vessels in the fleet were never intended to return home. They would be packed with stores, and when these were exhausted, the ships would be burnt, scuttled, or abandoned. Carracks were the first deep-sea cargo ships and were used by the Portuguese for around a century. Eventually, they were surpassed by galleons, which were faster and more capable of defending themselves. Caravels were also employed, but because of their limited cargo-carrying capacity, they acted more as scouting and as fast escort and messenger vessels.

The Portuguese dominated trade with the East through the sixteenth and into the seventeenth century. Between 1497 and 1650, over a thousand ships departed Lisbon for India. But the Portuguese king's desire, through the royal trading house, the Casa da India, to keep trade a royal monopoly limited their ability to exploit the potential of the trade to the full. The other European powers would gradually steal Portuguese intellectual property in the form of their navigational guides, which they called their *roteiro*. The French word is *routier* from which the English word *rutter* is derived.

Although the Portuguese were first and dominated for over a century, as the turn of the sixteenth century approached, their inferior financial model meant that they were gradually overtaken by the northern European powers. The introduction of the joint-stock company, which dates from the beginning of the seventeenth century, as a means of raising large amounts of risk capital, meant that ultimately the English, Dutch, French, and the Scandinavian countries would become involved, although the latter not so successfully.

England versus the Netherlands

The Netherlands, although Protestant, and therefore natural allies of England after Henry VIII broke with the Roman Catholic Church, went to war four times against England between 1652 and 1784. The first three wars were fought in the latter half of the seventeenth century and the fourth a century later. The Netherlands was an immensely wealthy and powerful trading nation in the seventeenth century, rivalling Spain. It had stolen Portugal's maritime intellectual property and come to dominate its trading activities by financing the Portuguese king. The conflicts with England can therefore be characterised as an established mercantile power being challenged by one that was on the rise.

The Anglo-Dutch wars were predominantly naval engagements and fought largely over trade and overseas colonies. The Netherlands had colonial interests in India, and Great Britain wanted into the lucrative spice trade out of what is now Indonesia. Together they had forced the Portuguese out, and they fought frequent skirmishes. Eventually, Britain's increasing involvement in India caused it to concentrate its energies on the subcontinent and leave the archipelago to the Dutch. But the fourth war, fought after the American War of Independence in 1780, marked the beginning of the decline of the Netherlands as a maritime power.

The Dutch 'Fluyts'

Dutch ships making the journey to the Indies were known as fluyts. These vessels, unlike their competitors, although sometimes lightly armed, were not built to do dual duty as cargo vessels and warships.

Inspired by the galleons, the fluyts had a high narrow aftercastle but a little forecastle. Generally three-masted, with the mizzen (rearmost) carrying the ubiquitous lateen sail, the bowsprit was well-developed and rigged square spritsails with fore-and-aft 'headsails'. These would have made the vessel more effective working to windward. As they developed, the fluyts eschewed the lateen sail and adopted a combination of square sails and a 'jigger' sail on the mizzen mast.

Compared to other European ships of the age, fluyts were relatively light and designed specifically to maximise cargo space. New tools were used in their construction, and Dutch shipbuilders had harnessed the power of windmills for sawing timber. They also made extensive use of the mechanical advantage provided by multiple pulley systems to reduce crew numbers. Less crew meant less space devoted to food and water, maximising cargo space. Their masts were high to harness stronger wind for speed but rigged in such a way that the topmasts could be easily lowered in the event of bad weather.

The fluyt had a high aftercastle, and the barrel-shaped hull featured pronounced tumblehome to reduce deck space. This had originally been done to minimise Danish duties on their frequent trips through the Sound (or Oresund, the strait forming the border between Denmark and Sweden) to their trading partners in the Baltic forest lands to access shipbuilding materials. Because of the Netherlands' shoaly coastline, the fluyts had minimal draft, which enabled them, on the other side of the world, to enter shallow anchorages and proceed up rivers not accessible to European ships.

The English privateer Sir Francis Drake admired the fluyts, noting that they handled very well, that their tall masts made them speedy, and they could be worked by smaller crews. As ever, economy in the form of lower transportation costs was a watchword with the Dutch, and the fluyts were a major factor in the rise of the Dutch mercantile empire.

The Netherlands had little in the way of an aristocracy, and its extensive middle class were talented traders. The superiority of the fluyts meant that towards the end of the seventeenth century, England was using Dutch ships captured in the Anglo-Dutch wars for trading and began to emulate the design in their own East Indiamen. So effective were the Dutch as traders that, by 1670, seventy years after the formation of the Dutch East India Company (the Vereenigde Oost Indische Compagnie, or VOC), the Dutch fleet totalled well over half a million tons—half the European total.

The Dutch retained their reputation for parsimony in the outfitting of their ships and the fit-out can be compared with the British East Indiamen, which, under the influence of the ship's husbands (about which more below), became increasingly luxurious.

British East Indiamen

Before and paralleling the rise of the various joint-stock trading companies, the main purpose of England's shipbuilding had been to produce fast, heavily armed conventional warships and 'race built' galleons. They were designed to protect the island fortress and raid the seaborne commerce of the Iberians. English galleons were designed for relatively short times at sea and, with stores and armament, had little space for trading cargo. England, and other north European countries, had had no colonies and therefore had no need of trading ships capable of carrying large amounts of goods.

So specialised were England's raiders that at one stage, Sir Walter Raleigh tried to set up a colony on Roanoke Island off the coast of the American continent. The intention was to provide a base adjacent to the Spanish shipping lanes that could grow to reprovision his raiders. Alas, when he returned to reprovision the infant colony two years after the original settlement was made, it was deserted. There was no trace of the over 100 people who had been landed there.

The English East India Company's (or EIC but nicknamed 'the John Company') successful development of trade with the East Indies meant a different type of vessel was required—one that could carry copious amounts of cargo, sustain itself for long voyages, and defend itself on the other side of the world. Commercial considerations had entered the minds of several northern European nations, and what emerged, because of their common purpose and destination, would develop into the largest ships ever built in the Western world—the East Indiamen. Apart from the 'country ships' that were equally skilfully built in India for the local Asian trade, the British East Indiamen were high-quality ships built on the Thames. Such were the profits they earned; they were refitted after each voyage, regardless of expense.

The first British East Indiamen were galleons, and as such, the hull featured a high stern castle and beaked bow. They carried a lateen sail on the mizzen mast, after which there was quite often an even smaller mast known as a 'bonaventure' mizzen, typically shorter than the actual mizzen and also rigged with a lateen sail. the fore- and main masts were square-rigged with a main course (mainsail) and a topsail. The main and mizzen masts were also a focus of evolution. The bonaventure mizzen appears to have been the first victim of development. The mizzen mast was beefed up and square sails added above the lateen sail. Then the lateen sail itself gradually morphed into a fore-and-aft gaff-rigged 'jigger' sail, enhancing manoeuvrability and ease of operation.

To achieve this, the forepart of the lateen boom was removed, and the after part became a gaff boom holding up the top of what was now a quadrilateral sail. The foot of the sail was attached to another fore-and-aft boom secured to the lower part of the mast. On the bow, to improve crosswind and upwind performance, the bow-rigged square 'spritsail' was abandoned. The bowsprit itself was strengthened, and fore-and-aft sails were attached to the stays supporting the foremast. The fore-and-aft stays supporting the main and mizzen masts were also eventually dressed with staysails, which contributed further to cross- and upwind performance.

The galleon rig was thus progressively adapted to improve the range of wind direction in which it could operate without losing too much performance. Much of this modification was inspired by the development of fighting ships. Technological progress occurs much more rapidly in times of war, and progress in sailing ship design was stimulated by the ongoing competition between England and France as they rose to be the dominant powers in eighteenth- and nineteenth-century Europe.

Hull-wise, the stern aftercastle reduced in size, becoming a moderately raised platform that became known as the quarterdeck, the precinct of the captain, the officer of the watch, and the helmsman. The forecastle was similarly simply a raised platform above the main deck, forward of the foremast, and traditionally the home of the ordinary sailors. The waist of the ship was extended and modified to simplify cargo handling and ship operations.

Instruments of Power: a Fleet of British East Indiamen at Sea

Source: Wikipedia Commons

In the first half of the seventeenth century, the EIC built its own ships. As wealth from the spice trade began to flow, it succumbed to allowing other interested investors, the so-called 'ship's husbands', to build vessels on its behalf. Rather than compete against one another for the business, ship's husbands predictably formed a cartel to exploit their position. The creation of what became known as 'the shipping interest' would become a significant factor in the EIC's eventual downfall.

For the time being, however, the burgeoning nature of the trade would lead to bigger and bigger ships that became a byword for luxury. They would anticipate the later ocean liners (or Western Ocean packets) to the extent that they were hybrids, built to accommodate passengers as well as freight. The EIC employed a large English staff to administer its overseas trading activities and, subsequently, civil administration of the Indian subcontinent, not to mention to command its private army. India (like Indonesia for the Dutch) became known as the 'white man's grave', so effectively did disease, boredom, and excessive consumption of alcohol harvest the tropic-tender northerners. The result was a continual replenishment of army officers and administrators and their families around the Cape of Good Hope to the land, quite often, of their graves.

The merchant galleons were a very successful design and plied the intercontinental routes for around 150 years, gradually evolving into fully rigged ships. They were well-armed and were often pressed into naval service when the need arose. The English East Indiamen took advantage of the requirement to, at times, fight as part of England's navy. The ships were painted with what was known as the 'Nelson Chequer'—horizontal alternating black-and-yellow rectangles along the hull. The yellow lines on a naval craft were broken at intervals by rectangular black gunports. When encountering an East Indiaman, enemy vessels or pirates could never be sure whether it was a naval vessel or a merchantman until they were at quite close quarters or, convinced it was the latter, how many of those black rectangles were real gunports. The ruse was so effective that the cannon would often be stowed deep in the ship to make way for more cargo.

The term 'East Indiaman' has attracted an air of romance, but it's unusual to refer to ships as masculine when sailors generally refer to them as feminine. The romance is likely associated with the period of great prosperity that flowed from the Indies trade. The ships were large, comfortable, and elaborately decorated, and profits from the voyages were shared between owners and the crew. Everyone in the crew had the right to a certain amount of cargo space and were able to trade on their own account, the amount varying according to one's position.

The lucrative nature of the trade also meant the ships were very well built and provided a level of luxury hitherto unavailable to sea travellers. The later East Indiamen were built at the famous Blackwall Yard on the Thames. It produced vessels of a high standard, including the later and almost equally famous Blackwall frigates, which would ultimately replace the East Indiamen.

Many East Indiamen were also built in India using the beautiful shipbuilding timbers available there (teak and mahogany, chiefly) and the high skills of Indian shipwrights. These latter vessels specialised in trading entirely within the Eastern region. This trade ultimately proved more lucrative than shipping goods back to the mother country, especially when the British began trading opium out of India into China.

Prototype Liners

Trade with, and the administration of, India and, later, dealings with China grew to a vast flow of goods back and forth from Great Britain, within Asia, and with other parts of the empire. It has been estimated that the East India Company was, at one stage, responsible for half of world trade. When the fleet left England annually, its procession down the English Channel was described as 'lordly'. As well as traders, on board was a host of army officers, troops, and colonial administrators and their wives and families. They were moved to and fro between the Indian subcontinent and eventually Britain's other possessions in Asia and the British Isles.

This vast trade in goods and people was carried out primarily by the East Indiamen that very effectively connected these two worlds. The later vessels were highly decorated and gilded, and the interiors were finished to a very high standard compared to the other ships—as much for the comfort of the captain and his officers as for passengers. Ultimately, they developed into big fully rigged ships where cargo capacity and comfort were more important than speed.

The practice of 'rigging down' the East Indiamen at night meant the crew didn't have to work the ship in darkness if the weather conditions changed dramatically. They would also rig down in the daytime at the slightest hint of bad weather. Rigging down slowed the ship's progress and made the voyages considerably longer. The Americans would change all that. They developed the practice of driving their ships day and night regardless of the weather. It would be a major factor in their rise to merchant marine supremacy.

During the century and a half that the East Indiamen dominated the trade between Europe and the Indies, they grew substantially in size. The early vessels would have been barely 400 tons, but under the influence of economics and safety, this figure rose gradually to 800 tons. Towards the end of the East India Company's reign, 1,200-ton ships were regularly being constructed. In 1795, the *Warley*, rated at 1,475 tons, slid down the ways. They were the largest ever to use the Port of London.

These were, for their time, inordinately large ships. They were also part of the company's undoing. The investors financing their construction (the ship's husbands) became, over time, very greedy. They colluded, and prices began to increase and construction quality to decline, as the builders sought to squeeze every last shilling from the company.

The 'Country Trade'

Although its original intention was trade between the home country and India, it was soon realised that Great Britain's superior ships, which were also well-armed (to the point where they were often commandeered in time of war), could trade profitably between the countries of Asia. What became more important was the fact that better ships could be constructed expertly in India from magnificent tropical timbers. These were not only superb shipbuilding timbers, but they were best suited to the tropics. They resisted the dreaded teredo worm, which played havoc with vessels built of European oak. Moreover, Indian shipwrights were highly skilled and cheap to employ, and many of their techniques (e.g. the tight rabbeting of each plank to its neighbour and the construction of watertight compartments) would be incorporated into British shipbuilding specifications.

Known, somewhat prosaically, as 'country ships', these superbly built and armed vessels set out to exploit the inter-country trade in Asia. Manned by Arab, Indian, and Chinese crews (called lascars), they were confined to Asian waters and not permitted to sail to England. Eventually, their activities contributed more to the EIC coffers than vessels making the journeys to and from England. Well-armed, they progressively pushed out the local Arab and Chinese traders in Asia. Lascars were good seamen. Cheap, compliant, and nimble, they were even tried in 'British bottoms' sailing back to England. (Until the repeal of the Navigation Acts mid-nineteenth century, only British-built ships, or 'bottoms', could trade into British ports.) The lascars, however, had a low tolerance for colder climes, and their agility declined inversely with the latitude.

EIC Denouement

Over the more than two centuries of their history, the British East Indiaman gradually evolved from the successful galleon shape and rig through to the penultimate configuration—the fully rigged ship, in time made famous by American transatlantic packets and the clippers. (Eventually, the ultimate merchant navy rig would be the four-masted barque.)

By the turn of the eighteenth century, however, the days of these great, lumbering windships were over. The John Company's monopoly, which Elizabeth I had provided originally, extended to all trade between the Cape of Good Hope and Cape Horn—well over three-quarters of the world and almost all its land mass. Parliament progressively whittled the company monopoly away until, in 1834, it was abolished altogether. Since its inception, it had grown venal, corrupt, and badly managed with company records literally years behind. During its decline, the trade came to be dominated by faster ships: the frigates. With competition increasing, their role on the route between Britain and the Orient was progressively confined to transporting EIC operatives back and forth. With the abolition of the monopoly, all ships were sold off or otherwise disposed of.

The French East Indiamen

During the latter years of the domination of the Oriental trade by the British East Indiamen, the international situation was changing significantly for the mother country. On the high seas, England's naval power was increasing but was constantly challenged by the French throughout the eighteenth century. Like the English, the French had a long history (despite their being part of the Holy Roman Empire at the time) of privateering against the Portuguese and the Spanish. French shipbuilders were noted for their designs, improving speed and manoeuvrability, and the quality of their workmanship. In time of war against England (which was a lot of the time between the late seventeenth century and the defeat of Napoleon in 1815) when French ships were captured, they were taken into the English fleet. Here they provided excellent models for improving English design. According to Arthur H. Clark, a marine historian and clipper captain, the leading nation in the modelling and construction of ships in the latter half of the seventeenth century was France:

> During this period the finest frigates owned in the British Navy were those captured from the French … the French forty-gun frigate Hebe which was captured by the British frigate Rainbow in 1782 [was] a most valuable acquisition and [according to the naval historian, William James] there were few British frigates up to 1847 which, in size and exterior form, were not copied from the Hebe. As late as 1821 the Arrow, for many years the fastest yacht owned in England, was modelled on the lines of a French lugger wrecked on the Dorset coast, which proved to be a well-known smuggler that had eluded the vigilance of HM Excise cutters, always escaping capture, although often sighted, through her superior speed.

Howard Chapelle, a foremost authority on the development of sailing ship design, points out that it was the French who were the first to become aware of the importance of length in ship speed:

> *The value of length was slowly becoming appreciated; French naval designers seem to have been the first to make practical use of this design element in order to obtain speed. French frigates and corvettes of 1745–51 were longer and somewhat sharper than the British 20- and 24-gun ships. Rigs were improving and some fast sailing small vessels were slowly evolving into distinctive types—the American schooner, the English cutter, and perhaps, the French lugger.*

It is one of the great maritime mysteries as to why the French, being such acknowledged designers of fast and effective warships, instead of designing their own merchant vessels, turned to the Dutch fluyts to trade with the East. But there is an argument that says that it was a very sensible idea. Why reinvent the wheel? The Dutch fluyts had proved their worth in international trade, and there was the added advantage that the fleet could be rapidly expanded by having some ships built in the Netherlands by the acknowledged experts. Many Dutch seamen were also recruited to captain and man the vessels even though the French company faced stiff competition from the VOC.

Models of the French East Indiamen that survive show them approaching the standard fully rigged ship, but fluyt-like, still carrying a lateen sail on the stern, a square spritsail on the bowsprit, as well as three headsails. They also appear to be fuller-bodied, wider at deck level than the Dutch fluyts, and more elaborately decorated.

France was determined to have a way station on the voyage to India, and while it succeeded in establishing colonies on two adjacent Indian Ocean islands, its preoccupation with establishing a base on Madagascar saw it fall short in its original raison d'être—supplying the much sought-after Indian spices, fine silks, muslins, and other kinds of cotton. The trading houses of other nations, chiefly the EIC and the VOC, stepped in to supply the unsatisfied demand.

Even though Portugal's practice of monarchical capitalism, making international trade a royal monopoly, had proved a disaster, France's first East India Company was also funded by the crown. It didn't adopt the more successful form of the joint-stock company (*La Compagnie Française pour le commerce des Indes Orientales*) until over sixty years after the British and the Dutch. The company founded colonies on what is now Reunion and Mauritius but did not establish a foothold in India until 1719. Reformed and consolidated with other trading enterprises in 1723, it pursued an aggressive policy against both Britain and India until defeated by Robert Clive at the Battle of Plessey in 1757. In 1794, after the French Revolution, the company was declared bankrupt, and its fleet was sold off.

The Frigate

By the mid-eighteenth century, the traditional East Indiamen were being replaced by a new class of trading vessels. These followed design trends being developed at the Blackwall Yard for the Royal Navy, themselves influenced by French designs.

A New Generation: the Blackwall Frigate *Kent*

Source: The State Library of South Australia

These were the same yards that had been building East Indiamen through their various iterations since the beginning of the seventeenth century. The new merchant navy ships were smaller and faster than their predecessors and built to look like single-deck, heavily armed Royal Navy frigates. Like the Royal Navy's fighting ships, they became known as Blackwall frigates. While they were fully rigged ships and had better lines and a higher length-to-breadth ratio, they lacked the finesse of the clippers that would be developed in the United States. The EIC's monopoly on trade with the East had been abolished by parliament in 1834, and there was no longer a need for big, cargo-carrying behemoths. The company traffic to the East was now in people, recruited to administer the largest colony the world had ever known.

Despite the distinct change in approach embodied in the Blackwall frigates, British shipbuilding design, and how its ships were operated at sea, had fallen behind, thanks to the lack of competition that existed before 1849. Rather than protection, America had honed its ship design and construction skills in an atmosphere of adversity and illegality, which bred new ideas on ship hull shape and operation that would stand it in remarkably good stead. During the course of the nineteenth century, America would rise from a source of agricultural products and raw materials on the other side of the Atlantic to dominating the world merchant marine.

A Many-Faceted Revolution

The first part of the nineteenth century, up until the economic bust in shipbuilding in the United States in 1857, was a remarkable era in maritime history. Much of it revolved around and was driven by American ability, ambition, enterprise, and hustle. Not all of it, however, by today's standards, was meritorious. The middle of the century was a period of enormous foment in which slave trading, opium running, trade with the Orient, Atlantic liner services, and globe-circling clipper services were all operating simultaneously. These activities took place against the backdrop of Great Britain's emerging industrial might, which provided the impetus for many of these developments.

The Abolition of the Slave Trade

After 1807, the slave trade (although significantly, not slavery) was banned by the British, and it encouraged the other main participants to follow suit. These undertakings were honoured more in the breach than in their observance. What it meant, however, was that ships seeking to continue slave trading had to be fast and weatherly. A primary requirement was that they be able to escape the frigates of the Royal Navy that Great Britain sent to police the trade.

Not only did the ships need to be fast and weatherly, but they also had to be able, when pursued, to continue under as much sail as possible for as long as it took to escape. The slave trade had evolved over a period when it was customary for sailing ships to 'rig down' at night. The Southern states of America had much to gain by the continued operation of the slave trade, and although Congress had passed laws banning it, they were poorly enforced. Shipowners from both the North and the South continued to engage in this very lucrative of businesses. Not only did they build faster ships, but to avoid apprehension either by their own or the Royal Navy, they drove them as hard as possible, day and night. In so doing, they built up a skill and a tradition of 'hard driving', which would be a key element in the success of the Western Ocean packets and later building and operating the great clipper ships.

The Western Ocean Packets (the Liner Services)

During the Revolutionary War of Independence, American shipbuilders had demonstrated their ability to build small, fast ships to harass British men-o-war and run the blockades they set up on American ports. After the war, America was alone and often at contretemps with its former mother country, especially because the Royal Navy would 'press' (kidnap) its very competent sailors whenever the opportunity presented.

When its difficulties with Great Britain came to a head in the Anglo-American War of 1812–14, the size of its former privateers was boosted and with it their effectiveness. Renowned for their speed, weatherliness, and manoeuvrability, these ships became known as the Baltimore clippers. They laid the foundations for a new approach to shipbuilding.

The baton was changing hands. No longer would the European nations dominate ship design, construction, and operation. In the new age that followed the final defeat of Napoleon and the Congress of Vienna in 1815, America emerged as the centre of maritime innovation and progress. Over the next fifty years, it would come to dominate the merchant maritime world.

Impatience at the dilatory nature of shipping services between the Old World and the New drove American shipowners to revolutionise transatlantic services. The so-called 'regular traders' across the Atlantic would sail down the east coast of the United States and into the West Indies, picking up cargo as they went until their holds were full. Similar diversions occurred on the return trip. Traders, especially cotton exporters and mechanical apparatus importers, were impatient for direct shipping. When the so-called 'liner' companies running direct transatlantic services in the form of the 'Western Ocean packets' were established, they proved successful, and a plethora of lines was established connecting the main ports in Europe with the major cities on the US east coast.

The ships sailed on set dates full or empty and had to confront widely varying ocean conditions according to the direction they were sailing and the season. At the outset, the liner vessels were small, fully rigged ships of around 400 tons, but they grew rapidly in size to accommodate the volume of the transatlantic trade. Speed was of the essence, and the masters were provided with strong financial incentives to make their passages as rapidly as possible.

The initial attempts were to simply increase the amount of sail and to carry it for as long as possible. This method of operation called for a particularly tough crew who could withstand this 'hard driving'. The Western Ocean packets were made all the more lucrative with the advent of famine and revolution in Europe providing a very lucrative back freight—emigrants. But brute force began to give way to art when it was realised there was a limit to the extra speed that could be obtained by simply cramming on more sail. America was fortunate in the rise of several inspired ship designers and builders who cut their teeth in building faster hulls for transatlantic packets and who would create the most famous of all sailing ships—the clippers.

The Emergence of America as a Merchant Marine Power

The history of merchant sailing ships is inseparable from developments in vessels whose prime purpose was to attack other ships or protect their merchant colleagues from aggressors. The age of the galleons is a prime example, and the East Indiamen were armed and built to resemble warships and even to act as such if the need arose. Once monopolies were rescinded, the merchant frigates that replaced the East Indiamen resembled their more heavily armed brethren but carried lighter armament.

After its war of independence, not only could America no longer rely on the Royal Navy to protect its merchant vessels, it had to guard those vessels against their former protectors. It was forced into global sea-power politics by the depredations of the Royal Navy and the Barbary corsairs, the former pressing American sailors and the latter enslaving and ransoming them. It was forced to establish the United States Navy. It lacked the resources to build the giant 'ships-of-the-line' employed by Britain in its wars with France. In any event, they were inappropriate for its purposes.

America chose instead a new concept in sailing ship: the frigate.

As a weapon of war, frigates were designed to hunt alone or in packs ('squadrons'), preying on each other's merchant ships or as prowling naval vessels, especially between the Mediterranean and along the English Channel. The vessels had a higher length-to-beam ratio than usual, were smaller than the heavily armed 'ships-of-the-line' (designed to fight set-piece battles), and apart from the latter, became the most powerful warships afloat. Following the end of the Napoleonic wars, their formidable speed, manoeuvrability, and combative power would, in its merchant form, ultimately replace the East Indiamen, although they would be less heavily armed than a naval frigate.

The American Congress approved the building of six super-frigates in 1794. Four were forty-four-gun vessels and the remaining two thirty-eight-gun craft. The Dey of Algiers would, meanwhile, sign a demeaning (for the US) treaty with the US before the ships were completed, removing one of the reasons for building them, and construction was temporarily halted. But relations with revolutionary France, formerly an ally, were deteriorating. French privateers began preying on unarmed American ships and by 1797 had taken 300 of them. The resulting indignation led to Congress approving three of the ships—the *United States*, the *Constitution* (which still floats, fully rigged today, in Boston Harbor), and the *Constellation*—to be finished, and a Navy Department set up to administer them. As hostilities increased, Congress approved the completion of the other three ships: the *Chesapeake*, the *Congress*, and the *President*.

Somewhat predictably, the success of the Dey of Algiers at extracting a big payoff and ongoing tribute from America inspired other Barbary coast rulers to use corsairs to try to extract a similar deal. In 1801, the Pasha of Tripoli declared war on the United States. The situation was eventually resolved, after considerable hostilities, with a ransom of the American sailors who had inadvertently become the Dey's prisoners.

The second of the two difficulties America was experiencing that led to the construction of the six frigates was impressment. The Royal Navy had 900 vessels at its disposal. America had seventeen. Some of Great Britain's ships had been built, and some captured, but it needed 150,000 men to crew them at a time when the population of England and Wales was only 11.3 million. Given the poor pay and even poorer conditions on British Naval vessels, impressment was a necessity, and American sailors and citizens were prime quarries—6,000 cases were registered by the American government.

To add salt to the wound, Britain, in its continuing war with its arch-enemy, Napoleonic France, was also arresting and confiscating any cargo that could conceivably be destined there. America declared war against Britain in 1812, with Britain regarding it as a minor conflict. Once the British emerged victorious over the French, it could turn its full force on the Americans. But its taste for war had declined, and the commercial interest was anxious for peace with America and a resumption of trade. Peace was finally declared in 1814 with the Treaty of Ghent. The English accepted that they could no longer impress American seamen and, with the peace, an American punitive expedition subdued Algiers, Tunis, and Tripoli, which agreed not to attack American shipping or take prisoners for ransom.

The Effects of the Peace

In the end, both nations desired to get back to what they were good at—generating wealth. The Anglo-American war was a watershed in that it saw a relatively small, primarily agricultural nation (7.2 million in 1810), withstand the naval might of the most industrialised and powerful nation in the world at the time. It demonstrated that America, with its relatively short maritime history but a talent for the sea and naval design, had emphatically arrived on the world maritime stage. It would be American nautical genius and initiative that would drive ship design and maritime achievement for at least the next half-century, through the instigation of the liner services and the development of that ultimate in wooden sailing ship design—the clipper. And it was all because the Americans brought a new sense of urgency to the world: time is money.

Driving ships hard twenty-four hours a day for days on end was to become the norm, not just a notion to be employed temporarily to gain a combat advantage in war, or for a slaver to escape apprehension.

Using their native genius and the natural advantage of a superb, cheap wood supply, they revolutionised wooden ship design. It was the limitation of wood as a material for the construction of ships that would bring their period of dominance to an end. They would be overtaken by their former enemy, which, with its industrial capability in the utilisation of steam and steel, would herald the beginning of the end of the utilisation of the wind and ocean currents to travel the world. The British, who had built the greatest empire the world had ever seen from the deck of a wooden sailing ship, would usher in its demise.

The East Indiamen operating far from home and the protection of their respective navies, and in an area infested with pirates, needed armament. The packet ships, operating in the North Atlantic, were fast enough and driven hard enough not to be armed. Most of America's merchant navy were unarmed, a situation that the Barbary corsairs had exploited. The next generation of sailing ships was fast enough and sufficiently weatherly to escape capture by a heavy, armed vessel. The installation and operation of cannon were expensive in terms of the extra manpower required for gun crews and the otherwise profitable cargo space they occupied. The notion of arming merchant ships went into decline assisted by the global influence of the Royal Navy.

The Clippers

The Setting

English merchant shipping, protected by the Navigation Acts, had little incentive to innovate. It was preoccupied with trade with India and China and harvesting the spoils of their enormous empire. For this, they employed the most potent navy in the world and a fleet of large, lumbering merchantmen.

Meanwhile, there was a revolution in how goods were produced going on in their own country, and it had little need for frivolities like tea, spices, and porcelain, but raw materials and, later, food. Consequently, Great Britain came to depend almost wholly on the American merchant marine to feed its industrial expansion, and it obliged wholeheartedly.

For now, the American Republic had no empire to exploit. It didn't even possess two-thirds of what would become the continental United States until mid-century. American entrepreneurs were driven simply by the desire to make money, and they had the resources in the form of abundant forests and a pool of innovative ship designers and builders to assist them in their endeavours. Their heritage to date had been the sea, and there was a ready pool of seamen, and especially hard-driving masters, who would exploit their innovations to the full.

Donald McKay's Magnificent Medium Clipper *Flying Cloud*

Source: from Jack Spurling Print in possession of the author

The Attributes

What were the qualities that American ship designers and builders came to realise were the keys to increasing the speed of a displacement hull of a sailing ship through the water? The work wasn't the result of one designer or constructor—it was the product of accumulated experience. They had entered a golden age, which extended from roughly 1820 to the peak reached for a few short years mid-century. The overwhelming advantage of the American designers was their experience with the Western Ocean packets and the coastal packets that fed cargo into the main ports on the American eastern seaboard. The great clipper ship designers all cut their teeth designing ships for the packet trade.

Full Body

Traditional hull design featured what was referred to as 'cod's head and mackerel tail', a bluff bow, with a wide midsection well forward of amidships and a gentle tapering towards the stern. It was based on the shape a melting block of ice forms when towed through the water. That design had long been abandoned by the designers of the packets in the interests of increased cargo space. Parallel sides continued the fullness of the hull further aft and, combined with a fairly flat floor, proved faster and more accommodating of cargo.

Minimum 'Deadrise'

As the transatlantic packets proved increasingly successful, feeder services developed to bring cotton from the South, food from the interior, and lumber from the maritime states. By chance, the cotton carriers had to have a flat bottom to navigate the shallow and shoaly waters of the Mississippi Delta to load in New Orleans. It was soon realised that a flat bottom slipped through the water faster than the traditional hull that was more 'V'-shaped in cross section—that had a more pronounced 'deadrise'. *Deadrise* is the term used to describe the angle that the bottom of a ship makes with the horizontal. Vessels with minimal deadrise (i.e. flatter bottoms), besides being faster, also had more cargo space: a big advantage for the shipowners.

Waterline Length

Perhaps the greatest advance, however, in displacement hull design was the recognition of the role that hull length played in obtainable speed. The French had been aware of this for some time, and their vessels, uninhibited (as in England) by pesky government regulation, quite often exceeded the 4:1 ratio of length to beam that had come to be the norm. Longer hulls could also carry more sail. It is now recognised that the maximum speed of a displacement hull is governed by a physical formula: hull speed in knots equals 1.34 times the square root of the waterline length in feet. ($HS = 1.34 \times \sqrt{WL}$ in feet.) Thus, a hull 200 feet in waterline length would have a maximum hull speed of $1.34 \times 14.1 = 18.9$ knots. A knot is a unit of speed equal to one nautical mile in an hour. One nautical mile is equal to 1.85 kilometres, so a 200-foot waterline-length vessel is theoretically capable of a maximum speed of around 19 knots, or 35 kilometres per hour. The clipper captain's job was to get as close to this maximum as humanly possible.

Champion of the Seas, an American clipper ship designed by Donald McKay for the Liverpool to Melbourne run, ran 861 kilometres in twenty-four hours on her maiden voyage—an average of 36 kilometres per hour—a record that stood for 130 years. Her length was 252 feet, and her waterline length would have been somewhat shorter. On that day's run, she must have been approaching the theoretical maximum, and it is no surprise it stood for such a long time.

Sharp Entry

In the interests of cargo capacity, the packets favoured the entry—the point at which the bow of the vessel meets the oncoming sea—to be fairly 'full' or relatively bluff. But it slowed the ship down because of the greater resistance it presented to the sea. Another aspect of the new designs was to substantially increase the sharpness of the bow. In an 'extreme' clipper, the flat bottom was confined to the after part of the ship, with the hull, as it progressed forward, made progressively sharper. The definition of 'extreme' is accepted to have been a ship with a forty-inch-or-more deadrise at half-floor (halfway along the length of the boat).

As well as the progressive steepening of the floor, another element of this 'sharpening' was 'hollowing out' the bow section above the waterline to make it concave. 'Hollow' bow sections were not new and had been a feature of the highly competitive New York pilot boats for some time. This design, however, proved deficient, not only in cargo-carrying ability but in that it possessed asymmetrical buoyancy, which strained and weakened the hull and led to 'hogging'. Hogging is the phenomenon where a hull sags at each end and the amidships section moves upwards. For this reason, the life of extreme clippers tended to be short, as did the currency of the design.

Constrained by owners to providing cargo capacity, they nevertheless implemented their ideas of flat floors and high vertical sides. Clipper ship design, therefore, retreated from the extreme model to carry the minimum deadrise and maximum beam (or width) further forward, thereby balancing the hull. The result was the medium clipper, the compromise that would still set speed records that would last for decades, all the while maintaining cargo capacity and profitability. A medium clipper could carry as much cargo as a British East Indiaman (hitherto the largest ships of their time) and do so while travelling half as fast again. While it was a compromise in hull design, the medium clippers still carried the outsize rigs and (in some cases) acres of canvas that typified the extreme vessels, and they were driven just as hard.

Concave Bow

The notion of a convex bow, which had been a feature of ship design for centuries, was another aspect that would be subject to revision in the interest of increased speed. The stem was carried forward in a curved line, thereby lengthening the bow above the water, presumably to increase foresail area. It also seems to have been a nod to the bow shape of the famous and fast Baltimore clippers that had regularly run the British blockade of the city of Baltimore during the Anglo-American War.

Champagne Glass Stern

The stern was also 'fined out' by the rounding up of the corners of the transom to produce the 'champagne glass' shape on their (backward sloping) counter (the actual stern face). While it may not have contributed materially to speed, it certainly increased elegance. The shape became an integral part of the clipper concept and complemented what is today still known as the 'clipper bow'.

Straight Run and Minimal Sheer

'Sheer' is the extent to which the bow and the stern sections of a vessel are higher than the centre section of the hull, that is to say, above the horizontal. The original slow-moving fifteenth- and sixteenth-century deep-sea vessels had quite pronounced sheer, both fore and aft. In the bow section, it prevented the bow from burying itself in a wave when the stern was being lifted and the ship thrust forward by an overtaking wave. Aft, it prevented the ship from being 'pooped'—the after section being swamped by an overtaking wave. The clippers were high-sided through the amidships section with a minimal fore-and-aft sheer. With their raked masts, elegantly protruding bow, and stern sections, the minimal sheer contributed further to the impression of speed, immortalised in the title of Carl C. Cutler's famous book, *Greyhounds of the Sea*.

The End of the Clipper Era

The overall effect of these changes and refinements resulted in a very individual shape. In their pursuit of speed through the water, clipper designers unconsciously produced a vessel of unparalleled grace and refinement. It engraved itself on the hearts of all those who mastered, crewed, or voyaged on these magnificent ships. And for all those who never had those opportunities, it remains the benchmark of naval architecture and the penultimate development in merchant sail.

A deep economic depression in 1857 almost wiped out America's wood-based shipbuilding industry. Great Britain, freed from the restrictions of the Navigation Acts, and with the templates created by the Americans (which they assiduously copied), got into the fast merchant ship business. The result was the short-lived but much romanticised era of the 'tea clippers'. To make their very large wooden hulls rigid, the American vessels were so assiduously reinforced that they had become a forest of timbers internally. The British builders, skilled in working with cast iron and steel, were able to create a strong metal frame and clad it with the superb boatbuilding timbers brought from India. The result was the 'composite hull'—relatively light and, with a typical clipper rig, quite fast, especially in light airs. However, they lacked the waterline length to break the speed records set by their transatlantic cousins.

Having completed the acquisition of their continental land mass following the Mexican–American War, post-Civil War, the Americans became preoccupied with their Western frontier and essentially abandoned the sea.

The tables turned.

America would become almost entirely dependent on British shipping between the Civil War and the First World War. But the clipper as a sailing ship form would not long outlast the opening of the Suez Canal that got the steamers into the Eastern trade. A new type of sailing ship would emerge, the product of new transport needs and the skill of British steel shipbuilding—the giant windjammer.

The Decline of the United States as a Merchant Maritime Power

The clipper era was one of feverish construction prompted by the high freight rates that accrued to fast ships, whether landing gold seekers at their destinations or bringing tea from China. Like all booms, it ended in overbuilding, and in 1857, a massive downturn in the industry wiped out most of the great clipper-building yards, a situation from which they would never recover. By the time shipbuilding recovered in the United States, the great era of wooden ship construction was over. When it emerged again in the twentieth century, the vessels it manufactured would be made almost entirely of steel.

The Advent of Steam and Steel

The latter part of the nineteenth century saw a period of rapid technological change. For merchant shipping, there was a move from the complete dominance of wooden sailing ships to the emergence of, firstly, iron and then steel construction. These new materials were used to build ships and especially ships driven by steam engines. This was essentially a symbiotic relationship due to the difficulty wooden hulls had resisting the vibration of the reciprocating steam engine.

In a very short period, the construction of wooden merchant sailing ships all but ceased. The superior strength of iron and then steel, besides resisting the vibration of a steam engine, was also superb at resisting the stresses on the hull generated by the rig of a sailing ship. In so doing, it ushered in what was perhaps the greatest age of merchant sail, the windjammers. But it was also its swansong.

The Windjammers

The windjammers were not an attempt to improve on perfection. They were designed, not so much for speed, although they were certainly no slouches, but for a specific task: bringing heavy bulk raw materials from remote locations. Because the earth's wind systems are at mankind's disposal anywhere on the globe, their niche was in lifting cargoes where steamers, the nemesis of the sailing ship, could not go. Early in the steamship era, they were limited in their routes and destinations by the availability of coal and the ferocity of the sea conditions. This was especially the case with the west coast of South America where an absence of coal, and the sea conditions likely to be encountered in rounding Cape Horn, precluded the use of steamers.

Whereas the construction of the Suez Canal was a major factor in the decline of the clippers, it was another 'dirty ditch' that would contribute to the demise of the windjammers. Even after the Panama Canal was opened, the windjammers would continue to bring nitrate from South America. It would be another triumph of the Industrial Revolution after steam: the chemical production of nitrate for use as a fertiliser, and the manufacture of munitions and explosives generally, that would seal their fate. The markets left to them were mainly wool and wheat out of Australia, where the absence of coal in the producing regions kept the steamships at bay.

The Biggest Sailing Ship Ever Built: The Windjammer *Preussen II*

Source: State Library of Queensland

It was a great final act. The last decades of the nineteenth century and up until the outbreak of the First World War in 1914 saw the construction of the greatest fleet of sailing ships the world has ever known. Not only were they more numerous, but they were also bigger than the clippers and constructed of a much more durable material—steel. Not only that, while the packets and the clippers were multipurpose vessels carrying cargo (both bulk and general), passengers, and mail, the great barque windjammers were expressly bulk cargo carriers feeding raw materials into the mature period of the Industrial Revolution, to manufacturing centres primarily in Europe.

Although few were built after the First World War, they were renowned for their durability, and some would continue lugging their cargoes from remote areas of the globe until after the Second World War. We are lucky that a number have survived into the twenty-first century as museum ships and restaurants. They're a testament to our fascination with a creation that exploited the earth's givens—wind, current, and tide—to the ultimate.

Some of the first windjammers were the largest sailing ships ever built—five-masted fully rigged ships—that is to say, square-rigged on all masts with a fore-and-aft sail included on the after mast. These were mighty vessels but in many ways French and German vanity projects. They were expensive to run, given their crew requirements in a time when wages were rising, and they weren't particularly good sailers. The rig that would emerge triumphant would be the four-masted barque: square-rigged on three masts and with a single fore-and-aft sail on the after mast. So effective were they that over 400 of these steel giants would be built. They provided a dramatic finale to an era that we shall never see the likes of again.

3
CHAPTER

The Age of Exploration

Introduction

The exotic products of India and the Spice Islands, even of China, were well known in the maritime pre-exploration period. Their existence had been established from information that had been travelling, along with the merchandise, on ancient land routes for centuries. The so-called Silk Road had delivered exotic goods into Europe since Roman times. Marco Polo even claimed to have been there. But these goods were expensive due to the risks involved, the multitude of middlemen, and the small quantities that could be carried on animals by the legendary trading caravans.

Long gone was the assumption that the world was flat and that if a ship proceeded too far, it would fall off the edge. Hellenistic philosophers had alluded to the earth being a sphere while Arab astronomers had made calculations as to its size some time before Columbus set out. His mistake was assuming their calculations were based on Roman rather than Islamic miles, which led to the conclusion that the world was much smaller than it actually is.

The cost of eastern goods was exacerbated by the stranglehold exerted on trade by the great eastern Mediterranean trading power, Venice. The city state monopolised the purchase of Eastern trade goods and their distribution throughout Europe. Its system was exemplary and lucrative. When Vasco da Gama made it to India and back, he demonstrated the much larger quantities that could be carried in the hold of a ship, even though there was still a considerable risk involved because of the length of the route and the perils of open-ocean sailing.

The larger quantities and uncomplicated supply chain meant that ship-borne goods were considerably cheaper than those imported using the land route. They were sufficiently cheaper to undercut Venice but still lucrative enough to make these voyages profitable. There was also an increased demand stimulated by the bullion flowing from Spain's American colonies. For safety's sake, ships sailed in convoys, but the cost of mounting an expedition was high. The spice trade required a lot of money to be provided upfront, and the profits would not be realised for over a year.

The Age of 'Discovery'

The period in which Europe became directly connected to Asia and the Far East was only coincidentally an 'age of discovery'. These epic journeys did not result in 'finding' India or China. What was unknown and 'discovered' were the giant continents of the Americas and the southern extent of Africa. The voyages to the East, or the completely unknown West, were made, not out of curiosity but from a hard-nosed desire to access Oriental goods more cheaply and in larger volumes. Direct access to the sources, whether by sailing East or West, would break the Venetian monopoly and avoid the constraints placed on the trade by the newly risen Ottoman Empire.

Geopolitics also played a role in the voyages to the East. Islam had spread West along the southern shore of the Mediterranean and, crossing at Gibraltar, had come to rule much of the Iberian Peninsula. There was some suggestion that sailing East might engender a meeting with the (mythical) Christian king Prester John. There is an Orthodox Christian community that has inhabited a part of Ethiopia since early Christian times and which still exists. There does not, however, appear to be any evidence that it was ever ruled by a Prester John. Nevertheless, it was thought that his assistance might be sought to combat Islam generally, and the Ottomans in particular, by dividing their empire.

By seeking to trade directly with the East, however, these voyages revealed the size of the African continent, the nature of India, and the Indonesian and Philippine archipelagos. They would also eventually establish direct contact with China and Japan.

What were truly voyages of discovery were those made to the West.

Although the Vikings had been there centuries before, no one in fifteenth-century Europe had the slightest idea of the existence of the Americas and that they stood between them and the Orient. The notion of a 'Great South Land', or Terra Australis Incognita, had existed conceptually or hypothetically long before any European set eyes upon it.

Columbus's encounter with the Americas was utterly unexpected.

The Immensity of the Earth

The early East Indian venturers became familiar with a lot of territory and trade possibilities (especially, for example, what is now the Indonesian archipelago and Japan) of which they were only vaguely aware. Columbus, on the assumption of a spherical globe, set out West, convinced that he could reach China more directly than sailing around Cape of Good Hope. He was unaware of how big the world was and what vast distance and enormous land masses blocked his way. Even if the Americas had not existed, his small vessels could not and did not carry sufficient stores to make the journey. He and his crew would have perished of hunger and thirst long before reaching the East. Even after he had discovered the West Indies, however, he still maintained he had reached China.

Navigators did not realise the immensity of the earth for another three decades. Ferdinand Magellan's heroic circumnavigation of the world (completed by his crew after his death in the Philippines) demonstrated that it was much bigger than Columbus had assumed. In exploiting the potential of the Philippines and the most eastern of the Spice Islands, the Spanish were risking Portuguese and papal intervention by continuing to sail West. They, therefore, shipped the fruits of their discoveries home via the Americas, utilising the wind gyre of the northern Pacific Ocean.

Five and a half decades after Magellan, Sir Francis Drake, attracted by the prospect these rich 'Manila galleons' presented for piracy, would be the first English navigator to circumnavigate the world. But he only did so after abandoning hope of finding a passage north around the Americas. There is the suggestion that Drake sought this route at the behest of Queen Elizabeth, and he certainly put a lot of effort into trying to find it because he knew he could not go back the way he had come. The Spanish would be waiting for his pirated, treasure-laden, and slow vessel. The only alternative for survival was to sail West. As such, circumnavigating the globe was a matter of necessity, not curiosity.

The maritime trade routes, once delineated, provided an overwhelming advantage over the land route. Compared to the pack animals of the middlemen-infested Silk Road, ships could carry a much larger volume of trade goods in a single-unit journey. The downside was that the loss of a single ship meant a considerable financial setback. To minimise the risks, voyages tended to be made in convoy. Ships crippled by storm or pirate attack could be abandoned, and their cargo, stores, water, and crew divided among the remaining vessels.

Why Europe?

At the turn of the fifteenth century, the world's population was less than half a billion people. Its estimated GDP was around 500 billion in constant (2011) US dollars. India and China were much larger economies than any country in Europe and, in many respects, more technologically advanced. India had a population of around 100 million, and China over 200 million. The entire population of Europe at the time, recovering as it was from the ravages of the Black Death, was around 90 million, of which France (15 million) was the largest.

However, Spain drove out Islam, the kingdoms of Aragon and Castile were united under Philip and Isabella, and the wealth of their South American colonies began to flow. It soon became Europe's richest and most powerful nation. The king of Spain was also the Holy Roman emperor, pledged to protect the Holy Roman Empire and, importantly but tragically for Magellan, to spread the faith. Even though the population of Spain and Portugal combined was only around 8.5 million, these two countries led the world towards globalisation.

Decades before European voyaging began, Chinese expansionism had brought vast areas of the East under its suzerainty. But at a crucial time in history, it turned inwards, abandoning its hold on Asia, leaving it and China itself open to exploitation. The Europeans sailed enthusiastically into the resulting power vacuum. Ironically, for China, the very gunpowder technology that it had developed would play a big part in its undoing centuries later.

China and Zheng He

The first great voyages of exploration were not, as we are commonly led to believe, European but Chinese. And one of the great 'what ifs' must be what would have been the path of world events had these voyages continued. Yongle, the third of the Ming emperors, was the instigator, and the voyages were conducted by Zheng He (1371–1433). Yongle sent large fleets of ships on seven separate voyages over almost thirty years that cowed a vast area of Asia and the Far East into acknowledging China as the dominant power and paying tribute accordingly. Had Yongle not been unseated in 1424, the course of world history might have been very different.

Zheng He and his Flagship

Source: © Chris Hellier/CORBIS

Asian countries were historically traders, and China, with its advanced technology and art, was a rich source of desirable trade goods. The right to trade was in the hands of the emperor, and he demanded princely tribute in return. To keep the trade routes open and the tribute flowing, Yongle exerted a soft (but sometimes hard) power to force recognition of China's domination. The emperor was not so much interested in conquest, but he demanded acknowledgement of his suzerainty by lavish gifts of jewels, bullion, and exotic animals.

Acceptance of the Celestial Empire (so-called because of the practice of heaven worship) as the dominant power in this vast region gained tributary states the right to trade with China. At the time, it was overwhelmingly the greatest and most advanced nation on earth. Tribute provided access to Chinese silk, porcelain, gunpowder, and technology and wealth flowed from access to such a large market.

During the latter part of the Ming era, China's mercantile fleet—estimated at 15,000 vessels—was more formidable than that of any other nation, whether they be East or West. Measuring up to 3,000 gross tons, Chinese ships were also much bigger than anyone else's. In comparison, the largest Portuguese carrack ever built was only half that size.

Chinese shipbuilding technology, which had developed in isolation, was unique. The dominant form of vessel was the 'junk'. Isolated or not, the technology had been honed over centuries and was, in many ways, in advance of the West. Junks had long employed such innovations as rudders (as opposed to steering oars), stayed masts, and watertight compartments, the latter not adopted by the West for centuries. Compartmentalisation also strengthened the hull. Like the fast dinghies of the twentieth century, Chinese junks had fully battened sails that retained an aerodynamic shape. The method of controlling these sails, by multiple sheets, was superior to anything in the West. The Chinese also employed 'lodestones' for navigational purposes.

The junk was flat-bottomed and carried up to five masts or, in Zheng He's case, up to nine. Their square sails were made of linen or matting reinforced with bamboo and rigged behind the mast. They were fast, easy to sail, and with their shallow draft, ideal for estuarine navigation.

In the first half of the fifteenth century, China's large merchant navy ranged all over the Indian Ocean, East Africa, the Middle East, and Southeast Asia. Chinese ships may even have got as far as the Atlantic, well before European craft were able to cover such prodigious distances.

Voyages of the Yongle Emperor's Great Admiral Zheng He

Source: Author research

A lot of what China achieved at sea can only be deduced from coin finds and local artworks, but there is a historical record from the early fifteenth century. Beginning in 1405, the fleets were under the command of the great navigator Zheng He, reputedly a high-ranking Muslim eunuch. Zheng He sailed as far away from China as the Red Sea, Hormuz, and Mozambique and may even have rounded the Cape of Good Hope in a westerly direction. In all, he made six voyages under the Yongle emperor, alerting the West to the trade possibilities of China.

Zheng He's main ships were enormous nine-masted junks, some of the largest wooden ships ever built, accompanied by a fleet of smaller auxiliary craft. His seventh and last voyage in 1431, under a new emperor, comprised sixty-three ships and 30,000 men. One of those ships was reputed to be 400 feet long (some sources say 600) and 150 feet on the beam with nine masts. This would make it the largest wooden ship ever built. (The largest wooden ship built in the modern era was American shipbuilder Donald McKay's *Great Republic*. It was 335 feet in length with a beam of 53 feet.)

Ming China was by far the largest and wealthiest nation on earth in the fifteenth century, and the voyages were conducted on a colossal scale. Besides trade goods, successive trips shuttled foreign ambassadors and tribute back and forth and ensured that lesser states continued to acknowledge their position and contribute accordingly.

The voyages were, however, an immense drain on the imperial treasury, and the hard-nosed mandarins controlling state finances soon began to resist. There was also resistance to imperial control of trade. Together, these factors brought an end to the expeditions. A period of unrest followed the fall of Yongle in 1424, and by 1449, China had turned decisively inwards, trade declined, and the great navy fell into disrepair.

The European Era

At the dawn of the age of European exploration, Europe was, on a global scale, a minor player split geographically between several interests and soon to be further riven on religious grounds. The Black Death had preoccupied the continent's rulers, but once it had dissipated, the mood changed and turned to the accumulation of wealth and the political power it could provide. Global voyaging procured exotic merchandise, such as silks and porcelain and the herbs, spices, and condiments that had been enhancing food in the East for millennia. There was also interest in medicines, such as camphor and opium, that had similarly long histories.

Portugal and Spain were governed by absolute and aspirational rulers and, despite their small populations, were possessed of an ingrained sense of superiority and greed. Out of necessity and because of their proximity to the open ocean, they developed navigational knowledge and skills, shipbuilding technology, metal-founding competencies, and advanced armaments. Together, these assets enabled them to cover vast distances on a trackless ocean to bring them safely to Asia and, more importantly, back home again.

Despite their navigational success, the Iberians—especially Portugal—lacked commercial acumen and a well-developed banking system. Another weakness was the absence of a comprehensive distribution system, similar to that of Venice and Antwerp, that would have enabled them to take full advantage of the larger European market.

Allied to greed, in an inhumane age, the Iberians were incredibly cruel, with little regard for human life. A feature of their exploits was a pronounced lack of respect for the societies, creeds, and cultures they encountered. In a complete absence of the rule of law, 'might was right'. It would be their commercial inadequacies; however, that would result in them, in time, being overtaken by more advanced European nations.

Arabs were the great navigators of medieval times, and their traders had developed skills and techniques that enabled them to dominate trading in the Indian Ocean. Their land forces had also reached the Atlantic via the Mediterranean by the late medieval period. In so doing, they alerted Europeans to the trade possibilities of the East. Their ships were not, however, capable of the prolonged voyages in the open seas to which the Europeans would have to resort in getting to Asia. Once there, it was the power of the Portuguese, Spanish, Dutch, and finally, the English ships that would push the Muslim merchants from the Indies.

Not only did they develop a bountiful trade between Europe and the East, but they also came to dominate the 'country trade' between Asian countries. The country trade would ultimately prove much more profitable than the high-risk 'return' trade to Europe. In time, Portugal, for one, financially stretched, would resort to trading spices into Hormuz. From there, the goods would go by land caravan and ship into the Venetian distribution system, which it had originally set out to circumvent.

The Politics of Expansion

At the beginning of this momentous era, it was inevitable that the two powers of the Iberian Peninsula would be the first to cross swords on who had exploitation 'rights' in this 'New World'. Meanwhile, although not nearly as large as Zheng He's craft, Europeans nevertheless built vessels that were demonstrably seaworthy, capable of surviving on the open ocean and doing so for prolonged periods, although losses were enormous.

The rewards were, nevertheless, sufficient to justify them.

For centuries, that meant simply surviving the rigours of the sea to safely deliver whatever cargo had motivated the voyage, not the speed at which it was accomplished. The original (mainly) Iberian carracks that led this first step along the road to globalisation were not fast, but their achievements attest to their seaworthiness and the courage and skill of the men who sailed them.

Portugal and Spain would come to have papally decreed monopolies on their respective hemispheres, and speed was not of the essence. The carracks were firstly the pioneers of international commerce and then its workhorses. In a period of lawless high seas, they were designed for defence, but this made them clumsy and poor sailers. Although some were quite large, in time, the sheer volume of trade they unlocked would provide the impetus for the next stage in ocean-going sailing vessel design, the galleon.

The notion of 'exploration' has been romanticised, but these were expensive, entrepreneurial, and above all, high-risk initiatives that promised extraordinary returns. Greed was the primary motivation rather than an insatiable curiosity or a youthful desire for adventure. They were avaricious, hard-nosed business ventures, mounted chiefly to find a cheaper and more productive means of landing the precious products of the East into Europe. Once these routes (to the Americas and then to Asia) were proven, the immense wealth that they unlocked triggered an increase in ship size to utilise and protect them.

The risks associated with fifteenth- and sixteenth-century long-distance voyaging were enormous. So great in fact that a ship needed to recover the costs of its construction and the mounting of an expedition from its first voyage. As well, the profits had to pay a handsome return to the merchants who instigated it. Only one small ship of Magellan's heroic circumnavigation fleet eventually reached Europe, but its cargo of pepper more than paid for the entire venture.

Had this very high ratio of return to risk not been the case, it is doubtful if the pioneering would have proceeded at the pace it did. The Asians had little interest in the trade goods the European adventurers had to offer and sought payment in bullion. It would be the riches (in the form of gold and silver) flowing from the first stage of the age of European conquest of the Americas that underwrote these voyages. Thus, it became less a case of trade and more of simply purchase by specie that drove the initial stages of exploration.

In time, it would turn into something much more one-sided: conquest and subjugation.

Portugal

Venice was the great trading power of medieval Europe, conveniently located at the western end of the Silk Road. A long history of courageous voyaging and successful entrepreneurship saw it dominate Mediterranean commerce and construct a highly articulated distribution system and trading empire. It took every advantage of its position and priced those goods accordingly.

Demand for spices and silks increased steadily through the fifteenth century. The fall of Byzantium signalled by the conquest of Constantinople by the Ottoman Turks in 1454 reduced supplies and pushed up prices. Although the Ottomans permitted Christians to continue trading with Asia, it was now slower and more dangerous. Pernicious Venetian pricing and declining trade good availability provided the incentives to find an alternative route to the East.

Portugal, where Eastern trade goods were most expensive due to its location Far West on the Atlantic coast, had a particular incentive. It meshed with its expertise in navigation, its unrestricted access to the open ocean, and its experience with open-sea voyaging. It would go on to establish the first and longest-lived of the European overseas empires, beginning with Ceuta in Morocco in North Africa in 1415. It would end with the relinquishing of Macau to the People's Republic of China in 1999. Portugal's navigational savvy derived from frequent trips down the West African coast—which it dominated—to trade slaves, gold, and ivory, an activity that was the particular preoccupation of its early fifteenth-century king, João I's third son, Prince Henry.

Prince Henry the Navigator	João I (King John I of Portugal)

Source: Wikipedia Commons	*Source: Wikipedia Commons*

Romanticised for his supposed ability to find his way on the open ocean, Prince Henry was neither a sailor nor a navigator. But he was possessed of a greedy enthusiasm for mounting seafaring expeditions south to Africa. To reduce the risks, he established a navigation school at Sagres on the south-western tip of Portugal in 1418. It provided instruction for Prince Henry's ships' captains in safely exploiting the trade possibilities for which Portugal was the most advantageously situated.

Prince Henry also sponsored developments in ship design and encouraged the collection and correlation of oceanographic data that facilitated progress to and from trading destinations—data that would be termed intellectual property today. Historians have accorded him the sobriquet of Prince Henry the Navigator, but he remained firmly on dry land financing and facilitating the voyages.

His father, João I, gave Prince Henry the exclusive right to trade in the aforesaid 'commodities' with Guinea and sugar from Madeira. The island, with its abundant supply of shipbuilding timbers, proved a very strategic asset. It was claimed by Portuguese sailors in the service of Prince Henry in 1419, settled in 1420, and is considered to be the first territorial find of the Age of Discovery.

Like the Ming emperors, the Portuguese monarchy regarded trade as a royal monopoly to be disposed of at whim. It led to the ineffectual system of 'monarchical capitalism' as a means of exploiting its venturing. Portugal was a small and relatively impoverished country. Unlike its northern neighbours, especially the Netherlands, it lacked an entrepreneurial middle class and a developed banking system. It was ill-equipped to bear the risk, provide the capital, and muster the commercial expertise required for long-distance trading.

Portugal was also unfortunate in that under the Treaty of Tordesillas, it was precluded from accessing the immense wealth that Spain obtained from the gold and especially silver mines of Peru. With a population of just 2 million, Portugal was also dwarfed by its much more substantial neighbour on the Iberian Peninsula. Consequently, after Prince Henry's death in 1460, little attempt was made to capitalise on the country's expertise and experience.

However, the international climate changed with the rise of the Ottomans, and with a new and more enterprising king, Portugal's interest in exploration revived.

Bartholomeu Dias

João I of Portugal died in 1433 and was succeeded by his son Duarte, who ruled for only five years (to 1438). Prince Henry died in 1460. Duarte's son, Alfonso V, died in 1481, and it was under his son, João II, that the great voyages of Portuguese exploration would take place.

King João II, smarting under the recent Ottoman domination of the Near East land trade routes and fascinated by the legend of Prester John, hatched a plan. He would send both land-based and seagoing expeditions to find the mythical ruler and to link up with him to overthrow the Turks. At the same time, he would try to open up a sea route to the East. The man he chose to make the sea journey was Bartholomeu Dias. His fleet was made up of three caravels.

Bartholomeu Dias (1450–1500)

Source: Alamy

Little is known about Bartholomeu Dias other than that he received an education that fitted him for life as a navigator and explorer. He rose to sufficiently high office in the court of João II to be recruited by the king for what appears today to be a somewhat harebrained expedition. Harebrained or not, it would trigger one of the great ages in human history.

For all he knew when he set out, Dias's voyage could have ended very badly (and almost did) or proved as frustrating as were the later repeated attempts to reach China via an assumed north-west passage. The African continent might have extended so far south that his progress would be blocked by ice. As it was, proceeding further south than the equator was made difficult by the adverse Benguela current and contrary winds. Navigators also lost sight of the Pole Star, which conveniently revolves tightly around the North Pole, providing a beacon for northern hemisphere navigators. But the recent acquisition of navigational technology from China in the form of the compass meant that Dias would always know roughly in which direction he was heading.

But as to the southern extent of the African continent, he knew nothing.

Dias's intention was, after avoiding the light airs of the Gulf of Guinea, to hug the coast, planting massive white stone crosses inscribed with the coat of arms of Portugal (*padrões*), claiming the land as he went. Being caravels, with their fore-and-aft sails, his ships could work into the wind when necessary, and this characteristic enabled him to make a coast-hopping way south which, by accident or design, would have kept him out of the main force of the north-flowing Benguela current.

In 1488, he finally succeeded, initially unknowingly, due to a fierce storm, in rounding the southernmost part of what is now South Africa. The Cape of Good Hope is not in fact the southernmost point, but it is the point when a ship begins to head more south-east than south. The *actual* southernmost point is Cape Agulhas.

Dias erected his first *padrão* in Algoa Bay, by which time he was heading north-east. His ships were the first Europeans to enter the Indian Ocean. As it turned out, compared to Cape Horn, Cape Agulhas lies at only a relatively balmy thirty degrees south latitude. However, replenishing food onshore had been prevented by hostile natives, and supplies were running low. Facing a mutiny by his crew, he was forced to turn back, having got as far as the Great Fish River, just north-east of where Port Alfred stands today. Here he erected another *padrão*. Dias's caravels might have been handy at coast-hopping, but they were limited in their cargo-carrying capacity and hence their operational range if prevented from making landfalls.

While not at a high south latitude, the Cape of Good Hope is an area of fierce storms and unruly, often mountainous, seas. It is known as one of the world's most treacherous coasts, and even in the twentieth century, ships were lost there. The sea floor rises suddenly to the continental shelf, which can cause freak-high seas. As well, sea conditions can be exacerbated by the meeting of the Atlantic and Indian Oceans. The convergence of two currents, the waves of which meet obliquely, forms very disturbed wave patterns. The turbulence is created by the warm Agulhas current—the world's second-fastest moving body of ocean, flowing down the east coast of Africa—meeting the cold Benguela current, which forms the southern portion of the South Atlantic gyre.

As well as the treacherous sea conditions, the navigational challenge is heightened by the fierce westerly winds. Just as a storm delayed Dias's realisation that he had rounded the Cape—a feat that put his name in the history books—so another storm would drown him there years later. Meanwhile, of the three *padrões* that he had brought with him on his initial voyage of discovery, he planted one in the vicinity of the Great Fish River, and one each at the Cape and Luderitz, in what is now Namibia, on his return journey.

Dias sailed back to Lisbon in late 1488 and reported his findings to the king. Present at this event was the Genoese navigator Christopher Columbus. He was now living in Spain but may well have returned to Portugal, where he had lived and worked for some time. He was trying to interest João II in his idea of reaching China by sailing West. But Dias's rounding of the Cape of Good Hope left the Portuguese king focused on capitalising on that discovery. Because of local problems, however, another Portuguese expedition to the East would not be mounted for another decade.

King João II, known as the 'perfect prince' given all he achieved for Portugal, died in 1495. He was succeeded by Manuel I, his cousin who, fortunately for Portugal, was also interested in exploration and its potential riches.

Part of the ongoing Portuguese navigational advantage was that they made meticulous written records of how to get to and from the places they reached. These *roterios* or 'rutters' were the basis of their subsequent domination of Eastern trade and were highly prized and closely guarded. It was the beginning of a long tradition of keeping accurate records of a ship's progress (their 'logs'), the detailed analysis of which, centuries later, would form the basis of the science of oceanography.

The Portuguese would be followed into 'their' hemisphere by legions of Spaniards, the Dutch, and ultimately British and American fortune hunters and imperialists. They were brave, avaricious, and often cruel and bloodthirsty freebooters, driven by visions of vast wealth. They exploited existing global wind and current systems to break down the often self-imposed isolation of Asian countries and to open up the world to trade and ultimately industrial development. For now, it was the turn of the newly united Iberian kingdoms of Aragon and Castile to flex their combined muscle.

Portugal, as a single nation and better located, had expelled the Moors, leaving it free to devote its expertise in navigation to seek further trading opportunities. The Spanish monarchs (Ferdinand and Isabella), who had also been preoccupied with expelling the Moors, came later into the business of maritime pioneering. But Spain's (or more precisely, Queen Isabella of Castile's) commissioning of Columbus was the beginning of a century and a half of territorial rivalry with Portugal.

Christopher Columbus

Christopher Columbus was born in Genoa in 1451 and began his working life serving on his father's cheese stand in the local market. He went to sea at age ten, later sailing to England and Ireland from where, in 1477, aged twenty-six, he returned on a Portuguese ship to Lisbon where his brother, Bartolomeo, was working at map-making. Columbus would remain in Portugal for nine years, marrying a Portuguese nobleman's daughter and spending time in the royal business of trading along the west coast of Africa. Unfortunately, his wife died in 1485, and he moved to Castile in Spain.

Christopher Columbus (1451-1506)

Source: British Library

An avid autodidact, the young Christopher taught himself several languages and read widely on, among other things, astronomy and geography. He was convinced that China could be reached by sailing west, but his concept of the size of the globe was seriously awry. The earth was much larger than he thought, and China much further away.

Moreover, a considerable obstacle in the form of the massive, joined continents of North and South America barred his way. But it was of little consequence. What he happened upon was ultimately of eminently more significance than an alternative route to China.

And it made Spain by far the wealthiest nation in Europe.

From his previous voyages north, Columbus had learned about wind systems, especially the persistent westerlies of the North Atlantic. He used the favourable, lower-latitude north-east trades on his outward journey looking to take advantage of the persistent higher-latitude westerlies (the other side of the North Atlantic gyre) on his way back. They affect an ocean-going sailing ship's ability to make its way to a particular location and back given their limited ability to work into the wind. The Atlantic posed another problem. Unlike the Pacific with islands scattered across its length and breadth, the islands in the Atlantic are around its periphery. There are no small land masses that might act as staging posts on a long voyage.

What Columbus found were those peripheral islands, outposts of the North American continent. They would prove much more significant for him and his financial backers than a shorter route to China. The reward wouldn't be spices but gold and silver and, later, land ideal for the cultivation of sugar cane and other subtropical crops, cotton among them. Although Columbus did not find a way to China, ironically, it would be these new supplies of bullion that would serve to finance the silk and spice trade with the Orient. As previously pointed out, the Orient wasn't especially interested in what the European explorers had to offer in exchange and insisted on payment in precious metals. Even though the distance had been conquered, trade with the Orient would have been considerably constrained by Europe's lack of precious metals.

Columbus's conviction that it was possible to reach China by sailing west was an idea initially floated by the Florentine astronomer Paolo Toscanelli in 1470. Columbus tried to interest the Portuguese monarch in the concept, but João II's preoccupation with Dias's rounding of the Cape of Good Hope caused him to return to Spain. After shopping the project around Venice, Genoa, and even to King Henry VII of England, he eventually succeeded in interesting Queen Isabella and her husband, Ferdinand II, in the enterprise.

They initially knocked him back, but to avoid him taking the idea elsewhere, they provided him with a pension. It was not until after three years of lobbying and persuasion, in 1492, four years after he had presented the plan to King João II, that the joint Spanish monarchs relented and agreed to finance the expedition.

It was a momentous decision and one the monarchy would be forever pleased they made. The riches that flowed as a result of Columbus's voyages to the Americas would make Spain the most powerful nation in Europe for more than a century. One can't help wonder what would have been the course of world history had King Henry VII of England relented in his miserly ways and agreed to sponsor the voyage. Nevertheless, his granddaughter and her freebooters would do a lucrative business preying on the ships moving these riches to Spain.

Columbus miscalculated the diameter of the earth partly because he assumed the astronomical calculations were expressed in the shorter Roman mile, rather than the Arabic measure. As a result, he felt the diameter of the earth at the equator was about 30,000 kilometres when it was actually 40,000 kilometres—one-third larger. It was just as well for him that he got it so wrong. There were no ships available at the time that could have carried sufficient provisions to survive such a long return trip, and potential sponsors would have likely discouraged him from setting out in the first place.

Ignorance, while not precisely bliss, created an environment in which the whole enterprise became sufficiently feasible to gain royal assent. As well as the sponsorship he obtained, the deal Columbus did with the Spanish monarchy gave him the potential to extract considerable wealth and power from his discoveries. But his pact was with unfettered royal power, and he would have difficulty holding them to their promises and realising its potential in the long term.

At the command of the monarchs, all of Columbus's ships were placed at his disposal by wealthy merchants. They embodied what would become the significant advantage they held over other vessels of the time. They had three masts that spread the load of the sails along the keel and permitted a variety of sail configurations depending on the prevailing winds. The largest ship (the *Santa Maria*) was a carrack, a large (for its time) square-rigged vessel with high fore- and aftercastles, square sails on the fore- and main masts and a lateen sail on the mizzen (after) mast. She was 19 metres (62 feet) long and measured 108 tons. A second ship (the *Pinta*) was a carrack-rigged caravel, and the third (the *Niña*) was a conventional caravel. Both were significantly smaller (around 40 to 50 tons) and more weatherly than the *Santa Maria*. The *Niña*, as a conventional caravel, was the fastest and most flexible of the three, although less so with a following wind. The names of the latter vessels were nicknames, but they were the ones by which they have become universally known. Portugal and Spain used both ship types in the Mediterranean while Portugal used them when exploring the west coast of Africa.

Employing his experience with wind systems, Columbus harnessed the north-easterly trades to sail in a south-westerly direction. Five weeks after leaving the Canary Islands off the coast of West Africa, he made landfall in the Bahamas. He used the northern side of the gyre to return home.

In all, he would make four Castile-sponsored voyages to the Americas and would consistently maintain that he had reached Asia. After exploring several islands in the West Indies, he returned to Europe where he was forced to land in Portugal due to bad weather. Here he met up with João II again who, somewhat ominously, pointed out that Columbus's voyage violated the Treaty of Alcáçovas of 1479 between Spain and Portugal, which had provided Portugal with supremacy in the Atlantic Ocean.

While in Portugal, Columbus paid his respects to one Eleanor of Viseu, who later became the queen consort. A ward of her court at the time was a youth also destined to write his name into the annals of maritime exploration.

His name was Vasco da Gama.

The findings of his first voyage to the Americas made Columbus what we would today call a celebrity, so much so that on his second voyage, he no longer had to implore influential people to sponsor him. So great was the thirst for the promised riches of the New World among the Spanish merchant fraternity that he led a fleet of seventeen ships, passengers on which included priests, soldiers, and farmers, across the Atlantic. The objective was no longer only exploration but colonisation. For his part, Columbus himself now rejoiced in the title of lord admiral and governor of the new lands.

His third voyage, comprising a fleet of six ships, was intended to both colonise and explore. Three craft went to resupply the island of Hispaniola, and Columbus took the other three vessels exploring. He was still looking for the passage through the Americas that would lead him to Asia. In so doing, he touched on South America near the mouth of the mighty Orinoco River, so big it indicated it drained a large land mass. That size notwithstanding, it wasn't anywhere near as big as the as yet undiscovered Amazon.

Upon returning to Hispaniola, Columbus got into a dispute with the settlers who insisted he had misled them as to the bountiful nature of the island. This controversy followed him back in Spain where he was imprisoned for a year (but freed after six weeks on the order of the king) and had to make a humiliating peace with the settlers.

Columbus found it difficult to realise the personal profits that had been promised by the Spanish monarchs, and the litigation conducted by his descendants would last until 1790. He was accused of incompetent, tyrannical, and brutal rule and prevented from taking any further part in the administration of the colonies. That he had failed in this vital part of the deal he had struck with the crown was used as grounds for denying him the enormous wealth that he stood to earn from it.

To his death, Columbus would maintain that the countries he had discovered were part of Asia. On his fourth voyage, he was still pursuing his dream of finding the Straits of Malacca, but it was marred by misfortune (frequent hurricanes) and being marooned for a year. He was caught in the same storm that sank twenty-nine of the thirty ships involved in the first treasure fleet to leave the Indies for Spain, laden with gold.

They now sit on the bottom of the sea somewhere in the Caribbean.

Just as Columbus was by now sick and ailing from arthritis and ophthalmia, so on this last sortie, the vulnerability of European ships to the teredo worm in tropical waters became apparent. But despite his understanding of offshore wind systems, his seamanship, the enormous risks he took, the privation he suffered, and the dangers he survived, he would die in his bed aged fifty-four in 1506. Just as he had wandered the seas for most of his life, so too would his remains. Although dying in Spain and being buried there, his remains were subsequently disinterred and moved to what is now the Dominican Republic, thence to Cuba and finally, in 1898, nearly 400 years later, back to Seville, their original resting place.

Although 'Columbia' was extensively canvassed as the name for the new continent, the Americas were not named for Christopher Columbus. That honour went to another Italian explorer, Amerigo Vespucci, who, in contradiction of Columbus, insisted, correctly as it turned out that the new lands were part of a whole new and hitherto unknown continent.

But Columbus was sailing for Spain, and Iberian mariners gradually accreted information on wind patterns and currents in their, at this stage, limited area of trading. These observations, directions, and principles, faithfully recorded in their rutters, had global application. They were able to use them to good effect navigating much further from home. In particular, they utilised the trade winds and observed the ocean gyres.

It is worth noting that the ships' companies, unlike today's merchant navy, had to be self-reliant. Accordingly, they were heavily armed, and their crews armoured and trained in hand-to-hand combat. Often thousands of miles from home, they had to be adept in protecting themselves not only from the hazards of the sea but also other mariners who derived a living from the watery world. They were not traders; instead, they thrived on preying on traders. Pirates abounded in Asian waters whose many islands provided cover to mount surprise attacks, and their light, speedy, and highly manoeuvrable craft made it almost impossible for a heavily laden merchantman to outrun them. They had no option but to stand and fight. Descriptions of pirate exploits make for gruesome reading. It paid Western traders to be heavily armed. Later, when the seas were comparatively safe, they would paint false gun turrets on their ship's sides to deter pirates.

The Treaty of Tordesillas

Columbus's voyages to the Americas upset King João II of Portugal because, under the Treaty of Alcáçovas of 1479 between Spain and Portugal, Portugal had hegemony in the Atlantic Ocean. Clearly, a clarification of the rights of these two great maritime (and Roman Catholic) powers of the time was necessary.

A significant secondary motivation of these pioneering voyages was to carry the true faith to the heathens of the world. The issue was arbitrated by Pope Alexander VI, who, in 1494, issued bulls promulgating a dividing line between Portugal and Spain, eventually set at 370 leagues west of the Cape Verde Islands (approximately 46.30 degrees west of Greenwich). Spain was given rights to all lands west of the dividing line and Portugal all lands to the east. Neither was to occupy lands already in the hands of a Christian ruler. Fortunately for Portugal, this line just clipped the easternmost piece of South America, what was to become Brazil (after *pau-brasil*, a redwood that would become the nation's national tree). Discovered by the Portuguese navigator Pedro Álvares Cabral in 1500, it speaks Portuguese today. The rest of the Americas fell to Spain, for it, a very lucrative delineation.

England and the Netherlands, as Protestant nations, had no rights under the treaty, nor did France which, although Catholic, was part of the Holy Roman Empire and possibly regarded as benefiting from Spain's hemisphere. Left out of the scramble for trading riches accruing from these westward exploratory voyages, France overcame its allegiance to the Empire and, like Spain, chose westward exploration, and possibly a direct route to China.

In 1534, Jacques Cartier landed on the American coast and sailed up the Saint Lawrence River, hoping to find the watershed and another great river flowing westward. Alas, the Great Lakes lay in front of him, and there was no great westward-flowing river. Nevertheless, the voyage added Canada to the French Empire and led to the establishment of the fur trade, which would prove to be a new and lucrative business. The French subsequently laid claim to much of what is now eastern Canada and an enormous swathe of what became inland US, extending west to the Pacific coast and south to the Gulf of Mexico.

The French presence in the north left a substantial length of coastline between what is now Canada, and the Spanish colonies in the Caribbean unclaimed. The voyages of the Verrazzano brothers, Giovanni and Girolamo, north and south of the Caribbean established the unbroken nature of the American coastline. The stretch between the West Indies and what is now Canada attracted English privateers seeking to establish bases on the American coast from which to attack Spanish shipping from the West Indies. Among them was Sir Walter Raleigh and his doomed colony of Roanoke. Eventually, the southern portion of this land would come under cotton plantations and provide abundant raw material for the later 'dark satanic mills' of England's cotton spinning revolution.

Non-trade Goods: The Columbian Exchange

Trade goods as such were not all that would be exchanged by the Portuguese and the Spanish with the New World. The natives of the West Indies and the Americas lived in a practically disease-free environment and had no immunological resistance to European illnesses. Smallpox, measles, chickenpox, cholera, whooping cough, bubonic plague, typhus, influenza, and malaria were taken from the Old World to the New, devastating whole populations.

In exchange, Old World sailors brought back not only immense riches but an array of vegetables and fruits that would diversify the plain European diet. Tomatoes, potatoes, sweet potatoes, maize, cassava, cacao, and vanilla, to name just a few, are central to the Mediterranean and world diet today. But the sailors also brought with them syphilis, reputedly from Hispaniola and, although not as devastating as the disease traffic in the other direction, caused considerable disruption in Europe. Many of the conquistadors were aristocrats, and the 'Great Pox' soon spread through all levels of society, especially the royal families of Europe, Henry VIII being a notable recipient.

The obvious gains in imports of especially gold and silver from the New World caused considerable inflation in Europe. But it provided the bullion necessary to acquire Eastern 'trade' goods.

Vasco da Gama

Bartholomeu Dias had reported back to King João II in 1488, when Europe was preoccupied with the rise of the Ottoman Turks. And so it was not until 1497 that another expedition was mounted to capitalise on his discoveries.

That expedition was commanded by the lad Columbus had encountered years earlier in Portugal—Vasco da Gama. Da Gama was born in the seaport of Sines on the south-west coast of Portugal. He was the third of five sons of a local nobleman and member of the Order of Santiago, which was to become a favoured organisation of the future king, João II. After studying navigation and mathematics among other subjects, da Gama followed his father into the order. In so doing, he came to the attention of the king. Although da Gama had little in the way of open-ocean seagoing experience, João II despatched him, in 1492, on a punitive expedition against the French in the port of Setubal and along the Algarve coast. The mission was a success, but João II died in 1495 and was replaced by his first cousin, Manuel I. Fortunately, Manuel was also an avid advocate of exploration and trade and appointed da Gama to lead an expedition around the Cape of Good Hope and, hopefully, to India.

Vasco da Gama (1469-1504)

Source: British Library

Portugal was a small nation of only around 2 million people, with the king highly reliant on the feudal aristocracy for his income. The Treaty of Tordesillas provided an incentive to use his pope-awarded right to navigation in the eastern hemisphere to create another source of income. Trade was a monopoly of the crown, and Portuguese royalty had been earning a tidy income from trading in gold dust, ivory, and slaves along the West African coast, activities that had been considerably expanded by João II. Trading in the valuable products of the East presented an opportunity to increase this 'monarchical capitalist' income and reduce the king's reliance on his feudal lords and lenders. Although useful in this respect, it would subsequently prove inadequate in the face of the joint-stock company.

That was in the future. For now, Manuel I decided to capitalise on the knowledge obtained by Dias, and in 1497, he mounted an expedition to the East Indies. Da Gama's first voyage consisted of four ships and 170 men. Significantly, two of the newly built vessels were carracks, with their considerably expanded carrying capacity and enhanced square-rigged 'following wind' performance. The third was a caravel, while the fourth was a supply vessel never intended to complete the journey.

Dias had proved that the route eastwards, although rough in its southern extent, lay at an otherwise relatively temperate latitude. It was, however, time-consuming, and the vessels required to pursue his route couldn't carry much cargo. If da Gama was to make it to India, he needed ships that could carry far more provisions and be capable of exploiting the South Atlantic gyre in the same way that Columbus had the North Atlantic system.

The accumulation of knowledge about ocean gyres, continental currents, and equatorial wind systems was progressively enabling the intrepid Portuguese navigators to bring the Asian hemisphere within the ambit of European trade. Da Gama would be the first navigator in modern times to achieve it. (The Egyptians and the Phoenicians may have circumnavigated Africa in ancient times, and there is a suggestion that the Chinese succeeded in rounding the Cape in a westerly direction, during the voyages of Zheng He.)

After the Cape Verde Islands, the fleet took advantage of the north-easterly trade winds to sail south-west around the doldrums of the Bay of Guinea and south off the coast of South America. Eventually, it picked up the westerlies that would blow them across the South Atlantic to a landfall on the southern African coast. It took five months to get this far, and the fleet had travelled 10,000 kilometres, probably the longest voyage ever made in the open ocean up to that time.

Having rounded the cape, once da Gama passed the Great Fish River on South Africa's east coast, he was proceeding further into the Indian Ocean than any other European ever had before. On reaching the Mozambique Channel, he arrived in an area in which the Arabs had been trading for centuries. Low on stores and with little in the way of trade goods, in a portent of what was to come, da Gama resorted to piracy using his heavy guns on practically unarmed Arab traders. Not surprisingly, his reception wasn't exactly warm until he reached Malindi where he secured the services of an Arab pilot. Only twenty-three days later, using the expertise of this seasoned mariner and his knowledge of the monsoon winds, da Gama reached modern-day Khozikode. What was formerly Calicut is located about 12 degrees north of the equator on the west coast of the Indian peninsula in the state of Kerala.

Da Gama's presents for the local ruler were paltry, and rather than a royal ambassador, he was labelled a common pirate by the local Arab traders. Consequently, his efforts at establishing a trading base came to nothing. Not only that, abandoned by his Arab pilot, his departure was marred by a lack of understanding of the trade winds which had governed trade for centuries and would continue to do so until the advent of steamships. Consequently, a passage that had taken twenty-three days on the way out took 132 days on the way back, and half of the fleet's crew died on the way. The depleted numbers were insufficient to man three ships, so one was scuttled.

Nevertheless, arriving in Lisbon two years after he set out, he was accorded a hero's welcome despite having failed to sign a commercial treaty in India and having lost two ships and two-thirds of his crew. It took da Gama half of the time taken for the entire enterprise to reach home partly because he left India at the most inauspicious time in relation to the trade wind cycle. The trade winds blow strongest during the winter. Leaving India during the northern summer meant that he was the victim of desultory breezes that made his journey across the Indian Ocean in a westerly direction so much longer than it had been in the easterly one. While the return journey took considerably longer, it added to the sum of knowledge about how to navigate global monsoon wind systems. The small volume of spices da Gama managed to bring back was, however, sufficient to demonstrate the promise of the sea route that he had pioneered, bypassing both Venice and the Ottoman Empire.

Vasco da Gama died on his third voyage to India. He was buried there, only to be disinterred and reburied in Lisbon twelve years later, presumably because the Portuguese monarch, Manuel I, felt his grave might be desecrated. Even after death, his bones again travelled the route he pioneered.

Pedro Álvares Cabral

Da Gama's first voyage was only moderately successful because the Indian magnates were not impressed by what they considered to be paltry trade goods. Still, it was a good indication of the potential, and Manuel I was enthusiastic. In 1500, he despatched a large fleet of thirteen ships and 1,500 men under the physically impressive but navigationally inexperienced Pedro Álvares Cabral on a major expedition to India. The fleet was made up of a mixture of *caravel redondas* ('round' caravels with fuller hulls to expand their cargo capacity) and carracks.

With little seagoing experience, Cabral was appointed commander as a reward. But under him were several very experienced seamen, including Bartholomeu Dias and his brother Diogo and Nicolau Coelho (formerly a captain in Vasco da Gama's voyage). Manuel I provided considerable monetary encouragement to Cabral, and this was also, no doubt, typical of the era. As well as cash equal to thirty-five kilograms of gold, he had the right to purchase thirty tons of pepper and a quantity of other spices on his own account. These he could sell to the crown, tax-free, upon his return. The expedition had the potential to make him a very wealthy man.

Taking advantage of the north-east trade winds, the fleet sailed westward and, whether by accident or design (probably the former as the object of the expedition was to reach India using the Portuguese half of the globe), made landfall in what is now Brazil. Although that landfall was west of the easterly extent of the South American continent (at what is today Porto Seguro), Cabral realised that he was still within the Portuguese hemisphere. He took possession of what he was convinced was a continent and despatched a ship home with the news. He continued south exploring the coast but eventually turned south-east on the South Atlantic gyre heading for the Cape of Good Hope.

Rounding the cape, which Dias had named Cape of Storms, true to its name, the fleet ran into trouble. Four ships and 380 men were lost. Bartholomeu Dias was captain of one of those ships.

The cape that he had discovered and named—and the rounding of which had made him famous—also took his life.

After sighting land and fixing their position, the fleet turned north. Still needing repairs, six of the remaining ships sought refuge near Sofala, continuing to Malindi. Here, pilots were recruited for the final leg of the journey to Calicut, which they reached in August 1500. Here, history came into play. The

Portuguese had spent centuries expelling Muslim conquerors from Portugal, and part of the motivation for their pioneering expeditions was to link up with Prester John in an alliance against Islam.

But while making good progress with the Hindu prince in Calicut, Cabral was reliant on Arab interpreters who became aware of the anti-Islamic bias of the letters from Manuel I. They rightly feared the loss of their trade and livelihood to the Portuguese. Hostilities ensued, culminating in a massacre of Arabs and the destruction of their ships by Cabral. The Portuguese felt they would always be numerically inferior in India, so they needed to put the fear of God into the locals, which they proceeded to do with their superior artillery. The precedent was now set for what would become the nature of European relations with Asia for centuries to come.

Cabral eventually returned to Portugal in January 1501. Seven ships made it home, two of which were empty and five fully laden. Six were lost. Nevertheless, the cargo showed an 800 per cent profit for the Portuguese crown. And this after counting the cost of mounting the expedition and of the vessels that were lost. Compared to the voyages of Vasco da Gama, it was hugely successful and provided the incentive for future expeditions and the establishment of the Portuguese empire in Asia.

As for Cabral, he became the first explorer to touch on four continents: Europe, America, Africa, and Asia. Although Manuel I planned a 'revenge fleet' under Cabral, he had fallen out with the king, and it ultimately sailed under Vasco da Gama. Cabral subsequently married well and spent the rest of his life in relative obscurity, although he has become somewhat of a hero in modern-day Brazil. He is credited with being the 'discoverer' of the country, although there is a suggestion that Spanish explorers may have touched cursorily on that coast before him.

The sturdy and capacious 'carrack'-type vessels that made up the majority of his expedition proved their worth, becoming the workhorses of the Asian and American trade with Europe for years to come. They were the first of the great three-masted windships, and they set seaborne commerce on a course that would become what is known today as globalisation.

Ferdinand Magellan

Ferdinand Magellan was a product of Portugal's superior navigational expertise. Noble, born in 1481, he gained his first experience of the sea sailing to India as a soldier. In 1505, he was under the command of Francisco de Almeida on a voyage to break Muslim sea power in the East. During this expedition, he visited the Moluccas, or Spice Islands, and was involved in subjecting them to Portuguese rule. Over the next four years, the Portuguese would gradually obtain control over the Indian Ocean.

But Magellan was firstly a soldier and was subsequently sent to fight in Morocco where he was wounded (and also accused of stealing). Although proved innocent, the incident ruined his reputation with the Portuguese king, Manuel I. He wanted to explore the Spice Islands and petitioned the king three times to do so. It became clear that the king had set his face against him, so he migrated to Spain and became a Spanish citizen. What was Portugal's loss would turn out to be a spectacular gain for Spain. Although his earlier life was spent as a 'marine', he became quite adept at all things nautical. The Spanish king, Charles I, saw fit to appoint him captain of a ship and head of an expedition to sail west in search of an alternative route to the Spice Islands.

Ferdinand Magellan (1480-1521)

Source: United States Library of Congress

Not satisfied with the immense riches in the form of gold and silver flowing back to Spain from its conquests in the Americas, Charles I also wanted a share in the riches of the Spice Islands. Under the Treaty of Tordesillas, however, Spain would have to find a new route. The only option was by sailing west. Also, depending on the circumference of the globe, it was possible the Spice Islands—presently claimed by Portugal—may have fallen to Spain under the Treaty of Tordesillas.

In fact, the reverse was the case.

The antemeridian of 46.30 west of Greenwich (133.70 east) would have given Portugal practically all the Moluccas (the present-day Maluku Islands), the source of the most valuable spices, and the entire Philippines as well. However, for the time being, the first step was to find an alternative westward route, and to that end, in 1519, Charles commissioned Ferdinand Magellan to do just that.

Having spent so much time lobbying the Portuguese king, it seems likely Magellan similarly lobbied the Spanish king once he became a Spanish citizen. He was still regarded as somewhat of a Portuguese, and as a safeguard against treachery, Charles I replaced most of Magellan's Portuguese crew with Spaniards.

For his part, the Portuguese monarch resented Magellan placing his native navigational expertise at the service of the Spaniards and tried to stop him. But commanding a fleet of five vessels (carracks, only two of which exceeded 100 tons), Magellan set off in 1519 and outran his former compatriot pursuers.

This turned out to be the least of his problems.

Magellan had been warned that his Spanish captains planned, at an appropriate time, to kill him. When the journey down the South American coast led to dwindling supplies of food and fresh water, three of the Spanish captains incited their crews to mutiny. As a measure of the man, Magellan succeeded in quelling the uprising, killing one of the captains in the process. The other two were found guilty of murder and treason; one was beheaded, and the other marooned.

In the sixteenth century, the term *self-reliance* meant very much just that.

When he embarked on the expedition, little did Magellan know that the voyage would take him to fifty-three degrees south latitude, further than any European had ever been. At that latitude, he discovered what turned out to be a protected corridor through the mass of islands that precede the most southerly tip of the Americas, a route that now bears his name. On the way, he made landfall at Rio de Janeiro and, further south, completed an extensive but disappointing investigation of the River Plate estuary. In the process, one ship was wrecked, and another deserted for home. Three vessels were left, and they were the first to enter the Mar Pacifico—the Peaceful Sea. It was something of a misnomer as it turned out, but it still stands.

The southerly extension of South America that lies less than 400 nautical miles from the opposing Horn of Antarctica would subsequently become known as Cape Horn. It is an area renowned for its gale force winds, contrary currents, and huge seas. This narrow stretch of ocean carries an enormous volume of water rampaging before the unremitting westerlies that circle the planet unobstructed at these latitudes.

Nineteenth-century ships would regularly take the outside track around the Horn, but so fierce are the conditions that heading west could take weeks. Ships had to sail against the wind, the current, and mountainous seas, and many a vessel (including William Bligh's *Bounty*) would be forced to abandon the attempt after sailing for weeks getting nowhere.

Having rounded the cape, Magellan did try to head west, but the persistent westerlies defeated him, so he turned north. After taking advantage of the cold north-flowing current along the coast, he was eventually able to head north-west. Assisted by the south-east trade winds, he finally reached the Spice Islands. Due to his inadequate knowledge of the size of the earth, Magellan expected this journey to be a short one. In fact, it took almost four months. Along the way, forty of his men died.

Renaissance religious thinkers wondered how was it that the new peoples discovered around the world had never benefited from the message of Christ. At the behest of the pope and following their religious conviction, early explorers, therefore, adopted a secondary justification for the mission: to bring the Holy Writ to the heathens. Renowned for his toughness, self-reliance, and navigational expertise, Magellan nevertheless bore this strong religious sense.

Having rounded Cape Horn; crossed the Pacific; eaten rats, sawdust, and leather; survived violent storms; and put down mutinies on three of his five vessels, he would now come violently unstuck. Upon reaching the Philippines, he was perturbed that a local chief of the island of Mactan resisted his efforts to convert his tribe to Christianity. Not one to take no for an answer, Magellan took sixty soldiers to teach the chief a lesson.

He was met by an army of about 1,500 natives.

Devout, trained as a soldier and very hands-on, Magellan was determined to get among the fighting. In what became known as the Battle of Mactan, Magellan was speared wading ashore. He died trying to free his sword from its scabbard, two years after he had departed Spain.

Magellan had already reached the Malay Archipelago by sailing east on a previous voyage, so he very nearly completed a personal rounding of the globe. With only two ships remaining, it was now left to his second in command, one Juan Sebastián Elcano, to complete what was the first circumnavigation of the world. Given the depleted nature of the resources at his disposal and the fact that he was still half a world from home, this was no mean feat of both navigation and leadership. By the time Elcano reached the port of departure, he had only one ship left, the eighty-five-ton *Victoria*.

The First Vessel to Sail Around the World: Replica of Magellan's Ship *Victoria*

Source: Fundacion Nao Victoria

That almost 250 of his original sailors perished, with only eighteen returning to Seville, demonstrates the risks confronted by these early navigators—not to mention their incredible fortitude in the face of adversity. But then the spices, loaded on to that tiny ship following Magellan's death, more than paid for the whole enterprise, the cost of the ships included.

As a footnote to this incredible voyage of survival, the *Victoria* continued to trade for another fifty years. She was eventually lost with all hands on a trip from the Antilles to Seville around 1570—seaworthy indeed! More importantly, Magellan's logs proved that the world was much bigger than had been previously thought and revealed the true expanse of the Pacific as the world's largest ocean.

Portugal does not figure largely in the events and politics of the modern world. Nevertheless, it is worth remembering that Dias, da Gama, Cabral, Magellan, Jorge Álvares, and António da Mota were all Portuguese. Álvares was the first European to arrive in China in 1514, and da Mota was the first European to reach Japan, after being accidentally driven ashore there. Without their exploits, the course of world history might have been very different. Sadly, Magellan's wife and child died while he was at sea, leaving little physical evidence of his existence behind him. History, however, has made eminently certain that he will not be forgotten. Not only are the straits he discovered named after him, but he is also remembered in the cosmos (the Magellanic Clouds), wildlife (the Magellanic penguin), space exploration (the Magellan spacecraft which mapped the surface of Venus in 1989), and in lunar and Martian craters. In modern times, it seems his name confers solidity and fiduciary responsibility and has been adopted by several investment funds.

Columbus was a Genoese (who died a Spaniard, as did Magellan). He is remembered in various place names in North America and the South American nation of Colombia. And Amerigo Vespucci, who got all the glory of having one-sixth of the world's land mass named after him, was also Italian. Vespucci has the disputed distinction of being the first man in modern history to view the Southern Cross. The Ancient Greeks could see this distinctive asterism, but due to the phenomenon known as precession, it subsequently disappeared to northern hemisphere dwellers. Vespucci would have had to sail across the equator to see it.

In 1514, Jorge Álvares was the first European to arrive in China, and a Portuguese colony was subsequently established in Macau. It was another three decades (1543) before, yet again, a Portuguese explorer, the storm-wracked António da Mota, was accidentally driven on to the coast of Japan at Tanegashima. The Portuguese would later found a trading port at Nagasaki. Their objective was less to take Japanese goods to Europe and more to trade Chinese silks, porcelain, and European firearms into Japan and take Japanese slaves, especially women, back to other parts of their expanding colonial empire and to Europe.

The advent of trade with China, at least, added a whole new and lucrative dimension to the business. East Indians favoured gold as payment for their pepper and other exotic trade goods, whereas the Chinese favoured silver. Gold was highly prized in India and could be exchanged for silver most advantageously compared to the rate in China. Western goods traders could therefore engage in bullion arbitrage as well, to their considerable advantage.

Increasingly, European ships would become involved in the 'country trade': finding products that were available in one Asian region and desired in another. Their fighting superiority meant they pushed Arab traders out and, at the same time, dealt with the pirates that infested the area. As the availability of prime shipbuilding timbers declined in Europe, even the ships would be built in Asia. Using the abundant supply of excellent woods (primarily teak and mahogany) and the superb craftsmanship of Asian (especially Indian) shipbuilders, they would build superb craft, better suited to the tropical environment.

Although other European powers would overtake the Portuguese, they made a significant contribution to the opening up of trade with Asia. For some time, their realm extended from India to Japan and embraced the Indonesian and Philippine archipelagos.

Portuguese was the first European language encountered by the Chinese, and Portuguese missionaries taught the Chinese to speak their language. It would be a bastard form of Portuguese that would become the lingua franca used by the Chinese to communicate with all the European powers that followed, at least until European scholars succeeded in comprehending the 'beautiful obliquities' of the mandarin language and notation, and English traders taught their local partners the language of the empire.

Sir Francis Drake

No survey of the navigators of the great age of maritime pioneering would be complete without recalling the exploits of Sir Francis Drake. His famous ship was also representative of the changes that were taking place in ship design that would result in the emergence of the new form: the galleon. He was a man admirably suited to his time, and it would be hard to find someone who so fully realised his potential. When he died, he was only fifty-six and had crammed an extraordinary amount into those scant few decades.

His second cousin was Sir John Hawkins, eight years his senior, whose family owned a fleet of ships based in Plymouth. Together, these two performed one of the most daring deeds in the annals of English maritime history—the raid on Cadiz that crippled an armada being assembled by Philip II of Spain to invade England. They would also die together—of yellow fever and dysentery in the tropical hellhole of Panama. (In later attempts to build a canal across the isthmus, disease would decimate management and workers alike. The aborted French attempt alone would kill 22,000 people.)

Sir Francis Drake (c.1540-1596)

Source: Courtesy Ann Longmore-Etheridge/Flickr

Drake was born in 1540 into a Protestant yeoman farmer family of twelve sons in Tavistock, near Plymouth, in England's West Country. He went to sea as an apprentice on a coastal trader and was bequeathed the boat when the owner died. Not satisfied with coasting, he sailed on his first Caribbean voyage at the age of twenty-three with Hawkins. That two such notable mariners and naval architects should be cousins was one of the great serendipities of the sixteenth century. Their bravery, seamanship, navigational skill, and sheer audacity were genuinely remarkable. Apart from their queen, they were the two most notable people of the Elizabethan era. At one stage, upon the completion of his circumnavigation of the world, Drake was held to be the most famous person in the world.

On one voyage with Hawkins in 1568, the family fleet was trapped by the Spanish in the Mexican port of San Juan de Ulúa. They managed to escape but lost all but two of their ships in the process. As well as trading trips to the Caribbean, Drake also deliberately set out on marauding voyages and in 1572 raided Spanish ports there. The Mexican adventure would not be the last time these two would come together to perform immensely daring and risky ventures. While they would ultimately die together, they had a lot of living to do before that.

Drake was famously the first Englishman to circumnavigate the world, although he did not set out to do so. He was so successful raiding Spanish shipping on a voyage that took him through the Straits of Magellan and up the coast of the Americas as far as Alaska that he was faced with little alternative. His ship, built to his specifications, and originally called the *Pelican*, was renamed the *Golden Hind* during the voyage. It is best described as a vessel constructed during the transition period from carrack to galleon and was rated at about 120 tons. She was 100 feet long (the same length as a modern super-maxi racing yacht) and accommodated some seventy crew who lived aboard for three years. The *Golden Hind* was purpose-built in 1575 for Drake's 1577 voyage.

The Second (and First English) Ship to Circumnavigate the World: Sir Francis Drake's *Golden Hind*

Source: Drawing by Ray Aker Courtesy of Point Reyes National Seashore

Freebooting was the intention under a licence from Queen Elizabeth, who may also have asked that he try to find the fabled north-west passage. (When he grew tired of looting and mayhem, that is, and needed to come home.) There was never thus the intention to circumnavigate the world, be absent for over a thousand days, and travel 36,000 miles, the longest single voyage undertaken in the world up until that time.

It was just that in the course of that voyage, it became a necessity.

After negotiating the Straits of Magellan, Drake made his way up the South American coast. He was intent on chasing down Spanish ships laden with bullion and gems from the mines in their South

American colonies, Peru, and Bolivia. He knew that these ships would be heading north for porterage of their precious cargo across the peninsula, and thence by galleon convoy to Spain. (Drake had previously attempted to hijack that porterage.) Also, the Spanish, under the Treaty of Tordesillas, could not take their spoils from the Philippines back to Spain via the Cape of Good Hope. Their treasure and spices were, therefore, shipped in what were known as the 'Manila galleons' to Acapulco on the other side of the Pacific. From there, their cargos would be portered across the isthmus to Vera Cruz for shipment to the mother country.

Drake, whose audacity seemed to know no end, raided ships on both these routes with alacrity, accumulating twenty-six tons of silver, half a ton of gold, and thousands of coins and pieces of jewellery. The haul was considerably beyond his, and his queen's, wildest dreams.

Now laden down with treasure and knowing the Spanish would be waiting if he tried to get home the way he had come, he opted to keep sailing north in pursuit of his secondary objective—the fabled north-west passage. After reaching present-day Alaska, Drake decided the search was in vain and that there was no option but to sail west towards Japan and, quite incidentally, to get home by completing a circumnavigation of the world. Possibly to assuage his vexation at having to take the long way home, he decided to call in at the Spice Islands where he uploaded some six tons of cloves, themselves almost worth their weight in gold at the time.

Drake sailed from the Portuguese-dominated Spice Islands along virtually the main Portuguese trade route and at immense risk. Nevertheless, his small ship was, although heavily laden, relatively fast and manoeuvrable—qualities he no doubt hoped would keep him out of trouble. After loading the spices and taking advantage of the north-east trades, he sailed across the north of Australia, south-west past India and Madagascar, around the Cape of Good Hope, up the west coast of Africa, and finally past Portugal, Spain, and France to home.

Having been away so long, he had been given up for dead, a not-to-be-unexpected outcome given the nature of the enterprise. Drake's cargo was reputedly worth 160,000 Elizabethan pounds, or half a billion pounds today. Elizabeth's share alone was said to be worth more than England's national debt at the time. Despite making such an enormous contribution, the disingenuous Elizabeth could not, she felt, afford to personally honour him for fear of further twisting the Spanish tiger's tail. So she had the French ambassador do it for her. Seventeenth-century queens made their own rules.

Queen Elizabeth's cautious treatment of the most powerful nation on earth could not, however, save her forever from its wrath. Not only were the English opportunistic and successful raiders of Spanish shipping, but they were also Protestant. King Philip II of Spain was now the Holy Roman Emperor with definite obligations towards the preservation and expansion of the Holy Roman Empire and the protection and propagation of the faith. As well as spreading the wealth Spain derived from its South American colonies, the English were also interfering in the newly conquered Netherlands.

Philip was encouraged by Pope Sixtus V, who promised a subsidy and other concessions should he successfully conquer pesky England and return it to the Roman Catholic Church. Philip intended to use the Netherlands as a staging point for the conquest of heretical Albion. The saga of the four Spanish armadas Philip despatched—and the role both Drake and Hawkins played in their defeat—has become the stuff of legend and came at the end of the renaissance Age of Exploration. The emphasis would, for some time, lie in the exploitation of the outcomes. The Age of Enlightenment would bring another flurry of European exploration, which would, apart from Antarctica, fill in the remaining blank spaces on the map of the world.

4

CHAPTER

The Age of Exploitation

Introduction

While the Portuguese may have pioneered the use of global wind and current systems, they could not retain their advantage. Their hard-won knowledge soon spread, first to the Spanish, then the Dutch, and finally (and ultimately most successfully) to the English.

The mineral riches of the Americas would make Spain the wealthiest country in Europe and sustain its power for centuries, but Portugal, whose brave and avaricious navigators had accumulated the knowledge whereby the vast riches of the East Indies were unlocked, was limited in its ability to fully utilise it. This was mainly due to the shortcomings of its entrenched system of monarchical capitalism.

The increased cost of the burgeoning trade activity saw Portugal lose its advantage to the wealthier and more commercially astute Venetians, Dutch, and English. Sensing Portugal's weakness, they provided the funds to mount voyages and picked Portugal's brains by sailing on her ships to trade on their own account. They left her a minor player whose possessions would ultimately be forcefully appropriated by cannier partners.

Portugal's undoing lay in its medieval financial *modus operandi*. The English and the Dutch were outliers in terms of the Treaty of Tordesillas, but they were accomplished seamen and traders. Best of all, they had a new financial weapon.

Portugal

Being first along the road (or should that be sea), Portugal had an immense advantage over its competitors. Greed, native daring, navigational skill—combined with its geographical position on the extreme western end of Europe—had given it a considerable lead.

King João II was keen to reduce his revenue dependence on Portugal's medieval aristocracy and saw the expansion of trade from the west coast of Africa—and the infinitely more lucrative trade of Asia—as a passport to financial independence. To achieve this, he felt he had to keep trade as a royal monopoly. Portugal was able to capitalise on its intellectual property for almost a century. Fortunately,

Spain was excluded for the most part from its hemisphere, and at the outset, the other European powers were preoccupied with the Reformation and the geopolitical tensions it caused.

Portugal was a minor player compared to the wealth of Spain and the mercantile might of the Netherlands. It was poor and somewhat commercially inept. Spain adopted the same monarchical trade monopoly, but it not only had a much larger tax base, it also derived immense wealth from its American possessions. Besides being chronically undercapitalised, Portugal lacked both an established middle class (the traditional 'traders' of Western society) and, compared with, say, Italy, the German provinces, and the Netherlands, a developed banking and insurance system.

Equipping trading fleets was an expensive business. The ships had to be built, crewed, and militarised. It then took a long time to realise on the investment (the round trip could take two years), so considerable working capital was required.

Not only was the expenditure significant, the risks—from storm, mutiny, freebooters (especially the English), and Asian pirates—were immense. To exploit their monopoly, the Portuguese kings had to progressively accept financial assistance from merchants from other European countries, most notably the Dutch and the Venetians.

The Dutch, especially, used them to learn the trade and the route. They came initially as paying passengers to travel on Portuguese ships and trade privately. Eventually, to keep up with expansion in the trade, Portugal had to borrow from the wealthier, more experienced trading nations. That was a slippery slope, and it would progressively surrender the enormous economic rent it derived from its overseas operations as its creditors increasingly sought more and more concessions in return.

In the beginning, in addition to repayment with interest, lenders requested part of the cargo space to trade on their own account on voyages they financed. They also took mortgages over the royal share to ensure repayment of their advances.

The 'Wharf between Two Seas'

The financiers increased their demands until, eventually, most of the cargo landed in Lisbon belonged to others. It would then be transhipped on to craft bound for the channel, the North Sea ports of the Hanseatic League, and Venice. In time, Antwerp became the primary point for the distribution of spices into Europe.

For all its skill, courage, and enterprise in pioneering the East Indian trade, Lisbon was ultimately reduced to the status of 'a wharf between two seas'. Rather than making the long trip back home around the Cape of Good Hope, what voyages Portugal did mount independently increasingly were made into the kingdom of Ormuz (also known as Hormoz) on the northern shore of the Strait of Hormuz. After a short overland journey, these goods would end up in the Venetian distribution system, the very device the Portuguese had originally set out to circumvent. The wily Venetians, far from being cut out of the exotic trade by Portugal's seafaring exploits and hard-won monopoly over Eastern trade, were better off as a result because the volumes they obtained were larger.

In time, the Dutch and the English would want it all for themselves and would wrest Portugal's Asian possessions from it. Meanwhile, the Portuguese had lost their intellectual property—how to find one's way to and from the various trading ports in Asia. It was a precedent so often repeated down the ages: the real innovators lose out to those with the capital and expertise to exploit them. Not only would Portugal, in time, lose its initial advantage and its papally arbitrated monopoly of the eastern hemisphere, it would lose its eastern empire as well. But that was a century and many battles away.

Initially, most of Portugal's trade was in pepper, but there were other exotic substances used as medicaments. Benzoin and camphor were aromatics, musk and garu were used in ointments, and betel as a digestive. Pepper was shipped in large quantities because it came to be used in everyday life to enliven the stodgy and often near-rancid traditional European diet. For this reason, when Indonesian spices became available, they would overwhelm all other commodities—except for pepper.

The Rise of England and the Netherlands

The hitherto unforeseen and rapidly expanding trade created a demand for more and larger ships. And this brought developments in design and navigational technology.

In 1521, Martin Luther split from the Roman Catholic church over the question of indulgences, and Henry VIII did so for entirely different reasons (but which could also be termed an indulgence) ten years later.

Just as the pope took no notice of them when making the Tordesillas arbitration, so the Protestant countries—England, the German provinces, and the Netherlands—did not feel obliged to abide by the Treaty of Tordesillas. Their growing maritime strength, forged through fighting Spain, led them to covet not only the gold and silver being extracted from the New World but the wealth accruing from the spice and silk trades. Along with the French, they would turn to raiding Spanish settlements in the Caribbean and their treasure ships crossing the Atlantic, where they were at their most vulnerable. They did so with considerable effect, redistributing Spain's wealth around northern Europe.

Spain had gained access to the Spice Islands from their eastern end in the Pacific Ocean, the archipelago they named the Philippines (*Las Islas Filipinas*) for King Philip II. During the seventeenth century, regardless of the Treaty of Tordesillas, the Portuguese and Spanish would continue to fight over the spice trade. The argument as to the demarcation line in Asia (the anti-meridian to the original line set out after the treaty) would take many years and not a few treaties to resolve. Ultimately, it would be of little benefit as the rising northern Europeans flexed their maritime muscle, seeking a place in a world that had been divided between the Iberian states. Spain would retain and bleed its American possessions for many years to come and retain its foothold in the East Indies.

But England, the Netherlands, and France would push Portugal out.

As well as being the first Europeans (through misadventure) to arrive in Japan, Portugal inadvertently made a big contribution to opening up trade with China. Pedro Álvares reached the Middle Kingdom in 1513 and gained permission for missionaries to enter Macau. The bastard Portuguese Chinese argot that developed there would become the lingua franca used by the European East India companies in their attempts to establish trading relations with China.

Spain

In 1510, the Spaniard Vasco Balboa established a permanent settlement in the far north of what is now present-day Colombia. Santa Maria was the first European colony on the mainland of the Americas. Balboa also crossed the isthmus between North and South America—present-day Panama—to be the first European to view the vast Pacific Ocean. From there, the Spaniards looted native wrought gold and silver and established the infamous silver mines of Peru, which they worked with local slave labour.

African slaves would have been preferred, but they were saved from this awful fate by their inability to work at the high altitude.

The influx of treasure into Europe would, on the one hand, cause rampant inflation. On the other, it would provide the bullion necessary for Portugal and Spain and later the various East India trading companies of northern Europe, to carry on trade in Asia, where specie was invariably required in payment for trade goods.

To capitalise on their discoveries, the Spanish organised what would become the first transatlantic trade cargo route in history, taking New World treasure—gold, silver, agricultural products, lumber, sugar, tobacco, and other exotic goods—to Spain. They returned with Spanish goods such as wine, oil, tools, textiles, paper, and literature. And religion. As we have seen, also riding as invisible and silent passengers in both directions was disease, most perniciously from east to west. The tropics would have their revenge, however, and Europeans would die in their thousands in Central America and the East Indies.

Meanwhile, in the Pacific, in 1521, Magellan was the first European to reach the over 7,000 islands later named the Philippines. Besides spices, they shipped gold and other valuable trade goods back to Spain. Vessels from the Philippines could not take the westward route home because that hemisphere belonged to the Portuguese. Faced with sailing around Cape Horn, or to central America and conducting a portage across the isthmus, the latter was by far the shortest and safer choice.

The ships used the North Pacific Ocean gyre to sail to Acapulco, heading north initially and then riding the gyre east to Central America. They returned by sailing east but north of the tropical 'dead' zone. The volume and often precious nature of the trade meant a need to increase the capacity of these vessels and their ability to defend themselves from northern European privateers, especially the likes of Sir Frances Drake.

The Spanish Armadas

Left out of the initial stages of the voyages of exploration and with no colonies to its name, the English used their seamanship, experience as corsairs in the English Channel, and sheer daring to raid Spanish and Portuguese cargo carracks and galleons. It was all done under several somewhat flimsy premises. But in Renaissance Europe, there were no 'big brothers' to come to England's aid, and she stood alone against the might of the Spanish Empire, which she was bound to antagonise to supplement her meagre tax base. Spain was the most powerful nation in Europe at the time, and inevitably, it would take up arms against its tormentor.

In all, King Philip II mounted four armadas against England, but it was the first that would prove the most formidable. In today's discussions of contemporary military strategy, much is made of pre-emptive strikes, but Elizabeth I and her audacious captains were right across it. Elizabeth realised that the future of her realm was now very much at stake, and the time had passed for trying to placate the Spanish king. She knew Philip personally because, for a time, he was married to her half-sister, the infamous 'Bloody Mary'. After Mary died, he even proposed to Elizabeth. She procrastinated while her privateers—Hawkins, Frobisher, Drake, and their ilk—played havoc with Spanish treasure ships, significantly boosting the English treasury.

King Philip II of Spain (1527-1598)

Source: British Library

Exasperated, Philip began building an armada to invade England.

In 1587, before the armada could set sail from Cadiz, and prompted by Hawkins and Drake, Elizabeth ordered an attack, sending three of her most modern galleons: Drake's flagship, *Elizabeth Bonaventure*, *Golden Lion*, and *Rainbow*. Drake called it 'singeing the king of Spain's beard', but it was a great deal more than that. Hawkins and Drake planned, and the latter mounted the famous raid, which lasted only sixteen hours but sank or severely disabled thirty Spanish ships.

Although this didn't deter Philip from his objective, it did set him back about a year, giving England a valuable respite in which to prepare. Not satisfied with that piece of effrontery, Drake then raided other ports along the Spanish coast and, hungry as ever for plunder, sailed out into the Atlantic seeking treasure galleons.

The real attack came in 1588, when Philip despatched a fleet of some 130 vessels, only thirty of which were what we would today call capital ships: heavily militarised galleons. The intention was not to defeat England on the high seas but to transport a land army to the Netherlands to meet up with the army of Spain's duke of Parma. The merged forces would then mount an invasion of England.

A Replica of the Spanish Galleon *Andalusia*

Source: Courtesy Fundacion Nao Victoria

The army general that Philip put in charge of the armada, the duke of Medina Sidonia, could have easily landed his troops on the south coast of England. But determined to obey the king's orders to the letter, Medina Sidonia continued up the channel, only to be routed by the English when he paused at Calais to contact the duke of Parma.

The Spanish were on a lee shore, and the English set fireships to blow downwind on to the Spaniards. Fireships were old vessels that were packed with explosives and flammable materials that were set to blow unmanned downwind on to the enemy. Panicked, the Spaniards, with no time to raise them, cut the cables attaching their anchors to the ships and, fighting to get up to windward, lost the formation that had been so successful in frustrating English attacks on their way up the channel.

The English had the channel blockaded, so the Spaniards had no choice but to sail north. There, harassed by the nimble English ships, they were forced to take the long way home around the north of England and west of Ireland against the force of the Gulf Stream. Plagued by storms and the loss of the anchors they had left on the seabed off Calais that would have allowed them to take shelter, only sixty-three ships made it back. A staggering 20,000 soldiers and sailors were lost. The English lost no ships and only about 100 men, which would suggest that saving England from Spanish conquest owed more to Drake's strategy of continual harassment until the weather gave him a decided strategic advantage than to the superiority of his ships.

It was the English race-built galleons' reputation for speed and manoeuvrability that led the Spanish to adopt a strategy of sailing in tight formation. This was effective until the weather put them at the mercy of Drake and his fireships.

Philip would make three more attempts to send armadas against England, but they all failed due mainly to weather conditions before they got anywhere near their goal. Their dismal performance led to developments in design to improve the speed, manoeuvrability, and seaworthiness of the traditional Iberian galleon. It was a successful concept, well designed, and subsequently developed to effectively transport the spoils of conquest and subjugation to the mother country. But Drake's more manoeuvrable ships acted like wolves, cutting out stragglers from the main herd and subduing them.

The Portuguese and especially the Spanish trading fleets were controlled by monarchs through an age of absolutism where wealth from trade was accumulated primarily by the royal family and its medieval aristocracy. The Iberian aristocrats were smart navigators, adventurous, brave, self-reliant, but at times immensely cruel. The motivation for their revelatory voyages was greed and an intense desire for financial self-aggrandisement achieved through brutality, rapine, conquest, and subjugation. What they found, they took. They appropriated the resources for their exploitation and fought to retain exclusive access. They exhibited little sense of trade being a two-way street, of enhancing the well-being of both parties to their long-term mutual benefit. Convinced of their racial and religious superiority and backed up by their military power, they saw no reason to act in any other way.

England

England was a small nation whose earlier monarch, Henry VIII, had wilfully excluded it from the Holy Roman Empire. Its hostile relationship with Spain was consistently expressed in terms of the necessity of the freedom of the seas. England also claimed the right to trade in the areas originally discovered by Iberian explorers. Peace with Spain would have given the English trading rights, but it would have deprived Elizabeth of what had become a very important source of income: the fee for providing 'letters of marque' to privateers, 'licensing' them to prey on Spanish and Portuguese ships.

Queen Elizabeth I of England (1533-1603)

Source: Courtesy of Ann Longmore-Etheridge/Flickr

These letters of marque also entitled her to tax the spoils. So involved did she become in piracy that she was secretly sharing in the financing of freebooter expeditions and, in some cases, would send her own ships privateering in the hands of her most able pirates. This way, she got almost all the loot from a successful capture, not just a minor share.

Under England's interpretation of maritime law, the issue of letters of marque was legitimate so long as a 'state of war' existed between the two parties. A state of war was defined as the absence of a formal peace treaty. As well as seeking to justify these raids under maritime law, Elizabeth also pleaded that many English buccaneers were based in the West Country, an area over which she had little control.

This activity has been described as state-sanctioned organised crime 'controlled by the oligarchs of Whitehall and Charing Cross' (the Queen's Council). Many of them were moonlighting as active merchants and contributing to privateer voyages. As such, they had a vested interest in 'managing' the relationship with the Spanish monarch and in the interim surviving the four armadas he sent against England.

In confronting the Spanish, English ships had been refined and were good not only at defensive pursuit and harassment but also at privateering, especially with regard to treasure-laden galleons from the West Indies. They forced the Spanish to amass convoys to make the perilous journey home. Success in waylaying a single galleon, besides making the perpetrators very rich, made a considerable contribution to the English treasury.

Elizabeth played a clever double game in this process. She did not want to unduly provoke Philip, but her domestic taxation base was narrow, and she needed the money to save her from having to increase taxes on the great lords of her realm.

For Protestant England, privateering was a means of sharing in the wealth of the New World. But to successfully raid Iberian shipping—either treasure vessels from the West Indies or spice ships from the East Indies—England needed advanced ships. They needed to be faster, more agile, commanded by capable captains employing superior tactics, well-drilled, spoil-sharing crews, and equipped with fast-firing armaments. Besides keeping England afloat financially, which was the main object of the policy, they were laying the foundations of her future naval supremacy.

For the time being, however, it was indeed a lucrative business. When Drake returned to England in the *Golden Hind* in 1580, Elizabeth's share of the loot was greater than her entire annual revenues from taxes and crown lands combined. The wise old girl did not seek to make foreign trade a royal monopoly as did the Iberian monarchs, but she liked her cut.

The Joint-Stock Company

Why, towards the end of the sixteenth century, did the English scale down milking Spanish treasure from the Americas and turn their attention towards the East rather than the West Indies?

An end of the age of English privateering came in 1604 after Elizabeth had shaken off her mortal coil in 1603, and James I came to the throne. England signed a peace treaty with the new king of Spain, Philip III, who had succeeded Elizabeth's old nemesis, Philip II. (Spain and Portugal had been united under the Spanish crown in 1580, a state of affairs that existed until 1640.) Certainly, that meant privateering would no longer receive royal cash and kind support that it had received during Elizabeth's reign. Nor was it now 'legal' using the previous justification.

Meanwhile, before Elizabeth's reign ended, English merchants, indeed merchants all over Europe and the world, were becoming much more aware of the wealth that could be generated from peaceful maritime commerce. As a consequence, trade was expanding rapidly.

The move towards peaceful commerce was led primarily by the Dutch, who were said to have owned no fewer than 10,000 ships at the end of the sixteenth century. The immense wealth being generated by the Eastern trade was brought home in England when, in 1587, English privateers, as was their wont, captured a large Portuguese galleon called the *San Felipe*. The immense value of the cargo was one thing, but what was to prove far more important were the charts and sailing instructions (the rutters) and the commercial documentation found aboard the ship. The latter opened the eyes of English merchants to the huge profits that were being made from trade with India, the Spice Islands, and China. It is said to have been the main impetus behind the formation of the East India Company in 1600.

Although small and a predominantly rural nation, England had an active merchant community, something, for example, Portugal, lacked but the Netherlands had in spades. In Portugal, the monarchy was absolute and monopolised international trade. In the Netherlands, monarchy didn't exist, and the aristocracy there were the merchant princes.

England was a hybrid. It was a monarchy, but one where the queen had come to depend on participation in the organised crime of privateering, and many of the aristocracy and the Queen's courtiers were 'on the game'. Besides financing privateering, large numbers of investors also risked their fortunes on individual trading voyages. To do so, they made extensive use of the 'joint stock' concept to finance individual voyages or to participate in regular trading on a more permanent basis.

In Roman Catholic Spain and Portugal, financing trading success depended on the personal wealth of the monarch. In Spain, this was less of a problem, but its constant wars with a variety of belligerents had a draining effect.

In Protestant England and the Netherlands, the notion of the joint-stock company increased in popularity. Joint-stock enterprises enabled international trade to be significantly expanded. They allowed large amounts of money to be raised while spreading the risks involved across a large number of shareholders, according to the size of their investment. The concept democratised investment in the lucrative pursuit of international trade, and unlike the kings on which Portugal and Spain's trade depended, the entity was potentially immortal.

This longevity was undoubtedly an important element in the effectiveness of the most famous example of the concept—the British East India Company (EIC), which traded with (and for a very long time, ruled) a vast area of Asia. The EIC existed for over 200 years and, in time, became responsible for half of the world's trade. Eventually, it was brought to an end, fat, inefficient, and corrupt, by its original creator—the British government. A similar fate befell its Dutch equivalent, the Vereenigde Oostindische Compagnie (VOC), and for the same reasons.

Longevity is an advantage, but it doesn't guarantee good management. In fact, there is a dynamic with these companies that invariably leads to their demise. Entrenched interests cannot resist the temptation to pursue their advantage to its utmost and ultimately kill the goose that laid the golden eggs.

The Muscovy and Levant Companies

One of the earliest entities to employ the joint-stock device was the Muscovy Company, which received its charter in 1555. It had been preceded by the Company of Merchant Adventurers to New

Lands whose three instigators were two explorer/navigators, Sebastian Cabot and Richard Chancellor, and Sir Hugh Willoughby, a soldier of some note. The objective was to find a north-east passage to China. Willoughby led the first voyage, but he and his crew froze to death, probably after succumbing to carbon monoxide poisoning trying to keep warm.

Willoughby's successor, Richard Chancellor, was more fortunate and reached Moscow where he received a warm welcome from Tsar Ivan IV. At the time, Russia did not have access to the Baltic Sea, and as the land trade was dominated by the Hanseatic League, the tsar was keen to open up a sea route to England. Chancellor returned to England with a promise of advantageous trading privileges.

The Company of Merchant Adventurers to New Lands was then rechartered as the Muscovy Company by Mary I. The Muscovy Company was appreciated by the isolated Ivan IV, and English trade was also established, somewhat arduously, with Persia via Russia. Diplomatic relations with Russia subsequently deteriorated and with them the possibilities of fruitful trading, but bizarrely, the entity survived into the twentieth century as a charity.

The Muscovy Company had, however, also uncovered the rich whaling grounds of the far northern seas around Spitsbergen, and Elizabeth I granted the company a monopoly charter on whaling in the area. Still anxious to find a north-east passage, the company despatched Henry Hudson on two voyages of exploration.

Needless to say, both were unsuccessful.

A period of anti-monarchical activity in England involving civil war and the beheading of Charles I saw the company fall further from favour in Russia. The Dutch, emerging as a potent competitor for England's overseas trade, succeeded in usurping its Russian trading activities. Nevertheless, the Muscovy Company provided a prototype for the form of commercial organisation that would soon bear fruit for England.

The Muscovy Company was not the only English joint-stock trading company to precede the EIC. The Levant Company was an amalgamation of the Venice Company and the Turkey Company, two joint-stock trading entities whose charters had expired but whose activities Elizabeth I wished to see continue. They provided trade and political links with the Ottoman Empire.

The new Levant Company charter was granted in 1580 after a treaty was signed with the Ottomans, giving England trading rights. In 1588, the Levant Company was converted to an established monopoly on a recognised trade route, headquartered in Aleppo in modern-day Syria. The company owned and operated an extensive fleet. They were heavily armed vessels to fend off the depredations of Barbary pirates as they made their way in and out of the Mediterranean Sea through the Strait of Gibraltar. Some of these vessels became part of Elizabeth's navy on the occasions it was marshalled to fend off successive Spanish armadas. The trade gave England access to a huge variety of goods, including pepper and other spices, medicinal substances, cotton goods, velvet, and carpets. Between 1581 and 1640, the Levant Company owned and operated over 100 ships on the route.

One of the company's governors was Thomas Smythe, a prominent merchant, politician, and colonial administrator who was schooled from childhood in the family business. He was an investor in the Levant Company and a foundation governor of the East India Company. Smythe would continue intermittently in a management role at the EIC for over two decades, during which time he amassed a fortune from his investments in trading and colonial companies. In many ways, he is the archetypal English merchant; not high-born so, with no political influence, he had no assets other than his commercial acumen, his appetite for risk, and his drive.

The British East India Company (EIC)

The Muscovy and Levant companies were essentially 'local' trading enterprises. England had yet to demonstrate ability in long-distance trading and colonising. Sir Walter Raleigh's attempt at establishing the first English colony on mainland America—the settlement on Roanoke Island south of Chesapeake Bay—had been a disaster. Moreover, England had a potent and experienced competitor in long-distance trading in the Netherlands, which incorporated its East India company, the Vereenigde Oostindische Compagnie (VOC), just a year after the English East India Company.

Overtures for peace between England and Spain began in 1600, and a treaty was eventually signed in 1604. The prospect of not being able to issue letters of marque meant Elizabeth needed to encourage trade to compensate for lost revenue. There was now an urgent need to replace state-sanctioned piracy with legitimate trade. The English appetite to do so was whetted in 1592 by Sir Walter Raleigh's capture of the Portuguese carrack *Madre de Deus*. Its cargo consisted of bullion, jewels, ambergris, cloth, tapestries, and a variety of valuable spices, as well as dyes, cochineal, and ebony. What would prove even more valuable were the ship's rutters. England, which had not been involved in exploratory voyages to India and the Spice Islands, now had the wherewithal to begin trading extensively with the Orient.

It would make the most of the opportunity.

On the last day of the sixteenth century, 31 December 1600, Elizabeth I granted a charter for a monopoly by a joint-stock company on trade from the Cape of Good Hope to Cape Horn.

The East India Company was in business.

The EIC came to act as an agent of British imperialism and, at its zenith, controlled India, Pakistan, Bangladesh, and after 1885, Burma as well. It gave (what was to become) Great Britain full colonial control of this enormous area of Asia—all this from its Initial Public Offering (or IPO, as we would say today), which raised only just over 30,000 pounds, the equivalent of 3 million pounds today.

The English set up their first colony in India at Bombay (now Mumbai) in 1615. They were followed by the Scandinavians, who established small settlements in the present Tamil Nadu, Serampore, and West Bengal, as well as in the Andaman and Nicobar Islands. Although they were to maintain a presence in India for over 200 years, they were undercapitalised and never a threat to the major powers. France, in the form of the French East India Company, was considerably later into the game, establishing a trading port in what is now Pondicherry, on the east coast of India, in 1668.

Given their history of animosity with Britain, this was bound to be a problem in the future.

It would indeed be the case until they were finally defeated by Robert Clive at the Battle of Plassey in 1757, effectively ending their influence on the subcontinent. (The Spanish, it will be remembered, were excluded from establishing trading bases in India and the Spice Islands by the Treaty of Tordesillas.)

The Tea Trade

The EIC was the first trading house to establish a foothold in one of the great ports of China—Canton, now Guangzhou. Chinese tea had arrived in England from purchases made by EIC employees in India and Batavia where it had developed a reputation as a medicine. Its reception in England convinced the EIC to redouble its efforts to open trade directly with China. It would not be until the early years of the eighteenth century that this was achieved.

The trade would be enormously successful, and profits gained would support the company while it fought off the French and the Dutch to establish its control of India. By the early 1700s, English East Indiamen were voyaging regularly to China to indulge in a trade that would drive commerce for many years to come—well after the EIC had lost its monopoly on the tea trade.

By the mid-eighteenth century, ships of all flags were regular visitors to the Celestial Kingdom to load the magic, caffeine-rich leaf. The English were by far the most enthusiastic tea drinkers in Europe, and by 1813, 10 per cent of the British government's revenue would be derived from import duties on tea. In the mid-nineteenth century, the British were importing around 2,300 tons of it. By 1866, shortly after the EIC began growing tea in India, imports of Chinese tea had almost doubled to over 4,400 tons.

England versus the Netherlands

The EIC mounted many modestly profitable voyages to the Indies in the early years of the seventeenth century but were unable to prevail against the Dutch in the Spice Islands. There, big profits were to be made trading aromatic spices such as nutmeg, cloves, mace (clove petals), cinnamon, cardamom, saffron, fennel, and turmeric. The Dutch ships were better financed, better armed, and more skilfully sailed than the vessels despatched by the EIC.

The competition between the two trading houses led to several decades of conflict in which, despite some successes, the English consistently came off worst. It would strongly contest the Dutch position in India and the Spice Islands until they signed a peace treaty in 1658 (with hostilities renewed a century later). The English would also make peace with the Portuguese when the Portuguese Princess Catherine married Charles II of England. Dutch aggression would subsequently push the pioneering Portuguese out of southern India and Ceylon.

Marine Manpower

The Royal Navy, although often providing the East Indiamen fleet with protection halfway across the Atlantic, nonetheless preyed on its own charges unmercifully. Like the EIC, the Royal Navy depended on a constant supply of ordinary manpower, which, because of the poor conditions and harsh discipline on board its ships, were rarely volunteers. Its practice of 'pressing'—literally kidnapping men from English seaside towns and their surrounds—did not always result in the acquisition of skilled seamen. Anything but.

On the other hand, East Indiamen, due to their superior conditions, had no trouble recruiting crews, even though they were almost continually undermanned. Supremely powerful, the navy could board any merchant ship and press members of her crew. The merchant captains were powerless to resist, and seamen would go to all sorts of extremes to feign disability or ignorance, but to no avail.

To this extent, the East Indian trade performed a valuable service for England in training up a reservoir of capable crew. But the value of the East India Company was much greater than training crew. Although the EIC ships were not as heavily armed as British warships of equivalent size (and quite often stowed their cannon in the hold to increase cargo space), they could be, and were, commandeered in time of war to participate in naval battles.

Porcelain: An Accidental Treasure

In trading tea out of China, it was the practice for Indiamen captains to load porcelain, tightly packed in the hull, to act as ballast. The English had never encountered such fine ceramics, and they, too, were soon all the rage. The captains could thus turn a tidy profit (which accrued to them personally) on goods they were shipping purely for the purpose of seaworthiness.

The British ships weren't allowed to moor against berthing faces but had to lie in a protected part of an anchorage or river (e.g. Canton's anchorage at Whampoa) and be loaded by Chinese stevedores who were experts at storing goods on seagoing vessels. Iron, lead, and various fabrics would be unloaded and the return cargo stored, beginning often with tantalum (a corrosion-resistant metal) or porcelain as ballast.

Next would come the tea, firstly the lower-quality product, which might be affected by water during the voyage. It was followed by zinc-lined chests of the best leaf: early picked 'Bohea' that would retain its taste longer than that of the later-picked coarser grades.

Bales of silk would fill the remaining space along with a variety of other trade goods such as drugs, quicksilver, camphor, crystallised ginger, lacquerware, scented wood, and precious stones—all needing to be paid for in silver bullion.

England's Balance of Payments Problem

The Chinese were not attracted to the trade goods offered by England and demanded payment for porcelain, silks, and of course, tea, in silver. The result was a massive trade deficit with China—and a drain on England's bullion reserves.

The English were still mercantilist to the core and sought to generate a surplus with all its trading partners. They felt especially vulnerable in relation to its rapidly increasing imports of tea, to which they were addicted almost as much as the Chinese were to opium. In 1784, the government had reduced the import duty from 110 per cent to 10 per cent, causing a big surge in demand. Its exports to China were worth only one-tenth of its imports.

Exacerbating the balance of payments problem was porcelain. Initially imported simply as ballast, it became so popular in England that the capacity of Chinese potteries had to be expanded many times over to satisfy demand. Charles Lamb, the noted English essayist, and himself an employee of the EIC in London, wrote a charming essay lauding the beauties of 'Old China'.

Eventually, the English would steal the intellectual property involved in the manufacture of porcelain, which required fine white clay and kiln temperatures up to 1,500 degrees Celsius. The high temperatures did not present a problem in coal-rich and newly industrialising England. Fortunately for it, deposits of high-grade 'China' clay were discovered at home, in Cornwall.

The porcelain trade with China was doomed.

There was, however, no way that the English could grow tea, at least not in England, and it was soon realised that India could be exploited for the same purpose. In 1849, a Scottish botanist, one Robert Fortune, disguised as a Chinese nobleman, succeeded in smuggling thousands of plants and seeds out of China. Not only the plants were stolen but also, in one of the greatest thefts of intellectual property in history, the expertise involved in growing and processing it too. Fortune took two Fujianese black tea farmers with him to India. There they would apply their expertise growing tea crops in the foothills of the Himalayas for the East India Company. Plantations would subsequently be established in Ceylon.

Another British practice that would not stand close examination today was its treatment of the cotton industry in India. Indian cotton hand weavers were wonderfully skilful and wove superb cloth in a wide range of weights and an extraordinary spectrum of colours. Not surprisingly, in the early days of the empire, they found a ready market in Britain and Europe.

Allied with its innate genius for the steam-driven mechanisation of manual tasks, Britain could now produce vast quantities of cotton goods far beyond its own needs and for which it sought export markets. However, the quality of British mechanised weaving at the outset was poor compared to that achieved by hand weavers in India, and it had difficulty competing. England's response was to discourage hand weaving in India and require the Indian cotton growers to, instead, supply their cotton for export to England. There it would be manufactured and returned to India as often inferior goods. Thousands of highly skilled craftsmen weavers and their families presumably went hungry. When cotton became available from the much closer American South, the cotton growers of India were forced to produce opium instead.

Indian opium had been reaching China surreptitiously aboard EIC ships, and not surprisingly, China banned it. The EIC feared that to continue to do so would prejudice its rights to buy tea, porcelain, and a host of other lucrative products. The British government was determined to perpetuate the trade in the face of equally determined opposition from the emperor of the Celestial Empire. The trade is examined in more detail in a separate chapter, but suffice it to say here, the British government had no intention of backing down.

The Decline of Portugal

Both the EIC and VOC, and later the French East India Company, intended to operate on Portugal's patch and to trade spices out of India and the Spice Islands. Under the Treaty of Tordesillas, if one subscribed to the writ of the Roman Catholic Church, trading rights to the eastern hemisphere were held exclusively by Portugal. There was no supranational body to arbitrate, and the papacy had no means of enforcing its proclamation.

When other (especially Protestant) contenders entered the field, it was always going to be a matter of might being right. There was never a clear-cut and decisive battle over who should hold the right to trade, especially with the Spice Islands. The conflict between the Netherlands (in the form of the VOC) and Portugal represented by Philip II (also Philip III of Spain) would drag on for years. For a while, it was a three-way fight with England, in the form of the EIC, also a contender. But the Dutch had superb ships, were expert global mariners, and were better equipped financially to take on the English company.

As a result, the English ultimately decided to cut their losses and concentrate on India. They would leave the Dutch and the Portuguese to fight over the aromatic spice trade. This did not preclude the English from taking the odd Dutch or Portuguese ship if the opportunity arose, and vice versa. Such would be the extreme lawlessness of the oceans until the British Navy emerged supreme to act as a sort of global marine policeman in much the same way as the United States Navy does today.

The Jewel in the Crown

As well as luxuries, India had sizeable deposits of potassium nitrate, or nitre, a salty-tasting white powder, the common name for which is saltpetre. As well as being useful as a fertiliser, meat preservative, and in cooking, saltpetre was a vital ingredient for the all-important strategic good of the day—gunpowder.

Saltpetre's ready availability to Great Britain was a significant factor in its rise as a naval power. The decision to cut its losses in the East Indian spice trade and concentrate on the Indian subcontinent was a fateful and ultimately lucrative one. England was on the road to establishing the largest and most profitable long-distance colony the world has ever known.

The Wind System Constraint

The need to grow England's national wealth, combined with the personal greed of the merchant adventurers, meant the trade be expanded as rapidly as possible, but there were constraints. Voyages to the East were, as ever, governed by a weather window dictated by the trade winds. Fleets would leave England in September in time to reach around thirty degrees north by midwinter and in so doing catch the full strength of the north-east trades, which would speed them across the Atlantic almost to Brazil.

They would then sail south on the South Atlantic gyre until they picked up the permanent westerlies around forty degrees south. Riding the bottom of the South Atlantic gyre across to Cape Town, the fleet would reassemble there and resupply. It would then confront the most dangerous part of the voyage—north up through the Mozambique Channel—and then exploit the south-westerly trades across the Indian Ocean to India. If the voyage was to end there, they would need to have done their business by the onset of the northern winter to, this time, ride the now north-easterly trades back across the Indian Ocean.

One only has to remember Vasco da Gama's difficulties when he tried to defy this cycle.

After re-rounding the Cape of Good Hope, they could sail directly north under the influence of the north-flowing Benguela current (the eastern side of the South Atlantic gyre) with its southerly winds, and later the north-east trades, to round the hump of Africa. With the wind systems limiting journeys to India to one a year, the logical solution was to build bigger ships and increase the number despatched.

The English East Indiamen

The EIC built ships in standard sizes, but that standard increased over time. The concept of a permanent navy to safeguard trade, made up of far-ranging ships designed and built specifically for combat (as the later English naval frigates, for example, were), had yet to emerge. The new breed of ships, as well as being able to carry considerably more cargo, also had to be sufficiently well-armed as to make them entirely self-reliant—capable of taking their own part on the other side of the world.

This meant large and robust ships, sailing in convoy wherever possible, carrying numerous cannon, crewed by men who were not only sailors but skilled in hand-to-hand combat and motivated by their share in the success of the voyage. The answer manifested itself in the magnificent British East Indiamen. If we set aside the giant junks which projected soft power for Ming China in the fifteenth century, the East Indiamen were the largest cargo ships ever built up until that time. Moreover, they played an integral part in expanding world trade with its wealth-creating effects and putting two parts of the world in constant contact.

The 'Shipping Interest'

The East Indiamen grew from 500 tons mid-eighteenth century to 1,200 tons and even 1,500 tons half a century later. An 800-ton ship, which for some time was the standard, could carry 1,000 tons of tea, which made any voyage very lucrative.

The EIC originally built its own ships, but it wasn't long before it handed the function over to private consortia, the so-called 'shipping interest', which would build the vessels and lease them to the company; the tradition developed of a ship being leased in perpetuity. As an old ship was scrapped, the owner had the right to build its replacement.

The shipping interest was thus a closed shop with no threat of competitive tendering. These so-called 'ship's husbands' encouraged the construction of larger and larger vessels pointing out that the increased profit more than justified the higher cost of a bigger ship. The system was widely abused with the ship's husbands colluding to increase the price of the ships and the lease payments. Many ship's husbands were substantial shareholders or on the board of the EIC and were well aware of the profitability of each voyage. They were in an ideal position to influence the construction of more and larger vessels.

It was a system that contributed to the EIC's eventual downfall. While individual voyages were demonstrably profitable, no account was being taken of the hefty overhead costs of maintaining its large private army and the numerous staff required to administer its rule of India.

Indolent Passages

The East India Company was a monopoly and, as such, there was little incentive for swift, hardworking passages, and the voyage was ruled by the weather window anyhow. The English East Indiamen were large and luxuriously fitted compared to other ships of the day, and their procession down the English Channel, accompanied by a naval escort, was described as 'lordly' and a spectacle not to be missed.

They were, however, poor sailers.

They were deep, bluff-bowed, and had rounded bottoms. They ploughed through the water at three or four knots and, if the wind was on the beam, would make about as much leeway as they did headway. Even in relatively calm waters and in heavy ballast, they were dreadfully cranky and prone to wallowing with an interminable lurching roll that could make even the most seasoned mariners seasick.

In addition, every evening, no matter how fine the weather, the royals and all the light sails were taken in and stowed, and the royal yards sent to the deck. If the evening weather looked at all threatening, the topgallant sails and the mainsail were taken in and a reef put in the topsails. At the slightest threat of bad weather, even during daylight, sail would be reduced. The ship was darkened at night because, wallowing under easy canvas, it was a sitting duck for an enemy man-o'-war, privateer or pirate.

Earlier vessels featured a lateen sail on the mizzen mast, but as the ships grew larger, this was gradually replaced with a spanker sail. Square sails were then rigged above it to create the fully rigged ship. It would remain the standard rig for well over a century.

Functionally, the East Indiamen began their reign as freighters, and they were armed like any warship, although more lightly. As profitability increased and the burden of the administration of the private colony grew, so the ships carried less cargo and more people. Many cannons came to be stowed deep in the hold to make room for more accommodation. Cabin divisions were flimsy, however, so they could be knocked down in the event of the gun decks having to be cleared for action. In this event, every man aboard, including passengers, was assigned an action station and was expected to fight to resist being boarded by an aggressor vessel.

Indian Influence on British Shipbuilding

The experience gained from the considerably increased ocean passage-making conducted by the East Indiamen, plus intimate contact with the, in many ways, superior methods of shipbuilding in India came together in one Gabriel Snodgrass. He held the position of the EIC's chief surveyor of ships for nearly forty years. An experienced shipwright, he had been to India and studied ship construction there. He would introduce many reforms to the construction of the ships leased by the company.

The ship's husbands also had a vested interest in building good ships. They owned them and leased them to the company. The loss of a cargo was a loss for the EIC, but the loss of a ship at sea was to their cost. In the latter half of the eighteenth century, Snodgrass exerted himself to improve on the general standard of English shipbuilding, often by employing techniques he had learned in India. Traditional butt joints between planks were replaced by the stronger interlocking rabbet joints, and watertight bulkheads were introduced. The shortage of 'grown knees' to support the deck beams led to them being replaced by iron. By the turn of the eighteenth century, new East Indiamen contained nearly 100 tons of wrought iron.

More importantly, changes were made to hull shape. It was realised that the extreme tumblehome favoured hitherto, because it brought cannon closer to the centre line of the ship, actually encouraged heeling. Again, drawing on the Indian experience, in particular the vertical-sided Bengal rice ships, Snodgrass argued that vertical sides made the ship stiffer. It also spread the shrouds, thereby improving the staying of the masts and enabling an increase in cargo capacity.

The wells between the fore and aftercastles were reduced in depth, and the decks cambered to assist draining in heavy seas. The importance of introducing this particular improvement was brought home in 1808 and 1809 when thirteen Indiamen were lost at sea. They were carrying cargo worth a million pounds. These vessels were deep-waisted and proved the worth of new designs that reduced the depth of the deck well and cambered it to shed water easily.

The End of the Indiamen

Later, after the monopoly was lost (to India in 1813 and to China in 1834), these 'lordly' old ships were no longer competitive and were gradually replaced. The new vessels were called 'Blackwall frigates' after the famous Blackwall Yard on the Thames, which also built vessels of this design as Royal Navy frigates. The frigates were smaller ships without the high aftercastle and with narrower sterns. They could sail faster and, resembling Royal Navy frigates (the most feared naval ships of their time), tended to discourage pirates.

Securing the Colony

The EIC would proceed to consolidate its position on the Indian subcontinent. The great Mughal (or Mogul or Mongol) Empire was established early in the sixteenth century by invading hordes from Uzbekistan. They were Muslims and came to exert their rule over vast swathes of a predominantly Hindu country. Their empire extended from the Indus Basin in the west, north-west to Afghanistan and north to Kashmir, all the way to Bengal in the east, as well as the Deccan Plateau in the south.

It was very wealthy, rivalling the Ming Empire in China, but it was unruly with local magnates constantly conspiring with and against other local rulers. As the centre (with a base around Delhi) grew weak, it degenerated into a series of local fracas as regional magnates endeavoured to expand their tax base in this wealthy country, at the expense of their neighbour.

When the British arrived and obtained, at a considerable price, various trading concessions, especially in West Bengal, their concern was to protect their position from the French, who had established themselves on the coast to the south of Calcutta (the capital of Bengal) and the Dutch further south and in Ceylon (now Sri Lanka). In each of its main trading centres—Bombay, Madras, and Calcutta—the EIC had recruited mercenary armies from the local population to protect its property and its rights to the land it had leased from the local rulers. Their military strength saw the British gradually get drawn into assisting one Mughal prince against another, and eventually propping up the emperor.

With the arrival of Robert Clive in 1744, the situation changed completely. Clive was a juvenile delinquent whose father despaired of him but succeeded in getting him a job as a clerk with the EIC. He was a layabout, not a trained soldier, yet by the age of twenty-eight, he had distinguished himself militarily in the Carnatic Wars. These involved the British, the French, the local Nawab of the Carnatic, and the Nizam of Hyderabad.

Robert Clive (1725-1774)

Source: Alamy

The outcome of the three wars was the permanent weakening of the French position in India. Another outcome was that Robert Clive made a fortune and decided to return to England to pursue a political career. When his fortune proved insufficient to fund the bribes necessary to obtain a seat in the 'Mother of all Parliaments', he returned to India intent on replenishing it.

Having previously defeated the French, Clive would subsequently subdue the Dutch and the local prince who had taken the lucrative province of West Bengal from the Mughals—all using locally recruited armies. From there, British influence would spread progressively over all of India and what is now Pakistan. In the process, Clive made himself possibly the wealthiest man in the British Empire. As historian William Dalrymple has put it, rather than, as traditional history would have us believe, the British government seizing vast tracts of India was

> *a dangerously unregulated private company headquartered in one small office, just five windows wide, in London, and managed in India by a violent, utterly ruthless, and intermittently mentally unstable, corporate predator—Clive.*

During the eighteenth century, trade with the Orient expanded beyond the EIC's wildest dreams. Meanwhile, its ability to manage such an embarrassment of riches was proceeding in the other direction. The number of ships despatched to the East rose from 30 to 40 in 1690 to 100 in 1717 and 150 in 1727. By comparison, the Dutch were sending forty ships, and the French thirty-five.

The rate of expansion was much faster than the meagre administrative resources of the London head office could cope with. As a consequence, its records fell hopelessly behind at first, months, and later, years. The absence of effective management sowed the seeds of the company's demise, even at the height of its trading activity. But masking this administrative incompetence was its popularity as an investment with its share price rivalling the Bank of England and paying 8–10 per cent per annum.

Thanks to the EIC's military superiority and assistance from the Royal Navy, it saw off competition from the Dutch and especially the French. By the end of the eighteenth century, both the Dutch and the French East India companies were bankrupt, and their assets either turned over to private traders or nationalised.

The EIC, on the other hand, although fatally flawed, had risen to become the supreme power on the Indian subcontinent.

Such was its dominance and its rapacity that it would close down the superb Indian cotton mills and force Manchester's coarse goods on to the Indians, insisting the cotton fields be planted to opium for shipment to China. Had it been organised as a coherent whole, the subcontinent was thirty times larger than Britain in land area, with a population probably twenty times larger and wealth considerably exceeding it.

Owing to its fragmentation, it became completely subjugated.

In time, it would turn into the largest and wealthiest colony the world has ever known.

But in a surprisingly *short* time, it came to be ruled by a small coterie of company servants. Their dictate was enforced by an army of 260,000 men made up overwhelmingly of locally recruited soldiers, officered and trained by a minimal number of Englishmen. At the time, the entire British Army was only half the size of this private force—surely the largest private army ever assembled.

The Importance of the 'Country Trade'

When Western powers arrived in the East it was suffering from an intense shipping shortage due to a surge in economic activity and foreign trade between the countries of that hemisphere. Arab, Malay, Indian, and Chinese traders had pioneered these trade routes and filled this niche in a system of more or less open competition for centuries. But their vessels were small, limited in their range, and lacked effective armament.

It was the power of the European ships—their size, armament, and sailing capabilities—that had been necessary to make the journey to the East, that led to them taking an aggressive attitude towards the local merchant navies. The Eastern countries would benefit little from the increased economic activity. The Portuguese, but especially the Dutch and later the English, pushed the local merchant navies from the Indies seas and vastly expanded what became known as the 'country trade'. Ultimately, for the Dutch and the English trading houses, the country trade became much more profitable than the 'return trade' to Europe and formed the basis of later domination and colonisation.

The European–Oriental trade drew on the wealth that had been injected into Europe from the Americas, especially the supplies of silver, without which Europe would have lacked the ability to buy such large quantities of Asian goods. Other than firearms (and opium in China), there was little Western countries had to offer Asia. Payment for goods was required in bullion—gold and silver—and as the tea, silk, and porcelain trade with China grew, especially silver.

Silver, however, was more highly valued in China than gold, which opened up opportunities for bullion trading, which the Western countries were quick to exploit. Later, the opium traders would ship opium to China in exchange for silver and bring it back to India where it could be advantageously traded for gold.

The Denouement

The British East India Company was in India for over 200 years and came to rule the country, complete with its own army, courts, and civil service. Ultimately, it would also enter a period of decline brought on by administrative incompetence, corruption, and avarice.

By 1784, it was two years behind in payment of its accounts and 5 million pounds in debt. It continued to pay excellent dividends, however, and was therefore popular as an investment. It was able to stay afloat by repeatedly raising capital. In this respect, it was similar to modern 'Ponzi' schemes. That year, the government installed a board of control, and in 1813, it lost its monopoly of trade in the East and was effectively reduced to managing India for the British government.

The investors were, however, politically powerful, and once nationalised, the government continued to pay shareholders dividends of 10 per cent per annum for forty years. The vast area over which it had held sway became a British colony, with Queen Victoria its empress. In the beginning, it assisted local magnates in their perpetual arguments with their neighbours and gradually gained control over them. In so doing, it created the largest colony the world had ever known and delivered it, holus-bolus, to the British crown.

The British government's hold on India would survive for more than a century. After the Second World War, Great Britain was in an extremely parlous financial position and completely dependent upon the United States to avoid bankruptcy. Needless to say, it could no longer afford to administer India, which was also becoming increasingly politically fractious. Arrangements had to be made for a hasty departure, which would result in one of the greatest dislocations of peoples in history.

Historically, India was Hindu but had come to be ruled by the Mughals, who were Muslims. Centuries later, the two religions were still quite separate. Vigorous attempts were made to come up with a political solution that would have retained British India as a single entity, but they failed due to Muslim fears of being dominated by the Hindu majority. The only solution the British could come up with was partition—the creation of separate countries. India and West and East Pakistan were born.

By 1885, Great Britain, through a series of wars, had also added Burma to the empire, making it a province of India. In 1948, it was granted independence, but its birth as a nation was far less disruptive than the massive relocation of peoples involved in the partition.

The Dutch East India Company (VOC)

The Netherlands was the great maritime and trading power of the seventeenth century. This was partly derived from its strategic location 'between two seas', the Atlantic and the Baltic. The Netherlands' trading relationships in the Baltic were very valuable. With few forests of its own, it was the source of naval stores such as shipbuilding timber (oak and pine), masts (from single robust Baltic pines), pitch (for caulking), and tar.

Formation of the VOC

The year 1602 was a notable one for international commerce. In that year, traders in the Netherlands (or the Republic of the Seven United Provinces of the Netherlands) formed the Vereenigde Oostindische Compagnie (VOC). By then, they were free from Spanish rule and any obligation to the Roman Catholic Church. They were Protestant (and therefore not bound by the Treaty of Tordesillas) and republican, unhindered either by grasping monarchs (such as Queen Elizabeth I of England or King Manuel I of Portugal) or the marriage politics of European royal houses. But the Netherlands had little in the way of national resources, and its population numbered only 1.5 million, less even than Portugal. Their main assets were grit (inbred through centuries of fighting back the North Sea), shipbuilding prowess, navigational expertise, and their parsimony and commercial acumen, the last most important of all.

Contrasted with England, they were wealthy and passionate traders and, when finally relieved of the cost of the long-standing conflict with the Holy Roman Empire, enthusiastic to use their strengths in carving out a share of trade with the Indies. It was a zeal that would carry them far and provide almost two centuries of prosperous trading and the accumulation of enormous wealth.

Their trading vehicle also differed in structure to the EIC. Not only was it much better financed, Dutch capital, once committed, was used to finance a succession of voyages, and annual dividends were paid on the continuing stream of profits accumulated by the company. In contrast, initially, the EIC had no capital of its own, and investors could choose to invest or not in a particular voyage. Compared to the Dutch, the EIC was undercapitalised, and it suffered from an alternative investment being available in Raleigh's Roanoake colony.

The VOC held its fundraiser in 1603, gleaning 6.44 million guilders, or about ten times as much as its English competitor. This was a measure of the Netherlands' necessary experience, expertise in, and enthusiasm for, long-distance trading and the profit-making opportunities it provided.

The Netherlands had a well-developed banking system, insurance sector, and stock market. It was the most commercially sophisticated economy in Europe. Moreover, the year after its incorporation, a VOC ship captured a large spice-laden Portuguese carrack, the value of which more than doubled its available capital. Simple arithmetic suggests that the value of the ship and its cargo was about 30 million pounds in today's terms.

Two inferences can be drawn: the incredible value of Eastern spices in the European market and the extent to which the EIC was initially considerably undercapitalised compared to its direct competitor. The Dutch also had another overwhelming advantage. Despite the enormous wealth Spain garnered from its American possessions, it spent much of it fighting its many enemies. The Dutch were, at this time, the wealthiest nation in Europe, and the riches flowed from its monopoly on the trade in aromatic spices.

Fine Spice Monopoly

By 1622, the VOC had a monopoly on nutmeg (*Myristica fragrans*) and mace (the coating of the nutmeg seed). Monopolising the clove (*Syzygium aromaticum*) trade took longer. It involved concentrating production on the island of Ambon by destroying all the trees elsewhere in the Moluccas. By capturing Makassar in 1667, the VOC eliminated the only source of 'contraband' fine spices. A monopoly on cinnamon (*Cinnamomum)* was achieved by pushing the Portuguese out of Ceylon.

Financial Superiority

Compared to the monarchical capitalism practised by the Iberians, the rise of the Dutch and English trading houses was very much merchant-based, formed and supported financially by a strong middle class whose livelihood was commerce. The Dutch, particularly, were both territorially aggressive and successful traders. They systematically defeated the Portuguese, pushing them out of India and Ceylon and then the Spice Islands. They turned what is now the Indonesian archipelago into a Dutch sea centred on Batavia (present-day Jakarta).

The same year as the VOC was formed, the Dutch arrived in India and concentrated their trading activities between Cochin (Kochi) on the south-west coast of the peninsula and up the east (Coromandel) coast, including Ceylon. They later (in 1656) invaded Ceylon, taking it from the Portuguese. To protect Ceylon from being retaken, they followed the invasion up by invading the other Portuguese trading ports around the peninsula. It was an age when naked aggression went a long way.

The Dutch persisted in India but were not nearly as determined to win there as they were in the Spice Islands. The result was several decades of conflict with England in which England rarely gained the upper hand. At one stage (in the Battle of the Medway in 1667), Dutch ships sailed up the Thames estuary to deliver a punitive raid on Sheerness.

A decision was made by the EIC to abandon the aromatic spice trade and concentrate on other, for the present time, less lucrative but ultimately more rewarding trade in the products of the Indian subcontinent. These included the ubiquitous pepper, medicinal substances such as camphor and opium, fine cotton textiles (such as muslins and chintzes), and silk and indigo—all luxury goods in Europe.

Its most important business, however, was in exerting military power.

The Dutch East Indiamen (Fluyts)

Dutch ships were utilitarian and lightly constructed, designed to maximise cargo space and rigged to be operated by small crews. Unlike other trading ships of the time, they carried little or no armaments and were not built to be converted to warships. They were built cheaply using new tools and sawing power harnessed from windmills. Their low cost provided economical transport for their wide-ranging trading activities and gave Dutch merchants a cost advantage over their competitors. The fluyts' shallow draft (necessary due to the shallow and shoaly water around their home ports) enabled them to put into rivers and ports not accessible to other vessels. They influenced European ship design, especially English, after the Royal Navy captured a number during the Anglo-Dutch wars.

The VOC did not build its own ships but rather, like the EIC, hired them. It dictated their design and maintenance, however, based on their trading experience in Asia. The ships needed to be safe, well-built and seaworthy, capacious, and crewed by seamen trained to defend the ship. Captains who did not adhere to the rules regarding well-maintained armaments and trained crews suffered financial penalties.

The fluyts made considerable use of the mechanical advantage provided by pulley systems and were designed specifically (for economy's sake) to be sailed by relatively small crews. They had tall masts, which increased their speed, but they had shallow drafts and substantial tumblehome, so the topmasts were rigged so that they could be lowered in heavy conditions. They eschewed luxury in the interests of cargo-carrying capacity. Originally designed exclusively as freighters, as the administrative needs of their empire grew, like the British East Indiamen, they became hybrids, carrying large numbers of passengers as well. When, in 1629, the company's new flagship, the *Batavia*, was famously wrecked on the Abrolhos Islands, it had 322 people aboard.

Some fluyts were built using the 'outside in' technique rather than by the traditional method of erecting a framework, which was then clad. The Dutch established the shape of the ship using the cladding inserted into a mould and then built the structure inside it. In the interests of manoeuvrability, Dutch East Indiamen, like their British brethren, forsook the notion of a high forecastle but retained the aftercastle and were nonetheless seaworthy.

Getting to the Spice Islands

To reach their capital, Batavia, Dutch East Indiamen, having rounded the Cape of Good Hope, would sail directly east before the prevailing wind. When they estimated they were on the same longitude as the Sunda Strait and Batavia, they would turn left. A lack of accurate timepieces meant they had no way of accurately determining how far they had come.

It was always going to be a guess.

One guess that was wrong was made by an East Indiaman captain, Dirk Hartog, who collided with the legendary Great South Land a century and a half before James Cook. Hartog happened upon an area that was dry, infertile, and sparsely populated and dismissed it as unworthy of further investigation.

Another misjudgement that had much more serious consequences occurred in 1629. The *Batavia*, captained by one Francisco Pelsaert, was on her maiden voyage to the eponymous city when, at night, it ran up on the Houtman Abrolhos Islands. Most (282 of the 322 aboard) survived the wreck and made it to land.

Replica of the Ill-fated VOC Flagship *Batavia*

Source: Wikimedia Commons

Pelsaert took the ship's boat and sailed to Batavia to organise a rescue, leaving a company supercargo (junior merchant) called Jeronimus Cornelisz in charge. By the time he returned, Cornelisz—an ex-Haarlem apothecary and would-be mutineer turned psychopath—had arranged the murder of at least 100 of the survivors.

Pelsaert returned literally in the nick of time to prevent further bloodshed.

Cornelisz and some of his closest collaborators were (after their hands were chopped off) hanged on the island. Of the original complement of the *Batavia*, only 122 made it to their destination. Two hundred were either drowned, murdered, or hanged. Pelsaert, whose timely arrival had saved many from certain death, was held partly responsible and deprived of all his worldly goods.

Rise to Trading Power

By the end of the eighteenth century, the Dutch East India Company was in trouble. It was making spectacular profits on its monopoly of the aromatic spice trade, but maintaining it was expensive. Capital expenditure on ships (thirty or forty sailed to Indonesia each year), forts, and factories, and maintaining a European workforce of 12,000 people, was taking a heavy toll. Losses were aided and abetted by alcohol and the tropical diseases so prevalent in the canals of the capital, Batavia. Disease was such a problem that ships of other nations calling to resupply would typically lose a quarter of their crew to sickness before the exercise could be completed.

In the more than two centuries of its existence, the VOC's operations increased considerably. In total, it fitted out 4,700 ships to sail to the East Indies, nearly 1,700 during the seventeenth century and a good 3,000 during the eighteenth. The company spent some 370 million guilders on ships and equipment between 1610 and 1700. That figure rose to 1,608 million guilders from 1700 to 1795. In terms of personnel, between 1602 and 1700, 317,000 people sailed from Europe. Between 1700 and 1795, this total reached 655,000—an average of upwards of 7,000 per year. For its time, it was an extraordinarily large trading enterprise, and in its first century, it was much larger and more lucrative than the EIC.

Decline

Despite the massive increase in its operations during the eighteenth century, the VOC never made a profit. Reserves accumulated during its first century of operation were gradually whittled away, and it was only able to continue with government support. Besides mismanagement, corruption in the VOC's ranks was also a problem with employees who, no doubt urged on by the possibility of imminent death, took every opportunity to enrich themselves at the expense of the company.

The Dutch had fought long and hard to keep the British out of the East Indies but in doing so neglected their position in India. The VOC had also been content to buy tea from Chinese ships trading into the strategically located port of Bantam on the western tip of Java. By the time it realised the importance of the tea trade, it was too late, and it would find it difficult to overcome Britain's dominance.

The VOC's financial situation became so dire that it was effectively nationalised by the Dutch government in 1800, and its various colonies in the Spice Islands integrated into a colonial government of the Dutch East Indies in 1826. The Dutch government would retain its hold on the colony until after the Second World War. Following a period of Japanese occupation, however, in 1948, the archipelago would become an independent nation as the Republic of Indonesia.

A Similar Fate

The VOC was a very successful trading entity creating immense wealth for its homeland. Similar to the EIC in India, it would become a private company ruling an enormous archipelago with its own army and civil administration. Eventually, however, as has been the case with so many long-lived human institutions, it would become corrupt and spend well beyond its earnings trying to defend this immense area of land and sea.

It, too, would experience the need to bring not only trade goods but a continuous supply of people to man this empire in the face of the depredations of tropical disease and pestilence that regularly harvested white people unused to the tropics. It, too, would eventually be nationalised (in 1796), and the Dutch government would control its vast territories for a century and a half, until after the Second World War.

The East Indies would benefit very little from its extensive period as a Dutch colony, and when they departed, other than their preoccupation with turning a fever-ridden swamp into a simulacrum of their canal-based European capital city, there was very little left to show that they had been there for over three and a half centuries.

The Spanish Empire

It is difficult to comprehend today that a country the size of Spain once held dominion over such a large area of the land on earth. But it did, creating the largest empire in history. It extended over much of the Americas and included, as well, the Philippines. And no region of the world has been more changed as a result of European colonisation than the Americas.

It is also difficult to comprehend the wealth that Spain extracted from the Americas in relation to the amount that existed in Europe. In both of its administrative divisions—one headquartered in Central America and the other in Peru, in South America—they would benefit from the diseases which travelled with them, which had a devastating effect on the local populations, reducing their ability to resist. It is estimated that the original population of the Americas ran to tens of millions and that 80 to 95 per cent of that population died from European diseases alone.

And then there were the locals who were worked to death in the silver mines. It deprived the colonisers of a labour force, however, to cultivate the land, necessitating the import of thousands of African slaves, at least into the lower-lying areas. The wealth the Spanish would derive from its American colonies would make it the most powerful nation in Europe.

The Spanish conquest began with Christopher Columbus's arrival in the West Indies and expanded to the conquest of the Aztecs in Mexico in 1519. From there, the Spanish North American Empire, designated the Viceroyalty of New Spain, spread over Central America and north into the south-western part of what is now the continental United States.

The Incas in South America were an older and more impressive civilisation than the Olmecs, the Aztecs, and the Maya of Central America. The Spanish arrived in 1532 and created the Viceroyalty of Peru that extended over all South America except for Brazil, which was claimed by Portugal under the Treaty of Tordesillas.

Spain's main objective was to find gold, and while they did find some, their big discovery was a mountain of silver in Peru, along with the mercury required to refine it. Between the sixteenth and the eighteenth centuries, it is estimated that Spain produced over 150,000 tons of silver, equal to 80 per cent of the world's supply during that period.

The increase in spending power that it created in Europe was not matched with a commensurate increase in output, and it led to inflation. The Spanish monarchy did not adjust its taxation base to account for inflation, and so the silver washed through its economy without providing an equivalent increase in actual wealth, it being dissipated for the most part in higher prices.

It did, however, provide a supply of specie that could be usefully traded in Asia for the highly desirable spices, tea, silks, medicaments, and porcelain it produced. Silver was the first global market. The high altitude of the silver deposits, however, meant they could not be mined by African slaves, so the locals, used to working in such conditions, were enslaved to do so. Millions of them would die in the silver mines from hunger and exhaustion and be buried where they fell.

Despite mismanaging the effects of such a large increase in purchasing power, Spain became immensely wealthy, and (unlike Portugal) the monarchy was able to exploit its colonial acquisitions without resort to newfangled financial organisations. It would do so for nearly 400 years, but besides failing to capitalise on the enormous increase in spending power, it was also involved in a series of hostilities in Europe, mainly against the rising wealth and mercantile power of the Netherlands.

As a consequence, the benefits of empire slowly waned. It lost most of its possessions in South America in the early nineteenth century as they fought for and gained their independence. By 1900, it had lost its colonies in the Caribbean and the Pacific and retained only its possessions in Africa. Its legacy is the Spanish language spoken over most of the Americas south of the United States (and a good deal there too) and the Roman Catholic religion, which is universal through the region and in the Philippines.

The Portuguese Empire

The Portuguese monarchy concentrated its colonial activities in India and the East Indies and eastern South America, which, under the Treaty of Tordesillas, it was entitled to colonise. With a small population, the Portuguese were by far the most avid of slavers, and it is estimated to have transported almost half of the slaves removed from Africa (about 6 million people), mostly to its sugar plantations in Brazil. Disease was rife and the working conditions extremely harsh, so much so that the lifespan of slaves imported to Brazil was shorter than those imported to elsewhere in the Americas.

The Dutch East and also its West Indies companies were intent on pushing Portugal out of India, the East Indies, Africa, and Brazil. It fought a series of wars against the Iberians in the first half of the seventeenth century, the era of the rise of the great northern European joint-stock companies. The Portuguese and Spanish crowns had been united under Philip II in 1580, and the conflict can be regarded as an extension of that waged by the Spanish against the Netherlands for eighty years.

By the mid-seventeenth century, the Netherlands had, for the most part, triumphed, with Portugal losing most of its Indian, East Indies, and African colonies. Spain/Portugal retained Brazil, however, and it would revert to Portugal after Portugal declared itself independent of Spain in 1640. With the massive import of slaves, the original colony expanded down the south coast of South America and along the Amazon, well beyond the boundary set by the Treaty of Tordesillas. In 1822, however, Brazil declared its independence from Portugal.

The Age of New Ideas

During the eighteenth century, an immense transformation was taking place as the next great agents of change—the Age of Enlightenment and the Industrial Revolution—began to exert an irresistible force upon the Western world. The Age of Enlightenment was an intellectual and philosophical movement, whereas the Industrial Revolution concerned material goods and how they were produced.

The former emerged out of the Renaissance and the preceding Scientific Revolution and paved the way for the Industrial Age by half a century. Drawing on the revival of pre-Christian philosophy and scientific concepts, the Enlightenment emphasised reason and observation as the primary sources of knowledge. It dealt with abstract concepts such as liberty, equality, progress, and tolerance. Undermining the authority of the church and divine right, it advocated constitutional government.

The Industrial Revolution drew on these notions, especially individual freedom and progress, to clear away entrenched ideas and open up society to accepting new ways of producing material needs.

First, water power in the form of water mills was harnessed along with the benefits of water, as opposed to land-based transport, in the building of canals. The population grew more rapidly, and output increased markedly, creating demand for resources, not all of which were readily available locally. Increased output also sought export markets.

The upshot was a demand for more and better transport. Capital was all important in building factories and stocking them with machines. A new concept arose: the time value of money. Speed in the industrial process was important so that monetary returns could be produced and reinvested or applied elsewhere. The various demands created by the new Industrial Age would produce a revolution in shipping, firstly in more efficient forms of sailing ships, and how they were operated. And later came the application of the revolutionary concept of steam power, in necessary conjunction with steel, to land-based and oceanic transport.

Meanwhile, the opportunities opened up by the ages of exploration and exploitation created an increased demand for new products and the labour to produce them. Slavery was an important part of increasing the supply of exotic goods, especially foodstuffs. Out of this universal evil came the maritime models and practices that would be vital to meeting the demands of the new industrial era.

5

CHAPTER

The Slave Trade

Introduction

Whether it was to build pyramids or empires, or just to make life more comfortable for the privileged, the enslavement of, and trade in, human beings is almost as old as civilisation itself. Although slaves were taken from anywhere to anywhere, for the last millennium, Africa has been the most popular source.

Arabs and Indians were slave trading up and down the east coast of Africa as early as the ninth century. Since then, it is estimated they captured and transported more than 15 million Negroes to other locations in the Middle East and the Indian Ocean rim. In the Middle East, plantations were being established to increase food supply, but manual labour had come to be regarded as demeaning by increasingly wealthy Muslims. As well as reclaiming land lost to agriculture, slaves were also sought as soldiers. The Gujarati, Hindus from India, were also prominent traders of East African peoples around the Indian Ocean rim. The main sources were the Bantu peoples from what is now Tanzania, Mozambique, and Malawi.

By the middle of the fifteenth century, the Portuguese had been trading slaves from the African west coast to the Cape Verde Islands, again to develop its plantation economy. It was a 'proto-triangular trade', shipping European arms and ammunition and cheap baubles out to the Guinea coast, slaves to the islands, and cotton, indigo, sugar products, and hides back to Portugal.

The West Indian and American Slave Trade

When Columbus landed on Hispaniola, it was a heavily populated island with several million inhabitants. But the Europeans brought with them a range of diseases against which the locals had no defence. Columbus intended to enslave them to serve his purposes as the newly arrived governor, but the population was reduced rapidly from disease to the point that it would be necessary to import labour.

The logical solution was to bring slaves from Africa who, unfortunately for them, possessed herd immunity to many European diseases. Again, with the discovery of gold and silver in Central America, especially Peru, disease would decimate the local population.

American Negroes could not, however, work at the high altitudes in Peru. What was left of the local population, bred to live and work in these conditions, were enslaved to work the silver mines.

Similarly, Europeans brought disease to the North American mainland, which was only sparsely populated by Indians, who did not take readily to being so imposed upon. Again, it was necessary to import African slaves to work firstly British and later French plantation economies. Initially, they grew tobacco (the consumption of which had boomed in Europe) and later indigo and sugar and still later, and most importantly of all, cotton. Had the West African Negroes lacked disease immunity, the slave trade, as it subsequently developed, would have been pointless.

The Portuguese had been trading West African slaves into Europe and their own offshore islands for hundreds of years. The discovery of the Americas, however, led to an exponential growth in what is, by modern standards, a despicable industry.

It would thrive legally for almost 200 years—and illegally for another 50.

The Novel Products

With the discovery of the Americas, the novel vegetable riches of the New World—tomatoes, maize, and potatoes, among others—held particular delight for Europeans. But these would grow in Europe, so they simply became part of the Columbian exchange.

What was not native to the Americas, but would grow very well in the plantations of the West Indies, was sugar cane. Sugar cane is a native of New Guinea, but its popularity led to its cultivation across Southeast Asia to India (where it hybridised with wild plants) and eastward into the Philippines. Sugar is produced by crushing the cane and extracting the juice, which is boiled until it thickens into molasses or further until it crystalises into raw sugar. The raw sugar is then refined to extract the molasses and other impurities. Molasses is mainly used by bakers (to make cakes and biscuits), distillers (to produce rum), and other processors (to make pharmaceuticals and animal food). It is further refined for table use.

Tobacco use was widespread among American Indians, and although it was possible to cultivate the crop in Europe, the production process and the quality of the leaf were far superior if grown in America. But growing and curing tobacco was labour-intensive. Sir John Hawkins brought the first seeds to England, but the first cured leaves of Virginia tobacco were introduced by Sir Walter Raleigh. Proponents of pipe smoking boasted of its health-giving properties, and demand for the product soared all over Europe. Its increasing use encouraged the development of plantations and, in turn, the demand for slaves to cultivate them.

Westward Movement

In England, the duty on tobacco was increased fortyfold, but demand did not wane. James I, who went out of his way to discourage smoking, nevertheless appreciated tobacco's moneymaking properties. He restricted the source to his colony of Virginia and made it a royal monopoly, charging fifteen pounds per year for a licence to produce it. Cultivation needed a lot of ploughing, sowing, weeding, harvesting, and curing. With the local population devastated, the only answer was slave labour. The first black slaves arrived at Jamestown, Virginia, in 1619.

Plantations are best established on flat, fertile land. For that reason, the later demand for cotton saw the area of cultivation spread westward rather than northward. Slaves were moved from Maryland, Virginia, and the Carolinas to the deep south: Georgia, Alabama, Mississippi, Louisiana, and Texas. By the time the slaves were freed by an amendment to the United States Constitution in 1865, there were over 4 million of them.

Europeans already knew how to sweeten their otherwise unappetising diet. Sugar could be obtained from sugar beet, but it was weak, and the yield was poor. Cane sugar was quite the reverse. Sugar cane had a much higher yield; it had a powerful taste, and the juice had another highly desirable characteristic—when fermented, it became the raw material from which to distil rum.

Rum would become an alcoholic staple in Great Britain and especially in the British Navy where it was used as a reward at the end of a hard day. Being deprived of it was a potent punishment. It was said that the British Navy ran on 'rum, sodomy, and the lash'. In its Australian colony, where there was a distinct shortage of specie, rum was widely used as currency, and an attempt to monopolise its supply led to insurrection.

It would be in the crude form of molasses that the raw material for sugar would be exported to England. There it would be refined into a variety of products, but the big money was in the distillation of rum and the production of refined sugar.

As would later be the case with opium, many British fortunes were built off the backs of slaves, the sugar refining company Tate & Lyle being an example. Slave labour could therefore be said to have built the Tate Gallery. Even Charles II formed a joint-stock company (the Royal African Company) explicitly to participate in the 'triangular trade'.

By 1800, by far the most financially profitable West Indian colonies belonged to Britain.

The 'Triangular Trade'

Beginnings

One of the first of many British navigators to exploit what became known as the 'triangular trade' was none other than the eminent Elizabethan buccaneer, later secretary for the navy, Sir John Hawkins. In 1567, accompanied by his younger relative and long-time associate, Sir Francis Drake, Hawkins mounted a large-scale expedition around the three-legged course. Such a trade was only made possible by the ability of sailing ships to cross and recross the Atlantic Ocean sailing a triangular course.

The Portuguese had first used this technique sailing from Lisbon to reach the Canary Islands and the Azores and thence to northern Europe. Columbus had just extended it south and west using his knowledge of the Atlantic wind systems that he had gained in the northern area of that ocean. Once used as the path of discovery, it subsequently became the basis of the trade route between Europe, Africa, and the Caribbean, and the east coast of America.

The Infamous Triangular Trade

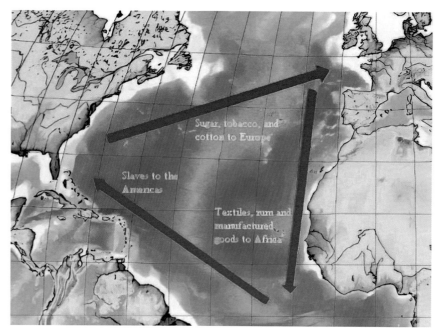

Source: SimonP. Wikipedia Creative Commons CC BY-SA 2.0

The First Leg

On the first leg of the triangle, ships sailed from Europe to the west coast of Africa laden with various European 'coast goods', such as copper, cloth, trinkets, and small arms and ammunition. These were then exchanged with Arab traders and local chiefs for unfortunate souls captured on raids into the hinterland.

Under the Treaty of Tordesillas, the line of demarcation dividing the trading rights for the entire globe between Portugal and Spain just clipped the South American continent—what is now Brazil. Portugal lost no time in capitalising on its acquisition and, with its long experience slaving out of West Africa, began shipping slaves to its new acquisition.

It would make a welter of it.

Of all the countries engaged in the slave trade, Portugal was the smallest but by far the most active. Over the time it was engaged in slaving into Brazil, it has been estimated that 6 million West Africans were transported against their will. The figure represents almost half of the people ever taken from West Africa to the New World.

The Infamous 'Middle Passage'

On the second leg, the infamous 'middle passage', the slaves were transported across the Atlantic to plantation owners in Brazil, the Caribbean, and later the American South.

It was the conditions on the ships making this middle passage that brought the triangular trade into such disrepute. A typical 'slaver', as the ships were known, had a lower deck on which the slaves were made to lie head to toe in four rows. They were shackled, and there was no space between them either lengthwise or sideways. The ship's hull was designed to continue these four rows for as long a part of the overall length of the ship as possible.

Above this deck was a gallery, or simply a shelf, on which more slaves were packed side by side, again shackled, with no space between them and barely any space above them. Even in the so-called regulated slave trade, there was only required to be two feet, seven inches between these two decks. Those unlucky enough to be lying under the deck beams had much less. Every possible small part of these deck spaces was packed with shackled bodies, although women and children, who were kept separate, were generally not bound.

The bottom deck might be packed with around 300 bodies and the shelf with another 130 or so men, women, and children. Some ships repeated this loading pattern over two decks, as shown in the lower left-hand corner of the illustration below. There was no provision whatsoever for toileting, and the conditions, which grew progressively worse as the voyage proceeded, must have been horrific, especially when bad weather led to seasickness. This torment could last anything between six weeks and several months. While the trade was legal, any ship, no matter how slow, could be pressed into the business.

Stowage of the British Slave Ship *Brookes* under the Regulated Slave Trade 1788

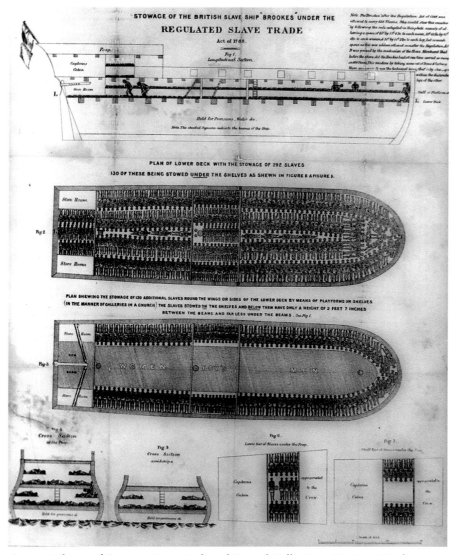

Source: Library of Congress Rare Book and Special Collections Division Washington, D.C. 20540 USA cph 3a44236 //hdl.loc.gov/loc.pnp/cph.3a44236

Every effort was made to cram as many bodies on board as was physically possible. The forecastle, normally accommodation for the crew, was filled with ships' stores. Most of the crew slept on deck, although this could have been as much to escape the stench as for lack of space.

Once the ship reached its destination, the survivors of this hell of malnutrition and disease, generally about 90 per cent of those originally loaded, were sold to plantation owners, although a 50 per cent survival rate was still profitable. They would spend what remained of their lives in a vicious regime of poor food, continuous hard work, and cruelty, their offspring the property of their owner and liable to be sold off at any time.

The ships were then thoroughly cleaned and prepared to take on a non-human cargo of mainly casks of molasses. They would sail the third leg of the triangle back to their home port, from which the whole process would begin again.

The main participants were, in order of the number of slaves transported, Portugal almost 6 million (mainly to Brazil), Great Britain 3.3 million, France 1.4 million, and Spain just over a million.

The Third Leg

Sugar cane, once harvested by the slaves, was crushed and boiled, also using slave labour. Previously crushed cane (bagasse) was used as fuel. The syrup obtained would be reduced, and the molasses stored in barrels for shipment to Europe.

The ships were designed to carry human beings and were not especially adept cargo carriers. Nevertheless, a merchandise cargo—products of the slave-based plantations, including barrels of molasses, rum, and sugar—would be loaded.

When the plantations in Virginia were established, the return freight would be made up of tobacco, hemp, rice, and later, cotton. In Europe, the molasses would be sold to distillers for the production of rum or refined into cooking and table sugar and other by-products such as stock feed.

Feeding the Slaves: Another 'Triangular' Trade

A dependable protein source was needed to feed the vast number of forced labourers. The fisheries of the shallow seas of the Caribbean were not particularly productive, and livestock was plagued by disease. The result was another 'triangular' trade that supplied salt cod from the bountiful fisheries off the North American coast as well as lumber and agricultural produce to the Caribbean. Molasses products were then taken back to Great Britain and British-manufactured goods brought across the Atlantic to what were, up until 1776, its American colonies.

Central America had promised enormous wealth to the original explorers, but it could only be appropriated at similarly enormous risk. Their immunity to European diseases did not make the African slaves (or their masters) immune to the various diseases prevalent in the tropical areas of Central America, and consequently, a constant resupply of manpower was required. Yellow fever was the grimmest reaper, but malaria was also a big killer, as was dysentery.

Even as late as the late nineteenth century, Frenchman Ferdinand de Lesseps tried to follow up on his success with the Suez in an abortive attempt to build a canal across the pestiferous isthmus, only to be beaten by disease. The fact that the mosquito was responsible was still unknown, and 22,000 people would die. The United States finally succeeded in building the canal, but only after the extensive use of DDT to kill the mosquitos and the implementation of strict sanitation measures.

Nevertheless, 5,600 workers perished.

The Impact of Banning the Trade

The vessels used in the slave trade were initially the quite utilitarian trading craft of their time, following the process of gradual development typical of merchant navies. When the British parliament declared the slave trade (but not slavery) illegal in the British Empire in 1807, it provided an enormous demand for fast ships to escape apprehension. The majority of the owners were Americans. According to maritime historian Carl C. Cutler,

> *The Act outlawing the slave trade in 1808 furnished another source of demand (other than privateering) for fast vessels, and for another half-century ships continued to be fitted out and financed in this trade by many a respectable citizen in the majority of American ports. Newspapers of the fifties contain occasional references to the number of ships sailing from the various cities in this traffic. One account stated that as late as 1859 there were seven slavers regularly fitted out in New York, and many more in all the larger ports.*

America's Involvement

Great Britain succeeded in signing treaties with the main slaving nations, Portugal, France, Spain, and Brazil, giving it authority to stop and search vessels suspected of slaving. Even being laden with what were termed 'coast goods' on the first leg of the triangle was regarded as being 'manifestly equipped' for slaving.

The US Congress had legislated to ban slaving, but it would not sign an agreement with Great Britain to allow it to police it. In 1815, newly emerged from the Anglo-American War of 1812–1814, the United States government felt any such treaty smacked of the 'search and seizure' practised during the war. It was a convenient rationalisation to avoid condoning the policing of a trade that was, by now, integral to the plantation economy of its Southern states, and a fruitful investment for Northern entrepreneurs.

The American flag was used on the first leg, and the vessel would be chartered (in fact, bought) by the slaving enterprise for the middle passage, which it sailed under another flag. It was a lucrative business. Now the trade was financed by American entrepreneurs, and the ships were built in America.

According to the American naval architect and author Howard Chappelle, a single voyage of the *Montevideo* in 1835 carrying 800 slaves netted the slaving enterprise $180,000. The 'charter fees' received by the American owner (in fact, the purchase price) were considerably more than the cost of the ship. The American owner, through his captain, also received 'earnest money', in this case, $9,000. Another American-built slaver, *Venus*, cost between $30,000 and $50,000 to build, and it is estimated her costs for the voyage added another $30,000 to $50,000. She loaded 860 slaves, which sold for $340 per head, earning total revenue of almost $300,000 and a profit in the vicinity of $200,000.

The Later American Slave Ship *Wanderer*

Source: US Naval Historical Center Dictionary of American Naval Fighting Ships
Wikimedia Commons

Like the opium trade to follow, the rewards of slaving were spectacular. Post-1808, slavers would place great emphasis on speed, weatherliness, and 'hard-driving' to escape the British Navy frigates sent to police them. When these were insufficient to outrun a pursuing frigate, it was common for slaves to be thrown overboard to lighten the ship.

The British Navy's frigates (as opposed to its 'ships of the line') were formidable vessels, heavily canvassed, well sailed, and renowned for their skills in pursuing enemy ships. The big difference between the slave trade and the opium trade was that Great Britain, the naval power of the time, was the sworn enemy of the slavers but aided, abetted, and protected the opium runners.

Basil Lubbock, the great chronicler of the opium trade, noted that several ships in the trade were ex-slavers and stated their year of apprehension as slavers. Captured ships were sold by Lloyds of London into the opium trade or could simply be repurchased by slaving enterprises.

Howard Chappelle suggests that there were only about seventeen or eighteen American-built vessels in the opium trade, which intimates most of the arrests went back to slave running. Some slavers, however, were sold to pirates who operated in the South Atlantic off the coast of South Africa.

The British claimed that, after about 1835, most of the slavers were of American origin, mainly built in Baltimore and on Chesapeake Bay. They were generally small, lightly built schooners, brigs, and brigantines. There was typically a substantial fore-and-aft rigged element in their total sail area and considerable waterline length in relation to their beam.

In Great Britain, it had been realised, in its pursuit of speedy smugglers (probably based on French luggers), that waterline length in relation to beam was a key ingredient in hull speed. In a typically British solution, it, therefore, legislated that the length-to-beam ratio of coasting vessels could not exceed 3.5:1. American designers suffered under no such constraints and were free to experiment with all sorts of design element combinations to build faster vessels.

They might also have a shallow draft, depending on where they shipped their human cargo. If the slaves were loaded off beaches, for this to be done quickly to avoid detection, they needed to be able to anchor close to shore. Some vessels were so shallow they may even have been equipped with centreboards. Where there was so much money to be made, vessel design conformed to the needs of the trade. Another trend also emerged, this time probably mostly cosmetic: the practice of concaving the bowline and raking the masts to give both the impression and the reality of speed.

The lessons in fast ship design then fed into the design of vessels to ship opium from India to China where the ability to outrun Chinese war junks and pirate prahus was paramount. The preoccupation with speed and weatherliness in the construction of these American vessels, itself inherited from building government revenue craft and highly competitive pilot cutters, fed directly into the construction of Western Ocean packets and clippers. American builders were still constructing slave ships well into the heyday of the clippers. These were key elements in the subsequent rise of the United States as the world's most powerful mercantile shipping nation.

America's key role in the slave trade set it up to dominate the world's merchant marine for the next half-century. It built fast ships and, out of necessity, drove them very hard, all while the other great naval powers of the day languished behind mercantilist rules and regulations.

The question arises as to why the United States government was so lax in its administration of its own law forbidding any involvement in the trading of slaves.

The answer, in a word, was 'cotton'.

The Role of Cotton

Cotton cultivation dates back 8,000 years in America and at least 7,000 years in Asia and was a common fabric in Europe in the Middle Ages. Its manufacture was introduced into the Mediterranean with the Muslim conquest. Columbus found Indians wearing cotton cloth in the West Indies, feeding his conviction that he had reached the Orient.

Cotton working was the largest manufacturing industry in the Mughal Empire and was responsible for a large part of its international trade. India had an estimated 25 per cent of the world market in the early eighteenth century. Renaissance and, later, Enlightenment Europe was dependent on imports from Mughal India. Indians were skilled spinners and weavers, and their light cotton fabrics, when introduced into England by the East India Company, were a hit. However, it was the cheapest cotton fabric, calico, that proved extremely popular among the poor, damaging demand for local woollen fabrics and causing its importation to be banned in 1721: a ban that was not lifted until 1774.

Great Britain's inventive genius had by then produced machines such as the 'spinning jenny' and the water frame. These devices permitted cotton goods to be woven quickly and in considerable volume, enabling Britain to compete with imports from India. Later in the eighteenth century, cotton goods made up 16 per cent of the country's exports. By the early nineteenth century, that proportion had risen to 42 per cent, and Britain was dominating the world market. India was forbidden to export to

Great Britain, and its population forced to accept inferior British goods. Once Britain could source raw cotton from America, the British East India Company discouraged the production of cotton in India by forcing its growers to produce opium.

The rapid development of British cotton manufacture was only made possible by the equally rapid increase in the production of the cotton staple, *Gossypium*, of which there are several varieties. Cultivation is, however, very labour-intensive, and keeping up with demand required an ever-increasing supply of African slaves.

In 1791, cotton production in the Southern states of the United States was 900 tons. The application of steam power to cotton manufacture in England increased demand for the staple dramatically. In 1789, as cheap sources of coal became available, steam engines were applied directly to driving cotton mills.

In 1793, Eli Whitney, an American inventor, came up with a mechanical 'gin' that substantially reduced the time taken to remove the seed from the cotton boll. By 1800, exports had reached 56,000 tons, over sixty times what total production had been just nine years earlier. By the middle of the century, production was 441,000 tons, of which 414,000 tons, or 94 per cent, was exported.

Alabama Fever

Burgeoning demand for land to plant cotton resulted in a land rush known as Alabama fever. Production spread West across suitable land in the American South, creating more and more 'slave' states. With the expanded production area came increased demand for African slaves. Although initially indentured labour, that practice soon morphed into regarding them as chattels. All children born of slaves were, by law, regarded as slaves, so, as they reproduced, they not only replaced themselves but did so with a multiplier effect.

After the initial outlay, which would be amortised over future generations, slave labour was essentially free, and the cultivation of cotton using free labour became enormously lucrative. Everyone, including children and the elderly, was expected to work, and work very hard, so much so that one-third of the slaves died after three years, creating a constant demand for their replacement. Cotton profits were limited only by the number of slaves available to produce it, and by the 1850s, they made up half of the population of the main cotton-producing states.

Cotton was king, not only in the American South but also in Britain and France, which were dependent on it for their raw material. It was so important to these European powers that it was considered by the Southern states that they would intervene in any civil war over slavery to protect their supply. The European manufacturers chose instead to diversify their sources. In 1861, India was supplying 31 per cent of Britain's imports, but by 1862, it was 67 per cent. By 1867, after the Civil War, America was again supplying two-thirds of Britain's needs.

The 'Cotton Packets'

Cotton was America's largest export by value just before the Civil War. It is not difficult, therefore, to see why the draconian laws on involvement in the slave trade were not enforced. Its dominant position in America's export economy continued up almost to the outbreak of hostilities.

As well as a source of wealth, the shipment of cotton out of the Mississippi Delta states was providing insights into fast hull design. 'Cotton packets' were being used to feed it out of the Delta to the main Western Ocean packet ports on the northern seaboard. To negotiate the shallow and constantly shifting shoals of the approaches to the cotton-loading ports, the ships were built with minimum deadrise, that is, with practically flat bottoms. That shape also worked to maximise the volume of cargo. It was noted that ships so constructed were also fast sailers in the open sea. This would go on to play a major part in clipper design.

'Hard-Driving'

The configurations employed made slavers not only fast in the wind conditions likely to be encountered on the middle passage. Their weatherliness also made them capable of escaping to windward from any square-rigged British Navy frigate that might be pursuing them. Complementing the design attributes of the vessel was the development of the skills and abilities of 'hard-driving'. A highly motivated form of seamanship, hard-driving involved pushing a vessel to the very limits of its capabilities and to have the nerve and will to hold it there day in, day out, with no let-up. The tradition developed in the slave trade where it could be a matter of life and death, or certainly massive financial loss.

Hard-driving, combined with an innate competitiveness, it seems, developed into something of a cult among American skippers in less reprehensible trades, such as the Western Ocean packets and the clippers. Blended with the genius of their wooden sailing ship designers and plentiful wood supplies, hard-driving would take America to the very peak of the global merchant marine.

6
CHAPTER

The Opium Clippers

The Need for Speed

The Portuguese introduced high-grade opium into China in the mid-eighteenth century, sourcing it from Turkey and delivering it in their great lumbering argosies. By the nineteenth century, transport of opium from India and, to a lesser extent, Turkey required small, fast, and weatherly vessels.

Loading opium in India, these craft could make more than one trip to China a year, but it did depend on their ability to make to windward against the monsoon. The most important requirement was speed. Ships needed to be fast in order to outrun the pirates that infested the shallow seas of Asia, whose numbers and ferocity increased to take advantage of the burgeoning trade. Speed was also handy to avoid Chinese war junks as they approached their base in Canton or distributed the drug along the Chinese coast.

The designs of opium clippers referenced the fastest ships that were available in the world at the time. There were several ways to achieve speed, and they were invariably employed in occupations where a large cargo-carrying capacity was not important or not the primary requisite. They typically ran fruit or other perishables, tea, passengers, and the mail, not to mention naval blockades. Other fast ships included smugglers, slavers, revenue cutters, pilot boats, and personal yachts. Another source of inspiration was in the construction of privateers, which, in wartime, would aim to capture another country's merchant vessels or escape from the enemy when discretion was the better part of valour.

Cutters: The Predecessors

At the beginning of the nineteenth century, England was still deriving a lot of government revenue from customs duties, which were sufficiently onerous to encourage widespread smuggling. Part of the remedy—and a typically British one—was to place restrictions on the design of small merchant ships (such as cutters, luggers, shallops, and wherries), limiting their length to beam ratio to 3.5:1. In addition, they had to be square-rigged.

Even within these confines, it was possible to build a fast craft. The cutter was a single-masted vessel which employed a lot of canvas in relation to its hull length. These vessels typically made use of big fore-and-aft sails rigged on outsize bowsprits and booms. They featured square sails, which, although a legal requirement, would have enhanced performance when sailing directly, or close to directly, before the wind. Their masts were tall, and some crossed two, three, and sometimes four yards. Although they had a low length-to-beam ratio, they had great deadrise (steep floors) and fine convex lines. Because of the length-to-breadth restriction, the hull form had to fill out quickly and had to be deep to provide resistance to the outsize rigs. Most cutters were between 50 and 150 tons, with the largest around 250 tons.

Schooners, Brigs, and Luggers

While fighting the Revolutionary War of 1776, the young United States was short of money. It imposed high tariffs on imports, encouraging not only smuggling but also the development of fast ships known as 'revenue cutters' to stamp it out.

By the end of the eighteenth century, to cram on more sail, a second mast was added, and schooners and brigs were built with 'cutter' hulls. The term *cutter built* implied the same as *clipper built* would in the mid-nineteenth century. It identifies a type of vessel. A 'cutter brig' was a two-masted vessel with square sails on the mainmast and fore-and-aft sails on the mizzen and forward of the mainmast, with the hull built on cutter lines.

The French were not constrained by clumsy legislation that limited the development of fast vessels for smuggling purposes. Not being bound by any length-to-breadth ratios, they built lengthy luggers with sometimes three masts, all gaff fore-and-aft rigged with topsails on each.

In the similarly unrestricted Americas, following the War of Independence, cutters were common in the West Indies, but mainland Americans favoured the Bermudan sloop rig (single mast, all fore-and-aft sails), as well as the schooner (generally two-masted with fore-and-aft sails), which gained early prominence. The longer waterlines and narrower hulls on both the French and American vessels permitted a finer entry and greater speed.

Britain's Manpower Problem

In fighting the post-revolutionary war against France, Britain had to expand its navy, but it was desperately short of crew. In 1793, total naval manpower was increased to 45,000. By 1794, the full complement required was 85,000; by 1799, it was 120,000. Conditions in the Royal Navy were brutal, and the food and pay woeful. Consequently, volunteers were rare. Ordinary seamen were often convicts who had opted to serve rather than be incarcerated. Similarly, bankrupts could avoid debtors' prison by entering the navy.

A large number of men were kidnapped (pressed) and forced to serve against their will. They were often poor physical specimens, sometimes illiterate, ignorant of the sea, and undernourished. They were the sweepings of British ports and towns near the sea. By contrast, American sailors, whether US Navy or merchant marine, went to sea voluntarily. They tended to be young, strong, literate, knowledgeable, well-fed, and reasonably well paid. They were also attractive to other countries—British naval vessels would regularly attack American naval or merchant ships and force their crew into serving in the Royal Navy.

The Anglo-American War and the Baltimore Clippers

During the French Revolution from 1789 to the late 1790s, shipbuilding in America was based at Chesapeake Bay on the mid-Atlantic coast, with the main centre being Baltimore. The vessels produced were fast brigs and schooners much admired by the French, who secretly purchased several to harass British shipping. In so doing, they enhanced the reputation of the 'Baltimore clippers' on both sides of the Atlantic.

Pride of Baltimore II – a Replica of the Original Baltimore Clipper Ship

Source: Richard Ellis Alamy Stock Photo

Provoked by the impressment of its sailors to fight for Great Britain, from which they had gained their independence only a few decades earlier, the United States declared war on Great Britain and Ireland in 1812. The 'Baltimore clipper' privateers played an important role in the conflict running the British blockade of Baltimore and attacking British merchant ships on the high seas.

As is usual in times of war, technology developed rapidly, and the vessel designs that emerged, especially of fast brigs and schooners, would provide the templates for many of the later slavers and opium clippers. Seventy-one of the ninety-nine vessels listed by the British historian, sailor, and soldier Basil Lubbock in his 'Register of the Opium Fleet' were either brigs or schooners.

Some of the American opium-runner Russell & Company's early ships were probably vessels that made their way into the opium trade after peace was made with Britain in the Treaty of Ghent in December 1814. The brigantine *Prince de Neuchatel*, built in New York between 1812 and 1813, provided the design for the *Red Rover*, an opium clipper renowned for her speed. Certainly, two of the opium clippers were ex-Royal Navy vessels, and six were captured ex-slavers. The migration of slavers to the opium trade may well have been caused by the Royal Navy beginning to pursue them after Great Britain banned the trade (though not the practice) in 1807.

The Basis of the Opium Trade

The Portuguese began importing Indian opium into China in the early years of the eighteenth century, and the Chinese government resistance to the trade began soon after. The Indians had been familiar with opium for centuries, and their product, like so much in India, was of very high quality. They tended to eat it, which meant the drug was absorbed by the digestive system, limiting its psychotropic effects.

Chinese opium, on the other hand, was of inferior quality, but the Chinese managed to amplify its effects by smoking it rather than consuming it internally. The British soon realised that the market for high-quality Indian opium would create enormous (and similarly debilitating) demand from Chinese addicts. The British, colonial rulers of India for so long, were considerable users themselves, usually in the form of laudanum. Those with any conscience at all would have been well aware of the consequences of shipping 4,000 tons a year of the stuff into China.

Nevertheless, the British government was persuaded to rise against China's temerity in its attempts to control the trade and proclaim any ban was against the principle of 'free trade'. Never mind that its own trade was hedged all around with all sorts of mercantilist restrictions protecting its landowners, shipowners, and investors, the Corn Laws and the Navigation Acts being prime examples, not to mention the EIC monopoly itself.

The Risks of the Trade

The main risk to the opium runners was piracy. The 'shallow seas' of East Asia, as novelist Joseph Conrad referred to them, abounded in ferocious pirates whose numbers expanded in step with the opium trade. Their crews were equipped with small arms and trained in hand-to-hand combat. Opium was a high-value, compact, and reasonably light cargo, so an opium clipper did not need to be a large ship. Also, being smaller reduced the possibility of being detected by the Chinese authorities. Opium clippers were immensely valuable prizes if they could be subdued. On the way to China, they were laden with opium, and on the return journey, they were rich in the ultimate prize, sycee silver (the purest form of the metal).

The variable weather in the areas through which the opium runners sailed made things difficult. Tropical lulls could leave ships vulnerable to ambush by oared pirate vessels sheltering in the myriad islands. With no wind in which to employ their major defensive weapons—their speed and weatherliness—the runners had no option but to stand and fight.

They were equipped with small cannon, but the pirates could counter their effect by girding their vessels with heavy matting. The pirates attacked in packs, and their prahus were fast and light.

An East Indian Proa or Prahu

Source: Wikimedia Commons

Prahus resisted the wind, not with a keel but an outrigger. They carried a large triangular sail and could be steered from either end.

The larger lorchas mounted a junk rig with battened sails on a European-style hull.

A Malay Lorcha

Source: Naval Historical Society of Australia

The other major risk was weather at the other end of the continuum. The runners needed to be very seaworthy, and their crews highly skilled seamen when confronted with the typhoons, which assailed the area in certain seasons. A combination of very strong wind and relatively shallow seas could spell disaster for the less experienced, poorly built, or poorly equipped vessel.

Opium runners tried to make two trips a year, which meant sailing on one thrashing into the teeth of the north-east monsoon. Many of the ships and the skippers had come out of the slave trade, and they had every opportunity to demonstrate their skill at hard-driving no matter what the conditions.

As well as the variable weather conditions, the shallowness of the mostly uncharted seas made for enormous tides and treacherous currents. The opium runners, like all true sailing ships, lacked any other means of propulsion, save the wind. The areas through which they passed required a very high standard of seamanship on the part of those in command and a highly responsive crew to avert disaster.

Small Fast Ships: the Barque Opium Runner *Sylph*

Source: Painting William John Huggins, Wikimedia Commons

Britain's Trade Deficit

Britain also had a financial problem to solve. The Chinese had been resisting reciprocal trade because they weren't interested in any of the goods (typically manufactures) that the 'barbarians' had to offer. Compared to the utilitarian goods offered by the Europeans, China was a veritable Aladdin's

Cave. But in having to pay for everything they wanted in pure silver, it is not surprising that Britain soon had a distinct balance of payments problem. Mercantilist to the core, the English were unused to running trade deficits as its burgeoning wealth bore witness. It therefore cast around for a commodity that would remedy the situation.

It quickly hit upon the perfect solution: opium.

The company whose banner proclaimed 'Heaven's Light Our Guide' persuaded the British government to grant it a monopoly on opium production in India. It then set about expanding production for export of this highly addictive substance to the largest market on the planet.

But there was a big problem: importing opium into China was illegal. The EIC could not risk their licences to trade in other commodities, especially tea, by selling it direct. The somewhat duplicitous solution was found by selling the drug to other (necessarily) British entities who would run it into China. Opium production was profitable for the EIC, and its sale to the (British) opium runners for silver went a good way towards redressing Britain's balance of payments issue.

After 1800, the EIC had to share its opium profits with (albeit British) third parties, but there was enough profit in the business to make both the producer and the runners very happy. Its monopoly on production ensured foreign (other than British) runners couldn't obtain supplies from India and leak silver from England's balance of payments.

To expand its income from the trade, the logical solution was to substantially increase production. The EIC forced the former cotton growers of India (and also cultivators of sugar, indigo, and various food grains) to grow prodigious amounts of opium.

It was an extraordinarily repressive system. The land farmed by a peasant (or 'ryot') was assessed as to its potential, and money advanced under contract to complete the cropping process. If the crop fell short of the assessment, the ryot could lose what he did produce and be sued for the value of the shortfall.

The peasants were kept in constant debt to the company and were thereby bound to it.

When the gum from the lanced poppy bowl was harvested and processed, it was stored in vast warehouses and shipped downriver to the ports where the opium traders would buy it at auction.

The Chinese government had, from the outset, sought to limit contact with the British. Foreign ships were not allowed to tie up to a wharf face. Instead, they were required to anchor in the Pearl River, behind Whampoa Island (now Pazhou Island). The difficulties involved in running opium did not favour big ships. What fully rigged ships there were were used as factory ships. The superior armament of these vessels prevented the Chinese naval junks from interfering, and the mandarins onshore, who were supposed to be preventing the trade, were paid more by the smugglers to neglect their duty than they could have ever been expected to obtain by doing it.

The distribution system was completed by the oared craft of the local Chinese merchants, which plied between the factory ships and the shore. The business was strictly cash or, rather, sycee silver, on the nail head. It wasn't a business that extended terms to its customers. Large factory ships, generally 'country' East Indiamen, were permanently anchored there. They would receive shipments from the opium runners and sell to the local Chinese merchants. Opium clippers also ran directly to other ports not served by factory ships.

From the Whampoa anchorage, the factory ships were serviced by small boats manned by Chinese stevedores. The opium runners cultivated agents ashore and bribed the local mandarins to the point where they were eventually able to establish warehouses (called 'factories' or 'hongs') within a restricted area on land known as the Thirteen Factories. Here Great Britain, the United States, Sweden, Denmark,

Spain, and the Netherlands had offices to conduct ordinary merchandise trade. The opium runner hongs facilitated trade but left their onshore stocks vulnerable.

The rapid increase in activity naturally drew the attention of the Qing emperor, Daoguang. He was aghast at the dissolution high-grade opium was wreaking in the general populace, not to mention the extent to which it was depleting the country's silver reserves. In 1838, he banned imports of the drug. To enforce the ban, he appointed an especially zealous mandarin, Lin Zexu, as an imperial commissioner and despatched him to Canton to destroy existing stocks.

Lin appealed to Queen Victoria and later the British public to put a stop to the trade. When this ploy failed, he either burned the considerable hong stocks or spoiled them in seawater. In all, about 1,100 tons of opium was destroyed, equal to about one-quarter of a year's supply. The British would later insist that their loss was worth 21 million pounds.

The EIC and the private runners immediately began lobbying the British government to take action against China.

The upshot was the First Opium War of 1839.

The Opium Wars

The prohibition on the import of opium was touted by the British as a blatant restriction of free trade. Furthermore, they asserted the destruction of the trader's stocks (variously referred to as 'her Majesty's assets' and 'the Queen's opium') was unconscionable. The opium interests then persuaded the British government to declare war on China. The Celestial Empire, in resisting contact with the West, had not acquainted itself with technological developments there, especially advances in making war. Ironically, it was the Chinese who invented gunpowder, but they could not resist British exploitation of the substance via advanced armaments mounted on superior vessels.

The result was a disaster for the Chinese.

Once defeated, they were at the mercy of the victors.

The First Opium War was settled by the Treaty of Nanking in 1843. Under the terms of the treaty, the Chinese government was required to compensate British traders for 'the Queen's opium' that had been destroyed (to the tune of 21 million pounds) and open up four more 'treaty ports' to allow importation of the drug. It was forced to defray the cost of sending the Royal Navy to fight the war and defeat them. And it was further required to cede Hong Kong to the British for 150 years, an arrangement that only expired in 1997.

Humiliation, indeed, for trying to protect itself from this nefarious substance.

And that wasn't the end of it.

The British, seeking even more trading concessions, contrived to start the Second Opium War of 1856–60 at a time when the failing Qing Dynasty was in the throes of trying to quell the Taiping Rebellion. Predictably, the Chinese were again defeated by the power of superior arms, and the government was forced, inter alia, to open up more ports to the importation of opium.

In 1867, imports of opium into China reached a massive 60,000 chests (around 4,000 tons). The French decided to similarly contrive to enter the hostilities and to seek similar concessions to the British. One of the concessions won by the British was free entry and travel for missionaries.

Today, it is difficult to reconcile the actions of the British government with their Christian values, but in the mid-1800s, their might made them right. Thanks to their sea power, they were the most powerful nation on earth.

As well as the obscene profits being made by the opium traders who bought their drug supply from the EIC, the EIC itself became dependent on the income from opium for its financial viability. According to an American missionary doctor by the name of Nathan Allen, over a quarter of EIC income was derived from opium sales in 1848–49. The drug was clearly propping up the company. While Allen may have been prescient, not even the extraordinary profits from opium sales could ultimately save the EIC. In 1857, triggered by the issue of cartridges for the new Enfield rifle that were believed to be greased with cow or pig fat, several sepoy companies rose in rebellion. The underlying causes were EIC taxation and land acquisitions, the imposition of Western customs, and what were regarded as increasing attempts to convert Indians to Christianity. Local rulers were also upset at the progressive restrictions being placed on their rights and privileges. What has become known as the Indian Mutiny was ultimately unsuccessful, but the die was cast, and in 1858, the British government nationalised the company.

In China, in the intense market scarcity following the Second Opium War, partners of one British trading house were reputed to have made between 400,000 and 800,000 pounds each—the equivalent of 42 million and 84 million pounds today. It must rank as one of the most profitable trades ever pursued in human history.

To put the magnitude of the enterprise in perspective, Nathan Allen noted that in 1850, China (the largest country in the world at the time with a population of 350 million) spent more on the drug than the entire revenue of the United States government. The figure was also more than any other country in the world spent on *any* raw material, save Britain's imports of cotton. Opium had been cultivated since biblical times, but trade in the substance—facilitated by the advent of globe-circling sailing ships and demanded by between 4 and 12 million addicts in China—made it one of the most important international commodities.

Allen goes on to say the EIC made 3 million pounds from the cultivation of opium in 1846—equivalent to over 350 million pounds today. Similarly, some of the great British trading houses, of which Jardine Matheson and Dent & Co. were the most prominent examples, made similar annual fortunes in shipping opium to China.

Jardine Matheson is the only company still extant.

Needless to say, it has erased its involvement in the opium trade from its official history.

The Opium Clipper Fleet

According to Basil Lubbock, the first private 'country' ship (i.e. other than EIC vessels) to enter the trade was the *Jamesina*, a 382-ton, ex-Royal Navy brig in 1823. She was large for the trade and, being ex-navy, was probably heavily armed and dependent on her ordnance rather than her speed.

Of the ninety-nine vessels listed by Lubbock, only six exceeded 400 tons, and more than half (fifty-three) were under 200 tons. One (the *Celestial*) was only 50 tons, and nine were under 100 tons. The last vessel listed as entering the trade (the *Chin Chin* of 263 tons) joined in 1860. The average tonnage of vessels was 211 tons.

This represented a fleet of small and fast ships, audacious in the amount of sail they carried, driven by greedy interests, and heedless of the social destruction they caused. According to Lubbock, the private trade spanned almost four decades, beginning in 1823, with the last vessels entering in 1860. As a business, opium running reached its peak in 1841–42 when twenty-six vessels entered the trade.

The Royal Yacht Squadron at Cowes on the English Channel was the source of a number of fast vessels that ended up in the opium trade. Three of the fastest built by immensely wealthy and highly competitive private sailors—*Harlequin*, *Pantaloon*, and *Pearl*—were all sold to active opium runners. Another source of inspiration, if not actual craft, were the French luggers that specialised in running contraband into England. These were famously speedy and weatherly vessels and influenced fast vessel design both in England and the United States.

Nathan Allen described the opium runner ships as follows:

> *[being] built and fitted expressly for this business and are said to be amongst the finest vessels anywhere to be found. Most of them are constructed in the form of schooners or brigantines, with low hulls, and being adapted to cut the waves with remarkable speed, are called 'clippers' or 'runners'.*

He went on to say,

> *The vessels conveying the drug from India to China are probably the finest boats in the world … one, the* Lanrick, *is superior in sailing on the wind to any man-of-war.*

The 'Clipper-brig' Opium Runner *Lanrick*

Source: Courtesy UK Government Art Collection

The *Lanrick* entered the trade at its height in 1843 and was owned by one of its most significant participants, Jardine Matheson & Co. The vessel measured in at 283 tons, and her length, at 108.4 feet, was four times her breadth of 26.9 feet.

Of a trip on the *Lanrick*, Allen said, 'Frequently we were running at eight or nine knots close-hauled and carrying royals, when a frigate would have reefed topsails and courses.' And of the ship's commanders, '[they] are generally educated men, of gentlemanly manners, very hospitable, of generous dispositions, well skilled in seamanship, and of a courage and boldness unsurpassed.'

According to Allen, the number of chests of opium (each weighing, on average, about 64 kilograms) landed in China rose from nearly 7,000 in 1820 to around 40,000 in 1838. It was also at this time that the Chinese authorities began to take more determined measures to halt the trade, measures which led to the First Opium War.

History provides us with two contrasting views of the trade. As Allen, the evangelising American, put it, opium was, 'a fearful desolating pestilence, pervading all classes of people, wasting their property, enfeebling their mental faculties, ruining their bodies and shortening their lives'.

Basil Lubbock had a different view. Besides documenting the trade, he subsequently did a great deal to romanticise it, without a thought for its consequences or morality: 'To read of a rakish schooner thrashing to windward in the teeth of a monsoon, of a taut-rigged brig battling it out in a howling typhoon, or of a tall skysail-yard barque fighting for dear life against a circling swarm of piratical prahus or lorchas'.

This was more than many an English youth could resist. The profits were often five hundred and even a thousandfold, with risks, Lubbock maintains, to match. When it wound down, he went on to lament, 'with a sigh that the glorious profession of seafaring has lost a good deal of its romance'.

The Prominent Opium Runners

Lubbock's register of opium clippers lists ninety-nine vessels. The two most prominent owners were English trading houses Dent & Company (fourteen vessels) and Jardine Matheson & Co. (twelve vessels, another source says nineteen). An American firm, Russell & Company, had eight vessels. In addition to their actual opium clippers, Jardine Matheson had (and no doubt the two other big companies had also) a vast fleet of smaller craft used for coastal and upriver distribution.

Jardine Matheson & Co.

Jardine Matheson is the only one of the big three opium traders still operating today. Although its promotional literature and official history make no mention of its involvement, opium is how it acquired its initial capital.

It was established by second sons Scotsmen, William Jardine and James Matheson, in Canton in 1832. Jardine was of humble origins, but he had graduated as a doctor at age nineteen from Edinburgh University and for fourteen years served on East India Company ships. As such, he was permitted to trade on his own account. He quickly realised opium was infinitely more lucrative than medicine.

Matheson was a graduate of Jardine's alma mater but was of more substantial origins. The two men were physically and temperamentally different, but as second sons (and therefore unable to inherit a share in any family fortune), they both had considerable incentive to succeed. The pair complemented each other in the aspects of the business each chose to handle, and it proved a long and prosperous partnership.

Jardine Matheson was also fortunate in its association with the fabulously wealthy and prominent Parsi businessman Jamsetjee Jejeebhoy, whom they had met in India and who often underwrote their business ventures.

William Jardine (1784-1843)   James Matheson (1796-1878)

Source: Wikipedia Commons

The partnership went from strength to strength, in time adding family members from both original partners. By 1830, as the influence of the East India Company weakened, it came to control half of China's foreign trade. Both Matheson and later Jardine were responsible for persuading the British government to declare war on China.

Jardine Matheson's big business was trafficking opium, but it also traded cotton, silk, tea, and a variety of other goods, including porcelain. After the First Opium War, it established its head office in the new treaty port of Hong Kong, an island ninety miles from Canton. Hong Kong was advantageous for three reasons. The move gave the company a base on one of the best harbours in the world. It enabled it to better organise its opium distribution into the rest of China, away from the mandarin influence in Canton. And Hong Kong gave it the ability to service its own and other ships.

From there, Jardine Matheson spread its trading activities all along the Chinese coast and into the Philippines and other Asian principalities. By the end of the nineteenth century, it had become the largest foreign trading company in the Far East and had expanded its activities into sugar refining and trading, shipping, cotton mills, and railway construction.

Dent & Co.

Dent & Co. was arguably the largest of the opium traders, a tough competitor to Jardine Matheson, and one of the wealthiest British–China traders of the period. It originally operated out of its hong (warehouse) in an allocated area of Canton on the banks of the Pearl River. It went on to establish offices in Hong Kong after the First Opium War and later on the Bund in Shanghai. The entity was originally launched by Sir Francis Baring, a scion of Baring Brothers & Co., the prominent banking family.

Sir Francis Baring (1740-1810)

Source: Wikimedia Commons

In 1831, Lancelot Dent became the senior partner in the firm. In 1839, Lin Zexu, the emperor-appointed mandarin tasked with cleaning up the opium industry, issued a warrant for his arrest, and this was one of the triggers of the First Opium War.

The collapse of a bank in London, in turn, prompted a general financial collapse. On the other side of the world, Jardine Matheson heard about the disaster an hour earlier than the other opium trading houses and was able to clean out its balances in the failed bank before anyone else became aware of the disaster. Dent & Co. were not so fortunate and were forced to close their Hong Kong and Canton offices. Nevertheless, it opened up on the Bund in Shanghai, where it also entered the silk and tea trades. Members of the firm were instrumental in the establishment of the now gargantuan Hong Kong & Shanghai Banking Corporation (HSBC).

Russell & Company

If there is one aroma capable of travelling on the winds and ocean currents of the world with great speed, it is the whiff of inordinate profits. The British monopolised the supply of high-quality opium out of India, but the Portuguese (who had pioneered the China trade centuries before), the Dutch, and the Americans had access to similar product out of Turkey.

The Americans' most prominent trading house was Russell & Company. Earlier on, they had found a product that would attract Chinese attention—ginseng root—which grew abundantly in the forests of the north-eastern United States. The Chinese believed that eating ginseng would make them immortal, an attraction similar to, but not as powerful, as that of opium.

Enterprisingly, the Americans had scoured the world for other products the Chinese would buy, and they supplied them with furs, seal skins, bêche-de-mer, shark fins, edible birds' nests, and the like. They were not, however, enough to pay for America's appetite for Chinese products (especially tea) and merchandise (especially silk). They, too, found themselves still having to ship kegs of specie to China and would finally resort to the opium trade, sourcing the product out of Turkey. The voyage was longer, but the profitability of the trade made the extra time more than worth it. The French and the Danes were also involved, but to a lesser extent.

In addition to opium, Russell & Company traded silk, porcelain, and tea. It was founded by Samuel Russell in 1824. Russell had been orphaned early in life but was apprenticed to a maritime merchant where he learned his trading skills. He later travelled as a supercargo on international vessels. After setting up his own business, he began trading operations in Canton. He was very successful, especially with opium, and was assisted by his local partner, the highly respected Howqua, the most prominent Canton merchant of the day. So renowned was Howqua for his fair dealing and honesty that one of the great American tea clippers was named after him. In 1836, having made a considerable fortune, Russell returned to the United States. By 1842, the company he formed was the biggest American trading house in China.

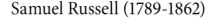

Samuel Russell (1789-1862)

Source: Wikipedia Commons

One of the company's partners was Warren Delano, great-grandfather of Franklin Delano Roosevelt, the thirty-second president of the United States. In 1823, he sailed to Canton, and within seven years, he was a senior partner. He maintained that the opium trade was perfectly legitimate and no worse than dealing in alcohol. He returned to America extremely rich where he gave his daughter Sara in marriage to James Roosevelt, the father of Franklin Roosevelt, who fathered FDR.

Six of Russell & Company's vessels were designated ex-slavers, obviously attracted to opium running when Great Britain began to prosecute slavers on the high seas in 1808. By 1891, however, Russell & Company was facing financial difficulties caused by increased competition from the English trading houses and their more advanced banking facilities. The opening of the Suez Canal also improved their logistics. To counter its failing fortunes, it went into shipping, but its situation did not improve, and it devolved into Shewan & Company in 1891.

Warren Delano (1809-1898)

Source: Wikipedia Commons

The Denouement

By the time of the Second Opium War, Chinese imports had reached 50,000 to 60,000 chests a year and, under the concessions obtained, would continue rising until the end of the nineteenth century. By then, the vessels being employed were either steam-driven or a combination of steam and sail. Gradually, however, the Qing government, although forced to legalise consumption of the drug, would regain control over its importation and consumption.

In 1907, the Chinese forbade the cultivation of opium locally and banned its importation. Britain's industrial and colonial power, and the fact that it was now producing all the tea it needed in India and Ceylon and porcelain in Cornwall, meant it no longer had a balance of payments problem with China. The Celestial Empire was thus able to agree with the British government in India to gradually reduce the export of the drug. It extended for ten years, and by 1917, the opium trade had ceased altogether.

Just as war results in leaps in technology, so the efforts of opium traders to minimise the depredations of pirates led them to build faster and more weatherly ships. The American involvement was significant. While running slaves had proved lucrative for America's maritime entrepreneurs, the risks involved in opium running, especially with their skill set, were felt to be less. At the very least, it provided a diversification. This would account for the number of American ex-slavers that became involved in opium trading.

At home, they were already amassing a fleet of Western Ocean packets and developing ships that would make them the masters of speed across the water for decades and the princes of international shipping and commerce.

Influence on Clipper Design

Except for the 'factory ships'—large heavily armed vessels that acted as floating warehouses in China—the opium clippers were much smaller than either the East Indiamen or the great American clippers that followed them. Nevertheless, their speed and weatherliness influenced the clipper designers. Their oversize rigs and greater use of fore-and-aft sails contributed to their weatherliness, which, other than outright speed, was their main advantage.

Their bowsprits were long and employed gammon knees—strong 'grown' knees attached to the bow and used to support the bowsprit. Extended and concave stems gave an impression of speed, as did the rake they added to their masts. Both of these design characteristics would carry through into conventional clipper design. These design aspects notwithstanding, their hulls had considerable deadrise, and their relatively diminutive waterline length, although longer in relation to their breadth than was usual at the time, limited their overall speed.

It was up to the clipper designers to discover the potential of ever-increasing size, especially length, and flat bottoms (minimum deadrise), which reduced the wetted surface and hence the drag the hull created.

7

CHAPTER

The Western Ocean Packets

Introduction

Following the American War of Independence, the Napoleonic Wars, and the Anglo-American War of 1812–14, the Western world seemed intent on settling down to some serious moneymaking. The tempo of commerce between the United States and Great Britain, and later the continent, quickened. British historian A. H. Imlah calculated that between 1820 and 1914, world trade grew more than fivefold—from 6 million tons to 32 million tons.

The period from 1820 to 1860 was the golden age of merchant shipping under sail. When the first steamship crossed the Atlantic in 1819, its entire cargo space was filled with fuel. In 1860, forty years later, world commerce had almost tripled (to 16.6 million tons), but 90 per cent of it was still carried in sailing ships. Of the increase of 10.6 million tons, 86 per cent was carried under sail.

America's embryonic manufacturing industry could not sustain its rapidly expanding Western frontier and increasing population. It needed British capital and manufactures. And the British dumped goods to keep it that way. That is to say, they sold goods at a price below the home price or below its full manufacturing cost. Britain's larger-scale manufacturing industry was more efficient, and it could undercut the prices of American producers.

Britain, for her part, had a narrow resource and agricultural base and needed raw materials, cotton, tobacco, fruit, foodstuffs, and lumber to feed its burgeoning urban population and manufacturing industry.

The British government had been running ships that sailed to Ireland and the continent carrying 'packets' of royal and other mail, which had been one of the necessary tendons of administration of the realm since Tudor times. For this reason, the vessels were known as 'packet' ships.

With the founding and expansion of the American colonies, the government ran a service from Falmouth to New York carrying the royal mail, other small freight, and bullion. But its ships would call at Bermuda or Nova Scotia when travelling in both directions. They did not carry freight and rarely passengers. They were small ships: brigs with two square-rigged masts with fore-and-aft sails on the foremast and a fore-and-aft 'spanker' or 'jigger' sail on the mizzenmast. They were sailed hard in the interests of delivering the mail expeditiously, and as so many were lost, they became known as coffin brigs.

The 'Liner' Service

Other ships plying the Atlantic, the so-called regular traders, were anything but regular. Not only would ships refuse to sail when the weather was bad, they would also, in America's case, sail down the eastern seaboard, sometimes as far as the West Indies, until they had a full cargo. Only then would they depart for Europe. Passage times and destinations could vary greatly depending on the cargo available at the various ports of call. The whole process was costly, and it made it impossible to fulfil contracts or guarantee deliveries.

By 1815, the Napoleonic Wars and the Anglo-American hostilities were over, and American entrepreneurs were in a hurry to take advantage of the many opportunities afforded them by the peace. The country's rapid growth in population and geographical area was not only creating demand for merchandise local facilities could not provide, it was also generating a surplus of raw materials that could feed Britain and Europe.

American commercial interests had become impatient with the dilatory transatlantic services available to them. With economic activity booming on both sides of the Atlantic, they were anxious to find a more efficient way to transport all manner of stuff in both directions.

America was short of capital and therefore painfully conscious of the time value of money. They were thus sorely aware of the need for speed. During the prolonged period of hostilities, whether avoiding the Spanish coastguard to land fish into the West Indies (which the planters needed to provide protein for their slave labour force) or outrunning British blockaders of American ports during the Anglo-American War, superior speed—and the ability to escape to windward—were necessities.

The Americans were also avid slavers and built ships that could outrun the British frigates sent to enforce its writ after Great Britain declared the practice illegal in 1808. As well, there was a move to try to profit from the East Indies trade outside the East India Company's monopoly. To do so, the 'free traders' needed faster ships to escape company vessels, and until the EIC developed a range of purely offensive brigs and sloops to deal with them, they were able to trade with some success.

There was a need for regular services across the Atlantic, vessels that sailed directly to and from particular ports on each side of the ocean, and that did so on a predictable schedule. They had to proceed as fast as possible, regardless of the weather—whether their holds were full or not. The need was most acute between cotton producers and traders and food and lumber producers in the United States, and metal machines and equipment manufacturers and woollen and cotton goods producers in Great Britain. Unlike the East Indiamen, the Royal Navy now reigned supreme in the Atlantic, obviating the need to waste valuable cargo space with cannon and ammunition.

The Beginnings

While Great Britain lauded itself as the home of free enterprise in the nineteenth century, its economy still featured many mercantilist traits and was riven with restrictions such as government-granted monopolies of which the East India Company was the most glaring example.

Until their repeal in 1849, maritime trade with Great Britain was governed by the Navigation Acts. Under these acts, all sorts of restrictions had been placed on its international trade to the supposed benefit (but ultimate detriment) of its merchant navy and the national exchequer. The acts decreed, for example, that goods entering the country had to be carried in 'British bottoms'. For this reason, American ships could not bring tea and other exotic trade goods into Britain. The exception was if the goods originated in the same country as the vessel. Because the main products carried by American packet ships, especially cotton, originated in America, American ships could exploit their merchant maritime superiority. And they went to it with a will.

In 1818, when the first Black Ball Line ship set out on a direct voyage to Liverpool, Britain was consuming less than 50,000 tons of raw cotton. By 1850, the figure had grown to 263,000 tons, a greater-than-fivefold increase. In 1818, the proportion of raw cotton sourced from the United States was 38 per cent, with the main source being India. By 1850, it was 74 per cent. The efficiency of the liner services was the main factor in this almost doubling of America's share of the burgeoning market.

The revolution in transatlantic transport began with a venture launched by a partnership between a New York merchant, Isaac Wright, his four partners, and several Liverpool connections. Ironically, three of the stateside partners were Englishmen who lived in New York, importing woollen goods from their mills in Great Britain.

Their service, later known as the 'Black Ball Line', was identified by the large black ball in the mainsail and on the burgee of its vessels. The Treaty of Ghent ending the Anglo-American War was signed in February 1815, and the Black Ball Line sailed its first voyage in January 1818 out of New York, bound on a winter passage to Liverpool.

The newly built ship was named the *James Monroe* after the incumbent American president. Simultaneously, her sister ship, the *Courier*, set sail from Liverpool for New York. Their synchronised departure has been described as the greatest improvement in transatlantic travel since the *Mayflower* and equivalent in significance to the later triumphs of Marconi and Lindbergh.

Superior—An Early (1822) Black Ball Line Packet

Source: from a painting by Clement Drew (1806–1889) Wikimedia Commons

In many ways, these vessels were the predecessors of ocean liners in that they carried both cargo and passengers. The Black Ball Line fleet was initially made up of four ships, and there was a sailing from both New York and Liverpool on the fifth and first of each month, respectively. By the end of the first year, each ship had made four round trips, not always full, but mostly on schedule. This was before international letters of credit. All international trade was conducted in cash, and so, besides the merchandise trade, another regular item of freight was bullion.

Vast fortunes would eventually cross the Atlantic almost daily.

Within three decades of that first packet sailing in 1818, more than fifty vessels were plying the Atlantic on regular schedules, and the port of New York alone was averaging three arrivals and three departures a week. And the emigration boom had barely begun.

In hindsight, given the circumstances that gave rise to it, it seems such a service was destined to be successful, but that was by no means apparent at the outset. The North Atlantic can be a wild place. These wooden ships relied on canvas for their motive power and hemp rope and sturdy timber spars to control it. And they had to sail as fast as possible.

The maintenance would have been horrendous, and if the trade had not developed rapidly to full holds and well-occupied passenger accommodation, there was a good chance the service would have failed. But the enthusiasm for the amenity, which so aptly met the needs of the time, meant the Black Ball entrepreneurs were able, at least initially, to charge high freight rates, and so the service prospered.

Before the 'Western Ocean packets', as they became known, an average direct crossing west to east (the 'downhill' run) took thirty days, and east to west forty-five days. The liners reduced these times to, on average, twenty-two days and forty days, although exceptional passages got down as low as sixteen days each way.

The ships were no different from the 'regular traders', but they were new, sturdy, and well-equipped. They were flush-decked with a raised galley and the longboat in a housed-over area amidships. The longboat carried the livestock: pens for sheep and pigs in the bottom, ducks and geese on a deck laid over gunwales, and hens and chickens on top. The cowhouse, which provided milk for the officers and first-class passengers, was lashed to the top of the main hatch. Some cows crossed and recrossed the Atlantic that many times they became rather adept sailors.

Impact of Competition

The Black Ball Line's first four ships—*Courier, James Monroe, Pacific,* and *Amity*—were all fully rigged ships of about 400 tons, but within twenty-five years, packet ship tonnage would more than double to upwards of 1,000 tons; so successful was the service. After 1850, the average tonnage would rise again to around 1,400 tons. The largest of the Black Ball Line ships was the *Great Western* at 1443 BRT (British Register Tonnage).

The Later (1851) and Largest Black Ball Line Packet Ship *Great Western*

Source: Painting by John Stobart courtesy of Bonhams Art Auctions

So profitable was the Black Ball Line that, in 1822, it spawned two competitors on the same route—the Red Star and the Swallowtail lines—running four ships each. Meanwhile, the Black Ball Line expanded its fleet to eight vessels. Thus, only four years after its inception, the number of vessels plying between New York and Liverpool had quadrupled, with weekly departures on each side of the ocean. In 1828, it was estimated by port officials that duties levied on ships arriving in New York were sufficient to run the entire United States government. By 1843, there were twenty-four packets on this route.

Nathaniel Palmer and the Dramatic Line

Nathaniel Palmer's life story is the stuff of legend. At age nineteen, as captain of the small (forty-seven-foot) sealing sloop *Hero*, he discovered the South Orkney Islands and was the first American to see Antarctica, parts of which are today named after him (the Palmer Archipelago and Palmer Land). He was to be instrumental in a major design innovation that would feed into the hull shape of the clippers—minimum deadrise or 'flat floors'.

Palmer was later the master of a ship feeding cotton from the Mississippi Delta to the packets sailing from New York to Europe. To cross the bars that gave access to the delta, these ships, called droghers or sailing barges, had shallow draught and minimum deadrise—that is to say, they were practically flat-bottomed, a shape that incidentally maximised their cargo space, a very important consideration.

Palmer was surprised at the speed of his vessel in the open sea and felt, contrary to the conventional wisdom, that a ship with minimum deadrise was faster than one with the conventional 'V' shape below the waterline. ('Deadrise', it will be remembered, is the angle a ship's bottom makes with the horizontal. A flat-bottomed ship is said to have minimum deadrise.)

Nathaniel Palmer (1799-1877)

Source: Antarctic-logistics.com

With his wide experience in both sailing and influencing ship design, Palmer was consulted by one E. K. Collins in 1835 over the design of four ships for a new packet line to Liverpool. Collins, it seems, was something of a Shakespearean aficionado. He already owned a ship named *Shakespeare* and named the four new packets after famous Shakespearean actors of the day. The new enterprise was called the Dramatic Line, and the four ships were *Garrick*, *Siddons*, *Sheridan*, and *Roscius*. These four vessels were designed with minimum deadrise, and they earned reputations for speed such that the leading naval architects of the day took careful note. They are acknowledged as being a key influence on clipper design.

The Dramatic Liners still retained an element of traditional design. They were 'bluff-bowed', with their widest beam forward of amidships. The four ships were built in 1836 and 1837, and within the next decade, the plan shape of new ships would change to introduce the other innovations that made the clippers so fast and so famous. The bluff bow would be replaced by a hollow (or concave) entry with the bow section rapidly broadening out to a long straight run. Like the packets, these ships had big rigs. The *Roscius* spread as much canvas as later crack clippers.

The original Western Ocean packets of the early part of the nineteenth century were not all that much different from the East Indiamen of the seventeenth century, 200 hundred years before. What had changed was not their technical advance, so much as their numbers, their cargo-carrying capacity, and the practice of hard-driving.

At the height of the packet trade in the 1840s, there were some 1,600 ships arriving in the British Isles each year—an average of over four a day. The packets used the same natural forces, configuration, and methods as ships from two centuries previous but did so more efficiently. No packet line held a monopoly. Far from it. They were in constant competition with rival lines, and maintaining their reputation for speed and reliability was vital.

Also changed was the fact that the Industrial Revolution was now in full swing, and international trade had expanded enormously. The packets became part of a vast integrated intercontinental supply network that relied almost entirely on the sail-driven international merchant marine.

The Eastward and Westward Courses

Being fully rigged ships, the packets were naturally constrained by wind and current systems and utilised the North Atlantic gyre, first observed by Columbus over 300 years earlier. The west-to-east voyage was driven by the prevailing westerlies and assisted by the eastward-flowing Gulf Stream, which acts as a gigantic conveyor belt across the northern Atlantic. At its maximum, it carried a ship along at almost five knots, or nine kilometres per hour, which at times would be at least as much speed as the ship was deriving from its sails.

The trip from east to west was longer. For a limited time of the year, the packets could swing south towards the equator in a large arc until they picked up the north-east trades. Initially, they were assisted by the westward-flowing North Equatorial Current, which makes up the other side of the North Atlantic gyre. Eventually, when far enough east, they would pick up the Gulf Stream, which would again take them north up the north-eastern seaboard of America.

With increased competition, going faster became more and more important, and captains would add canvas to make the absolute most of the wind, especially on the eastbound journey, which was the shortest and most directly before the wind. The packets established an average time of twenty-two days from New York to Liverpool and forty days for the return journey where winds could be adverse and the distance considerably longer. Nevertheless, they rarely deviated from these times by more than a day or two. The ships sailed to schedules, summer and winter, and as competition between the lines increased, so too did the ruggedness of their construction.

The same genius that was being applied to packet ships would exert considerable influence on the clippers, which, from 1849, were being used primarily on the California run. Building vessels for the packet lines had made American designers very attuned to ways to increase speed. America was building an enormous enterprise in the construction of wooden ocean-going merchant vessels. In time, their shipping companies came to dominate the world's merchant marine.

The Packet Captains and Crew

The traders may have instigated these services, but they relied enormously on the skill and fortitude of the men who manned them: the captains, mates, and their doughty crews. The captains needed courage and skill and were superb seamen. But they were entrepreneurs in their own right with all sorts of perks to bolster their compensation and competitiveness.

For the crews—the so-called packet rats—life was very different. Mostly Irish, they were excellent (and often mutinous) seamen, and it took tough captains and officers to control them.

Using the techniques of hard-driving originally developed in the slave trade, these ships were sailed hard twenty-four hours a day, regardless of the season. The crew was well paid as far as seamen's wages went, but with very little in the way of mechanical aids, a passage relied on their courage to 'go aloft' in all weathers, at all times of the day and night, and on their muscle power, grit, and fortitude. In bad weather, the crew could be soaking wet for weeks on end, and their time aloft could be a life-and-death struggle with flailing canvas and whipping ropes as they strove to shorten (take in) sail in a gale.

The upshot was that when in port, they tended to make the best of its comforts, especially the salving effects of copious amounts of alcohol and the purchased attentions of the opposite sex. Needless to say, they were generally skint by the time their next berth was due to depart, and so they had little option but to do it all over again. Although they lived a dissolute life, they were nevertheless proud of their ability to withstand the conditions under which they worked.

The packet rats were considered the toughest men afloat—manning the first ships that sailed to schedules. With the captain's reputation and bonuses at stake, time was of the essence, and shortening sail (making the exposed sail area smaller by reefing, or tying the whole sail to the yard) was generally done as a last resort and consequently in atrocious conditions. Captains were known to lock the sheets on to prevent the crew from easing them. When the need became inevitable to save the ship, it was the crew who suffered the consequences.

Feeder Services

After a modest start, the freight service began to boom and diversify. Other merchant interests saw the success of the Black Ball shuttle, and before long, services were operating from other ports: Train & Co. plying between Boston and Liverpool, and others from Philadelphia and Baltimore to ports further eastward, such as London, Le Havre, and Antwerp. Similarly, coastal liner 'feeder' services were set up to ply the east coast of the United States, a notable one being specialised (shallow draft) vessels bringing cotton from the Mississippi Delta. Besides New Orleans, other feeder services operated from Charleston, Savannah, and Mobile.

The sailing packets reached their peak operating almost entirely as freighters in the period 1835–40. New York, where the packet services had begun, became the foremost port on the American eastern seaboard, with many of the feeder services terminating there. From the early vessels of a mere 400 tons, many packets were now measuring 1,000 and even 1,500 tons. The value of the merchandise they were unloading at South Street Pier rose in value from $84 million in 1825 to $146 million in 1836. In 1840, 414,000 tons of sail tonnage was registered there, second only to London, and with 500–700 vessels operating from the city. The packets were laying the foundation of America's rise to merchant marine greatness.

The Erie Canal

Inland waterways and rivers also connected with the transatlantic packets. The construction of the Erie Canal, which had begun in 1817, became a part of this extensive network and would provide a disproportionate boost to the transatlantic trade. The canal connected Buffalo on the Great Lakes with Albany on the Hudson River. By doing so, it enabled the port of New York to service an enormous expanse of territory that extended almost halfway across the United States.

A Vital Artery—the Erie Canal

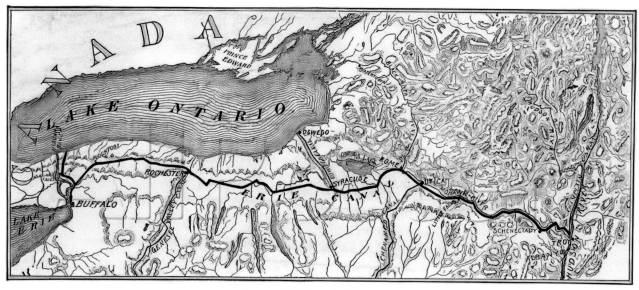

Source: Wikimedia Commons

Over 360 miles long, the Erie Canal's locks lifted barges over a 565-foot range of hills, crossing swamps and using aqueducts to cross rivers. It took eight years to build and was completed in 1825. The canal carried just over 200,000 tons in its first year, but by 1850, it was shifting over 3 million tons.

Western farmers from as far west as Lake Superior could send all sorts of primary produce to New York. In return, they could afford to buy an amazing variety of manufactures from Europe. The canal also provided an artery along which a prodigious number of immigrants would reach the western plains.

The barges were initially pulled by mules, and the life towing them was immortalised in the song 'Fifteen Miles on the Erie Canal'—the lament of a bargeman and his mule named Sal which was revived in the 1950s. Although by the 1880s the service was overtaken by the railroads, it had repaid its 7-million-dollar cost within a decade.

At the other end of a packet's voyage, more often than not, was the Port of Liverpool, the gateway to England's industrial heartland. Liverpool was the destination of an untold tonnage of raw materials and source of the myriad manufactures that were so earnestly sought on the other side of the Atlantic.

Liverpool was also the site of the world's first enclosed dock, isolated from the tidal Mersey River. The number of these docks would be expanded to twenty-eight by 1860. They were all connected by lock gates and crossed by swinging bridges that enabled goods traffic and pedestrians to flow in and out but allowed free movement of ships twenty-four hours a day.

So busy was the port that by the mid-nineteenth century, a Liverpool merchant allegedly counted some 300 ships entering the dock system on a single tide. The port was fed by scheduled feeder services similar to those that extended down the eastern seaboard of the United States. Initially, these services utilised the extensive canal network that had become an integral part of England's inland waterways, beginning in Roman times. This unified transport network would soon be supplemented by that irresistible change agent: the steam railway.

What began as a regular port-to-port service soon evolved into a vast, integrated network. The key element? These mighty, ocean-spanning vessels—the packets. They heralded the start of the regularised globalisation of trade and passenger movement we take for granted today.

Casualties

Despite their reputation for speed and timeliness, not every aspect of the service was so triumphant. Wealthy passengers 'fared' well, but the poor suffered incredible indignities. During the five decades of the packet heyday, out of the hundreds of ships that made the journey, one in six ended its career in disaster. The chief cause was storms, especially as the ships approached land, but fire on board was an even more terrifying possibility.

In 1822, as the Black Ball Line packet the *Albion* was making her way to Liverpool from New York, she was struck by squalls that soon reached hurricane force. The hurricane lasted two days and smashed her against the cliffs near Kinsale, County Cork, in Ireland. Of the fifty-four people on board, forty-five, including the captain, drowned. In the same storm, sixty ships were sunk or damaged in Liverpool harbour, and salt spray coated trees five miles inland; so strong were the winds.

Famine Creates Emigrant Back-Freight

Although the liner services began as freight services, before long, they were blessed with the holy grail of merchant shipping—a burgeoning back-freight, this time in people.

When plants are taken from one environment to another, they quite often thrive because the disease and insect regimen that was based on them do not make the trip. Thus, Tasmanian bluegum does well in South America partly because the local pest regimen has no appetite for the potent sap of the species. One of the major inhibitors to growth in its native environment is thereby removed. Similarly, radiata pine is a scrubby tree in its native habitat on the west coast of the United States but thrives in a plantation environment in Australasia.

So with the potato. It is native to America, and its introduction into Europe was part of the Columbian exchange. Free from its native pests, it was extremely successful to the point of becoming a staple in several countries, most notably Ireland.

In 1845, its American nemesis, the potato blight, somehow made its way from South America to Europe, either via Mexico or possibly in among fertiliser imported from the west coast of South America. It struck with a devastating effect on the European potato crop in 1845. Its impact was especially dramatic in Ireland where the agricultural workforce was almost entirely dependent upon it.

Famished Children, West Cork 1847

Source: Skibbereen by James Mahony, Wikimedia Commons

The country's population was reduced by 20 to 25 per cent, and it dramatically altered its demographic and its political and cultural landscape. About a million people died from starvation, and many more emigrated, mainly to America. Too weak to work and with meagre participation in the cash economy, they had pitifully little money. Landlords would often pay their former tenants' fares to America to be rid of them. The demand so created for shipping was prodigious, and the transatlantic liner companies took great advantage of it.

Irish Immigrants Embarking for America

Source: Wikimedia Commons

From around 8,000 people in 1820, total emigration to the United States rose to 372,000 in 1852. Those leaving Ireland (including Northern Ireland) increased from 3,600 in 1820 to a peak of 221,000 in 1851.

Liberal Revolutions in Europe

Another source of emigrants was the liberal revolutions in Europe in 1848. Triggered by a desire for democratic reforms, and beginning in Sicily, these upheavals spread to France, Germany, Italy, and the Austrian Empire.

Many Europeans, especially the young, saw America as a land of freedom and opportunity, and following the upheavals, they flocked to emigrate. They did so to avoid the repression that followed, the implementation of pogroms, and conscription into the armies of the newly militarised Prussia, Austria, and Russia.

The famine in Ireland raged from 1845 to 1847, and the impact of the blight on the European food supply may have been a factor in the political upheavals of 1848. Whatever the case, the demand for shipping services they created followed immediately upon that generated by the potato famine. People departing Germany in 1820 numbered less than a thousand and peaked at 215,000 in 1854. The flow would peak again in 1873 at 150,000, in the aftermath of the Franco-Prussian war of 1870–71, but by then, the steamers dominated the transatlantic emigrant trade.

The chart shows the growth in emigration to the United States and documents the bonanza it created for the packet lines.

Emigration to the USA: 1820-1880

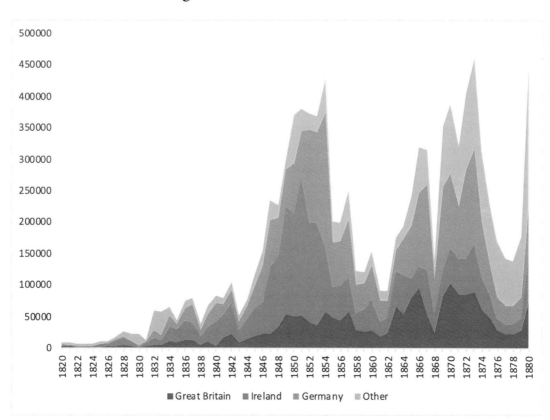

Source: Historical Statistics of the United States, Series C89-119

Emigrant Numbers

The more the conditions deteriorated in Europe, and especially Ireland, so the numbers of those wanting to get out swelled. Between 1845 and 1855, 2.1 million people left Ireland, reducing its population by a quarter. Ninety-five per cent of emigrants headed for the United States. Between 1846 and 1850, two million people crossed the Atlantic, more than half as many again as those who made the journey in the seven decades from independence (1776) to 1845.

Abysmal Conditions

In their haste to make the most of this 'human rush', the packet owners and captains paid very little heed to the plight of their cargo. It is a measure of their desperation and the conditions on board that, in 1847, it was estimated that some 17,000 people died at sea during the passage. Diseases such as smallpox, dysentery, and typhus were rife. Some passengers, infected with cholera, were able to board after a cursory medical exam. Ten per cent of the passengers often died on a single voyage, and on a bad passage, the number might rise to 16 per cent. Some ships lost a quarter, or more, of their steerage passengers to disease. They may not have been the healthiest of people at the outset, suffering from malnutrition and a variety of diseases, but the abysmal conditions on board, often described as worse than on slave ships, were mostly to blame.

Given the foetid conditions, on-board doctors would often refuse to go down to the steerage decks. Regular packet ships would store cargo in the 'tween' decks (the space between the upper deck of the ship and the cargo hold) on the journey east and erect flimsy accommodation facilities and cram it full of immigrants on the westward run, the longest and most uncomfortable of the two voyages. The emigrant trade has been described as maritime commerce at its most heinous—exploiting poor wretches already weakened by famine.

Regulation Fails

Initially, the liner owners were in the freight business, and passenger fares were generally a perk of the skipper, but as the trade in emigrants grew, packet owners took their share and limited the largesse available to the skippers. But the captains had to provision the passengers, so it comes as no surprise that at the top end, the accommodation was very acceptable, the food sumptuous, and the fares expensive. At the low end, however, the accommodation was abysmal with food to match.

There was a whole range of other indignities to which poor passengers would be subjected in the course of the voyage: tainted water, itself in extremely short supply; limited access to cooking facilities; practically non-existent sanitation and ventilation; and cramped conditions (sometimes six or more to a bed made for four). The list goes on and on, and all exacerbated in times of bad weather.

Then seasickness struck, and the hatches—the only source of ventilation—were battened down, denying the emigrants access to the only fresh air available to them. Attempts to regulate the conditions on the packets were simply disregarded by the owners, and the conditions of departure and arrival made it impossible to enforce them. For example, thirty ships might leave Liverpool from all over the extensive dockland on a single tide.

Fire Hazard

The other main hazard was fire. It could be caused by lightning, crew carelessness with candles or lanterns, passengers using unsafe methods to cook food, or spontaneous combustion. Sometimes the fire would spread quickly, as was the case of the White Diamond Line's 1,300-ton *Ocean Monarch*. Built in 1847, she was designed by Donald McKay and was the largest American, and second-largest ship, on the Atlantic run. In 1848, shortly after leaving Liverpool bound for Boston, she caught fire. The vessel was still in the Mersey estuary where help was readily to hand. Nevertheless, she sank thirteen hours after the fire was first reported, with a loss of 178 lives.

Packets were made of wood as were their lifeboats, which were at best flimsy and at worst rotten, and there were never enough to hold all souls on board. The proportion of ships that were overcome by storm, or by fire, will never be known.

Their final mention in the maritime annals was usually 'went missing'.

They all simply set sail from one side of the crossing and failed to reappear on the other. With no form of ship-to-shore communication, their fate will be forever unknown.

Repeal of the Corn Laws

Meanwhile, back in Ireland, English landlords continued to export grain, butter, livestock, and all manner of vegetables to England, while the people all around them starved, often to death. The philosophy of the day was that the market would provide, and it was adhered to, even when people were obviously suffering.

The notion of 'market failure' would not arise until the late twentieth century.

Nineteenth-century economic credos, meanwhile, were not renowned for their humanity. There was no shortage of food, but British landlords' rents were underwritten by the high price of grain. They were protected from foreign competition by what were called the Corn Laws, which had been introduced after the defeat of Napoleon in 1815.

Poor tenant farmers, who paid their rent with labour, were dependent on the potato for sustenance and could not afford to buy grain. By the mid-1840s, it must have appeared to the packet line owners that they could do no wrong, as so much went right for them. In 1846, the British government was forced to acknowledge that, with so many starving and malnourished people, supplies of cheap grain were urgently required, and the Corn Laws were repealed. Cheap grain from America flooded in. The packet ship owners were able to cash in on this new eastbound cargo, which, besides being lucrative, provided a diversification away from cotton.

In Europe, the revolutions were severely repressed, and many of those who could afford it sought a better life for themselves and their families in 'the land of the free'. But it was not only political refugees who saw promise in the United States. There was also demand for a considerable range of passenger accommodation for time-short businessmen and spirited, generally young, Britons and Europeans. They all sought a more adventurous future, and one less constrained by privilege, across the Western Ocean.

Steam and Steel Spoil the Party

The packet owners certainly made the best of their time in the sun, extracting every last penny, it seems, from the trade, especially the emigrant sector. By the middle of the nineteenth century, an average of more than a quarter of a million passengers were making the crossing every year. In some years, it was more than half a million.

But there was a chill in the air.

While the sailing packets were predominantly American-owned and American-registered vessels, the steamships that began to cross the Atlantic were primarily British-built, reflecting that country's mastery of steam technology, engine building, iron founding, and steel construction.

The first steamship to cross the Atlantic carried neither passengers nor freight. Its entire hull space was taken up with coal, water, and machinery. But the British worked hard at improving this most disruptive of technologies, extracting every last joule of energy from steam. Consequently, the first commercial steam packet made the run in 1838.

The sailing packets' Achilles heel was the time they took to complete the east-to-west run, having to avoid the permanent influence of the prevailing westerlies by sailing in a wide southern arc and into less certain wind systems.

The steam-powered packet, assisted by sails when the conditions permitted, on the other hand, could chart the shortest course and make quite acceptable headway directly into the prevailing westerlies. Moreover, they could keep to schedules better than the sailing ships, even on the 'downhill' run from west to east.

The sailing packet liners gained acceptance because they sailed to schedules, full or not. The steamships began to make inroads into their business because they could do the job better.

The End for the Western Ocean Packets

It was the misery often encountered on that most lucrative east–west crossing that proved the sailing packets' ultimate undoing. By 1863, 45 per cent of emigrant passages were made on steamships. Just three years later, that proportion had increased to 81 per cent. The sailing packets were progressively relegated to their original industrial cargoes of grain, cotton, and coal.

Nevertheless, there were a few still sailing at the end of the American Civil War in 1865. Of the five biggest sailing liner companies still scheduling after the war, three of the largest—Red Star, Blue Swallow Tail, and Dramatic lines—had closed by 1878. In that year, the pioneering Black Ball Line was still loading six ships, but at year's end, it, too, succumbed.

The last sailing packets to cross the Atlantic as liner services were ships of the Red Swallow Tail Line. It closed in 1880, and its last two ships, the *Sir Robert Peel* and the *Liverpool*, were sold to become merchantmen. The latter had served thirty-seven years as a liner. The diminutive *James Monroe* that had inaugurated the service in 1818 couldn't compete with the new and larger ships, and she was also sold as a merchantman. She must have been a tough little vessel because she was still sailing in 1850 when wrecked off the coast of Tasmania. The final sailing packet to cross the Atlantic on a scheduled run arrived in New York in May 1881.

Ironically, the 1396-ton vessel's name was *Ne Plus Ultra*—'nothing further'.

Influence on Clipper Design

The naval architects of the day cut their teeth designing packet ships, and many of their innovations flowed through to clippers. Although they had bluff bows in the interest of maximising cargo space and had to be, of necessity, more ruggedly rigged, the flat floors that would prove so successful in the clippers were originally employed in packet ship design. It was an effective development for sailing ships, which increased both their cargo capacity and speed.

In return, the clipper designers brought their aesthetic sense, so apparent in their later creations, to packet design. Size became a consideration. By the mid-1850s, one packet ship in eight was being built as a three-decker. But as these ships grew bigger, so the sources of suitable timbers got further from the shipyards, and freight became a more important factor in vessel cost. It was one of the first hints that limitations were emerging on the construction of very large wooden ships. The amount of structural timber required to maintain rigidity in such large hulls would also begin to impact the ease of loading and unloading the vessel. Wooden construction was approaching the limit of its capabilities and, with it, America's ability to sustain its leadership in merchant shipbuilding and maritime commerce. There would, however, be a last hurrah—the clippers.

The packet ships introduced a new age in merchant sail. They made a great improvement to transatlantic merchant sail services by departing to regular schedules, sailing direct to specified ports and making every effort to keep to scheduled arrival times at the end of the voyage. They showed the way towards the modern steam and later motor ship services of today. Unfortunately for them, they depended on the wind and the weather, which don't operate to schedules.

8

CHAPTER

The Rise of the Clipper Ships

Introduction

The clipper ships were the fastest sail-driven merchant ships the world has ever known. They were also some of the most profitable. But their time in the sun was short-lived.

There are a number of explanations of the origin of the word *clipper*, but the most common appears to be as a term given to a ship able to sail at a good 'clip', that is to say, a good speed. A more classical reference comes from Arthur H. Clark (himself a former clipper ship captain), who quotes the seventeenth-century poet John Dryden, in *Annus Mirabilis* (inspired by the Great Fire of London in 1666), using it to describe the flight of a falcon as the source of the term:

Some falcon stoops at what her eye designed,

And, with her eagerness the quarry missed,

Straight flies at check, and clips it down the wind. (Stanza 89)

The history of clipper ships and the search for speed across water is also a history of the maritime development of two nations: an old bull in the form of Great Britain and its progeny, the United States. The young bull held pride of place through the golden age of the clippers—the 1850s—but in the latter part of the century, the old bull reasserted itself through its mastery of working iron and steel, but only after the young bull had left the scene.

Initially built on the north-east coast of the United States, the clippers were the epitome of the marine architect's art and the acme of commercial sailing ship design. In their most highly developed form, the need for speed was the dominant force driving their design, but in their earlier incarnation— the so-called 'extreme' clippers—a lack of forward buoyancy, limited cargo space, and high maintenance limited their profitability.

Shipowners wanted a compromise, and so designers modified their hull shapes to accommodate more cargo and provide increased forward buoyancy. In these so-called 'medium' clippers, they were able to retain and refine the revolution in hull design that so improved their speed through the water.

America's packet ships dominated world merchant shipping and the design and operation of sailing ships. The country was blessed with an abundance of prime shipbuilding timbers and a workforce skilled in utilising them. They were most usefully employed in the construction of the sturdy wooden vessels that poured off the drawing boards of their inspired designers. Shipyards in the north-east, and especially in New York and Boston, enlarged the ships, increasing the length-to-beam ratio, flattening the floors, and moving the point of the maximum mid-ship section (the widest beam) further aft.

Under the old tonnage measurement rule (which was not abandoned until 1868 in the United States), ships could be built deeper without increasing the charges the owner had to pay. So the first attempts at enlarging the ships were made by increasing the depth. Unfortunately, this resulted in clumsy, less seaworthy vessels and ones that had difficulty in shallow waters.

Another approach was clearly needed.

The Agents of Change

The arrival of the clippers extended the golden age of American shipping and shipbuilding. Not only were the hull lines of these 'ocean greyhounds' revolutionary, the shipbuilders also worked out how to strengthen the hull to withstand the strains imposed by larger size, heavier cargoes, and the immense rigs used to drive them at maximum speed.

During this period, the American packet ships dominated the transatlantic traffic. The packet trade had been stimulated by the Industrial Revolution, drawing in raw materials such as cotton, food, and a huge variety of other materials. Likewise, worldwide demand for the products of that revolution—iron and steel, coal, machinery, textiles, and other manufactures—grew rapidly. As a consequence, the marine transport requirements between the New and the Old World increased, particularly between Great Britain and the United States.

Over and above the increase in international commodity and merchandise trade, five key events led to frenzied demand for American shipping: the famine in Ireland beginning in 1845; the 1848 revolutions in Europe; the discovery of gold in California in 1849; the repeal of the Navigation Laws in England, also in 1849; and the discovery of gold in Australia in 1851.

In a mere six years, the Western world was utterly transformed.

Hot on the heels of famine and revolution came the great gold discoveries. Getting the 'diggers' and their equipment, sustenance, and comforts (mainly alcohol) to the goldfields boosted demand for fast ships. Concurrently, the flood of gold into the international economy resulted in a shipping boom.

During this period of rapid change, the British navigation laws were abolished. Under the acts, all goods landed in English ports from its colonies had to be carried in 'British bottoms' or in vessels owned in the country of origin of the goods. These laws had been enacted in the 1600s when they had been very successful in reviving English shipping. Under the strict mercantilist regime of the time, they were designed to hoard a national store of gold and silver in order to keep the benefits from trade (including freight) within the empire.

The system protected English shipping from the competition, secured its supply of raw materials, and guaranteed a market for it and its colonies' exports. The acts were also a handy way of extracting as much value as possible from those colonies.

In this mid-century ferment, the British parliament was forced to repeal two pillars of the old mercantilist regime. Preceding the repeal of the Navigation Acts, the Corn Laws—which prohibited the import of grain into Great Britain—had been revoked in 1846 to increase the nation's supply of food.

The prairies of America and Canada were opening up their spectacular grain-producing potential, and with the construction of the Erie Canal, that grain could be landed on the east coast for export to Europe. The United States was now the pre-eminent maritime power of the time. These two repeal measures exposed British shipping, protected for the last two centuries, to American competition.

A Transatlantic Trade Boom

Undersea cables and telegraph undermined the need for small fast ships to carry news and commercial documentation. Larger ships were needed to provide transport for the burgeoning goods and passenger trades, especially across the Atlantic. Responding to the capitalist dictum of 'time is money', there was increased emphasis on speed and the ability to load and unload efficiently.

A symbiotic relationship had developed between the textile mills of Lancashire and the cotton growers of the Southern states of America. Between 1830 and 1859, American cotton exports to Great Britain expanded from 554,000 bales to 3,535,000—a more than sixfold increase—and provided half of the utilisation of the foreign trade fleet.

The passenger trade, both steerage and stateroom, increased even faster—from 25,000 passengers in 1830 to 460,000 in the peak year of 1854—an over eighteen-fold increase. The gold discoveries were completely unanticipated and provided a lucrative market for ships able to provide a speedy passage around Cape Horn to the Californian goldfields.

It was not only the punters seeking their fortune.

The gold- and scarcity-inflated goods trade was also very profitable. A trip to California from the eastern states of America was regarded as a coastal voyage, which was protected from foreign competition. At the height of the trade, freight rates were from five to six times their normal level, and a ship could repay the cost of its construction on its first loading. As a result of the Mexican War, America had also recently annexed California, bringing that trade under the United States monopoly.

The years from 1830 to 1856 represented a period of expansion and prosperity for shipyards building wooden sailing ships. The shipowners made fortunes, especially after 1847. The expansion culminated in a boom between 1847 and 1856 and a long-remembered collapse, beginning in 1857. From 1831 to 1846, 1,480 fully rigged ships and barques were built, and in the period from 1847 to 1857, 2,858 much larger vessels of the same rigs were delivered. In terms of gross tonnage, the annual construction in the latter period was about twelvefold that of the years 1815–29. The peak year was 1855, when an incredible 381 fully rigged ships and barques were delivered.

Such a rapid expansion, while a considerable achievement, was bound to come to an end. By the time the industry could look forward to signs of recovery, the Civil War was upon it.

The Designers and the Builders

The first American clippers are considered the pinnacle of sailing ship design because the emphasis was placed on speed at the expense of cargo capacity and operating costs. The practice of hard-driving, developed in the slave trade and pursued into the packet ship era, meant the crews needed to be large, and the wear and tear on the hull, spars, and sails made the ships very expensive to run.

It is said that 'cometh the hour, cometh the man', or in the business of designing superb sailing ships, cometh *the men*. The design innovations that contributed to the speed of these vessels came mainly from the drafting tables of four great American marine architects: John W. Griffiths, Samuel H. Pook, William H. Webb, and Donald McKay (the latter probably the greatest of them all).

The intellectual 'father' to three of these great designers was Isaac Webb. Webb had begun work as an apprentice to the shipbuilder Henry Eckford in New York in 1810, along with several other young men who would make their names as shipbuilders. Starting out as a tradesman, Webb opened his own shipyard, Isaac Webb & Co., in 1831 and employed John W. Griffiths, William Webb (his son), and Donald McKay as his apprentices. Two other Eckford apprentices, Jacob Bell and David Brown, would also form their own yard, Bell & Brown, and it, too, became a prominent shipbuilder.

Isaac Webb, it was said, had an unusual ability to pass on his insights into the construction of fast ships, but unfortunately, like many great men of artistic ability, he had no head for finance. When he died insolvent at forty-six, his son William took over the yard.

There were also design influences flowing from the practical seamanship side of things: from famous skippers of hard-bitten experience, such as Nathaniel Palmer and Robert Waterman, the latter another notable hard-driver.

As well as dramatic changes in hull shape, the ships these designers produced embodied other critical factors, chiefly their lofty masts and the enormous sail area they could spread. But ships don't make rapid passages in and of themselves, no matter what their design. As with the bonus-driven skippers of the packet ships, many of whom migrated to the clippers, it was the cult of hard-driving that was the main determining factor, certainly compared to the British practice of the time.

The Fastest Sailing Ships

Although the *Ann McKim*, built in 1834, showed the way, the American clipper era opened properly with *Rainbow*, launched in 1845, and which logged a maximum speed of 14 knots. If she could have kept it up over twenty-four hours, she would have covered 336 nautical miles. In 1854, barely a decade later, Donald McKay's *Sovereign of the Seas* logged the highest speed ever recorded for a sailing ship when she temporarily reached 22 knots running her easting down on a trip to Australia. (The term 'running her easting down' traditionally refers to the wild ride before the wind across the Indian Ocean between 40 and 50 degrees of south latitude. It extends from the Cape of Good Hope to Australia—an area commonly referred to as the 'roaring forties'.)

Sovereign of the Seas—The Fastest Ever Merchant Sailing Ship

Source: From a Jack Spurling lithograph; author's own collection

Another of McKay's ships, *Champion of the Seas*, recorded the greatest distance ever covered by a sailing ship in twenty-four hours when she ran a breathtaking 465 nautical miles in a day—an average of over 19 knots.

To put this achievement in a modern context, in 2017, an ultra-modern ocean-racing yacht, *Comanche*, won the Sydney to Hobart Yacht Race in record time. It covered the 629 nautical miles in about one day, nine hours. A mere shell with a highly skilled crew, made of the very latest materials (carbon fibre, Nomex, Kevlar, etc.), efficient electrically driven sail-handling, and the latest in navigational technology and weather forecasting, it averaged 19 knots for the journey.

Champion of the Seas achieved the same speed over twenty-four hours *160-odd years before*.

There are eleven other instances of sailing ships logging over 18 knots. Ten of these were American, with the only other one the Canadian-built *Marco Polo*. David McGregor, an English author and authority on clipper ships, points out, however, that the records established by *James Baines*, *Champion of the Seas*, and *Lightning* were all made when under the command of British skippers. The British proved fast learners, and their newly acquired skill at hard-driving would stand them in good stead in the 'tea races' that would follow.

Donald McKay's Transatlantic Record Holder *Lightning*

Source: Jack Spurling lithograph; author's own collection

There are thirteen other cases of sailing ships travelling more than 400 nautical miles in a day. All except the *Marco Polo* were American. Before the clipper age, the British rigged down at night, whereas the American skippers drove their ships every hour of voyages that often lasted over 100 days. It was this hard-driving—and the intense competition between shipping lines and their skippers—that pushed sailing ship design and development to its limit.

The record for the highest speed ever attained under commercial sail in less than a twenty-four-hour run was achieved by the Donald McKay-designed clipper *James Baines* in 1856. It was clocked at an astonishing 21 knots—equal to 39 kilometres/hour. Built in 1854, she had a short and brilliant career. Two years after setting that record, she burned to the waterline. Sadly, for her owner, James Baines, her insurance policy had expired three days before.

The Mighty Clipper *James Baines*

Source: Jack Spurling, courtesy of John Oxley Library, State Library of Queensland.(NB: Note the stunsails set on almost all of the yards on the fore and main masts.)

The Transition from Packet to Clipper

The transition from packet hull to clipper hull was, thus, not a sudden break but more a process of evolution. The packets constituted a breakthrough because they provided a regular non-stop service between America and England, and they were so successful that a whole network of transport modes emerged to feed into their services. But competition soon developed, and inevitably, the speed of the passage became a factor.

At first, going faster was limited to cramming on more sail and driving the ship hard, but designers soon began to realise that what went on *below* the water was as much a factor in the speed of the ship as what went on *above*. As a consequence, they began to experiment with hull shape and length.

Fast ships had already been built, most notably during the Anglo-American War. These were the famous 'Baltimore clippers', small schooners that were used to run the blockade, smuggling, and slaving. They were based on French luggers that visited American ports during the war. The French ships were designed for speed and weatherliness because their primary business was smuggling and privateering.

The *Ann McKim*, an enlarged Baltimore clipper rigged as a ship, demonstrated exceptional speed, but she could carry very little cargo. One of the vessels that constituted a more recognisable transition from packet to clipper came from a specialised form of the packet used in the feeder services for the transatlantic vessels. They were the 'droghers', shipping cotton from the southern states to New York.

The catalyst for change would come from one of the most colourful characters of the era, Nathaniel Palmer.

The Flat-Bottom Revolution

Nathaniel Palmer was instrumental in the design, and supervised the construction of, the four packets that made up the Dramatic Line. They were considered the fastest ships of their day, and their design lines began to feed into vessels being built to exploit the growing tea, porcelain, and silk trade with China, the so-called 'China packets'.

Palmer captained the first three of the Dramatic Line transatlantic packets to be launched, but soon, he, too, felt the (no doubt, financial) pull of the China trade. To take advantage of it, he built the *Paul Jones*, a fast, flat-bottomed packet designed for the conditions on the China run. But on the return journey, he faced the fierce south-west monsoon, an experience that got him thinking about weatherliness: the ability to make good to windward.

On board this particular journey was one William Low. Low was a member of the tea trading house A. A. Low & Bros, which was connected to the prominent Chinese trading house (and opium runner) Russell & Company. Palmer explained his ideas to Low, who agreed to build a ship embodying them. The result was the *Houqua*, named for Low's respected Chinese merchant in Canton. The ship, built in 1844, was a distillation of Palmer's years of experience as a master mariner. It would earn an enviable reputation as a fast passage-maker.

John W. Griffiths

John W Griffiths was the son of a shipwright but had little practical experience of the sea. Instead, he applied science and mathematics to ship design. It was the blending of these two approaches that set ship design on a new path.

John W. Griffiths (1809-1882)

Source: Wikimedia Commons

The young Griffiths began his working career first as an apprentice shipwright with the prominent shipbuilder Isaac Webb and later as a draughtsman for Smith and Dimon, also noted shipbuilders. Part of his approach was to follow the Englishman Mark Beaufoy by tank-testing his hull models. They were towed through a long water tank, and their performance carefully observed. He subsequently gave the first lectures in America on what was to become the profession of naval architecture.

Regarded as somewhat eccentric, Griffiths nevertheless attracted the attention of shipping company Howland & Aspinwall, and in 1843, they contracted Smith and Dimon to build the *Rainbow*. After some dispute over the placing of the masts, she was not launched until 1845 but would later come to be known as the first of the extreme clippers. She measured 757 tons OM (old measure) and was 159 feet long with a beam of 32 feet—a length-to-beam ratio of 5:1.

Howland & Aspinwall hedged their bets and bought both the *Ann McKim* and one of Nathaniel Palmer's old flat-bottomed packets, the *Natchez*. The company put both on the China run to gauge their performance. Both came home within a hundred days. Clearly, the future lay in synthesising the design principles embodied in these two ships, and that thought process led to the *Rainbow*. She was a departure from fast ship design to date, sacrificing cargo-carrying capacity for speed like no other vessel had done.

Profitability

One of the hardest-driving skippers in the business, the New Yorker Robert Waterman, had brought the *Natchez* home from Macao in seventy-eight days. The next year, Griffiths followed the *Rainbow* up with *Sea Witch*, claimed by some to be the most beautiful clipper ship ever built. She was 192 feet long by 33 feet beam (a length-to-beam ratio of almost 6:1) and was rated at 908 tons old measure.

Griffiths had consulted with Waterman on her rig and sail plan. Even the hard-driving Nathaniel Palmer conceded that she was 'very heavily sparred'. He added (ever the practical seaman) that she would sail at great expense (presumably from manning) 'to say nothing of the wear and tear'. As an experienced marine master, Palmer was sensitive to the economics of running ships, and he was prescient about one of the great weaknesses of the clipper. *Sea Witch* had the tallest masts of any ship afloat (her mainmast was 140 feet high) and spread more canvas than a Royal Navy seventy-four-gun ship of the line.

Rainbow proved to be an extraordinarily fast vessel. On her maiden voyage, she set a record of seven months, seven days for a round trip to China. On her second voyage, she went out against the north-east monsoon in just ninety-two days and came home in eighty-eight.

Meanwhile, *Sea Witch* came home from Canton in an all-time record of seventy-seven days, which she later reduced to seventy-four days—a record that stood until broken by a trimaran, *Great American II*, in 2003. *Sea Witch*, however, did not have the advantage of modern technology, satellite navigation, or global weather forecasting—*and* she was carrying a full cargo! *Sea Witch* went on to set more records than any other sailing ship of her size, before or since. Highly profitable, she is said to have made $200,000 in one voyage to China.

On the same day as *Sea Witch* arrived from Canton, *Rainbow* set out on her fifth voyage, this time for Valparaíso in Chile and China. She was never seen again and was assumed to have foundered off Cape Horn. *Sea Witch* was wrecked off Havana in 1856. These ships were potentially very fast, and hard-driving made them so, but they were often pushed past the limits of their capability.

The Navigation Acts and the Tea Trade

The infusion of *Camellia sinensis*, a small evergreen shrub of the flowering plant family *Theaceae*, had been cultivated by the Chinese for 3,000 years and is native to the south-east of the country. The tea-drinking culture in America dated back to the Dutch colony of New Amsterdam. A tax on tea was one of the causes of the American Revolution, after which it was free to trade with China on its own account.

The biosynthesis of the operative drug, caffeine, is at its greatest in the young tea leaves, and the fresher they are consumed, the greater the hit. The tea trade did not require large cargo capacity. The money was in getting the best young leaf to Europe (mainly England) as quickly as possible. Speed was of the essence, and this was made more urgent by the belief that the leaf's taste deteriorated through prolonged exposure to a marine environment. It followed that the ships that could get the product to the market quicker earned the best freight rates—a consideration that led progressively to the development of the 'extreme' clipper.

America had come up against the force of the British Navigation Acts before, and they were one of the triggers of the American War of Independence. The Acts forced Americans to buy expensive British sugar and molasses when French products were cheaper. With the Industrial Revolution, this restrictive attitude gradually gave way to the philosophy of free trade. It suited industrial England, at that time the 'workshop of the world', to obtain raw materials and food as cheaply as possible to sustain its industry and workforce.

America, with its abundant land, individualism, and pronounced work ethic, was a major source of cheap food. The Erie Canal had opened in 1825, giving America's east coast ports access to supplies of grain from the vast western plains. With the repeal of the Corn Laws, using American ships was the most economical way to land it in England. In 1846, the year of their repeal, Great Britain imported 800,000 tons of cereal grains. The following year, the figure exceeded 2 million tons, and by 1913, the figure was over 10 million tons.

The repeal of the Navigation Acts also meant that American ships could engage in the English tea trade, for which their fast, hard-driven vessels had a distinct advantage. Before the repeal of the acts, there had been no incentive for British shipbuilders to improve their designs. Once the American clippers entered the China tea trade, however, they were very much playing catch-up, not only in design but in the practice of hard-driving, which was a large part of the Americans' success.

Not to be outdone by Howland & Aspinwall—and even though there were now upwards of fifty ships on the China run—another prominent shipping company, A. A. Low, commissioned a ship from Nathaniel Palmer. She was the *Oriental* and was destined to become famous as the first American clipper to dock in Great Britain after the repeal of the acts. On her second China passage, *Oriental* made Hong Kong in eighty days, ten hours, the fastest run ever from either the United States or England.

She was immediately chartered by Russell & Company to carry 1,600 tons of tea to England at a price that netted the Lows a profit of $48,000, nearly two-thirds of what it had cost to build the ship. She came home in ninety-eight days, then a record, and it was at that point that she caused such a sensation in the London docks. Onlookers were stunned to see such a beautiful, relatively small ship that set half as much canvas again as one of their mighty ships of the line, complete such a passage. In dry dock, the ever-canny British shipowners took great care to have the Lloyds Register surveyors take off her lines (carefully record her underwater shape) as a step down the catch-up path. Meanwhile, the *Times* newspaper thundered,

> *We must run a race with our gigantic and unshackled rival. It is a race of a father who runs a race with his son … Let our shipbuilders and employers take warning in time … We want fast vessels for the long voyages which will otherwise fall into American hands.*

No love lost there, but British shipowners had, under the monopoly of the East India Company on long-distance mercantile shipping, allowed their designs to fall way behind those of the Americans. It was not only their ship designs that had lagged. So too had their approach to passage-making. East Indiamen were known to rig down at night no matter the weather. The British perpetually erred on the side of caution, whereas the Americans took pride in their reputation as maritime daredevils.

The Californian Gold Rush

The American designers had forty years of immediately relevant packet design experience behind them, and they were about to be given another enormous boost.

It has been estimated that up until 1500, only forty tons of gold had ever been mined in the history of civilisation. By 1908, that figure had reached 5,000 tons, and most of it had been produced by three great gold rushes: California in 1848, Australia in 1851, and Transvaal in 1886.

The clipper ships, which had been in a process of development in the mid-1840s, arrived just in time to take advantage of the boom. The gold rushes would stimulate the ships' development from relatively small vessels to the largest and fastest wind-driven merchant ships to exist up until that time, or since.

California was then one of the most isolated and poorly developed places on earth. Yerba Buena, now known as San Francisco, was a mere village, yet in the next five years, hundreds of thousands of people would arrive to try their luck on the diggings, to make the more sustainable fortunes by selling supplies and services to the miners, or to take advantage of the economic boom that flowed from the rush. California's first census was in 1850 when some 93,000 souls were counted. By 1860, the number had grown to 380,000, a fourfold increase in just ten years.

San Francisco in 1851 During the Gold Rush

Source: Library of Congress via Wikimedia Commons

By the end of 1849, 775 vessels had arrived, but there were few houses and very little food. Everything was in short supply, and prices skyrocketed, presaging a massive and lucrative transportation opportunity.

The east coast shipbuilders rose to the occasion in a very memorable way.

America declared war on Mexico in 1846, and as part of the 1847 peace settlement, it obtained, *inter alia*, the area which subsequently became the state of California. It was a fortuitous initiative. Not long after, in 1848, gold was discovered at Sutter's Mill on the Sacramento River, forever transforming the west coast of the United States. In the first two years, a quarter of a million people would scurry to the fields. The rush would last until 1855, and it was those seven years that constitute the golden age of the clippers.

In the early days of the gold rush, a sea voyage to California could take 200 days, a journey that was immortalised by the young Harvard undergraduate Richard Henry Dana Jr. in his great account of the voyage, *Two Years before the Mast*. The treacherous overland trip across the United States through Wyoming's South Pass was arduous due to the harsh terrain, variable weather conditions, and risk of attack from hostile Indians. For Midwesterners, however, it was the most expeditious.

The fastest way to reach California from the east coast, on the other hand, was by sea. One way was by clipper to Panama to make a difficult and disease-ridden journey on horseback or by mule across the rugged isthmus and await a passage to California on the other side. The distance was 5,000 miles. Many more people chose this route in preference to the overland trail.

The only other alternative was a single voyage around the dreaded Cape Horn—a distance of 14,000 miles—by fast clipper ship. Not only was it around the Horn, but the trip went around it the wrong way—into the teeth of the prevailing westerlies. All gold seekers were in a hurry, and the better-heeled could afford the fastest journey. It called for fast ships, and the faster the ship, the more it could demand in fares. In the year up until April 1848, only four merchant ships and nine whalers called into San Francisco. By 1849, 775 vessels left Atlantic ports for the city of gold.

Designer Response

The marine architects and shipbuilders of America's north-east coast responded quickly to the discovery of gold, building a fleet of ships designed for speed at all costs. Initially, the trade was mainly passenger-driven, and the ships that had been designed for the tea trade were the logical answer. They were pressed into service, but California had little capacity to feed, house, equip, and slake the thirst of the miners.

Big, fast ships, with considerable cargo capacity, were at a premium.

Nevertheless, in January 1850, the (relatively small, at 752 tons) tea clipper *Samuel Russell* sailed for California, weighed down with freight. The passage netted the owners $72,000, more than it had cost to build her. The trip took 109 days, but *Sea Witch* then made the journey in ninety-seven days, the first vessel to break 100 days for the passage.

Samuel Hartt Pook

These ships had been built in New York and, being relatively small and 'exceedingly sharp' in their design, their cargo-carrying capacity was limited. Owner attention turned from New York to the shipbuilders of Boston where the keels of two considerably larger clippers were shortly laid down. The first was the *Surprise* from the pen of Samuel Hartt Pook (1827-1901), the twenty-four-year-old son of an established ship designer, Samuel Moore Pook. The second was from the desk of Donald McKay, who was destined to become the most famous clipper designer of all time. Samuel Hartt Pook's 1,361-ton *Surprise* broke *Sea Witch*'s record by a day on its first trip to California.

Samuel Hartt Pook (1827-1901)

Source: NH47374 Courtesy of Naval History & Heritage Command

Samuel Hartt Pook had ship design in his blood, his father having designed ironclads (warships covered with armour plating) for the US Navy. The young Pook was born in New York but spent his youth in Portsmouth, New Hampshire, where his father was employed at the naval shipyard. He served an apprenticeship under his father but then, in 1850, left to develop his reputation as a merchant ship designer in wood.

It was an exciting time for a young ship designer. Tea clippers had been plying the China run for several years, and that was thrilling enough, but the discovery of gold in California called again for ships that were not only fast but capable also of carrying substantial quantities of cargo.

Enter the 'medium clippers'.

The first ship credited to Samuel Hartt Pook was *Surprise*. However, disputes about his contribution to other vessels built at the Samuel Hall yard, where he was working, led to him going out on his own as a specialist designer. Although his designs were not as radical as those of John W. Griffiths, who gave up designing just as Pook's heyday began, he gained a reputation as a creator of solid performing vessels. Two of his designs set records: *Northern Light* (San Francisco to Boston) and *Red Jacket* (New York to Liverpool). *Defiance*, launched in 1852, surprised everyone with her speed on her way to New York to pick up cargo: she sailed from the Fire Island Light to Sandy Hook at twenty knots.

Unfortunately, Pook's *modus operandi* left him open to exploitation, with plans passed on from builder to builder and location to location, without compensation or recognition. It may have been this inability to capitalise on the fruits of his talent, or that he saw steam as the future, that led Pook to abandon freelance sailing ship design. In 1861, he began designing ironclads and in 1865 took up permanent employment with the US Navy, eventually becoming chief naval constructor.

Donald McKay

Although he became the most famous clipper designer in history, Donald McKay was born in Nova Scotia in 1810, the son of a farmer. He began his nautical career crewing on a fishing schooner but soon moved to New York to take up an apprenticeship with the prominent shipbuilder Isaac Webb. McKay was a quick learner and sought to expand his knowledge working at different yards, learning design, and drafting from his first wife, Albenia Boole, who came from a whole family of shipbuilders. Albenia died in 1848, and McKay moved to New England, eventually taking up employment with a shipbuilder in Newburyport, Massachusetts. He partnered with other builders building packet ships, the last of which was for Enoch Train as an inaugural vessel on his White Diamond Line. Train was so impressed with the ship he encouraged McKay to move to Boston and set up a shipyard there with his financial backing. That backing enabled him to invest in modern equipment such as steam-powered sawing, lathes, and derricks.

Clipper Ship Designer Extraordinaire: Donald McKay (1810-1880)

Source: Wikimedia Commons (Southworth & Hawes via Metropolitan Museum)

The first ship to slide down the ways at the new yard was *New World*, a 1,404-ton packet that was the largest in the world and the first three-deck packet to sail the Atlantic run. She was followed by *Stag Hound*, which was, at 1,534 tons, the largest and longest merchant ship afloat at the time and the first 'extreme clipper'. She spread nearly 6,000 square yards (over an acre) of canvas, which brought her undone when, sixty days out, she was dismasted. She put into Valparaíso for five days to repair the damage and still made California in 113 days. Her round trip netted her owners a tidy $80,000.

The Largest Clipper

The 1,782-ton *Flying Cloud*, which would prove to be the fastest clipper afloat, was also the largest merchant ship at the time she was launched. Donald McKay built big ships. Several more of his vessels would be the largest in the world at the time of their launching. But the biggest ship he ever built (and perhaps the biggest wooden ship built in the modern era) was the mighty *Great Republic*.

Donald McKay's Biggest Clipper: *Great Republic*

Source: James E. Buttersworth

Great Republic was launched in 1853, a four-masted, four-decked, but ill-fated behemoth designated a 'clipper barque'. Rated at a massive 4,555 tons (old measure), it was as if some divine power had decreed that she was just too big. At 335 feet long, 53 feet beam, and 35 feet deep, she had a length-to-beam ratio of 6.3:1. Her mainmast mainsail yard was 120 feet long, more than twice the beam of the ship, and she would have set stunsails outside of that.

At Christmas 1853, while loading in New York for what would have been her maiden voyage, she caught fire. Embers from four other wooden ships which, themselves had been set alight from embers blown from a bakery that was in flames onshore, were responsible. Three of the four other ships were destroyed. *Great Republic* was towed away on fire and scuttled short of her waterline to save the hull. It was a blow for McKay because she was underinsured.

Nathaniel Palmer bought the hull and had her rebuilt. But he rebuilt her with only three decks, which reduced her capacity rating to 3,357 tons. He also modified her sail plan so that she could sail with half the crew that was originally intended. Even in her reduced state, she was still by far the largest merchant ship in the world.

The Limit of Wooden Construction

When first built, the *Great Republic* consumed 1.5 million super feet of pine (one square foot by one inch thick), 2,056 tons of white oak, 336 tons of iron, and 56 tons of copper. The amount of pine was about three times the volume required for a large clipper ship. It was clear McKay was reaching the limit for a ship hull made of wood.

So much timber was required to stiffen a hull of this size that the interior was described as being like a 'forest'—a jumble of struts and stanchions that inhibited the loading and unloading of cargo. It was a problem the British clipper builders would overcome by using their material of choice—wrought iron—when they began to produce the last generation of clippers. These were the so-called composite ships that used iron extensively in the keel and frames of the vessel to overcome the deficiencies of the wooden American clippers.

The British had been caught flat-footed by the American ship designers. On the other hand, the Americans had stuck with wood long past its practicality and neglected to hone their skills in the working of iron, and later steel, which, like steam, was the future. They built ships in primitive conditions on the bank of a river or harbour with mainly manual labour and limited mechanisation. Great Britain, the most highly industrialised country in the world at the time, was pouring in money to industrialise the shipbuilding process as much as possible.

Larger size or, strictly speaking, longer length, held out the possibility of higher speed. McKay's penchant for flat-bottomed design meant that his ships were generally classified as 'medium clippers'. The enormous rigs he designed to power those hulls meant that his vessels were destined to write his name into the history of wooden merchant ship design. Besides building some of the largest and fastest clippers, over his life, McKay designed no fewer than seventeen packets, thirty-six clippers, six schooners, and eight other sailing craft as well as various naval vessels.

Matthew Maury, Scientific Sailor

In 1850, there were twenty new clippers on the California run. By 1851, forty more were engaged on the route. The skippers were hard-drivers and believed this was the best way to get a ship from one place to another as quickly as possible.

In another case of 'the man and the hour', enter Matthew Fontaine Maury.

Matthew Maury (1806-1873)

Source: www.history.navy

A US naval lieutenant, Maury had, for his outspokenness about the need for reform of certain of the navy's procedures, been buried as superintendent of the charts and instruments department. Among other things, his office was the repository of all the logbooks of naval voyages, and he realised that, far from being a pile of mouldering records in which there was no interest, here was a valuable resource.

In his days as a sailing master, Maury had been frustrated by a lack of charts on the currents and wind systems for the most frequented passages, including around the Horn. In 1847, he published his first *Charts and Sailing Directions*. This document drew on the information of wind current and even ocean temperature he had so patiently extracted from the logbooks and recommended the best routes to Europe and South America and around Cape Horn to California.

From his painstaking research, Maury was able to make recommendations for each month, and even sometimes each week, of the year. Hungry for more data, he urged merchant masters to keep daily records of 'all observable facts relating to winds, currents, and other phenomena'. To gain their cooperation, he offered copies of his charts in return for their logs.

Remarkably, the first four vessels to follow his directions shaved ten days off the trip to California! On the trip covering 11,000 nautical miles to Australia around the Cape of Good Hope, he is credited with reducing the voyage time from an average of 125 days to a little over 90. As the distance via the

Suez Canal was not much shorter, a clipper ship, using the perpetual westerlies of the Great Southern Ocean, could compete favourably with the steamers. Even the youngest of mariners could access the experience of a thousand experienced skippers who had sailed the route before them.

Shortly after *Stag Hound* sailed for California, Donald McKay began work on another clipper at his East Boston shipyard. She was named the *Flying Cloud* and, at 1,782 tons, was the largest merchant ship afloat at the time. Her length-to-beam ratio was almost 6:1, slim indeed.

On her maiden run to California, with her navigator referencing Maury's *Charts and Sailing Directions,* she completed the voyage in eighty-nine days, twenty-one hours. She would later do it in eighty-nine days, eight hours.

Flying Cloud would become Donald McKay's most famous ship.

Eighty-nine days was now the magic number, and *Flying Cloud* held the record for 135 years, from 1854 to 1989, when it was broken by a racing yacht. But for a cargo-laden merchant sailing vessel completing the voyage without the aid of modern technology in the form of GPS or global weather forecasting, the record still stands.

Eleanor Creesy, Maury, and Flying Cloud

The record-breaking voyage of the *Flying Cloud* is notable for another reason. The navigator was a woman. Eleanor Creesy was the wife of the captain, Josiah Creesy, and had learned navigation from her master mariner father, John Prentiss. An experienced ocean navigator and devotee of Matthew Maury, she often sailed with her husband. She was astounded at the speed of the ship in the early part of the voyage and was constantly checking and rechecking her calculations.

One day, *Flying Cloud* covered 389 nautical miles, a greater distance than anyone on earth had ever travelled in a day up until that time. Josiah Cressy acknowledged his wife as the better navigator, and the two continued to sail together until the Civil War when he volunteered to skipper a small clipper ship. After the war, they retired inland, Josiah dying in 1871 but Eleanor living on until 1900 when she died aged eighty-five.

Sadly, *Flying Cloud* was wrecked off the South Australian coast in 1870.

Donald McKay's Beautiful Clipper: *Flying Cloud*

Source: From Jack Spurling lithograph; author's own collection

The old-time hard-driving skippers were sceptical of Maury's sailing directions, but in time, it was demonstrated that they saved time, and time was money. Soon many skippers from many countries were saving logs for him. It was pointed out that on the outward passages to Rio, San Francisco, and Melbourne, Maury's instructions were saving shipowners over 2 million dollars per year. Not only was he saving international maritime commerce money, he was also laying down the basics of what would become the science of oceanography.

The Quest for Speed

As the ships grew in size, so the number of crew required to man them expanded. Crew wages ranged from 8 to 15 dollars a month, which was a pittance for such hard, back-breaking, and potentially dangerous work. Ships found it difficult to find crews in San Francisco as men left to try their luck at the goldfields. The harbour became increasingly cluttered with ships, with some completely abandoned. At one stage, it was a veritable forest of masts, with over 300 ships unable to sail for lack of crew. The scarcity also hurt ships sailing for Europe with the 'packet rats' deserting to work their passages to California. Skippers were reduced to 'shanghaiing' or drugging and kidnapping crews for the voyage back east.

In 1852, sixty clippers were launched, again bigger than they had been hitherto. Two of those ships were Samuel Hartt Pook's *Defiance*, distinguished by its completely flat floor, and Donald McKay's *Sovereign of the Seas*. McKay's ship was rated at 2,421 tons and had a mainmast reaching 201 feet above the deck. It is not hard to understand why these ships were commonly described as being 'over-hatted'.

In 1854, *Sovereign of the Seas* became the first ship ever to cover more than 400 nautical miles in twenty-four hours. In fact, she covered 421 nautical miles and at one stage was flying along at 22 knots, or 25 miles per hour (41 kilometres per hour).

During the first leg of her maiden voyage, skippered by McKay's brother Lauchlan, a noted hard-driver, she was dismasted but still made San Francisco in 103 days. On a subsequent leg of the voyage, she made a record passage from Honolulu to New York, with a cargo of whale oil, in eighty-two days, having earned $135,000 in nine months. This last leg of the voyage back to New York was made with a crew of only 34 hands out of a normal complement of 105. She lost a lot to desertions in San Francisco.

Sovereign of the Seas then broke the record to Liverpool making the passage in thirteen days, thirteen and a half hours. In 1853, she was chartered by James Baines of the Black Ball Line. There was no connection to the American packet company for the Australia trade, but she was in the tea trade when, in 1859, she was wrecked in the Straits of Malacca on a voyage from Hamburg to China.

Sovereign of the Seas was an exemplar that burned brightly, but briefly, along with *Flying Cloud*, as two of the great manifestations of the era of the medium clippers.

The Australian Gold Rush

In 1851, within two years of the Californian gold rush, a returning Australian, one Lawrence Hargrave, decided to try his luck 150 miles inland from the city of Sydney, for no other reason than the topography reminded him of California. He struck gold, and just as the discovery at Sutter's Mill was suppressed for some months, so the wealthy landed interests (the 'squatters' or graziers) tried in vain to keep the news from getting out.

Word quickly got around, and soon even richer fields were discovered north of Melbourne. The presence of the big American clippers meant that this rush could be supplied much faster than had been the case in California, and in turn, it meant that those ships had a new market.

Besides getting diggers and supplies to California, the clippers were also employed in getting thousands of hopefuls to Australia. In 1851, Australia's population was about 400,000. By 1861, due largely to the ready availability of ships, it had almost tripled to 1.1 million. In the state of Victoria, home to the most productive goldfields, the population rose from 77,000 in 1851 to 538,000 a decade later, an almost sevenfold increase. In 1861, Victoria produced a third of all the gold mined in the world. By 1901, at the time of the federation of the Australian states, Victoria's population had swelled to 4 million.

Extending the Boom

Servicing the Australian goldfields, which were much richer than those in California, extended the clipper boom, and with Australia a British colony, it was time for the British shipping companies to get into the market. The vast distances without access to coal kept the steamers at bay.

An Englishman, James Baines, had the clipper *Marco Polo* built in Canada (then a British colony) for his Black Ball Line, sending her to Australia and back in five months, twenty-one days and covering 438 miles in one day. Before *Marco Polo*'s record voyage, ships sailing to Australia turned east at between thirty-seven and forty degrees south. Matthew Maury recommended that vessels continue south until they reached the 'roaring forties', those wonderful westerly winds that blow constantly and unobstructed around the globe at these latitudes. Once they unloaded and reloaded in Australia, his advice was to repeat the process for the leg across to Cape Horn. Each voyage thus became a circumnavigation of the globe.

'Great Circle' Routes

These voyages were further shortened, distance-wise, by sailing what were referred to as 'great circle' routes. Great circle routes sailed the shortest distance between two points on the surface of the spheroid (a slightly squashed sphere) earth, as opposed to a straight line drawn through the earth's interior. Euclidean geometry's rhumb line (the shortest distance between two points is a straight line) was replaced by 'geodesics' where straight lines are replaced by 'great circles' on a globe whose centre is the centre of the earth.

Following strict great circles to and from Australia would have taken sailing ships into very high latitudes, so high as to be impracticable. The risk of losing a ship to storms, which increased in their ferocity the further south you went, was amplified. You also need to be wary of icebergs. Experience showed that following the 50 degrees south latitude line was a more reliable route, even though 55 degrees south is 160 nautical miles shorter on the voyage from Australia to Cape Horn. For those not of a navigational bent, it will be appreciated that because the earth is a spheroid, sailing around it more towards the bottom is shorter than sailing around it on a latitude where the circumference of the earth is much greater.

The Dominance of the American Wooden Clipper

James Baines had several more ships built in Canada and some in England, but their performance was not up to that of the *Marco Polo* or the American clippers. There was only one place to have large fast ships built, and he had no option but to turn to the United States. Donald McKay's *Sovereign of the Seas* had just sailed from New York to Liverpool in under fourteen days (with the designer on board), and Baines didn't hesitate, commissioning him to build three passenger vessels for the Australia run.

The result would be *Lightning, Champion of the Seas*, and the *James Baines*. Baines would order a fourth ship, the *Donald McKay*, later. The latter three vessels were three-deckers, with *Lightning* the smallest of the four. The competition from steamers was becoming more and more apparent, so much so that Baines challenged any ship, sail or steam, to make a faster passage than the *Sovereign of the Seas* (which he had chartered) to Australia. Although her voyage was not particularly meritorious, it beat the opposition.

The fit-out on these four ships, however, reflected the increased competition from steamships and was a distinct contrast to the emigrant packets of the 1840s. There were comfortable, well-ventilated quarters for the steerage passengers and sumptuous accommodation for the cabin patrons. As well, they were big, strongly rigged ships capable of considerable speed. On her maiden voyage from Liverpool to Melbourne in December 1854, *Champion of the Seas* sailed 465 nautical miles in one day, a record that has never been beaten by a merchant sailing ship.

It is interesting to note that all the very fast one-day records (more than 400 nautical miles in twenty-four hours) were made in an easterly direction 'running their easting down' before the prevailing westerlies to Australia and then home. Of these, only four were made in the northern hemisphere. All the rest were made in the 'roaring forties' or higher latitudes. Carl C. Cutler, the acknowledged world expert on the era, called the ships that frequented the route 'the greyhounds of the seas'.

The *Donald McKay*, at 2,598 tons, was the largest of Baines's ships and, except for the *Great Republic*, the largest merchant ship afloat. Moreover, she carried more canvas than the *Great Republic* and was fitted with a rigging innovation that allowed the crew to reef her topsails without going aloft. When one considers the difficulty of this task in heavy weather, especially as the rigs got bigger and bigger, and the crew who would have been lost overboard performing this task, it is surprising that the development of such an innovation took so long. The shipowner's bank balance and the ego and remuneration of the skipper were the overriding considerations of the clipper era.

Except in exceptional locations (like the entry ports for goldfields), the crew was disposable. It is not difficult to see why these great ships began losing men to the steamships: no 200-foot masts to climb, often in heavy weather; no pounding ice from frozen lines in gale-force winds; no living in wet clothes for weeks on end—all for continually declining wages. These were the conditions that applied as sailing ships sought to stay relevant in the face of steam propulsion.

Baines's rival on the Australian run was the White Star Line. The company had commissioned a large clipper from the design desk of Samuel Hartt Pook—the *Red Jacket*, measuring 2,305 tons. On her first run from New York to Liverpool, she came in in thirteen days, one hour—eclipsing *Sovereign of the Seas*'s time and establishing a record that still stands to this day.

Shortly after, *Red Jacket* raced *Lightning* to Melbourne and beat her by an incredible *ten* days. At the same time, she made the fastest sailing voyage ever between England and Australia—sixty-seven days, thirteen hours. Not to be outdone, the skipper of *Lightning* on the outward run, the infamous Captain James 'Bully' Forbes, set out to race *Red Jacket* back to London.

Red Jacket had left Melbourne under a legal cloud and with a badly stowed cargo of wool. Moreover, she struck a series of adverse weather conditions. Meanwhile, Forbes pushed *Lightning* hot in her wake and made Liverpool in sixty-seven days, the fastest passage ever. His round-trip time of five months, eight days, twenty-one hours set a record that still stands.

It is extraordinary just how much the egos of the top clipper captains were instrumental in setting records and in driving their ships to their limits to beat a competing vessel (and its skipper). But that sort of competition pushed the design of sailing ships forward and produced the fastest and, as form follows function, most beautiful ships the world has ever known.

Clipper Building Boom

Urged on by the money a clipper could earn, the demand for sharp (fast) ships reached extraordinary heights, and in 1853, no fewer than 125 new vessels slid down the ways. In Boston, five were launched in a single day! In that year, 145 clippers sailed for the goldfields, but the signs were emerging that the California trade was about to experience the fate of all booms, the inevitable bust.

If there is one immutable tradition in the shipping industry, it is the propensity to overbuild tonnage. A shipbuilding boom is always followed by a bust and an ensuing recession until world trade expands to take up the excess capacity. The chart below sets out one version of clipper ship construction. These numbers differ slightly from those quoted in the text, but the chart eloquently illustrates the rapid build-up to the peak year of 1853—and the equally rapid decline that followed.

American Clipper Construction: 1845-1857 (GRT OM)

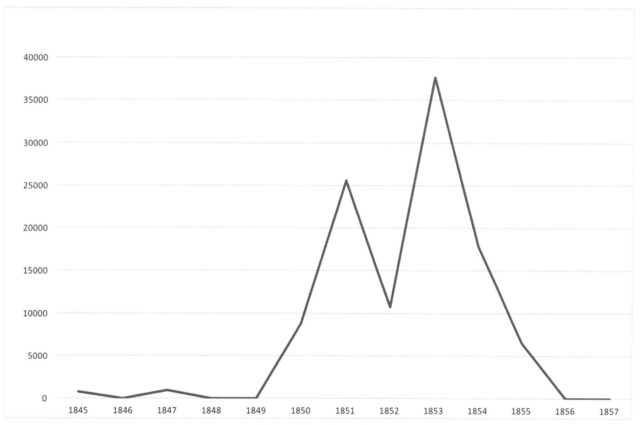

Source: Lars Bruzelius

The clipper building boom began immediately after the discovery of gold in California, and the first ships were launched in 1850 when a total of upwards of 9,000 gross register tons was launched. It is indicative of the relatively primitive, but flexible, means by which these ships were constructed that designers and builders could respond so immediately to the demand.

In 1851, launchings almost tripled to over 26,000 tons. They dropped to around 11,000 tons the next year, probably because an appreciable tonnage, for the most part built in 1852, was not finished until early the next year. The result was the launch of almost 38,000 tons of vessels, the boom's peak, in 1853. That the figures are distorted in this way is indicated by only 18,000 tons hitting the water the next year (1854). The average for the four years 1851–54 was around 23,000 tons per year, a remarkable feat of wooden shipbuilding.

But all good things must come to an end. In retrospect, it is obvious that the stimulus provided by the gold rushes that had been driving clipper ship construction was declining, and the need for fast, high-maintenance ships was sinking with it. Existing vessels would go on to service the emigrant trade to Australia with cargoes of wool and wheat on the way home around the Horn.

9
CHAPTER

The Decline of the Clipper Ships

The Glut and Depression

The year 1855 saw a considerable decline in clipper launchings with only about 6,000 tons being completed. The boom was over, and it had resulted in a massive overbuild. As the alluvial gold accessible to the amateur scrabblers was worked out, passenger and goods traffic associated with the original 'rush' declined precipitously. Too many shippers had entered the trade, freight rates were falling, and ships were being laid up for longer times.

The glorious 'greyhounds of the sea' dispersed.

No ships were built in 1856. By 1857, the whole industry was in deep depression. Wooden shipbuilding in America would never recover. The gold rush in Australia sustained the boom through the first half of the 1850s, but it too began to decline. The market had become glutted, and by 1855, there were 340 active clippers available.

One of the last great clippers to be built was the *Andrew Jackson*, a late entrant into the California trade but one that made a journey to San Francisco of eighty-nine days, one of only three ships to do so. America, which a few short years earlier had been at the very peak of her powers as a maritime nation, and whose magnificent ships had swept the oceans like those of no other nation, was headed for nautical decline. Worse still, the Civil War was not far off. In its aftermath, America's attention would turn inward towards the Great Western Plains and the conquest of the vast space between the eastern seaboard and its western extremity.

All was not completely gloom and doom. California began shipping wheat to the Atlantic ports, giving the clippers a backload, and the tea trade picked up with twenty-four American clippers loading tea for England in 1855.

The emigrant trade to Australia and New Zealand also enabled some of the ships to continue to earn a living. It was a long-distance trade at which the clippers excelled, and it lacked coaling stations for the steamers. Some, however, would eventually be reduced to transporting coal to waypoints on steamer routes and to fuel steam tugs in busy Asian ports. The cotton and timber trades across the Atlantic were still viable, but the highest-paying work had been usurped by the steamers.

A Last Hurrah

There were, nonetheless, international conflicts, such as the Crimean War and the Indian Mutiny, that gave temporary respite, siphoning off excess tonnage. Here the enormous carrying capacity of the medium clippers (that could carry twice their registered tonnage in displacement terms) meant they could earn a living transporting men and materiel to the theatres of war.

In 1853, to protect their interests in the Middle East and India, Great Britain, and France declared war on Russia, and in 1854, they laid siege to the city of Sevastopol. Getting a large number of troops and their equipment to the Black Sea required big ships, and the government chartered several now-idle American clippers for the job. One of the vessels was the *Great Republic*, now newly rebuilt by Nathaniel Palmer.

On her arrival in London, she created a sensation when it was found that no dock could accommodate her. Lying in the stream, the skipper was asked 'whether he had left any lumber in America, or whether he had brought it all with him'. While this comment may have been made in jest, the *Great Republic*, even in her cut-down state, measured 3,357 tons and was 334 feet long on the deck and had a 53-foot beam. Overall, including her 86-foot-long jib boom and the overhang of her protruding spanker boom, she measured 450 feet. Originally designed as a four-masted barque with four decks, she was rebuilt as a fully rigged ship with three decks plus poop and forecastle decks. The utilisation of the clippers gave the Anglo-French forces an advantage in sea-based logistics that was crucial in the battle for Sevastopol and their eventual victory.

The Crimean War was another case of cometh the hour; cometh (in this case) the woman. Born in 1820 in Florence, Italy, to wealth and high social position, Florence Nightingale was a nurse and social reformer. She arrived in Sevastopol in 1854 at the head of a corps of nurses to find literally thousands of wounded British soldiers languishing in appallingly unsanitary and inhumane circumstances. More men were dying of typhoid than their wounds. It is hard to imagine a more intimidating set of circumstances, and her resolution of this situation is the stuff of legend.

There was another woman who earned a reputation as the 'Florence Nightingale of the ocean', and her rise to fame occurred not long after the original Florence was making her name in the Crimea.

In 1856, the extreme clipper *Neptune's Car* was on a voyage to San Francisco when, off the Horn, the captain, Joshua Patten, fell sick with 'brain fever' and went blind. His first officer was under arrest for insubordination, and so the captain's nineteen-year-old wife, Mary Patten, took command. She had learned navigation on a previous voyage and, with the assistance of a faithful but illiterate second mate, fought the big clipper around the Horn and brought her safely to San Francisco, caring for her husband all the while.

James Baines (1822-1889)

Source: The Colonial Clippers, Basil Lubbock James Brown & Son

The immense carrying capacity of these ships was again demonstrated in 1857, when three of James Baines's ships, *Lightning, James Baines,* and *Champion of the Seas,* were chartered by the British government to transport troops to Calcutta as part of their attempt to put down the Indian Mutiny. As an indication of just how famous these ships were, when two of them, *James Baines* and *Champion of the Seas,* were in London loading 1,000 soldiers each for the voyage, Queen Victoria asked that they not depart until she could visit.

She was given a tour of the *James Baines* and, on her departure, expressed her pleasure that 'so splendid a merchant ship belonged to her dominions'. The monarch seems to have chosen her words carefully, presumably to avoid reference to the fact that despite the ship being owned by one of her subjects, the magnificent vessel was both designed and built in the United States—a colony her grandfather, King George III, had lost through revolution barely eighty years before.

Crossing the United States and the Suez Canal

In 1858, the first stagecoach clattered into San Francisco twenty-four days after leaving St Louis, about one-quarter of the time taken by clipper around Cape Horn. Although much faster, each coach could carry a tiny fraction of the freight and passengers.

The year 1869 was pivotal for sailing ships. The Suez Canal opened, and the first passengers travelling by rail from the eastern states arrived at the Pacific Railroad's Alameda terminus at San Francisco Bay. The opening of the Suez Canal gave steamers an advantage in passages to the Orient, and the coast-to-coast railroad connection in America revolutionised the settlement and development of the country's interior. It would make the transport of people and merchandise from the east quicker, safer, and cheaper.

Moreover, the capacity of the railroad to move prodigious amounts of both people and goods sealed the fate of the 'Cape Horners', as the great clippers on the west coast route were known. Just as sailing ships had proved superior in these respects to land caravans at the dawning of the Age of Exploration, so the railroad would constrain the routes available to sailing ships over three and a half centuries later.

Idle clippers were forced into the coal, case oil, and lumber business—or the detested guano trade.

A Sad End: The Guano and Coolie Trades

After ending the slave trade, the British had been the first to experiment with 'indentured labour' when they imported 200 Chinese to work sugar plantations in Trinidad in 1806. While Indian coolies were mainly transported between British colonies, between 250,000 and 500,000 Chinese 'coolies' were transported to British, French, Dutch, and Spanish colonies in the Americas, Africa, and Southeast Asia in the period 1847 to 1874. During these twenty-seven years, 125,000 Chinese were sent to Cuba alone. They were also brought to work on plantations in Australia or build railway lines in the United States and Canada. Others ended up in Peru where most suffered a fate worse than death.

On one ship, destined for the sugar plantations of Cuba, there were floggings, suicides, and finally, mutiny, with the coolies trying to set the ship on fire. By the time the ship arrived in Havana, 130 coolies had perished, seventy killed when the mutiny was suppressed, and the others died of dysentery. The coolie trade even claimed the beautiful John Griffiths-designed *Sea Witch* when, in 1856, with some 500 coolies on board, she piled up on a reef a few miles from Havana: an ignominious end for one of the greatest clippers ever built.

The infamous guano trade arose from the trend towards more intensive agriculture in Europe. Guano is made up of the faeces and bones of seabirds (mainly the Guanay cormorant) and seals, accumulated on islands which they had used as breeding and feeding grounds since time immemorial. It was found to be rich in nitrogen, phosphate, and potassium, the three key nutrients for plant growth. Farmers could abandon traditional practices like crop rotation and planting leguminous crops that had been applied for millennia to increase agricultural yields and, instead, fertilise with guano. The practice became known as high-farming.

Coolies were brought from China to the Chincha Islands (Islas Chinchas). These specks of rock, some 13 miles off the coast of Peru, held the most valuable sources of guano in the world, with some deposits up to 150 feet thick. It only remained for them to be excavated and loaded on to ships.

The trade was lucrative, and the more lucrative, the more reprehensible it became. Some of the unfortunates were indentured (paid a small lump sum) for five years of labour. Others were simply kidnapped. In fact, they all became slaves, and most never saw their native land again. They were either worked to death, died from breathing guano dust, contracted dysentery, or committed suicide. They were shipped in terrible conditions that approximated the slave trade, treated cruelly, and half-starved. But they brought the ship owner between 50 and 80 US dollars per head when delivered into the hellhole that was the Chinchas.

The Infamous Islas Chinchas

Source: https://creativecommons.org/licenses/by-sa/3.0/

Mining guano was in full swing before the clipper era, and it was only after the gold rushes that the clippers became involved. The Peruvian government ran the industry, and royalties became its main source of revenue. Ships engaged in the guano trade came from all over America and Europe and would sometimes be held up for up to three months, waiting to load. After the mid-1850s, with clipper shipowners desperate for cargoes, they sent them to China for coolies or to the Chinchas for guano.

Just a few short years before, the clippers had been the queens of international mercantile trade. Their owners must have been very short of profitable utilisation to get involved in the coolie trade. But shipowners, especially those desperate for cargo, showed themselves to be quite capable of turning a blind eye to inhumanity, as they had shown in less desperate circumstances in the Atlantic emigrant trade. It was pretty much a last-ditch stand, however. In a few years, most of them would be out of business, consumed by the economic cataclysm in the industry that began in 1857.

To load guano, the ship would be drawn up close to a cliff, and the guano shovelled by the coolies into chutes that terminated in the ship's hold. The ship became enveloped in a cloud of yellow dust that got into every nook and cranny, completely coating the ship and its rigging in a way that was very difficult to remove. The north-flowing cold current off the west coast of South America renders it the most arid desert in the world. The only (very meagre) sources of water were distillation and condensation. Under these circumstances, the ships would have to wait for the rainstorms off the Patagonian coast to finally rid themselves of it.

The coolie trade was a scandal and widely criticised in the international media as simply another form of slavery. England banned its ships from being involved in the trade in 1855, so the Peruvian government simply bought up American clippers and carried on.

In 1856, however, it, too, succumbed to international criticism and made it illegal.

It was not until 1862 that Abraham Lincoln introduced legislation to end it for American ships. The vessels that had been so perfectly designed for speed and grace were ending up, rigged down, in a trade where neither was a consideration. The guano industry would not only support the last of the wooden clippers, but the demand for fertiliser and munitions would provide work for a new generation of great windships. They were the giant riveted iron and steel 'windjammers', and the source of the minerals would be the rich nitrate fields of northern Chile.

Ironically, despite the ability of chemical fertilisers to increase agricultural yields very quickly, their long-term application causes soil hardening and decreased organic matter and pH. Chemical fertilisers also run off during heavy rains, leading to environmental issues such as algal blooms. These problems are factors in the increasing popularity of organic horticultural products, the cultivation of which has revived interest in guano.

Vale Clipper Americana

Beginning with the liner companies sailing packets back and forth across the Atlantic in 1818 and ending with the outbreak of the American Civil War in 1861, American designers and shipbuilders and merchant navy crews dominated the seas for much of the nineteenth century. English shipbuilders, safe behind the protective wall of the Navigation Acts, saw no real need to improve on their ships' speed or weatherliness, or how hard they drove them. In the forty years before the repeal of the acts, the American designers, shipbuilders, and captains all made a quantum leap in ship design that swept away the competition.

It would not be until the Civil War (which would practically destroy its merchant marine) and the spanning of the continent by rail that Americans would turn inwards towards their frontier. To young men who would have ordinarily gone to sea for travel and adventure, the frontier held the promise of adventure and prosperity without the high risk and poor pay and, at times, appalling conditions, so typical of maritime careers.

The Californian gold rush stimulated demand at the start of the clipper era, and because it was regarded as a coastal trade, the Americans had it to themselves. But they were already so far ahead in their ability to create fast ships that no nation on earth could hold a candle to them. They continued to excel in the tea trade after the Navigation Acts were repealed and in the gold rush and emigrant trade to Australia, which were also open slather.

In the late 1850s, the Peninsular and Oriental Steam Navigation Company (today's P&O) extended its line from Suez to Australia and began to give the clippers some serious competition. However, the McKay-designed American ships (*Lightning, James Baines*, and *Champion of the Seas*) continued to perform well on the direct route to Australia, serving for over thirteen years. *Red Jacket* went on to make the trip for another decade.

Throughout much of the 1800s, America led the world in merchant sailing ship design and construction. Their pursuit of profitability and speed, however, meant that these wooden ships had become so large that their cargo spaces were turning into a forest of timber beams and props, making them difficult to load and unload. Also, supplies of vital shipbuilding timbers, which had given them such an advantage in the early decades of the century, were declining. Moreover, wooden ships could not be built to carry the tremendous leverage of the clipper rig for more than five or six voyages without being rebuilt. Their maintenance was high, and increasingly, their rigs had to be cut down because the hulls were no longer strong enough to withstand the enormous forces generated by their original set-up. Cut down, they required less crew.

With the recession of 1857, few shipowners could afford to build new ships or even refit older ones. Many of the east coast shipyards were wiped out, a reduction in shipbuilding capacity that was also a reason for the inability of the industry to revive following the Civil War. While the Americans had hitherto considered themselves a maritime nation, after the gold rushes, their attention turned inward and westward, towards the riches of the ever-expanding frontier. According to Carl C. Cutler,

> *America, which had been sea-minded for two centuries, was nautically decadent in 1855 . . . The mere opening of the West called for too great an effort and drained too completely the mental and financial resources of the East. There can be no doubt, however, that the internal strife which preceded the Civil War and continued for many years thereafter, accelerated the downfall of the merchant fleet and effectually retarded its revival. By 1860, the process could go little further. There was an attack on anything resembling public interest in matters pertaining to shipbuilding or in the exploits of the ships themselves.*

American ships so dominated the oceans that resentment in Great Britain grew about the amount of business going to US shipyards and shipping companies, with James Baines being accused of being anti-British. To pacify public opinion, in 1855, Baines ordered an enormous 2,600-ton emigrant clipper from Alexander Hall & Sons of Aberdeen, Scotland. She was named the *Schomberg*, after the emigration commissioner in Liverpool, an influential person when it came to securing emigrant contracts.

The Big but Ill-fated British Wooden Clipper *Schomberg*

Source: Lithograph by T G Dutton1855 Wikipedia Commons

The *Schomberg* was the most luxurious and well-built clipper of the period, as well as being the largest wooden sailing ship ever built in Britain. The four layers of diagonal planking that gave her a minimum hull thickness of 13.5 inches meant her frames could be more widely spaced. She had four decks. Her mainsail yard was 112 feet long, and she carried five sails on each mast.

Extravagant claims were made for the new vessel, and Baines gave Captain James Forbes command for her maiden voyage to Melbourne. Forbes, ever the boaster, claimed he would make the trip in sixty days. After crossing the equator, *Schomberg* sailed into calm and light airs that lasted for a fortnight, making such a feat impossible. When it became clear there was no way he was going to be able to make good on his boast, Forbes sulked and lost interest in the voyage.

The ship made landfall along the infamous 'Wreck Coast' on the south-east coast of the state of Victoria. When warned by the mate that the vessel was perilously close to land off Cape Otway, Forbes failed to take immediate action. The wind dropped, and the *Schomberg* drifted on to an uncharted reef (now called Schomberg Reef) on 27 December 1856. All mail, crew, and passengers managed to be offloaded by a passing coastal steamer, but the ship broke up on 6 January. Part of the vessel washed ashore in New Zealand—some 2,414 kilometres away.

An inquiry roundly condemned Forbes, and he lost his job with the Black Ball Line. He gradually sank, through a chain of minor commands, into obscurity. The *Schomberg's* fastest run was 368 nautical miles in twenty-four hours—an average of 15 knots.

The Rise of the English Tea Clippers

With the financial depression of 1857, the Americans withdrew from the tea trade, and the dominance of sail on the China run would not be seriously challenged by auxiliary steamers. Auxiliary steamers were steel sailing ships equipped with large steam engines but also with substantial sailing rigs that enabled them to set sails and take advantage of the wind when it favoured them. Being neither chalk nor cheese, however, they struggled to make a profit.

Meanwhile, true steamers, after allowing for machinery and fuel, did not yet have the fuel efficiency to carry sufficient cargo to make enough money. For another decade, therefore, a new generation of British clippers had the tea trade to themselves. Their designs were American, but they lacked the waterline length to break the world records set by the big American timber ships. Although not as many were built, they would, nevertheless, capture the nautical imagination of the British.

Great Britain, with its industrialisation of the steel shipbuilding process, had become far and away the largest shipbuilder in the world, especially of steamships. It would also reign over production in the last great age of sailing ship construction—the great windjammers.

The East Indiamen that had dominated the British trade with China lost their monopoly in 1834, opening up the trade to competition between fast sailing ships, but it would still be protected from the American behemoths until the repeal of the Navigation Acts in 1849. The *Schomberg* was not the end of clipper construction in Great Britain, and lacking native timbers, it began to build a series of 'composite' vessels that used wrought-iron framing. For the planking, they turned to another of Great Britain's comparative advantages in shipbuilding: the iron frames were clad with mahogany and teak, excellent shipbuilding timbers imported from India, Pakistan, and Burma.

The shipbuilding depression in America, built as it was on the gold rushes, had little effect on Great Britain, and its continuing thirst for tea led to the construction of a new generation of small clippers. After the repeal of the Navigation Acts, American clippers had entered the tea trade, shipping people and merchandise around the Horn to California and then sailing to China to load tea. The big, fast ships were excellent at landing the new harvest rapidly into England and received premium rates. Not only did they deliver the cargo quicker, enabling the merchant to get the best prices, but it was also believed that the shorter the sea time, the tastier the tea. An American clipper might receive £6/ton freight, whereas the slower English ships earned a mere £3.10/ton. Although the trade was lucrative, only 139 passages were made, and only three ships made more than three passages. The end of the gold rush traffic to California ended American involvement.

The big weakness of the American clippers was that they were made of softwood. Over time, it absorbed water, making them slow and sluggish in light airs. A crack clipper would only be good for about five years before it became strained and waterlogged.

British clippers were also made of wood, but it was hardwood and less prone to absorbing moisture. Moreover, they were designed for the tea trade, which did not involve negotiating Cape Horn, and as such, they did not need to be as big. Given the shortage of hardwood in England, some were built as 'country ships' in India using the superb materials available there. *Sylph*, *Waterwitch*, *Rob Roy*, and *Lady Grant* were all this provenance and were scaled up cutters in their hull lines. These vessels had fairly low length-to-breadth ratios and, contrary to the American practice, steep deadrise.

The pioneer builder in Great Britain was Alexander Hall & Sons of Aberdeen. They first made their name with *Scottish Maid*, a schooner with fine lines and a length-to-beam ratio of almost 5:1. But she was small, measuring only 142 tons. The first fully rigged clipper ship by Hall was the *Colloony* built in 1846, but again, she measured only 287 tons.

Generally, British ships were less than half the tonnage of their American counterparts, and their length limited their outright speed. They were fast passage-makers, however, able to keep up quite reasonable speeds in a greater variety of conditions. They also benefited from the ready availability of cheaper copper sheathing and superior cordage developed for the Royal Navy. In the 1850s, there were only three British clippers greater than 1,500 tons—the ill-fated *Schomberg*, *Tayleur*, and *Eastern Monarch*—whereas there were seventy in America, twelve of which exceeded 2,000 tons.

American clippers had to be built big to cope with Cape Horn. Their main market was California, and to ply that trade, they had to round the Horn twice, one way from east to west against the prevailing wind. Built for the China tea trade, the smaller British ships travelled to China via the Cape of Good Hope. Smaller vessels were also better able to accommodate both the nature of the anchorages at their trading destinations and the stevedoring facilities and practices available there. The Chinese ports, such as Canton and Shanghai, were generally large river mouths that were poorly charted and with constantly changing obstacles such as shoals and bars. Chinese stevedores, working from lighters, were also accustomed to loading smaller ships, which they did with amazing skill, packing cargo so tightly it rarely moved no matter what sea conditions were encountered.

Iron and Steel Replace Wood

British shipbuilders had been suitably awed by the design of American merchant ships when they first started to appear in British ports after the repeal of the Navigation Acts. The extent to which Great Britain had fallen behind became even more evident when London tea merchants preferred the fleeter American vessels to their own. American competition motivated British shipbuilders to apply their comparative advantage in working iron in a new approach to sailing ship construction. The technique of composite construction—using iron to provide structural strength and wooden cladding—eventually gave way to riveted cast-iron plate and, ultimately, steel.

On the other hand, only four iron-hulled deepwater sailing vessels and twelve steel-hulled ships were ever built in the United States. The iron vessels were built at shipyards on the Delaware River while the steel craft were constructed by the Sewall shipyard in Maine, which had made the necessary capital investment in steel ship construction.

Wood had always been plentiful and cheap in America whereas iron and steel were expensive due to import taxes. Steel remained too expensive for mercantile shipbuilding until the 1880s, by which time interest in sailing ships was very low. Those that were built were made of wood up until production ceased altogether in the early years of the twentieth century.

As a footnote to this era, the *Wavertree*, a fully rigged, 2,150-ton windjammer launched in 1885 in Southampton, England, was one of the last wrought-iron sailing ships ever built. Now a museum on New York's East River, she is the only surviving iron-hulled sailing vessel left in the world.

England had been using iron in ship construction from as early as 1675 when the shortage of good English oak was already becoming apparent. In 1781, an English warship, the HMS *Agamemnon*, a 64-gun vessel with a crew of 500, required the felling of 2,000 mature oak trees for her construction. In one year, the Royal Navy used up 1.5 million loads of timber. England was importing American oak from Canada and hardwood and softwood from the Baltic, but they were believed to be inferior. The best oak came from Bosnia, which seemed to have an inexhaustible supply.

In 1787, an English ironmaster constructed a barge seventy feet long and nearly seven feet wide from riveted iron. People were incredulous that iron could float on water! The serious use of iron in shipbuilding started around 1818 when the East India Company, unable to obtain enough 'grown knees' to connect deck beams to the vessels' frames, began to employ iron angle brackets. An iron steamship by the name of the *Aaron Manby* was built in 1821 and an iron sailing ship in 1838.

By 1852, more than 150 iron ships were listed at Lloyds, of which 100 were steamships. The most famous of these was the SS *Great Britain*, built in 1845 and, until 1854, at 330 feet, the longest passenger ship in the world. The first screw-driven ocean-going iron ship, her launching was full of portent for sailing vessels when she crossed the Atlantic uphill and against the prevailing westerlies in just fourteen days. Auxiliary vessels required both steamship and sailing ship crews and were seldom successful.

Ironically, the SS *Great Britain* was converted to an all-sail ship in 1881.

From the design example so explicitly provided by the great American wooden clippers, British naval architects would go on to produce a range of China clippers, albeit less than half the size of their transatlantic counterparts, and would not seek to emulate the achievements of the great American ships. Nevertheless, they weren't smaller and slavish imitations of the American giants and were good passage-makers given their ability in light airs. They were designed more carefully for a specific trade—tea—and because of passages needing to be made against the monsoon, weatherliness was an important factor.

The Americans came at clipper design from the direction of the Western Ocean packets providing liner services: large wooden ships designed to carry lots of general cargo and people. The early British flyers eschewed flat floors and minimum deadrise, preferring steep floors and hollow garboards (the planks immediately above the keel). An early example was *Cairngorm*, built by Alexander Hall & Son for Jardine Matheson. But length was still important.

The *Annandale*, built shortly after, was 227 feet long and had a breadth of 32 feet, a ratio of over 7.1:1! Another, *Queensberry*, had a ratio of 7.2:1. These length-to-beam ratios were only made possible by the composite construction—wrought-iron frames and multiple diagonal plank sheathing. They would not have been possible in an all-wooden American ship. A later iron-framed and iron-clad ship, *Tempest*, raised the ratio to 7.5:1, which was probably the highest ever achieved. The American clipper *Romance of the Seas* took the ratio to its limit for a wooden ship. Its length was six times its beam.

The British clippers had another advantage. American ships built of wood contained a virtual forest of beams and struts cluttering the cargo space and inhibiting loading and unloading. Henry Moorsom, whose method of measuring the tonnage of sailing ships was applied after 1836 (and became law in Britain in 1854), calculated that the cargo-carrying capacity of a ship built of iron was 16 per cent more than one built of oak (hardwood) and 23 per cent more than one built of fir (softwood).

Traditionally, tonnage, a measure of the ship's internal volume and hence its cargo-carrying capacity, was measured by multiplying the length by the beam by the depth. Depth was assumed to be half the beam. This system was subject to abuses that affected the stability and seaworthiness of the vessels as builders strove to minimise the breadth measurement but maximise carrying capacity. This was replaced by the 'Moorsom system', which calculated the number of units of 100 cubic feet available for carrying cargo.

Although British ships adopted the 'new measurement' (NM) method from 1836, America continued to measure by the 'old measurement' (OM) throughout the great age of the clippers, up until after the Civil War in 1865. The upshot is that American tonnage figures tend to overstate the size of the ship compared to their British counterparts. Thus, *Champion of the Seas* measured 2,447 tons OM but only 1,947 tons NM. *Flying Cloud* was 1,782 tons OM but only 1,139 NM. Going in the other direction with British ships, *Cairngorm* measured 939 tons NM but 1,246 tons OM. *Eastern Monarch* was a large British clipper measuring 1,631 tons NM but 1,849 tons OM. This would have made her about the same size as the *Flying Cloud*.

There does not seem to be a consistent relationship between the two methods of measurement, but American ships were consistently considerably larger than their British counterparts, regardless of the system used. And as noted above, a British ship could be physically smaller than an American ship and still carry the same tonnage because of the larger internal space available using composite construction or simply iron or steel.

Problems with Iron and Steel Construction

But the British would not get it all their way. Building in iron or steel had its problems. Ships made of iron and steel could produce compass irregularities. There were several disasters due to 'navigational errors', which were subsequently realised to be compass deviations. This problem could be easily fixed by correcting the compass with large moveable balls of iron adjacent to the binnacle (the compass housing).

The biggest drawback of ships built of iron, however, was their propensity to accumulate marine growth, which slowed the ship down—a problem that was particularly acute in warm tropical waters. Wooden ships avoided this problem because they were generally clad in copper. This option wasn't available to iron ships because of electrolysis. Seawater would, in the presence of copper, stimulate galvanic action and cause the iron to corrode.

The concept of a 'composite ship' using the strength of steel and the ability of wood to accept copper sheathing gave ship designers the best of both these worlds, and many of the great British clippers benefitted from the concept. The first composite ship is said to have been the *Assam*, built in India in

1839. Over the next twenty years, there would be more than thirty applications for patents relating to the construction of composite ship hulls.

In the 1860s, the concept would be used in several very famous British clippers including *Taeping, Ariel, Sir Lancelot, Titania, Sobroam, Fiery Cross, Thermopylae,* and *Cutty Sark*. All except *Cutty Sark* (it means a short nightdress or shirt) have regrettably disappeared from the earth.

The Great Tea Race

In the great tea race of 1866, five ships—*Ariel, Fiery Cross, Serica, Taitsing,* and *Taeping*—loaded 5 million pounds of tea between them in China, and by 30 May, all had made it to sea. The prize for the first ship home was 100 pounds for the captain and an extra month's pay for the officers and crew. By the time they reached the English Channel, *Ariel* and *Taeping* were the front runners, but it was *Taeping* that won. *Ariel* was only twenty-eight minutes behind in a race that took ninety-nine days and ranged over 14,000 miles. Incredibly, *Serica* berthed a little over an hour later, so close was the racing between these magnificent ships.

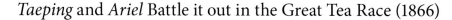

Taeping and *Ariel* Battle it out in the Great Tea Race (1866)

Source: Montague Dawson Courtesy of Bonhams Art Auctions

The great tea race was held only seventeen years after the 1849 repeal of the Navigation Acts. The British industry had lost no time in catching up with the modern standards of merchant marine construction and practice set by their transatlantic cousins.

A Beautiful End to the Line: *Cutty Sark*

Source: Painting by Gregory Robinson Courtesy of Royal Museum Greenwich

Cutty Sark was one of the last of the tea clippers ever built and, coming at the end of a long line of development, one of the fastest. The year she slid down the ways (1869) was also the year the Suez Canal opened. It spelled the end of the tea trade for her after only three years. Sailing ships cannot negotiate the canal, and the shorter route to China meant steamships could easily compete.

Cutty Sark was reassigned to the wool trade with Australia, one where the vast distances and advantageous wind systems still favoured sailing ships. She sailed this route for a decade, but the increasing efficiency of steamships meant that even this route was eventually closed to her. In 1895, she was sold to a Portuguese trading company and continued to operate commercially until 1922, a tribute to the durability of the composite hull concept. After spending some time as a training ship moored in the Thames, in 1954, she was finally brought up on to land for restoration.

Cutty Sark is now a museum ship in Greenwich in London. Even on dry land, she has endured her share of indignities, chief of which has been fire—twice. Her iron frame saved her from complete destruction, and luckily, at the time of the worst conflagration, all her spars had been removed for restoration.

Although designs had improved, with seagoing labour still fairly cheap in Britain, few concessions were made to labour-saving. Roller reefing (where the sail is wound around the yard rather than having to be tied to it) appeared around 1850 but was generally only applied to the topmost sails, but Britain's superior steelwork ability meant better gearing on anchor winches. Wire standing rigging became common, which obviated the need to be continually tightening or slackening hemp ropes. Generally, however, their deck layout and running rigging were unchanged.

Increasing competence in working iron and a shortage of wood eventually brought the age of the composite clipper to an end. With the fouling problem solved, Great Britain resorted to building clipper ships in iron.

In 1854, Lloyds had developed the first rules for the classification of iron ships. The iron clippers proved to be sturdy, fast, durable, and above all, 'tight' (that is to say, watertight). They would be the forerunners of the big four-masted, mainly barque-rigged sailers that would so dominate the last quarter of the nineteenth century and the early twentieth.

The first high-class all-iron ships appeared in the 1850s, just as the wood-based industry was climaxing. The iron *Lord of the Isles*, which made the best tea passage in 1855, was a harbinger of a new age. Great Britain could now compete with the United States in ship construction backed by ample quantities of cheap materials and advanced technique.

America versus Great Britain

The following chart shows the construction of clipper ships in America and Great Britain from 1845 to 1870.

American vs. British Clipper Tonnages Built: 1845-1870 (GRT)

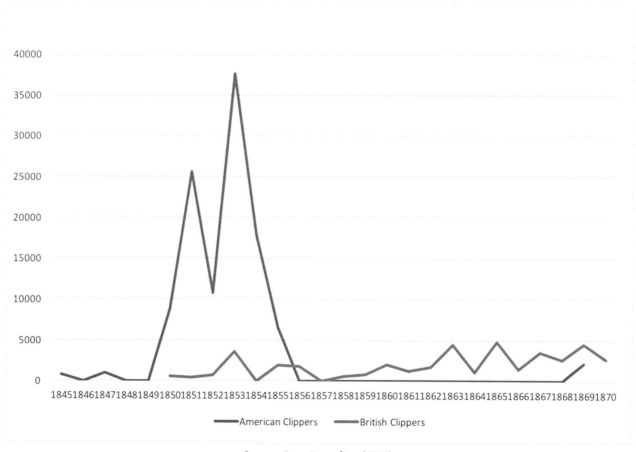

Source: Lars Bruzelius (GRT)

As previously indicated, the continuing use of old system measurement in the United States overstates the American tonnage figures by about 25 per cent, but because there is no consistent relationship between the two measurements, it is not possible to make a valid adjustment. What the chart does show is the astonishing boom in wooden sailing vessels in America in the context of the rise of the iron and, later, steel clippers in Great Britain.

The chart also shows the old system measurement of some eighty-six American vessels (average old system tonnage measure 1,490 tons), and fifty-six British craft (average 770 tons) using the Moorsom system. Even allowing for the differences between the two systems, the British ships tended to be smaller. The chart also demonstrates the frenzy in wooden ship construction after the gold discoveries, compared with the steady growth in Great Britain. In America, it all ended in tears, whereas Great Britain was becoming the greatest shipbuilding nation the world had ever known.

Despite the belief that tea tasted better when transported in a sailing ship, with the opening of the Suez Canal, the British tea clippers would eventually be pushed into the longer globe-circling trades such as emigration, or the coolie, guano, and nitrate trades. In the early, more leisurely days of the nitrate trade, wooden clipper ships could see out their days in the business, but Europe's demand soon increased in what has been called 'the white gold rush', getting nitrate into Europe for both fertiliser and munitions manufacture. The era of the giant steel windjammers was at hand, and it would be dominated by industrialised shipbuilders in the north of Great Britain, particularly on the Clyde River and its surrounds.

The age of the great globe-circling clippers was over.

Sailing ships, no matter their physical beauty and undoubted romance, were nevertheless commercial carriers hired by hard-nosed businessmen renowned for their philistinism when it came to the mighty dollar. Sailing ships were approaching their ultimate stages of development. Steam, that most destructive of technologies, was improving in leaps and bounds, and in hindsight, the end was inevitable.

Carl C. Cutler provided us with a benediction:

The day was at hand when the last beautiful creation was to spread her broad pinions and sail way into the blue never again to be seen by the eye of man in the full glory of their unshorn power and beauty.

John Fowles, the renowned novelist, added, 'The last of the sailing ships, that splendid and sharply individualised zenith of five thousand years of hard-earned knowledge and aesthetic instinct.'

The classic clipper represented a brief, brilliant period in merchant ship design. It was an era that needed high-paying cargoes such as gold seekers and tea to recoup the cost of driving oversparred vessels so hard and rebuilding them frequently. In America, the clippers were followed by a class of ships called the Down Easters, again the work of these same designers, which Howard Chappelle maintains were 'the highest development of the sailing ship; combining speed, handiness, cargo capacity and low operating costs to a degree never obtained in any earlier square-rigger'.

The 'Down Easters' represented the last gasp of big American wooden sailing ships. They were workaday freighters named for the provinces that lay to the east of the main east coast ports. Shipbuilding moved to Maine, and it became the centre of the American industry in the 1870s and 1880s. This area was less affected by the great recession of 1857, and yards were able to continue building. Moreover, wood supplies, on which they were dependent, were less depleted than further South. They took advantage of the lessons learned during the clipper era in strengthening wooden hulls and employed the improved fittings developed during that time.

Measuring around 2,500 gross tons, the Down Easters were fully rigged ships that carried all manner of cargoes, but mainly grain from America to Europe. Though not as heavily sparred as the clippers, they were, nevertheless, 'medium sharp' and carried enough sail to bear them along at considerable speed.

Their weakness was their operating cost, a factor that led to the morphing of the rig firstly to a barque (four masts, three square-rigged and the aftermost mast with fore-and-aft sails only), then to a barquentine configuration. The barquentine has only the foremast square-rigged, and the two other masts carried fore-and-aft sails, reducing manning yet again.

As well as high costs, it would be the increased use of steamers that contributed to their demise. Thus, even the age of the Down Easters soon ended, and Chappelle maintains sailing ship development in America ceased after 1890.

Following the repeal of the Navigation Acts and stimulated by the dominance of its former colony in the international merchant marine sphere, Great Britain developed its own fleet of clippers, smaller but more accommodating of cargo by their composite iron/wood and then steel/wood construction. They were purpose-built to bring tea from China, India, and Ceylon.

With the decline of clippers, there was all the more reason to concentrate on building steamships. Strangely, sailing ships continued to ply the tea route because many tea aficionados felt the heat and vibration of steamer transport spoiled the taste! But using its expertise in steel fabrication and its mechanical genius, Great Britain would go on to become not only the world's dominant builder of steamships but the major constructor of the largest fleet of sailing ships the world has ever known: the four-masted barques, better known as the windjammers.

Eventually, it would forfeit its strong position in sailing ship construction, forced out by French government subsidies to build large square-rigged ships. It was more profitable for Great Britain to exploit its position as the undisputed world leader in the construction of steam-powered vessels.

Brevity and Romance

The Western Ocean packet liner services began in 1818 and ended around 1881, after a somewhat drawn-out demise, but these ships plied the Atlantic profitably for half a century and carried untold tons of freight and millions of people (mostly) to and from the New World. They made an enormous contribution to the wealth and prosperity of peoples on both sides of the Atlantic.

Also, and importantly, the packet ships were a training ground for the seamen who would command the great ships of the next stage of windship development—the clippers. They would only last less than half that time, their brevity matched only by their romance. Howard Chappelle places it, in America at least, at a mere thirteen years—from 1846 to 1859—but *Pilgrim*, one of the last built, was constructed in 1873. It would be a period in which the design of a merchant sailing vessel reached its highest point, making them the most revered sailing ships ever to plough the oceans of the world.

But it was also a time in which hard-driving of their outsize rigs was lifted to new levels. Upon their inception, at least, they only served the top end of the market. Demand for their services was driven by the world's lust for gold and the Occident's thirst for tea. During their era, the baton of innovative sailing ship design would be passed from America to Great Britain, where it would remain for the rest of the merchant sailing ship era.

10
CHAPTER

Steam and Steel—Creative Destruction

The Steam Revolution—a Simple Process

Fire and water are antithetical elements. Brought together, but kept separate, the fire's heat evaporates the water, producing steam. Wafting out of a kettle spout, steam is innocuous, homely even, but if its escape path is blocked, the pressure inside the kettle increases as the steam is compressed. Allowed to escape and expand in a controlled manner, steam can be made to do an enormous amount of work. The higher the pressure that can be achieved within the kettle (or boiler), the more work it can do.

Even though the steam revolution is over 200 years old, civilisation still employs this elementary process—using steam turbines—to generate some 90 per cent of its power requirements, regardless of the fuel used.

The problem these days is the fuel.

Two centuries ago, the problem was constructing vessels that could *confine the process.*

Metallurgists were the heroes of the day, making progressively stronger steel boilers that allowed pressures within to be raised—in turn producing more energy. The coal used to make the heat required was simply solar energy accumulated over millions of years. That stored energy could be used in a variety of ways: pumping water, driving machines in factories, transporting goods and people on land, and propelling ships across the oceans.

Sailing ships also utilise solar energy, in the form of wind, but they must use it immediately, as and where it is available. Without the control obtained by using stored energy, while they were more economical, they were, alas, less dependable.

Steam power was one of the most destructive, creative, and transformative technologies of all time. It destroyed the old craft system of cottage production, already under attack from the watermills. It allowed factories to be moved away from watercourses, permitting the growth of the first industrial towns and, ultimately, the giant conurbations of today.

Steam engines were installed in paddle-wheel canal barges before they pulled trains on railway lines. But steam trains quickly transformed the landscape, laying siege to the canal network that itself had improved the transport of goods, especially bulk raw materials. Within a very short period, the countryside would be criss-crossed by railway lines. The network created a revolution not only in the transport of goods but also of people.

This great driver of the Industrial Revolution was enormously useful. But it did have its critics.

'Creative Destruction'

'Creative destruction', it is maintained, is a phenomenon at the centre of economic growth in market economies. The term was coined by the Austrian political economist Joseph Schumpeter in 1942. He derived it from the work of German philosopher Karl Marx. Marx saw it as a process linked to the accumulation and destruction of wealth under capitalism. It can also be applied to how capitalism destroys previous economic structures and creates new ones. Marx lived and wrote at a time when the economic nationalism of the old mercantilist order was succumbing to capitalism. He published his major work, *Das Kapital*, in 1848, around the time Britain repealed two bastions of the old mercantilism, the Navigation Acts and the Corn Laws.

The Navigation Acts had sought to ensure that all the wealth generated in the British Empire flowed back to the mother country. They regulated and promoted English ships and shipping, and trade and commerce between other countries, and with its colonies. The catalogue of restrictions they embodied had been accumulating for two centuries, and as a consequence, the English shipping industry developed—or *failed* to develop—because of the isolation the acts promoted.

This lack of progress was a major factor in the rise of America as a mercantile power. Free from restrictions and the social discrimination of English society, the Americans established a culture of innovation and competition that led to the superiority of their trading vessels and sailing practice. Luckily for Britain's maritime future, the Navigation Acts were repealed in 1849.

The Corn Laws had been progressively passed to protect British landowners (the overwhelming domestic political power of the time) in the first half of the nineteenth century. The laws safeguarded them from competition from (mainly) American grain and other foodstuffs, which could be landed in England more cheaply. High food prices kept land rents high and landowners wealthy.

Raw materials such as timber and cotton, which Britain needed to feed its emerging industrial power, weren't subjected to the same restrictions. It was the emerging middle class whose wealth lay in industry, not land, and who wanted cheap food for its workers, that was behind their repeal. In addition, expensive food made the working class less able to purchase their wares.

The immediate trigger for the laws' repeal was the famine in Ireland in 1846, a humanitarian disaster that would fill the American packet ships with food on the way out and with emigrants to 'the land of the free' on the way back.

Even before these two acts were abolished, though, there was a decline in protectionism around the world that led to a great expansion in trade. The East India Company had lost its monopoly in 1834, and Britain, thanks to the First Opium War, had gained a permanent trading foothold on the island of Hong Kong. These developments were then amplified by the discovery of gold, first in California in 1848, and Australia in 1851.

Wind (and the sails and rigging that harnessed it) was the motive power behind the world's international trade and had ruled supreme for millennia.

Yet it took only about a century to obliterate it.

A sailing ship is very efficient. It gets the wind for free and harnesses it with rigging set on an empty shell that is well-suited to carrying cargo. But that efficiency is also its Achilles heel. Because it gets the wind for free from nature, a sailing ship has no control over when it blows, from which direction, and at what strength. Similarly, the ocean currents created by the globe's wind and thermal systems can vary considerably, though not as much as the winds that create them.

Our observations of the natural maritime environment had enabled us to go and explore the world. Mariners left Europe and travelled vast distances, limited only by their ability to carry or replenish their supply of food and water.

What was more important was knowing how to find your way back.

The Development of the Marine Steam Engine

The presence of water in mine shafts had long defeated efforts to reach deeper deposits of minerals such as coal. A steam engine designed and built by Thomas Newcomen succeeded in keeping the water at bay and unlocking deeper deposits. But it was inefficient. It relied on the contraction of steam rather than its expansion. And having to be alternatively heated and cooled, it consumed huge amounts of fuel in the process.

It wasn't until the Scottish inventor and engineer James Watt began exploiting the expansion of steam and added a separate condenser that the steam engine was set on its long journey of technical development, one that would have such wonderful consequences for humankind—but such dire consequences for merchant sail.

The first steamship took to the water in 1801 in the form of a small, ten-horsepower stern wheel steamboat, the Charlotte Dundas, operating on the Forth and Clyde Canal in central Scotland. It was a 'beam' engine, with the piston working one end of a beam on a fulcrum and a rod connected to a crank on the other side to which the paddles were attached. In so doing, a reciprocating motion was converted into rotation with the regulating mechanism working off the beam. It was an immediate success.

The First Practical Steamboat: *Charlotte Dundas*

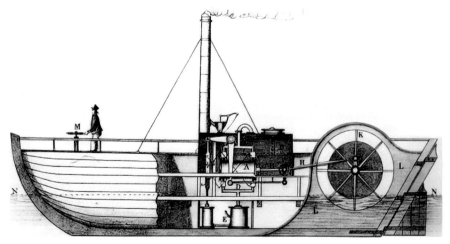

Source: Wikimedia Commons

These engines were heavy and had high centres of gravity, which could destabilise a vessel. It was not until Boulton & Watt replaced the overhead beam with side levers that steam engines gained acceptance in watercraft, especially highly manoeuvrable stern wheeler tugs. But side levers were heavy, and British inventor and engineer Joseph Maudsley eventually replaced them with the piston rod acting directly on to the crank of the paddlewheel.

A subsequent development was the 'diagonal' engine which was placed low in the hull and lent itself to 'compounding'. This is the process by which the expansion of high-pressure steam would be used several times, through separate expansions, substantially increasing their economy of operation.

Steamships were the product of the Industrial Revolution, which also enabled the environment to be altered in their favour. Sailing ships could, to a large extent, depend on the massive westerly wind systems that circle the globe above and below 40 degrees latitude. Industrial progress, however, sped the construction of the Suez Canal, which eliminated the need to venture to those latitudes at all. It also simultaneously shortened the distance between the West and the East, defraying the clipper ship's speed advantage. The technology embodied in a sailing ship, although extraordinarily efficient, was age-old, and the new destructive technology of steam was remorselessly running it down.

In spite of the improvements in their size, speed, and regularity, sailing ships helped create the environment that would destroy them. The emerging world was one in which the speed of the process of innovation was snowballing, with one technology quickly replacing another.

Entrepreneurs sought to benefit from their particular innovation and circumstances before it was overtaken by others. America was on the rise as a commercial and maritime power, and its creed of 'time is money' began to dominate.

Not that sailing ships were slow. It would be decades into the next (twentieth) century before a steamship could equal the speed of a clipper or windjammer in full flight. The issue for sailing ships was the *consistency* with which a steamship could maintain its pace. But in the early days, a lot of space in a steamship was taken up with machinery and the coal required to drive it. A sailing ship on the other hand had an almost empty shell available with which to earn its keep. They were literally mobile warehouses.

A Symbiotic Relationship—for a Time

Generating power without having to rely on the winds and tides, steam—in the form of harbour tugs—helped sailing ships combat the often unpredictable weather conditions when leaving and entering port. But it would be some time before steamships would cross the Atlantic and still have enough cargo space to pay their way.

Ocean transport now entered an 'intermediate phase'. It would run parallel to the glory days of pure sail, when the so-called 'auxiliary' steamships carried substantial sailing rigs that enabled them to take advantage of favourable wind conditions, saving space and expensive fuel. Steam was the handmaiden to sail, providing auxiliary and emergency power until it was sufficiently economical and reliable to be independent.

The later solely propeller-driven (angled blades set on an underwater shaft) ocean-going ship did not emerge fully formed. The technology developed for inland waterways—paddlewheels—was the first to be employed in ocean crossings, but such vessels were vulnerable in big seas and were susceptible to damage.

Nevertheless, by the 1820s, the English Channel, Irish Sea, and the North Sea had all been crossed by steamships. By the 1830s, the Mediterranean circuit ran to Malta, Egypt, and eventually Constantinople (Istanbul). After 1835, steamships were running to India after cargo porterage across the Isthmus of Suez. And by 1840, there were regularly scheduled crossings to the United States, although many still preferred the packets, which didn't have the continual thumping of the engine and grime associated with early steam navigation.

Regular sailings in paddlewheelers also took in France, Holland, Belgium, Hamburg, Cadiz, and Lisbon. They even went as far as India and China—the British used steam-driven warships in the First Opium War.

The English multidisciplined engineer Isambard Kingdom Brunel launched his revolutionary propeller-driven, sail-assisted SS *Great Britain* in 1845. At the time, she was the longest passenger ship in the world. Then in 1847, 325 years after Magellan/Elcano achieved it, a steamship finally managed to circumnavigate the world. However, it was a warship, not a trader—the HM sloop *Driver*, a paddle-driven auxiliary ship with a hull resembling a clipper—and she took five years to complete the task.

It had taken Magellan/Elcano three years back in 1522.

The universality of the wind, the patchy global availability of coal, and the limited cargo space if too much coal was taken aboard would continue to make long merchant voyages the preserve of the great windships for some time yet.

By 1852, at the height of the glory days of the clippers, a bimonthly paddle-steamer service on the west coast of South America linked Valparaíso with Atlantic steamers via the Isthmus of Panama. All the services were initially conducted by auxiliary vessels—paddle steamers assisted by sails. It wasn't long after Brunel's 'success' with SS *Great Britain*, however, that propeller-driven steamers were dominating the Mediterranean and Levant trades.

Steel and Sail

In the mid-1850s, as the United States reached the zenith of its success with wooden sailing ships, Britain was only just getting underway. Despite the arrival of auxiliary steamers, British shipbuilders were opening up a new age of sail, combining the obvious economies of sailing ship operation with their skill in iron and steel founding. It would be another three decades, or more, before the steel solely steam-driven cargo ship could supplant the sailing ship on the long routes to India, China, and Australia.

The problem for iron steam-driven vessels was the developmental time it took to combine three elements—hull design, engine efficiency, and propeller propulsion—into an effective unit. Victorian engineers had had enormous success with the working of iron into (for that time) spectacular bridges. They were also very good at squeezing surprising reliability out of rail-based steam engines.

The design and casting of propellers, however, was a new science with no counterpart on land.

Even when these knotty problems had been solved, mainly by the Admiralty experimenting with public funds on small naval vessels, the auxiliary steamers still had to contend with two other major issues: corrosion and biofouling. For this reason, composite hulls—iron frames clad in timber, which allowed the fixing of copper sheathing—would remain popular until the 1870s.

The Impact of Explosive Shells

Meanwhile, the development of explosive shells and the damage they could cause to wooden ships convinced the British Navy to find solutions to the problems of corrosion and biofouling. Explosive shells had been around for a long time, having been used in China as early as the fourteenth century. However, in their early nineteenth-century incarnation, they were somewhat ineffective. Spherical shells fired from smooth-bore cannon required a powdered fuse to be lit and for the gunner to have a good sense of timing; otherwise, the shell could explode in the cannon and blow it and him to pieces. Moreover, imperfections in both barrel and ball could cause inaccuracies. 'Breech-loading' (through the inboard end of the cannon as opposed to the muzzle) had also been around for some time, but the inability to obtain a gas-tight seal between the breechblock and the barrel had limited their effectiveness. This seal had been achieved in muzzle-loaders by ramming a cotton wad in on top of the charge.

The real advance came with the successful marrying of a rifled barrel to a gas-tight breech-loading cannon. These advances enabled the use of cylindrical shell casings that not only permitted a larger projectile for the same bore gun, but the rifling imparted a stabilising gyroscopic spin to the projectile, preventing it tumbling in flight. The outcome was improved accuracy and effective range and hitting power.

Packing the cylinder with explosives and, with impact detonators on the tapered nose, made for a fearsome weapon. It could wreak havoc on a wooden ship that had been built to resist the impact of solid circular shot. The arrival of impact detonating shells shot from a rifled barrel was immense. Clearly, much stronger hulls were required, and the only answer was to build them from steel. And with that came the problems of corrosion and biofouling.

Corrosion

Saltwater corrosion could eat through iron plates and cause ships to sink. This was the case with the British warship HMS *Jackal*, which foundered at Greenock, west of Glasgow, Scotland, from corrosion having eaten away her plates, apparently unnoticed. Similarly, in 1862, HMS *Triton* had her plates corroded to such paper thinness that, according to her commander, she was only kept from foundering by her fouling, practically sailing home on her barnacles!

Biofouling

Biofouling due to barnacles and algae clinging to the hull slowed vessels down considerably. The iron ships were often up to two or even three months late in a four-month voyage due to excessive biofouling, which was especially bad in tropical waters.

It was much more serious than it was on a copper-sheathed wooden sailing ship that relied on the wind for motive power. An iron steamship relied on coal, and its consumption (and cost) increased by up to 60 per cent on a badly fouled vessel. A man-of-war on commission in foreign waters for an extended period might become so fouled as to become unmanageable and unseaworthy before she could get home to be cleaned.

The English philosopher and reformer Jeremy Bentham recommended that the construction of iron ships be limited to 40 per cent of the fleet. The problem became so great that the navy considered the disposal of all its iron ships, but the vulnerability of wooden ships to the new ordnance convinced them to persevere.

According to the Woods Hole Oceanographic Institution, zinc sheathing was tried in place of copper. Zinc's exfoliation protected the ship's plates from fouling. Experience showed, however, that it became brittle and, being what's known as a 'sacrificial anode', was wasted away too rapidly by galvanic action to be of any real use.

Sheathings of Muntz metal (60 per cent copper, 40 per cent zinc), lead, galvanised iron, and nickel were tried, as were alloys of lead, antimony, zinc, and tin, but none proved effective. Warships were clad with wood over the iron plates and then sheathed in copper. This process worked but was too expensive for commercial use. Non-metallic sheathings of felt, canvas, rubber, ebonite (rubber hardened by vulcanising), cork, and paper were also tried. Even various forms of glass, enamels, and glazes were the subject of (unsuccessful) experimentation. Cement was also used but more as a guard against corrosion than as an antifouling agent.

The failure of sheathings led to renewed interest in antifouling compositions. Arsenic and sulphur mixed with oil had been used since ancient times. Tar and pitch and combinations of the two, sometimes mixed with sulphur, were also experimented with, mostly to protect wooden hulls against sea worms. A combination of cement, powdered iron, and copper had received a patent as early as 1625—the first use of copper as an antifoulant—and other chemical mixtures followed, but again, none were all that good. By 1865, over 300 patents for coatings had been issued in England alone. All were useless.

Introduced in Liverpool in 1860, 'McIness', presumably named for its inventor, was the first practical composition to come into widespread use. It was a metallic soap composition applied hot, in which copper sulphate was the toxic element. This antifouling paint was spread over a quick-drying priming paint of rosin varnish and iron oxide pigment (which was a protectant against corrosion). Shortly after, a similar hot plastic composition appeared in Trieste, Italy. Known as the 'Italian Moravian', it was one of the best antifouling paints of that time. Despite being both expensive and difficult to apply, it was used well into the twentieth century.

Steam engines were originally powered by burning wood, but an equivalent weight in coal made four times as much energy and was cheaper to produce. And despite its weight, coal was also easier to distribute. Wooden ships, however, could not withstand the vibration caused by a steam engine and could only be used for short periods or in emergency circumstances.

HMS *Erebus*, one of the wooden ships used by Sir John Franklin on his ill-fated voyage in search of the Northwest Passage, had been retrofitted with two steam engines. Their remains enabled the wreck's identification when, in 2014, it was discovered on the bottom of the ocean in the Canadian Arctic.

The Rise of Iron and Steel

These difficulties considerably extended the working lives of wooden merchant ships. In 1850 in Great Britain, the net tonnage of iron ships built was 12,800, as against 120,000 in wood. In 1860, the numbers were 64,479 versus 147,000. In 1870, however, the net tonnage in iron was 255,000 as opposed to 161,000 in wood, and in 1880, 495,367 in iron and a mere 20,000 for wood. In this latter year, only about one-fifth of the iron ships being built (about 100,000 net tons) were sailing ships. Sailing vessels could be iron or wood, but steamers needed iron hulls to provide the strength to carry heavy steam engines and their associated propulsion gear. They also needed to be strong enough to resist the vibration.

Advances in Boiler Pressure

According to Gerald Graham, an English academic, steam pressure in marine boilers in the 1830s averaged about 5 lbs/inch^2. By the 1840s, it had doubled to around 10 lbs/inch^2. In the 1850s, with the introduction of tubular boilers, it had doubled again to 20 lbs/inch^2.

One is reminded of Moore's law in computing, whereby the number of transistors in a dense integrated circuit—in other words, the computer's processing power—doubles every two years. With boiler pressure, the period was much longer, but by the 1860s, pressures began to increase towards 50 and 60 lbs/inch^2. They were accompanied by the adoption of compound cylinders and circular boilers sufficiently strong to take the increased pressure.

At the same time, surface condensers that allowed the continual use of fresh instead of sediment-bearing saltwater appeared. The introduction of the 'compound engine' constituted a notable advance in marine engineering. It involved passing steam from the first cylinder (where the initial pressure was high) to a second cylinder of greater bore where there was naturally less pressure per unit of area. While the amount of energy extracted from a given amount of steam was not doubled, it was considerably increased. Fuel consumption was thereby reduced by 60 per cent.

The breakthrough made the voyage to China to load tea economical for steamers. It is idle to contemplate what might have been, but had subsequent pressures of 125 lbs/inch^2 (obtained in 1870) been achieved twenty years earlier, the great age of English tea clippers may never have taken place.

These advances gave considerable pause to the builders of sailing ships. For the two years after 1869 (the year the Suez Canal opened), the construction of sailing ships almost ceased, and in 1871, it was 'unprecedently small'. In 1870, it was declared by the Royal Institute of Naval Architects that a vessel of 2,000 tons plying to Bombay, a distance of 12,000 miles, averaging 9 knots and burning 14 tons of coal a day, could carry 1,400 tons of cargo out and 2,000 tons back.

The days of sailing ships earning high freight rates on valuable commodities were drawing to a close, but their lives as commercial carriers would be extended because they were, among other things, the cheapest means of getting replenishment coal to ports and depots along the steamer routes.

The Polish–British writer Joseph Conrad's short story 'Youth' recounts the experience of a British sailing ship loaded with coal and destined for Bangkok suffering a spontaneous combustion of the cargo. After frantic attempts by the crew to put out the fire, the ship finally burst into flames. The young Conrad was the third mate and put in charge of one of the ship's boats to complete the voyage.

As well, carrying coal as ballast on the outward journey lowered the freight rates that sailing ships could accept for bulk return cargoes of food and raw materials. Alternatively, they would carry export coal to depots and destinations all over the world and back-freight raw materials for British industry.

The expansion in the grain trades in the latter part of the nineteenth century would also see the need for sailing ships. In 1882, there were 550 sailing vessels, mainly British, engaged in transporting grain from the west coast of the United States to Europe.

Similarly, the Australian trade would be dominated by sail throughout the 1880s. In 1874, Australia's grain exports were less than a million tons. By 1888, they exceeded 2.3 million tons. Grain and wool also provided excellent back-freight for emigrant ships. Until the Suez Canal significantly lowered its access rates in the 1880s, sailing ships dominated the rice trade from Saigon, Bangkok, and Rangoon. In times of economic bust, sailing ships could afford to lay up and await better times, a difficult thing for higher-capital-cost, high-maintenance iron steamers.

One more step along the road to the superior efficiency of the steam engine was required before steamships would come to totally dominate sail.

It came with the assistance of the science of metallurgy.

Even with the replacement of the paddlewheel by the propellor as a means of propulsion and the development of the compound steam engine, the sailing ship had still managed to remain the dominant cargo carrier.

In 1885, according to the Lloyds Register, there was, at 3.9 million tons, still 44 per cent more sail cargo-carrying capacity than there was in steam. But in the 1870s, the English Bessemer and German Siemens plants developed 'high tensile' steel that enabled boilerplates and tubes to withstand pressures as high as 200 lbs/inch^2.

But still, the production facilities lagged behind the science. It would be some time before the new product became available to shipbuilders along with more powerful furnaces and more efficient condensers. And of course, it was more expensive. Nevertheless, when the new product became available, it paved the way for an astounding new invention.

The 'Triple Expansion' Marine Steam Engine

In 1881, the owners of the White Star Line, George Thompson & Co. Ltd, launched the SS *Aberdeen*, which was fitted with 'triple expansion' steam engines.

Cutaway View of a Triple-expansion Steam Engine

Source: Creative Commons, Vienna Technical Museum, CC BY 3.0 Sandstein

Benefitting from the higher boiler pressures available, steam was now passed through three stages of expansion. With 4,000 tons of cargo, the SS *Aberdeen* left Glasgow on 7 April and, after bunkering at the Cape of Good Hope, arrived in Melbourne forty-two days later using a steam pressure of 125 lbs/inch^2.

Additional advances helped engineers cope with another major problem: corrosion in the boilers. These improvements all added up to considerable savings in fuel, wear and tear, and even space. With the improved steel, boiler pressures were subsequently increased to 200 lbs/inch^2, a pressure that required only a fraction more than a pound of coal per horsepower per hour. The old low-pressure engines had required 10 pounds.

The adaptation of the high-pressure triple-expansion engine to an iron-hulled ocean carrier marked the end of an epoch which, for the greater part of the nineteenth century, had seen the bulk of commercial cargoes carried by sail. Steam pressures would subsequently reach as high as 300 lbs/inch^2, and quadruple-expansion systems were invented; however, they provided little further gain. The compound steam engine had reached the limits of its practical development.

Steam Turbines

The steam turbine engine, which was introduced in 1897, was the last contribution of British shipbuilders. It provided an alternative to the reciprocating engine, especially where high speeds and power output (such as warships and large ocean liners, like the *Mauretania* and the *Lusitania*) were key considerations. It was widely accepted in the construction of warships, especially after geared turbines became available in 1910.

Although fourth- and fifth-stage expansions were developed in reciprocating engines, they were incredibly complex. The standard triple-expansion steam engine of about 2,500 horsepower would be surprisingly long-lived, its main advantages being reliability and simple maintenance. Thousands of single-propeller general cargo ships powered in this way would be built before and during the Second World War, including the famous 'Liberty' ships. By then, however, coal had long given way to oil. It reduced the space required for bunkers and was easier to transport and load. It also reduced labour costs by eliminating the stokers and trimmers so vital to coal-fired steam engines.

Mineral oil had been discovered by the Chinese around 600 BCE and was transported in pipelines made of bamboo. In the modern era, oil was discovered in Pennsylvania in 1859, but it was its discovery in Texas in 1901 that set the stage for the new oil economy. Petroleum was more flexible than coal, and the kerosene that was refined from crude oil made a more reliable and relatively inexpensive alternative to whale oil and 'coal oils' for fuelling lamps.

The Transition to Metal Construction

By the latter part of the nineteenth century, the United Kingdom was the largest shipbuilder in the world. Data on the transition from wood through iron to steel provide the best picture of the transition in merchant marine construction.

The chart below sets out merchant shipbuilding in the United Kingdom by type of material for most of the more than six decades preceding the First World War.

All Vessels Constructed in Great Britain by Material: 1850-1908 (000's net tons)

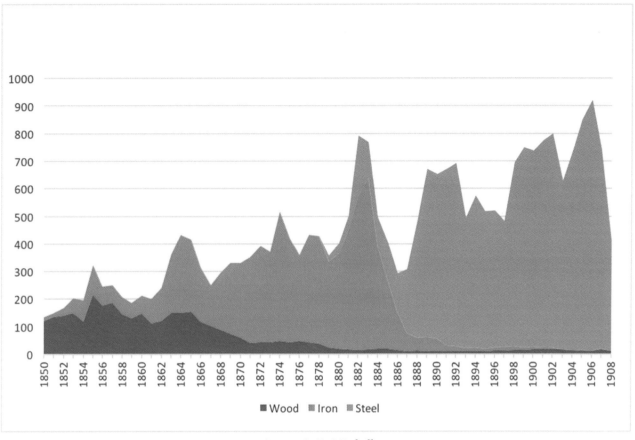

Source: B. R. Mitchell

Beginning in 1850, wood was by far the main construction material. It remained so until 1862 when it was overtaken by iron, which then dominated until it was, in turn, overtaken by steel in 1886. Construction in steel had begun around 1880 (before then, the figures were lumped in with iron). Of the over 900,000 net tons of ships constructed in 1906, 98 per cent was in steel. By this time, sailing ship construction, although mainly in steel, was very small. In 1906, it was only 31,800 tons or 3 per cent of the total.

The Inevitable Symbiosis—Steam and Steel

The advent of improved steam engines and the symbiotic relationship they had with iron and steel in the construction of marine hulls helped vastly expand the volume of world trade. Increased trade meant increased wealth. And increased capacity in ocean-going shipping fed the rapid industrialisation of Great Britain, then other European countries and the United States.

In 1850, in Great Britain, the total net tonnage constructed in all three materials in both sail and steam was 134,000 net tons. In 1882, albeit in boom conditions, it had reached almost 800,000 tons—an almost sixfold increase in just over thirty years. By 1885, it was 422,000 net tons (a threefold increase), and by 1892, it peaked at 926,000 net tons—a sevenfold increase in just forty-two years.

There was also a doubling in the seven years between 1885 and 1892 in what must have been one of the greatest shipbuilding booms of all time. By 1908, that figure had more than halved, and out of a total of 414,000 net tons of merchant tonnage constructed, sail constituted a mere 7 per cent. At the height of the merchant shipbuilding boom in 1892, sail had constituted 28 per cent of the capacity constructed.

The development of large-scale iron and steelmaking ran parallel with that of the steam engine and very closely allied with it. Working iron began over 3,000 years ago, originating in several places in Asia and also with the Hittites, living in what is now Turkey. But it was extremely expensive to make, and its use was confined to armour, weapons, tools, cutlery, and the like. It was also brittle and not as hard or as durable as bronze.

It may have been the disruption of trade routes and the supply of tin and copper associated with the decline of the Bronze Age civilisations that caused metallurgists to turn their attention to making iron harder and more malleable. This was achieved by controlling the amount of carbon in the smelting process and getting rid of impurities.

Glasgow About 1860

Source: Alamy.com

It was the Industrial Revolution's need for large quantities of a cheap, strong, malleable metal that stimulated a range of metallurgical experiments. In the mid-1850s, these led Bessemer to the steelmaking process that subsequently bore his name. Along with the Siemens-Martin process, steelmaking was turned into a highly capitalised heavy industry.

It was not until the mid-1860s, however, that improvements were made to remove the high level of phosphorous in British and European iron ores. This development, known as the 'open hearth' process, improved on the Bessemer method, and it eventually overtook it as a method of steel manufacture. Production rose dramatically. As a result, it ultimately outran Great Britain's ability to produce iron ore. In 1855, production was less than 10 million tons, and imports were negligible. By 1913, locally produced iron ore had risen 60 per cent to 16 million tons, and imports were over 7 million tons. Total iron ore inputs were now 23 million tons—a 130 per cent increase on the figure for 1855.

Marine Diesel Power

Today, steam power remains the primary method of generating electricity. But for ships, the diesel reciprocating engine would soon take over. In 1898, diesel power became widely available, and the adoption of the internal combustion reciprocating engine, invented by Rudolf Diesel in the mid to late 1890s and powered by oil, was rapid.

Powering ships using diesel engines went on to be developed by the Danish firm Burmeister & Wain when they acquired the production licence in 1897. The engines were fired on crude oil and provided two and four-stroke options, with the choice dictated by the vertical and horizontal space available in specific trades. A two-stroke engine expels spent gas on the same revolution of the crankshaft as it draws in a new fuel charge (two strokes of the piston). A four-stroke engine expels the exhaust on one revolution and draws in and compresses the new fuel charge on a separate revolution.

Although invented at the end of the nineteenth century, it would not be until the 1930s that ships powered by diesel engines became widespread. The diesel engine could be directly coupled to the propeller shaft or used to generate electricity, which in turn drove electric motors, which then drove the propellers. This configuration offered a great deal of flexibility in manoeuvring, with multiple propeller housings able to be swivelled and even turned 180 degrees to influence the speed and direction of the vessel.

A Secondary Symbiosis–Steel and Sail

The symbiosis of steam and steel triumphed after centuries of domination by sail. Construction in steel, however, gave sail a new resilience and produced the largest class of sailing ships the world has ever seen: the mighty windjammers. They could go almost anywhere on earth where there was saltwater and would prove tougher than the steamships that had displaced the earlier clippers. Steel was necessary to house steam engines, but ironically, it extended the life of merchant sail by another half century. Their rugged hulls and rigs would still be lugging heavy cargoes immense distances, some half a century after launching.

11

CHAPTER

The Windjammers—A New Era

American Dominance

T he United States dominated both shipbuilding and maritime commerce between the Old and the New World up until the mid-1850s. Following the American and Australian gold rushes, the industry suffered a deep recession. Gold had resulted in a massive overbuilding of deepwater sailing tonnage, as the early years of the following chart shows. It would prove to be the beginning of the end of the wooden sailing ship as a means of deepwater transport.

Ship Construction in the USA; Sail and Steam: 1850-1915 (Gross Tons)

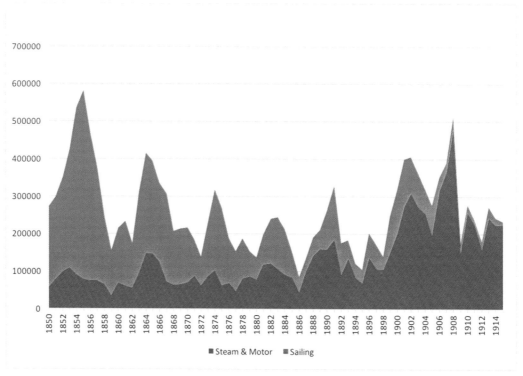

US Bureau of Census and Statistics: Shipbuilding—merchant vessels built in the US

Sailing ship construction boomed in the first half of the 1850s, peaking at over half a million gross register tons (GRT) in 1855. There was something of a revival towards the end of the Civil War and immediately thereafter, but the tonnages constructed were only around half those in the middle of the century. They were different ships too—the 'Down Easters'—rugged, practical full-rigged freighters designed for longer lives in steady trades, in this case mostly shipping grain to Europe. In time, for economy of operation, they would also adopt the four-masted barque rig that so typified the windjammers.

The locus of sailing ship construction had moved from New York and Boston to Maine. The Down Easters notwithstanding, and apart from the 'schooner boom' (see below), there was a hiatus in American wooden shipbuilding. Towards the end of the century, steel steamship construction began to push total tonnage constructed up again. This revival lasted until 1908. The annual average tonnage constructed in the five and a half decades after 1860 was 250,000 tons—less than half the amount built in the peak years of the 1850s. What growth there was was all in steam-propelled steel vessels with the construction of sailing ships all but ceasing in the lead-up to the First World War.

America Abandons the Sea

Apart from the Down Easters, the majority of ships built during this period were small vessels intended for coastal or lake trade. After the Civil War, America prospered, but its involvement in its foreign trade stagnated, as the following chart demonstrates:

American Imports and Exports; US Ships vs. Foreign Ships: 1840-1915 ($M)

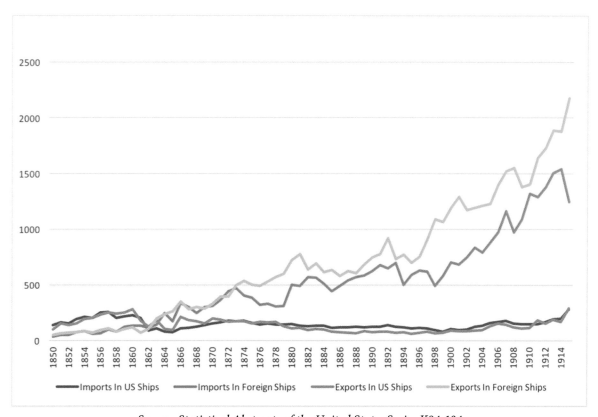

Source: Statistical Abstracts of the United States Series K94-104

In the early years of this sequence, all of America's foreign trade was by sea. Even in the last years before the First World War, the proportion exceeded 90 per cent. Following the Civil War, as American eyes turned westward and away from the sea that had been their fortune hitherto, so the value of trade—both imports and exports, carried in 'American bottoms'—stagnated.

Between 1850 and 1915, the value of American waterborne imports increased *eight and a half times*. But the proportion carried in American ships only doubled, having sunk to a low of only half the 1850 level during the 1890s. The value of waterborne *exports* in the same period grew a massive sixteenfold, yet the value carried in American ships only tripled. In the 1890s, it sank to two-thirds of the 1850 level.

Judging by the increase in trade generally, America was obviously prospering, but having turned so determinedly towards frontier pursuits, it was paying its trading partners handsomely to handle much of its foreign trade. What is also extraordinary about these figures is the extent to which American trade grew from the period when its 'Yankee' clippers were conquering the world to the years before the First World War. It was America's 'Gilded Age'—what would be termed an economic miracle today. According to an index of industrial production, compiled by the American economist Joseph H. Davis and published in 2004, United States industry in 1915 was *nineteen times* what it had been in 1850.

But despite this extraordinary growth, America paid a heavy price for abandoning the sea, having to play catch-up when it entered the First World War.

Its shipbuilders were masters of the art of wooden ship construction, but the nation turned inwards at a time when the industry was changing dramatically: from wood and sails, through combination iron and wooden sailing ships, to iron and steel hulls and steam propulsion.

Although some American shipbuilders experimented with iron and steel using experience gained building 'ironclads' during the Civil War, their costs were too high. Real wages rose 60 per cent between 1860 and 1890. They couldn't even compete in wooden ship construction any more. To make matters worse, the price of British ships (generally iron-framed wooden-clad clippers) fell below the cost for which America could build a wooden ship. Iron steamships drove the wooden sailing ships out of the protected coastal trade, but they couldn't compete with deepwater vessels.

The Big Schooners

In the late nineteenth and early twentieth century, American wooden sailing shipbuilders went big to compete with steam, building giant fore-and-aft gaff-rigged 'schooners' for the rising coastal trade. In this format, wooden sailers could compete with the steamers, at least for the time being. The construction of large wooden schooners was an entirely American development with no counterpart abroad, and it flourished up until the early years of the twentieth century. Their main trade was carrying coal along the east coast and timber from the west coast to the South Pacific.

The first three-masted schooner, the *American Eagle*, of only 386 tons, was built in 1865 in Maine. By 1880, when the first four-master, the 996-ton *William L. White*, slid down the ways, schooners were steadily increasing in size. Eight years later came the first five-master *Governor Ames*, which, at 1,788 tons, doubled that size. In 1900, several six-masters including the *George W. Wells* and the *Eleanor A. Percy* were built.

The peak in wooden schooner gross tonnage came in 1902 with the 3,739-ton *Wyoming*—the largest schooner built at the time. Later that year, the even bigger steel seven-masted 5,218-ton *Thomas*

W. Lawson slid down the ways. It arrived at the end of a schooner-building boom, was not a success commercially, and was wrecked soon afterward.

The Seven-masted Schooner *Thomas W. Lawson*

Source: Courtesy of the Boston Public Library, Leslie Jones Collection

The schooners' simpler rig and slightly better ability to work up to windward made them handier to navigate than square-riggers in coastal work, but they were less effective on long deepwater voyages before the wind. This meant that with its fewer control lines, the simpler rig could be operated with the assistance of steam donkey engines. These were small steam engines that could be harnessed to a variety of heavy tasks. The number of crew needed was thus considerably smaller—from 25 per cent to 55 per cent fewer than that required by a square-rigger.

Even a big six-mast schooner could sail with a crew of only twelve to fifteen hands compared to twenty-seven or thirty on a square-rigger. Only with this reduced crew requirement could they hope to compete with the steamers and the railways. In the right conditions (say, with the wind just aft of the beam), they could sail very quickly, completing voyages in two days that took three to seven in a steam-powered collier. Like the great clippers, their hulls were very full, with hard bilges and very little deadrise, maximising the volume of cargo they could carry.

Between 1900 and 1904, 332,000 gross tons of wooden schooners were constructed. In the five years between 1900 and 1905, ninety-two vessels of 1,000 tons or more were built, compared to only forty-two of equivalent-capacity steam craft. In the years preceding the First World War, there were still some fifty of these four- and five-masted wooden ships operating.

Altogether, they were effective components of the country's transport system during this period. Their big weakness was the possibility of an inadvertent 'jibe' when running before the wind. A jibe occurs when a sudden change in wind direction brings the wind on to what was the leeward side of the sail, causing it to sweep from out at an angle on one side of the ship to the same angle on the other. In a stiff breeze, this sudden movement of the giant sails and booms could happen with spar- and mast-breaking intensity.

Shipbuilders also learned that, as schooners grew larger, their ability to work to windward declined (they became less 'weatherly'). On the other hand, square-riggers, which had, with the addition of improved staysails, become increasingly 'close-winded' during the latter years of their development, could be almost as weatherly as a full fore-and-aft schooner rig. Changing the sails on the foremast back to square sails—creating what is known as a 'barquentine rig'—improved downwind performance and produced the best of both worlds for coastal work.

Post-1906, however, construction of wooden sailing ships, no matter the rig, went into terminal decline in America, beaten out by steamships towing barges. There was a brief respite during the First World War when 323 wooden cargo ships were built under government contract. There was also a short period of construction of barquentines and schooners on the west coast, using carefully prepared Douglas fir to replace the white oak so valuable on the east coast. But apart from these two spurts of activity, the age of merchant wooden shipbuilding was over in the United States.

It wouldn't be until the First World War when modernisation, heavily subsidised by building warships, led to a recovery in the construction of deepwater ships. Between 1914 and 1921, America's merchant ship construction increased tenfold—but that growth was based on steam and steel rather than wooden ships.

Chief among those providing international shipping services to America was, of course, Great Britain, and its domination through this period flowed from its mastery of iron founding and cheap steel production.

From being overwhelmed by the advanced nature of the American clippers immediately after the repeal of the Navigation Acts, Great Britain rose rapidly to create a new generation of iron and steel clippers. They would almost equal their wooden American counterparts and, more importantly, lead the world in iron and steel steamships.

In 1856, Great Britain's share of total foreign tonnage registered as entering American ports was 73 per cent. By 1878 (the latest year for which this series is available), it was still 65 per cent—an enormous turnaround on the situation at the time of the repeal of the Navigation Acts.

From Wood to Iron and Steel

Earlier, we saw how iron took over rapidly from wood in the construction of all vessels, only to be even more rapidly taken over by steel.

In steamship construction, wood was never a realistic material because of its inability to resist vibration. Iron dominated, but as soon as cheap steel became available in the early 1880s, it took over quickly and almost completely.

The chart below shows the dramatic increase in steamship construction in Great Britain during the period 1850–1908.

Steamship Construction in Great Britain by Material: 1850–1908 (000's net tons)

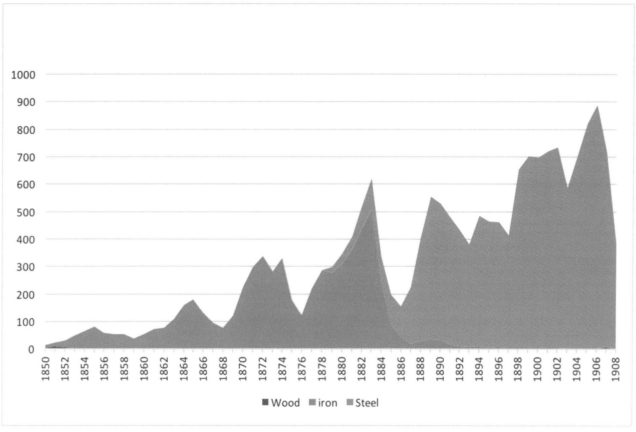

Source: British Historical Statistics; B. R. Mitchell

In the first three decades of this period, iron construction rapidly expanded the net tonnage of ships being built, but it precipitously fell once cheap steel became readily available. Steel construction began some years before 1878. By 1887, construction in iron had almost completely ceased. Steel took over, and after a brief hiatus in shipbuilding generally in 1886 and 1887, it continued the growth dynamic that had been established by iron.

The chart also shows how output fluctuated wildly in the early decades although, as the tonnages increased, the amplitude of the cycles decreased. It should be emphasised that this data is for merchant ship construction, and the reason it drops off so dramatically after its peak in 1906 reflects the extent to which production facilities were being devoted to the construction of warships in the run-up to the First World War.

Industrialised iron and steelmaking were disruptive technologies for those engaged in building wooden ships. However, American naval architects such as Donald McKay had taken wood to the limit of its capabilities. The Industrial Revolution and its accompanying increase in production, population, and trade meant ships had to simply be larger. Building in wood, increasingly, could not satisfy that need. As sailing ships grew in size, they outran wood's engineering properties. It is the sheer strength of steel that greatly extended the effective life of the sailing ship, and it did so by probably half a century.

Sailing Ships: From Wood through Iron to Steel

The chart below sets out the construction of wooden, iron and steel sailing ships in Great Britain between 1850 and 1908. It shows how iron displaced wood as a sailing ship construction material, only for it to be replaced by steel as superior production methods, and economies of scale brought costs down in the latter half of the nineteenth century.

Sailing Ship Construction by Material in Great Britain: 1850-1908 (000's net tons)

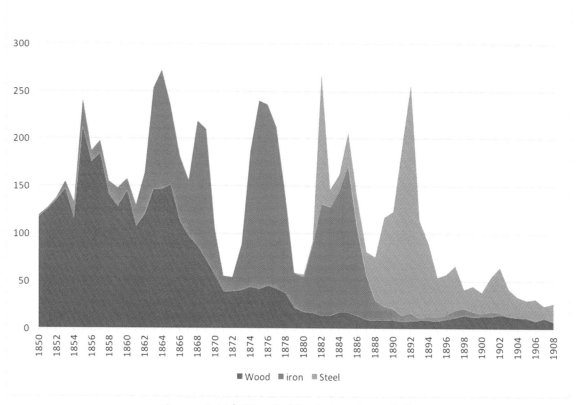

Source: British Historical Statistics; B R Mitchell

The chart demonstrates the decline in wood as a shipbuilding material—from a peak of 212,000 net tons in 1855 (the height of the clipper era in the United States) to a mere 8,000 net tons in 1908. Iron was used well before 1850 but had all but died out by 1908. Steel usage began before 1850, but cost kept the tonnage small. There was a pronounced peak in iron construction in the period 1854–57, but usage declined rapidly as steel became cheaper.

Taken overall, the chart shows the extent to which sailing ship construction declined from 1870 onwards, all the while fluctuating wildly. It fell from a peak of 273,000 tons in 1864 to a mere 27,000 net tons in 1908. This is typical of a 'capital goods' industry, but it would seem to be exaggerated in sailing ship construction. Sailing ships were less complicated than steamships and could be built much quicker, which may have resulted in the wild swings in construction.

The clippers lost much of their raison d'être after the inauguration of the Suez Canal in 1869. It opened up the Chinese and the Indian tea trades to the steamers. It was in the later years covered by this chart that sailing ship design changed from clippers to much larger and more utilitarian vessels. Steam was a threat, but there were still markets that could only be serviced by sail—or were more efficiently and effectively serviced by sailers. To do so in the rapidly expanding world economy required a much larger and tougher vessel than the clipper.

Iron and then steel made that possible.

The arrival of this new generation of ships can be seen from the increased output in the fifteen years from 1880 through to 1895. These were the mighty windjammers. In terms of sheer strength and lugging capacity, they were the most potent wind-driven machines of all time. They represented a revolution in sailing ship design in their size, cargo capacity, and strength.

Sail versus Steam

In Great Britain in 1850, almost 25,000 sailing ships with a net tonnage of 3.4 million tons were on the British register, compared to 1,200-odd steamships with a net tonnage of a mere 168,000 tons, most of which would have been small paddle-driven craft.

However, towards the end of the century, the situation had begun to change.

According to historian A. H. Imlah, by 1914 international trade had expanded enormously—almost doubling from 17.5 million tons in 1890 to 32 million tons. In 1880, the tonnage carried in sail was only marginally below what it had been in 1860, and the deep-sea trade was almost all in sailing vessels. By 1914, the role of sailing ships had, however, reversed. By then, they were carrying only around 13 per cent of total world trade, as opposed to almost all of it in 1860.

World Trade: Sail vs. Steam/Motor Vessels: 1820-1914 (net tons M)

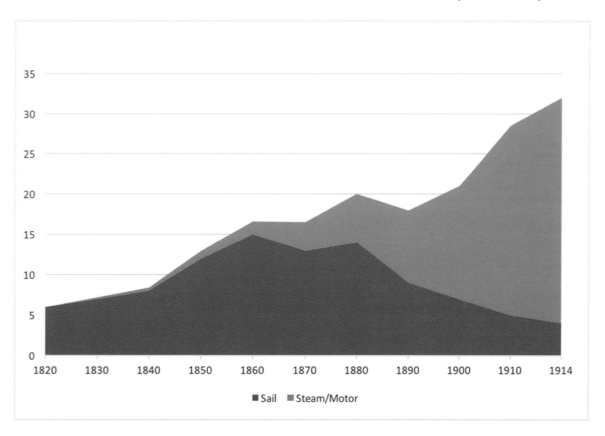

Source: Economic Elements in Pax Britannica. A. H. Imlah HUP 1958. NB figures for 1830 & 1850 are interpolations.

By 1914, the number of sailing ships registered in the United Kingdom had dropped by two-thirds to just over 8,000. The net tonnage was 847,000 tons, which suggests that most of those left were quite small. By comparison, the number of steamships on the register in 1913 had increased tenfold, to 12,600, with a net tonnage of 11.3 million tons. Proportionately, in 1850, sail's share of a total carrying capacity of 3.6 million net tons was 99 per cent. By 1913, full carrying capacity had increased from 3.6 million net tons to 12.1 million net tons, and steam made up 93 per cent. The proportion represented by sail had declined to just 7 per cent (0.8 million net tons).

The decline is reflected in the tonnage being built in sail versus steam:

Great Britain; Sailing vs. Steamships Built and First Registered: 1850-1914 (000's net tons)

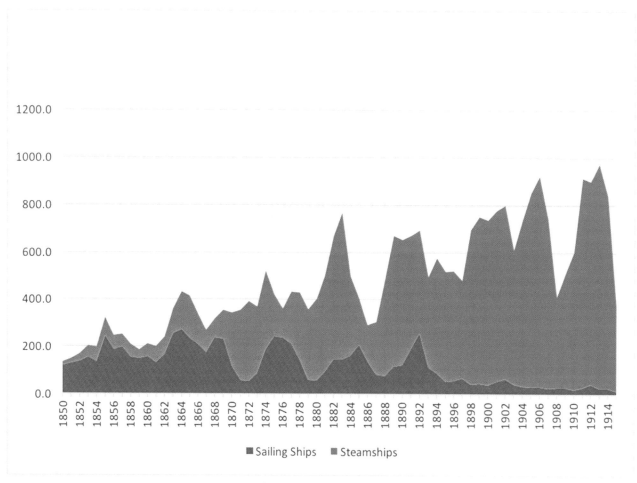

Source: British Historical Statistics B. R. Mitchell

In the year 1850, 119,000 net tons of sailing ships—overwhelmingly made of wood—were built in the United Kingdom. That same year, a mere 14,600 tons of steamship capacity were constructed, mostly in iron. The ratio of sail to steam was 9:1 in favour of sail.

Shipbuilding expanded steadily after the repeal of the Navigation Acts in 1849. In 1850, only 134,000 net tons of shipping capacity were built. In 1855, 370,000 net tons were added, an almost tripling over five years, but these volumes were insignificant in terms of what the British industry would go on to achieve before the First World War.

In 1915, the second year of hostilities, there was a sudden reduction in merchant marine construction as shipbuilding facilities were turned over to building warships. In 1913, the ratio of steam to sail was 38:1 in favour of steam.

The Crossover

The following chart shows a ten-year moving average of British sailing and steamship production from 1859 to 1915:

Great Britain; Sailing vs. Steamships Built and First Registered: 1850-1914 (000's net tons 10-year m.a.)

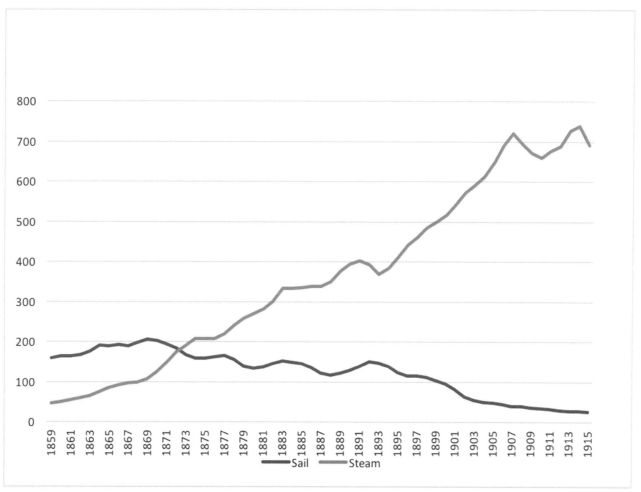

Source: British Historical Statistics B. R. Mitchell CUP

Sailing ship construction peaked in the decade preceding 1873. During the same period, however, steamship building was on a strong upward growth path. From 1873, when the two series intersect, sail was in more or less steady decline, but steamship construction was burgeoning. Interestingly, some of the sailing ships built in the latter part of this period were still operating decades later when many of their steam counterparts had worn out or been overtaken by technological change.

Although sailing ship construction was now in decline, in 1885, there were still 3.5 million tons of registered sail capacity in Great Britain, compared to 4 million tons of steam. It would not be until triple-expansion steam engines became widely available that steam would turn the tables on sail decisively.

Great Britain Reasserts Itself—the Age of Steel and Sail

After the Civil War, America became obsessed with its so-called 'Manifest Destiny'—appropriating all the land 'from sea to shining sea'—and this preoccupation meant that the baton of sailing ship development passed decisively to Great Britain. Although the construction of sailing ships was in decline compared to steamers, Britain, freed of its mercantilist inhibitions, became the main source of innovation in sailing ship design and development. The success of the windjammers can be attributed in large part to these innovations. Gone were the cast-iron frames and wooden cladding of the composite clipper. In came giant cast-iron and later steel hulls, flat-bottomed and slab-sided, with lofty steel masts and yards and wire standing rigging. Except for those sections of running rigging handled by the crew, manila rope was replaced by wire rope and chain.

Some vessels were equipped with the latest labour-saving machinery such as patent winches and donkey engines, halving crew numbers. Bracing the yards (the windward end of the transverse spars) is one of the most demanding tasks on a sailing ship, and the use of winches reduced manpower and the time taken to complete the job. Above-deck catwalks, known as 'flying bridges', protected crews from being sent overboard when the decks were awash, as they quite often were below 40 degrees south. On occasions, there could be upwards of *700 tons* of water on the deck of a big windjammer in a high sea.

Another innovation was the addition of a raised deckhouse amidships. It included accommodation for the officers and also the crew, no longer relegated to a forecastle, or 'foc'sle'. Nets were also rigged above the bulwarks to further protect the crew from being washed overboard. Cowlings protected the helmsmen, traditionally located above the rudder, from huge waves that regularly overtook eastbound ships in the high latitudes. Some of the later-built ships even moved the wheel to the midships bridge.

Double the Carrying Capacity

Most importantly, the new breed of vessel had twice the carrying capacity proportionate to the tonnage of a clipper ship and were virtually warehouses in motion. Windjammers specialised in carrying (for their time) huge cargoes long distances and from remote locations. On the rare occasions that they reached port, the ready availability of port steam tugs improved harbour turnaround times.

While steamships are often portrayed as the nemesis of the sailing ship, there was a time when steam was in its maritime infancy, and the world depended on big sailers to do the heavy lifting. The availability of steam tugs considerably improved the productivity of big sailing ships, dependably hauling them in and out of port. Even when steamships had taken over much of the business of sailing ships, the big windjammers relied on this relationship for home port turnaround.

A Typical Windjammer: the *Chile* Trading in the South Pacific

Source: Courtesy of the Boston Public Library, Leslie Jones Collection

By the turn of the twentieth century, windjammers were a common sight in the great harbours of the world. There are countless photographs showing forests of masts in Hamburg, Liverpool, London, Cardiff, Antwerp, Bordeaux, Dunkirk, Hong Kong, San Francisco, Vancouver, Shanghai, Rio de Janeiro, New York, Boston, Newcastle (Australia, where they loaded coal), and Melbourne. In 1908, there were more than 3,500 sailing ships registered with Lloyds of London alone. All the great maritime nations of the world were involved, but several stood out: the United Kingdom, initially as an operator and later primarily as a builder; Germany; France; and the Scandinavian countries.

As W. L. A. Derby, maritime historian and author of *The Tall Ships Pass*, wrote,

> *Lacking the daintiness, the handiness, and the sweet lines of their progenitors, [the windjammers] nevertheless represented, in their prime, sail's epitome of combined strength, seaworthiness, economy, and longevity.*

Dedicated Freighters

'Windjammer' may well have originated among steamship hands as a pejorative term referring to any type of sailing ship. Another suggestion is that the ships were so large and ungainly that they had to be 'jammed' up into the wind. The general description was any type of large, steel- or iron-hulled sail-powered freighter that was optimised for the long haul of bulk commodities. They were freighters first and foremost, with little if any facilities for carrying passengers.

Certainly, for their day, they were big (some could load 8,000 tons of cargo) and somewhat ungainly in that they were slab-sided and much less refined in their design compared to the elegant clippers. Typically made entirely of steel and shaped to maximise cargo capacity, there was little room for the graceful curves that made the clipper so aesthetically pleasing.

Despite the Suez Canal and improvements in steamship capability, a small group of hard-nosed investors still believed that traditional sailing ships were a more economical and profitable means of marine transport than steamships. As the ships were very big, they conceded that they needed to be suitably modified to take advantage of advances in shipbuilding and mechanics, such as winches and donkey engines. Their enthusiasm for sail kept alive the concept of great vessels navigating the vast oceans of the world using nothing but the wind, and the skill and fortitude of those who drove them.

The windjammers ranged from three- to five-masted fully rigged ships and barques, though by 1890, a consensus had emerged that the four-masted barque rig was the most suitable for the trades in which these ships were engaged.

According to Swedish maritime historian Lars Bruzelius, there were 434 four-masted ships built between 1853 and 1926. Of the 183 vessels built before 1890, ninety were fully rigged ships. Of the 251 built between 1890 and 1926, only seven were fully rigged ships, and the rest were four-masted barques. These figures did not include the fully rigged ships that were subsequently converted to the barque rig. It still provided plenty of power, and by not square-rigging the fourth mast, they were able to keep labour costs down.

Creative Ferment

The latter part of the nineteenth century was a period of considerable creative ferment in ship construction and propulsion. There were many hybrid vessels built that used various combinations of iron and wood in their construction and sail and steam for motive power. Sails were common on steamships, and a few steam engines were even installed in wooden hulls, although much less successfully. Iron or steel auxiliary steamers were neither fish nor fowl, and many were converted to either one or the other.

The difficulty was that an auxiliary steamship needed two crews: one to handle the sails and another to tend the steam engines. The development of the windjammers as a specific ship type arose from this upheaval in vessel design. Their construction was driven, at least in part, by the conviction on the part of some notable diehards that sailing ships were the most efficient and profitable means of transport and could compete with steam on specific routes that did not require adherence to timetables. Embedded in this conviction was invariably an intense love of the sailing ship concept as a rare manifestation of man's mastery of the sea. It was the rapid change in this period in history, and the limitations of steam, that saw windjammers emerge as a distinct and, as it turned out, long-lived, vessel type.

The reality was that sail, henceforth, could only survive as long-distance carriers with capacious iron or steel hulls loading cheap, raw material bulk cargoes from locations that were either inaccessible or dangerous to steamers. Typical cargoes were nitrate, wool, grain, coal, and 'case' oil. Using the wind as fuel, they would then deliver them to the markets of the Industrial Age, primarily in Europe.

After the American Civil War, which destroyed so much of its merchant navy, Americans were neither equipped nor inclined to build ships that satisfied the emerging market for sailers. As a result, this new generation of ships was primarily built in Europe where skill in metallurgy and metalworking had proceeded afoot. Being built of iron or steel, they also required an industrialised process in which considerable capital and expertise had been invested. It was a world away from the crude construction methods that had been employed in building even the largest of the American wooden clippers.

America's Mercantile Decline

Only four iron-hulled and twelve steel-hulled sailing ships were ever built in the United States. Steel was expensive there, labour costs were high, and America lacked the capital to exploit it on the necessary scale—or chose to invest it elsewhere. Great Britain's shipbuilding industry, by contrast, now involved a high level of expertise. It had also made a considerable capital investment in tooling and construction facilities. This was Victorian Britain's forte, where its industrial entrepreneurs excelled.

In 1857, of the 4.8 million tons of cargo entering American ports, American vessels carried 3.5 million tons, or 72 per cent. It was the largest share American ships would appropriate for the next two decades. By 1878, the inbound cargo tonnage carried in American vessels had fallen to 3.1 million tons, whereas total cargo tonnage (reflecting the massive expansion of the American economy) had increased to 11.5 million tons. The American share of total tonnage entering its ports had dropped by almost two-thirds.

The new sailing vessels were built initially of iron and then of steel in the industrialised shipyards of Europe, overwhelmingly in Great Britain, but later in France and Germany. In the latter years of the nineteenth and the early decade or so of the new century, these shipyards would turn out an enormous fleet of these great vessels.

America would re-emerge as a formidable steel shipbuilder, but it would not be until towards the end of the nineteenth century and not in merchant ships. By then, it would be too late to compete with, for example, the British industry, where wages for skilled labour were now lower, and highly effective industrial organisation and capital investment kept costs to a minimum.

Wrought iron was an expensive material for shipbuilding, and the transition to steel came in the late 1870s as cheaper supplies became available. Historian B. R. Mitchell writes that by 1885, there were 154 sailing ships made of iron and only thirty-two of steel. Because steel was so strong compared to wood and better able to withstand vibration, the symbiotic relationship between steam and steel consolidated. The uptake of steel construction in steamships was therefore much more rapid.

In 1885, 182 metal steamships were constructed, 159 of them in steel. By 1908, the last data available in the Mitchell series, the number of sailing ships built of iron had dropped to a mere eight vessels, while the number in steel totalled 141. These would have mainly been windjammers. In steamships, the transition was again more dramatic. There were no steamships built of iron in 1908, and a massive 473 in steel.

The Limits of Steam Navigation

Steamships, however, were constrained in the markets they could exploit profitably. Steaming long distances without the opportunity of re-bunkering (loading fresh supplies of coal) required large amounts of coal, which limited cargo space. They were also less capable of handling the sea conditions on any route that involved rounding Cape Horn.

Here they were extremely vulnerable.

An overtaking wave might crumple a funnel and swamp their boilers, leaving the vessel without power and steerageway and at the mercy of mountainous seas. Unlike a sailing ship, it is not possible to 'jury' rig a steamship. ('Jury' rigging is the process of making makeshift repairs with only the tools and materials at hand.) A steamship either had steam, or it didn't, and it was entirely dependent on its propeller shaft.

For sailing ships, however, tales of them losing substantial parts of their rig and still being able to proceed are legion. They could make way so long as they had at least part of a single mast still standing.

The 'White Gold Rush'—Chilean Nitrate Deposits

Due to an accident of geology, the guano deposits on the islands off Peru were in roughly the same global region as another source of high-grade nitrate. It took the form of highly mineralised geological deposits inland from the coast of northern Chile, about 500 nautical miles south of the guano deposits on the Chincha Islands.

Known since ancient times and used by pre-Colombian Indians as fertiliser, commercial-grade nitrate ore occurred on the eastern side of the coastal range in the driest of the world's deserts, the Atacama. Here, an almost complete lack of rain and a paucity of nitrogen-consuming plants led to the accumulation of high-grade ore, which is now believed to have been formed by the upwelling and evaporation of ancient mineral-rich groundwater.

The deposits occur from just north of Iquique at 20 degrees south of the equator, for a distance of over 400 miles further to the south—in a belt about 12 miles wide. During the heyday of the nitrate trade in the latter part of the nineteenth century and the early part of the twentieth, the deposits were exploited by British, French, German, and Chilean interests. They were dispersed through five major centres or districts: Tarapacá, Topophilia, Baquendano, Aguas Blancas, and Taltal.

Most deposits occurred at an elevation of less than 2,000 metres but had to be transported over the coastal range on the backs of donkeys and llamas, which were later replaced, as demand escalated, by railway lines and cable cars.

The deposits were discovered by Westerners in the 1830s, and they became the world's main source of nitrogen for fertiliser, explosives, and a variety of industrial chemicals. The deposits were also the world's chief source of iodine (previously extracted from seaweed) up until the mid-twentieth century.

From around 16,000 tons in 1843, shipments of nitrate rose to nearly 3 million tons during the First World War. But by the beginning of that conflagration, manufactured nitrate in Europe had exceeded exports from Chile, foreshadowing the end of what was one of the main trades for the windjammers.

Copper Ore

Chile was also a source of copper ore, another strategic material in demand in an increasingly belligerent Europe. Again, the distance was too great, and the route necessitated rounding Cape Horn where the conditions were too hazardous for steamers.

In geological terms, Chile's elongated Western margin is bounded by an earthquake-inducing, mountain-building, ore-producing 'subduction' zone. It contains some of the largest copper deposits and, more latterly, copper mines, in the world. The earthquakes and consequent tsunamis however created a significant hazard for ships loading minerals. The city of Arica was destroyed three times by tsunamis in the nineteenth century. The waves were so high and so powerful they could lift large ships hundreds of yards above the high-water mark.

Another hazard to navigation was the strong north-flowing current. If a sailing ship was becalmed adjacent to its destination, it could be carried many miles past. The only hope was to sail south-west and then east to intersect the coast below the port and hope the wind did not desert them again at the entrance. The whole process could take a month. The alternative was to abandon the charter altogether. The continental shelf is very narrow in this area, and yet another hazard was drifting towards the shore in water where it was too deep to anchor.

Despite these difficulties, demand in Europe meant that guano and nitrate ports sprang up on the offshore islands and at intervals along the mainland coast. Pisco, Callao, and Lomas were located in Peru, and Pisagua, Tocophila, Antofagasta, and Iquique in Chile.

The Dangers of the Nitrate and Coal Trades

Coal exported from Europe—particularly the great coal fields of England and Wales—provided a cargo for the windjammers on the outgoing voyage, resupplying bunkering points along the steamer routes, especially into the Orient. Windjammers could also load coal in Newcastle, New South Wales, and transport it to the west coast of the Americas where guano or nitrate could be loaded for the trip around Cape Horn to Europe.

Coal was, however, dangerous to transport. It only needed to be damp at the time of loading—or become damp during the voyage—and it could spontaneously combust. Unless the fire could be starved of oxygen, it might explode or heat a metal ship to the point where it was no longer possible to operate it.

Nitrate is very deliquescent and quickly soluble in water. But cargoes were also prone to catching fire. Peculiarly, the accepted way to extinguish a nitrate fire in the hold of a ship was with water containing dissolved nitrate! When a ship was being loaded, casks of this concoction were always kept at hand. Despite the precautions taken, Basil Lubbock cites several vessels that were destroyed by fire.

Early British Dominance

The early years of the nineteenth-century nitrate traffic out of Chile were dominated by British investment in facilities and by British ships. Nevertheless, it was considered the trade where, out of its huge merchant marine, its old ships went to die. Although more British ships were operating on the west coast of South America than of any other country, none of the British shipping companies specialised in the trade to the extent of F. Laeisz & Co. and A. D. Bordes, prosperous shipping companies from Germany and France, respectively. As the demand for the chemicals increased, these two companies competed to modernise the management and loading of the ships.

The companies' biggest contribution would, however, be in the vessels that they built to move the burgeoning tonnages to Europe. In the early stages of the massive increase in output, these companies initially turned to Britain for its expertise in the construction of large steel ships. Great Britain obliged, providing the models for the giant vessels that would ultimately be built in France and Germany.

Germany brought discipline and drive to the business. Laeisz's ships were invariably discharged and loaded in a quarter of the time it took other vessels, driving the stevedores and employing a disciplined system of lighters. Laeisz also insisted that the ships race home. The days of rigging down at night were long gone.

Other Markets

Another market for the windjammers was 'case' oil, or kerosene, refined from the crude oil discovered on the east coast of America in the late nineteenth century. It was increasingly favoured over whale oil for lighting purposes and was in demand everywhere. For convenience of unloading, it was transported in crates ('cases') of two four-gallon rectangular drums, what later came to be referred to as kerosene tins.

At least one windjammer, the *Falls of Clyde*, later in her working life had large tanks fitted into her hull. She plied between Hawaii and California, bringing kerosene from the mainland and returning with molasses for cattle feed. Built in iron on the Clyde in 1878, she is still afloat in Honolulu, almost 150 years later, although in dire need of restoration. The *Falls of Clyde* was one of the first merchant marine tankers.

Primary produce exports from the antipodes were also difficult for steamers even though they did not have to negotiate Cape Horn. From Australia, the windjammers carried coal, wool, and wheat, cargoes that were more secure for sailing ships due to the permanent isolation of the Great South Land. It was sheer distance to their markets, rather than pesky land bridges, that made them ideal grist for the windjammers. Bringing timber from the Pacific north-west to Europe was also a regular windjammer trade—general freight out and lumber home. The same was true of rice from Asia.

The Windjammer Rigs

The windjammers' giant rigs were designed to make them easier to work than the clippers. Unlike their forebears, the windjammers never set 'studding sails', the lower yard extensions so beloved of clipper ship designers and skippers. It was held they were too difficult to set for only a very marginal advantage. Consequently, whereas a clipper would appear on the horizon like a vast triangle of sail, the windjammer looked more like a giant obelisk.

Another concession to their size was to split topsails and royals into two sails—an upper and lower of each—for ease of handling. Still another rig, known as a bald-header, eschewed royal sails altogether and split both topsails and topgallant sails into two. Nevertheless, the largest (main) sails still weighed a ton dry, and very much more wet. The highest sail set was an upper royal, as opposed to the skysails and moonrakers of the crack clippers.

These modifications notwithstanding, a typical windjammer set more sails than any other ship—thirty-four in all—the area of which, for example, on the German *Herzogin Cecilie*, could exceed an acre. To put it in a modern context, her sails would have covered almost three-quarters of a full-size soccer field!

Herzogin Cecilie set eighteen square sails (six on each of the fore, main, and mizzen masts) and often sixteen fore-and-aft sails, five on the bowsprit, three between each of the square-rigged masts, and another two on the fourth 'jiggermast', mounted stern-most. For the officers and crew, managing this prodigious area of canvas with no other means of propulsion but the high winds that were a necessary part of their livelihood was a triumph of skill, resilience, and seamanship. It is an art that has long since disappeared.

In reaching their golden age, the windjammer owners would create the biggest sailing ships that have ever graced the oceans of the world. Not only were they the largest, they were also possibly the greatest. They performed tasks that were beyond the capabilities of their predecessors but also their steamship contemporaries and were a vital element of the merchant marine of the age.

12
CHAPTER

The Windjammers—Zenith and Decline

The Seven Five-Masters

F. Laeisz & Co. experimented with two enormous ships, the *Potosi* and the *Preussen II*, which were launched in 1895 and 1902, respectively. The *Potosi* was a five-masted barque, and the *Preussen II* was a five-masted fully-rigged ship. Although the *Potosi* would set a record for the voyage from Chile to England around Cape Horn, the vessels proved unpopular with crews. The ships were so large for their time that Laeisz found it difficult to find cargoes on outward voyages.

Altogether, there were seven of these giant five-masters built. In terms of length and sail area, the *Preussen II* was the largest sailing ship ever built, but both the *R. C. Rickmers* and *France II* had larger carrying capacities. With her five square-rigged masts, *Preussen II* carried over 73,300 square feet of sail, about 1.7 acres, equivalent to 1.2 soccer fields, or five and a half Olympic swimming pools. All the other five-masters were barques with only a spanker set on the fifth mast.

The *Preussen II*—the Largest Sailing Ship Ever Built

Source: Courtesy of State Library of Queensland

Their Place in History

The great windjammers lacked the grace, speed, and romance of the clippers which they succeeded. Not only were they bigger, there were many more of them. They were developed at a time when population and economic activity were quickly expanding. They were handmaidens of an industrial revolution, designed to bring necessary raw materials from the far corners of the earth.

It would be that same revolution that would ultimately destroy them.

Built of stronger material, they could withstand severe ocean conditions better than the clippers. They would also survive longer. Entering into service in the latter part of the nineteenth century, many were still working up until (and in a couple of notable cases, after) the Second World War.

They were the last of the great windships that had served mankind for centuries, if not millennia, and their demise was the definitive example of 'creative destruction'.

The Seven Five-masted Windjammers

Name	Year	Builder	Hull	GRT	LOA(ft)
France I	1890	Henderson Patrick, Glasgow	Steel	3784	435
Maria Rickmers	1891	Russell & Co, Glasgow	Steel	3822	443
Potosi	1895	J Tecklenborg, Geestemunde	Steel	4027	436
Preussen II	1902	J Tecklenborg, Geestemunde	Steel	5081	482
R C Rickmers	1906	Rickmers, Schiffbau Bremerhaven	Steel	5548	479
France II	1913	Chantiers Ateliers, Gironde	Steel	5633	481
Kobenhavn	1921	Ramage/Ferguson, Leith	Steel	3901	430

Source: Wikipedia.org List of Large Sailing Vessels

The fate of *France I* is unknown. The captain of the *Maria Rickmers* died when the ship was in Singapore, and the first mate took control en route to Saigon to load rice for a voyage to Bremerhaven. She was last seen passing Anjer-Lor in the Sunda Straits. The *Potosi*, after a long and eventful life and renamed the *Flora*, caught fire off the coast of Patagonia and, floating derelict and as a hazard to navigation, was sunk by naval gunfire.

Preussen II collided with a cross-channel ferry in 1910. She was one of three Laeisz 'P' Line ships that would be the subject of steamer collisions in the English Channel. The other two were *Pangani* (fatally) and *Padua*.

R. C. Rickmers was equipped with auxiliary steam engines, so was not a pure windjammer. She was seized by the British in 1914 and, renamed *Neath*, was subsequently sunk by a German submarine in 1917. *France II* was the second-largest sailing vessel ever built after the *Preussen II* and the largest in terms of carrying capacity. She stranded on Teremba Reef, New Caledonia, with a cargo of coke in 1922 with no loss of life. The *Kobenhavn* was the largest sailing ship afloat at the time of her construction in 1921. She disappeared without a trace in 1928.

The five-masters did not last as long as their four-masted brethren, although it seems to have had more to do with misadventure rather than any fault of the particular ship type. They were, however, considered to be less manoeuvrable. It was the more moderately sparred four-masted barques that proved most suited to the cargoes and routes available to them. They were the sailing ships that would hold out the longest against the challenge of steam.

The Rise of the Four-Masted Barque

Freighters doubled in size from the packet and clipper era. Steamers took the transatlantic packet business, and there now being no need for extreme speed, the clippers fell by the wayside. Size, sturdiness, lugging power, and durability became the watchwords.

The other important development in the latter quarter of the nineteenth century was the abandonment of the fully rigged ship rig in favour of the barque rig. Again, 1888 is a useful data point. In the years prior, of the 137 four-masted ships built purposely as sailers (i.e. excluding vessels converted from steam), ninety-eight were built as fully rigged ships.

But times were changing.

Seagoing labour was becoming scarcer and more expensive.

Rigging the after mast with simply fore-and-aft sails reduced crew numbers and labour costs. It also made for a more manoeuvrable vessel. From 1888 to 1931, when a total of 290 four-masted vessels were built, only twenty were fully rigged ships. The other 270 were rigged as barques.

According to Lars Bruzelius, there were an incredible 422 four-masted sailing ships built in the modern era, beginning in the middle of the nineteenth century, up until the first half of the twentieth. Beginning seriously in the latter quarter of the nineteenth century, four-masted vessel fabrication would describe an arc that would last into the twentieth century.

Four-masted Vessels Built 1874–1931

Source: Lars Bruzelius

Before 1874, there were five four-masted ships built in wood, mainly in Canada and the United States. They included Donald McKay's *Great Republic*. Between 1853 and 1865, there were nine ships built as steamers that were subsequently converted to sailing ships. Another followed in 1880. Between 1874 and 1930, there were 405 sailing vessels built as four-masted barques or fully rigged ships. Many of the ship rigs, however, were subsequently converted to the more economical barque sail plan.

As the chart shows, construction of four-masted ships began seriously in 1882, when nineteen were launched. In the next six years, production averaged eighteen vessels a year. Then 1889 saw the beginning of a four-masted metal sailing ship boom. In that year, construction jumped to twenty-six, then to thirty in 1890, and forty-three in 1891. In 1892, an amazing fifty-eight vessels, more than one a week, hit the water. In that year, Great Britain built 287,000 gross tons of sailing ships, and four-masted vessels made up 60 per cent of the total.

Steamship construction passed that of sailing ships around 1873, but there was a very distinct revival in sail during this period. The stimulus was that Europe was drawing in massive amounts of raw materials and food—nitrates, fertilisers, wool, and wheat—but from destinations too dangerous or where coal was not readily available, and hence outside the range of steamers.

Around one-third of the 405 purpose-built four-masted sailing ships were built between 1874 and 1887. During this period, the construction material was overwhelmingly wrought iron. Of the 133 ships built, only sixteen were made of steel. Three were built of wood (two in Maine and one in Canada), and the remaining 114 were made of iron.

Selected Great Four-masted Barque Windjammer Merchant Sailing Ships

Name	Year	Builder	Hull	GRT	LOA
Falls of Clyde (FRS)	1878	Russell & Co., Glasgow	Iron	1807	280
Polymnia	1886	Blohm & Voss, Hamburg	Iron	2129	291
Garthpool (Or Jutepolis)	1891	WB. Thompson, Dundee	Steel	2842	309
Lawhill	1892	Caledonian Shipbldg, England	Steel	2942	347
Olivebank	1892	Mackie/Thompson, Glasgow	Steel	2824	326
John Ena	1892	R Duncan & Co., Glasgow	Steel	2842	313
Herzogin Cecilie	1902	Rickmers A.G., Bremerhaven	Steel	3242	334
Pommern (Or. Mneme)	1903	J. Reid & Co., Glasgow	Iron	2423	312
Ponape	1903	Bacini, Genoa	Steel	2342	284
Moshulu (Or Kurt)	1904	William Hamilton, Glasgow	Steel	3109	335
Hans	1904	Hamilton & Co., Glasgow	Steel	3102	335
Archibald Russell	1905	Scotts Shipbuilding, England	Steel	2354	292
Pamir	1905	Blohm & Voss, Hamburg	Steel	3020	375
Viking	1906	Burmeister Wain, Denmark	Steel	2959	294
Peking	1911	Blohm & Voss, Hamburg	Steel	3100	322
Passat	1911	Blohm & Voss, Hamburg	Steel	3091	317
Sedov	1921	Krupp Germania, Keil	Steel	3476	329
Kruzenshtern (Padua)	1926	JC.Tecklenborg, Bremerhaven	Steel	3064	375

Source: Wikipedia, Lars Bruzelius, et al. FRS: Originally a fully rigged ship or: Originally

The *Falls of Clyde* was originally built as a four-masted fully rigged ship but was later converted to a barque. She is the only surviving iron-hulled four-master still afloat, though barely so. With *Wavertree* (a three-masted fully rigged ship), she represents the transition from wooden clippers and packet ships to the big iron windjammers.

The *Falls of Clyde*

Source: Courtesy Sunday Times

Polymnia stranded at Cape Horn on a voyage from the Chilean nitrate port of Pisagua to Falmouth, Cornwall. *Garthpool* (formerly *Jutepolis*) was 'bald-headed', setting double topsails and double topgallant sails, but no royals—a means of reducing handling costs. She was reputedly the last of the British-registered deepwater sailing ships and was wrecked in the Cape Verde islands in 1929.

Lawhill was another bald-header. She had many owners and served in a variety of trades before finally being broken up in 1959 after a working life of sixty-seven years. In 1911, the *Olivebank* caught fire carrying coal and grounded due to the volume of water taken aboard to extinguish it. Refloated, she served until 1939 when she hit a mine and sank with the loss of fourteen of her crew. *John Ena* was built for the San Francisco Shipping Co. of Honolulu and spent her working life in the Pacific before being broken up in San Pedro, California, in 1934.

The *Herzogin Cecilie* was named after the German Crown Princess Duchess Cecilie of Mecklenburg-Schwerin, spouse of Crown Prince Wilhelm of Prussia. *Herzogin* is German for 'duchess'. She was one of the fastest windjammers ever built, having once logged twenty-one knots over a short distance. Famed for her performance in the Great Grain Races from Australia, she won four times before 1921 and four out of eleven times between 1926 and 1936. That latter year, she famously grounded on the channel coast in dense fog, and although got off, she subsequently broke her back, capsized, and sank. While grounded her namesake came to visit her.

The Great *Herzogin Cecile*

Source: State Library of South Australia

Pommern, originally the *Mneme,* was steel-hulled and bald-headed, and the only Flying 'P' Line vessel to be built in Great Britain. Subsequently acquired by the Swede Gustav Erikson, she carried grain from Australia to Europe. Surviving two world wars unscathed, after the Second World War, she became (and remains) a museum ship at Mariehamn in the Åland Islands off mainland Sweden. *Ponape* was the only Flying 'P' Line ship to be built in Italy and one of only two to be built outside Germany. She was a war prize in 1914 and broken up in 1936.

Moshulu, originally the *Kurt,* was, at the time she was built, the largest barque in the world and one of the last four-masted steel barques to be built in Britain. Immortalised by Eric Newby in his book *The Last Grain Race,* she is the largest of the four-masted barques afloat today (as a restaurant at Penn's Landing in Philadelphia). She rounded Cape Horn fifty-four times in her career. (*Hans* was a sister ship to the *Kurt* and built the same year.)

After a long life, mainly in the nitrate trade (including confiscation during the First World War), *Hans* was re-rigged as a six-masted schooner in 1943 and renamed *Cidade da Porto.* She was broken up in Lisbon in 1948. *Archibald Russell* was the last deepwater sailing ship to be built in Great Britain. Constructed in 1905, she served in a number of windjammer trades including timber, grain, nitrate, and coal. Eventually ending up in the hands of Gustav Erikson, she was detained in the United Kingdom after Finland entered the Second World War on the German side. Post-war, she was returned to Erikson but was broken up in 1949.

The *Pamir* was built for F. Laeisz & Co. by Bloom & Voss in 1905 and used primarily in the nitrate trade. She was also sold to Gustav Erikson, who put her into the wheat trade with Australia. She had the distinction of being the last commercial sailing ship to round Cape Horn, in 1949. In 1957, crewed mainly by cadets and with an inexperienced captain, she capsized and sank in the vicinity of the Azores with a loss of all but six of her crew.

The Long-lived *Pamir*

Source: Wikimedia Commons

Viking was unusual in that she was built originally as a sail training ship in 1906 and later acquired by Gustav Erikson for use in the usual windjammer trades. She is now preserved as a museum ship in Gothenburg, Sweden. *Peking* was another 'P' Line ship seized as war reparations in 1921 and subsequently bought back by Laeisz and employed in the nitrate trade. She reverted to her original purpose as a training ship and was eventually sold to South Street Museum in New York City as a museum ship in 1976. In 2017, she was returned, at considerable expense, using the semi-submersible ship *MS Combi Dock III*, to Hamburg Port Museum, the city where she was built, where she is being restored.

Passat, like *Pamir*, was built in 1911 by Bloom & Voss for the Flying 'P' Line. Given to France as war reparations after the First World War, she was bought back by Laeisz in 1921 and sold to Gustav Erikson in 1932. Again, like *Pamir*, she was in the grain trade in 1957 when a cargo shifted, and she had to seek refuge. After the *Pamir* disaster, she was laid up in Hamburg.

The *Sedov* was built as a sail training vessel in 1921 called *Magdalene Vinnen II*. Renamed *Kommodore Johnsen* in 1936, she was given to Russia as war reparations in 1945. She was yet again renamed, this time as the *Sedov* after a noted Russian polar explorer, and is still used as a sail training vessel. In 2013, at ninety-two years old, she concluded a trip around the world.

The *Kruzenshtern* was originally the *Padua*, which was built in 1926 for the Flying 'P' Line and employed in the windjammer trades. She was surrendered to the Soviet Union in 1946 as war reparations and renamed for a prominent nineteenth-century Baltic explorer. She is still in use as a sail training vessel.

Europe's Dominance

All these metal ships were made in Europe, demonstrating the extent to which America had fallen behind. Not only were North American shipbuilders, who had so dominated shipbuilding up until the depression of 1857, still building in an outdated material, they also weren't competitive. An inquiry found that the American shipbuilding industry had been forced out of foreign trade because its costs were too high. Demand for wooden sailing ships in the coastal trade, however, remained strong because it was protected from foreign competition.

Almost all the famous American shipyards were closed by 1870, and a number went bankrupt. The legendary William H. Webb yard, responsible for so many of the great clippers and Atlantic packets, built its last ship in 1869. At Philadelphia and Baltimore, wooden sailing ship construction practically ceased. The locus of shipbuilding moved decisively north to Maine and Canada, focused on the grain trade to Europe—the 'down easters'. A large grain ship needed 200 to 300 full-grown oaks alone for framing, and wood supply had become a problem, being brought mostly from the Ohio Valley and the Great Lakes region. American shipbuilding was losing one of its main competitive advantages.

Thus, even the age of the down-easters came to an end.

Sailing ship development in America ceased in 1891.

By 1870, Great Britain's cost/ton in iron was equivalent to the Maine shipbuilders' cost in wood. As a consequence, iron shipbuilding in Great Britain boomed. Besides costing the same to build, iron ships were stronger, more durable, required less maintenance, and were more watertight.

Steel would eventually replace iron, increasing the vessel's strength and greatly reducing weight and cost. By the 1880s, steel was cheaper than iron (about USD50/ton), and because of its superior strength, less of it was needed. Steel sailers could be built in Great Britain for between USD50 and USD65/ton, a reduction of 40 per cent on the cost of iron ships in the early 1870s. Between 1887 and 1931, of the 269 four-masted vessels that would be fabricated, only six would be built of iron. The last iron ship, the *Altair,* was built in 1890.

Glasgow Windjammer Central

Another interesting observation from the Bruzelius database is the extent to which the north of the British Isles, especially Glasgow, dominated sailing ship construction. Before 1888, of the 137 four-masted ships built in the Western world, only six were built outside northern Great Britain, and these, all wooden ships, were built in France, Canada, and the United States before 1875.

Glasgow increasingly became the largest single centre of construction. Of the 131 four-masters built before 1888, fifty-three went down the ways in Glasgow. In the latter period, from 1888 to 1931, of the 290 vessels built, 100 were built in Glasgow. There was a concerted diversification of supply centres during the latter period as other yards in the north—Greenock, Whitehaven, Workington, Sunderland, Belfast, Dumbarton, and Liverpool—expanded their share. In this period, 223 vessels (or a massive 77 per cent) were built in the north of Great Britain.

Indeed, three of the great five-masters—*France I, Maria Rickmers*, and *Kobnhaven*—were built there.

However, the dominant builders were located elsewhere in the north of the United Kingdom as the following chart shows.

Windjammer Construction by Location: 1874-1914 (GRT)

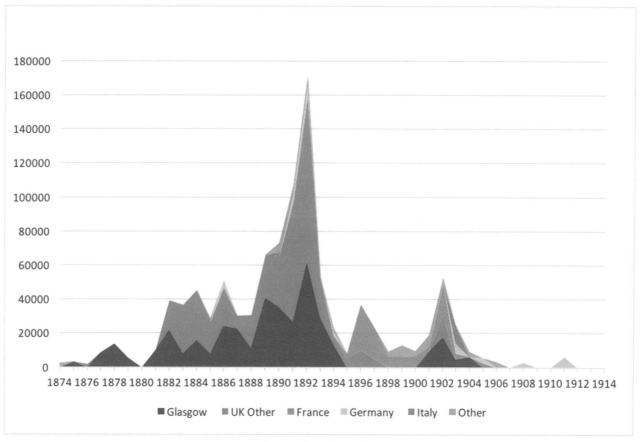

Source: Lars Bruzelius

Over the entire period of the Bruzelius database—from 1874 to 1931—shipyards in the United Kingdom built 80 per cent of the vessels recorded. The French subsidies encouraged only around 9 per cent of total construction, most of it in the two decades between 1891 and 1911. For their part, although they built some of the mightiest sailing ships ever launched, the German shipyards were responsible for only 5 per cent of windjammer launchings.

The Bruzelius database lists over a million gross register tons of windjammer capacity as being built between 1874 and 1931, the overwhelming (98.5 per cent, or 1.025 Mt) of which was constructed between 1874 and 1914. The comparable figure for the clippers was only 151,000 tons. The main stimulus for the American clippers (nearly three-quarters of the capacity constructed) was gold discovery, first in America and then in Australia. As such, the impetus was short-lived. The main market for the windjammers was much more substantial—the demand by the 'new' agriculture for enormous quantities of fertiliser to feed rapidly growing suburban populations. The main market for the British clippers was bringing tea from China, but it was aborted by the rise of steam power and the opening of the Suez Canal.

Windjammer construction reached a very sudden peak in 1892 when an incredible 67 new vessels met the sea in what was an extraordinary frenzy of sailing vessel construction. Only one-third that number (22) were launched the next year (1893). In 1892, 171,402 gross register tons were launched. The figure for the year before was 107,381 tons, but the year after only 52,918, and the year after that (1894), less than half that (23,324 GRT). Clearly, the boom was over.

To put this paroxysm in perspective at the height of the clipper building boom in America (1853), 37,620 tons (old measure) slid down the ways. Although the tonnage measurement systems used in each country mean the figures can't be directly compared, the general magnitude of the UK's achievement in industrialised shipbuilding is obvious, and it occurred only thirty-five years after the American craft-built wooden ship peak.

Over the four decades between 1874 and 1914, over one million tons of sailing vessel capacity were launched, overwhelmingly (81 per cent) from the north of the United Kingdom. The boom in clipper construction was much more short-lived, lasting really for only six years (1850–1855) in the USA and for two decades from 1850 to 1870 in the UK. American shipbuilders produced 111,000-ton capacity in only six years. Construction lasted for twenty years in the United Kingdom, and the output was only around 40,000 tons.

Impact of French Subsidies

A factor affecting Glasgow, and which weighed heavily on sailing ship construction in Great Britain towards the end of the period, was subsidised competition from France.

In 1881, the French government established a system of sailing shipbuilding and operating bounties. Builders of steel square-rigged sailing ships received 60 francs per ton, and shipowners received 1.5 francs per gross ton per 1,000 miles sailed.

These subsidies were increased in 1893, offsetting many of the disadvantages suffered by French builders. They stimulated the building of large square-rigged ships, especially in the 1890s. Given that A. D. Bordes, the French trading company, was such a significant operator in the nitrate trade and needed to buy steel sailing ships to support its position, it follows that the company was active in instigating this assistance.

In some cases, bounties could almost cover the entire cost of construction of a ship, and the operating subsidies would have reinforced its competitive position against Germany in the European nitrate trade. It was the increased rates introduced in 1893 that made the difference, but it took two years for the French industry to gear up for steel sailing ship construction on this scale.

The first French windjammer to appear in the list of four-masted vessels constructed in the western hemisphere in the latter half of the nineteenth century was the *Madeline*, a barque of 3,000 GRT launched in 1895. Over the next eight years, fifty-six four-masted barques would be launched, and twenty-nine of them were built in France. Also, one five-master, *France II*, was built there. The last four-masted sailing ship built in France, just eight years after the subsidies were introduced, was the *Gabrielle d-Ali*, which was launched in 1903, and about which little is known.

Just as suddenly as France appeared in the list, however, she disappeared, presumably because the subsidies had been withdrawn.

The French government assistance was highest in relation to the construction of large square-rigged ships. It appears its advent was sufficient to discourage the sailing shipbuilders of Great Britain, and they gradually withdrew from that sector of the industry. While the subsidies applied in France, there were only eighteen four-masted sailing ships built in Great Britain. After the subsidies were terminated in 1903, and French builders withdrew, only five more four-masted sailing ships would be built in Great Britain.

The short-lived French government intervention succeeded only in killing off large sailing shipbuilding in Great Britain. By this time, however, it was losing its competitiveness in all forms of vessel construction due to its outmoded industrial practices. The decline notwithstanding, the French subsidies provided no long-term benefit to its own sector.

With France gone and Great Britain on its way out, Germany was able to capitalise on its experience in the field. It had built five four-masted barques previously, the first being the *Richard Wagner* in 1886. Of the twenty-one four-masters built after 1903, eleven were German. Also, German shipyards built the largest sailing ships ever constructed (*Potosi*, *Preussen II*, and *R. C. Rickmers*) in what was a brilliant twilight of a romantic era. Although they built magnificent ships, the German yards were not particularly competitive, receiving hidden subsidies in the prices paid for German government vessels.

The Golden Age of the Windjammer

Despite the long-term decline in sailing ship construction, it was the last decades before the First World War that saw the golden age of windjammer building. Great Britain, although progressively preoccupied with building steamships, had dominated the construction of sailing ships and built most of the windjammers. According to British historian Sidney Pollard (although the data is undated but is assumed to be just before the First World War), the proportion of British-built ships in the world's sailing fleets was 92 per cent. That figure notwithstanding, only one of the famous Flying 'P' Line ships, the *Pommern*, was built new in Great Britain (on the Clyde in 1903). The remainder were German. Laeisz, nevertheless bought several English-built ships second-hand: the *Peiho*, *Parma*, *Pinnas*, and *Perim*.

Gustav Erikson, who never built a ship new but assembled a great fleet of used vessels in the last gasp of the golden age of the windjammers, respected the quality of British shipbuilding. Of the forty-one ships that passed through his hands, eighteen of them had been built in the United Kingdom. Among them were many legendary vessels, including the *Grace Harwar*, *Lawhill*, *Olivebank*, *Moshulu*, and *Archibald Russell*.

Three shipping companies are synonymous with the windjammer era: two that built many ships new—F. (Ferdinand) Laeisz & Co. and A. D. Bordes & Co.—and Gustav Erikson.

The Flying 'P' Line

Ferdinand Laeisz started out making hats and entered the shipping business building a small wooden brig, which he named after his son, Carl. This venture was unsuccessful, and the ship was sold five years later. But he inspired his son, who joined the firm in 1852.

The company again entered the shipping business with a barque which they called *Pudel* (puppy) after Ferdinand's wife Sophie's nickname. *Pudel* set a precedent, and all future ships, of which there were many, had names beginning with the letter *P*. In a tribute to their speed and reliability, the fleet became known as the Flying 'P' Line.

Carl Ferdinand Laeisz (1853-1900)

Source: Wikimedia Commons

Pudel was a small fully rigged ship and bore little relation to the giants that were to follow her. Nevertheless, owning her whetted Carl's appetite for shipping, and he became very successful in the business, specialising in the nitrate trade out of Chile.

Laeisz also had some outgoing cargoes that preferred sailing ships. Germany was a great maker of musical instruments, from the smallest woodwinds to giant grand pianos, for which there was a good market in South America. As had previously been the case with the flavour of tea, it was held that the heat and vibration of a steamer spoiled the tune of the delicate instruments. Sail transport was therefore preferred. When Laeisz's giant *Preussen II* collided with a steamer in the English Channel in 1910, she was carrying, among other things, a shipment of grand pianos.

Thus, in what became a sailing legend, a firm that originally made hats went on to become the world's largest operator of windjammers. The Flying 'P' Line has been described by Robert Carter, the

Australian marine historian and artist, as 'without doubt, the most successful fleet of sail-driven ships ever assembled under one flag'.

Great Britain's Dominance

Although one 'P' Line ship, the *Pommern*, was built in Great Britain, all but one of the other directly commissioned 'P' Line ships were built in Germany (*Ponape* was built in Genoa, Italy). The fact that they could be built in Germany was a sign of its increasing competence and an indication that German shipyards were catching up with Great Britain in both ability and reputation.

It is a recognised economic phenomenon that whatever country is second along a developmental road benefits enormously from the mistakes of their predecessor. A case in point is the very rudimentary system of screw threads. Many prominent manufacturers in Great Britain, being first along the road, had to develop their own thread specifications. The result was a plethora of designs, none of which was interchangeable.

Germany would set up a series of manufacturing standards (the Deutsches Institut für Normung or DIN) based on the French metric system, which meant it didn't matter which company built a machine; its fixings were interchangeable. Japan would also adopt the metric system in its manufacturing facilities.

These sorts of inefficiencies aside, up until the First World War, Great Britain was, according to the Lloyds Register, the dominant shipbuilder in the world, although by then, its share of the market had fallen.

According to British historian Sidney Pollard, in the period 1892–96, Great Britain launched a yearly average of over a million gross tons, equal to 79 per cent of world launchings. Between 1901 and 1905, its average annual launchings increased to 1.4 million gross tons, but its share of world shipbuilding construction fell to around 60 per cent. In the five years immediately preceding the First World War, its annual launchings averaged upwards of 1.7 million gross tons, and it managed to maintain its share of the world market, which was half as much again as the entire rest of the world.

These figures understate the dominance of the British industry, which was building for a world market. Many British-built ships were destined for other countries: France, Germany, Austria, Holland, Norway, Italy, and Greece, not to mention the British Empire. In the five years preceding the First World War, the annual average volume of ships sold abroad was over a million gross tons.

The New Kids on the Block

Germany

Germany was Great Britain's closest competitor, its average gross annual tonnage increasing from 87,000 tons in the period 1892–96 to 328,000 tons in the five years preceding the First World War. Compared to Great Britain, this was small and equal to only 14 per cent of the global market. Modern and technically advanced, German shipyards were too high-cost to gain foreign orders and relied on building for government-subsidised shipping lines.

The first of the 'P' Line ships (after *Pudel*) was the *Palmyra*, a steel-hulled, fully rigged ship of 1,779 gross tons. Named for the ancient city in Syria, she was built by Blohm & Voss in Hamburg in 1889.

Originally commanded by the legendary square-rig skipper Robert Hilgendorf, she sailed many voyages between Europe and the nitrate ports on the west coast of South America. She stranded on the south coast of Chile in 1908, with only the captain and the first mate surviving.

In 1890, A. D. Bordes ordered the construction of the first 'super barque', *France*, a five-master, from Henderson & Sons in Glasgow. *France* was the first five-masted barque and, at the time of her construction, the largest sailing ship in the world.

Not to be outdone, in 1894, Laeisz launched the *Potosi*, another massive five-masted barque measuring 4,027 gross tons. She was built by Joh C. Tecklenborg in Geestemünde (Bremerhaven). Besides being large, the *Potosi*, named for a city in Bolivia, had excellent sailing characteristics and was very successful in the nitrate trade. In 1904, she made a voyage from Chile to England in just fifty-seven days, a record at the time. Between 1895 and 1914, she made twenty-seven round voyages to the Chilean coast.

Potosi set six square sails on each of her four square-rigged masts, with nineteen set fore-and-aft for a total of forty-three sails. Her total sail area was 1.3 acres, and she could load 6,400 tons of nitrate. She was equipped with a donkey engine to do the very heavy work and carried forty-four crew fully manned. Capable of nineteen knots, the *Potosi* was one of only seven windjammers in the world with the powerful five-masted barque rig.

As sailing ships go, the *Potosi* had a chequered career and a sad ending. Arrested in Argentina at the outset of the First World War, she was given to France as war reparations. France sold her to Argentina where she was renamed the *Flora*. In 1925, carrying coal, she caught fire. She was floating derelict and still ablaze off the coast of Patagonia when, constituting a hazard to navigation, she was sunk by naval gunfire.

The five-masted barques, splendid as they were, were built largely for prestige, and although excellent sailers, their size made them difficult to handle. In addition, having been built for the nitrate trade, outbound freights were hard to find.

In her prime, the *Potosi* was so successful for the Flying 'P' Line that she was followed up in 1902 by the *Preussen II*, again five-masted, but this time set up as a fully rigged ship with square sails on all five masts and a fore-and-aft spanker sail on the after mast. Named for the German state of Prussia, the *Preussen II* was the only five-masted fully rigged ship ever built and, at 5,081 gross tons, attained the practical limit for square-rigged ships. While she was the fastest of the windjammers, achieving twenty knots, she was less manoeuvrable. She set 1.7 acres of sail and was manned by up to fifty men with the assistance of two donkey engines to power her winches, pumps, loading gear, and a generator.

Unfortunately, for posterity, she was sunk after a collision with a cross-channel ferry off Dover in 1910, a fate which befell other sailing ships when steamer captains failed to appreciate their speed. The steamer tried to cross *Preussen II*'s bow and, failing to do so, brought down the big sailer's forward rigging, with disastrous consequences. Although towed to Dover, both her anchor chains broke in a gale, and she ended up on rocks where her back was broken. Her bones are still visible in Crab Bay on low spring tides.

The turn of the century was the heyday of the 'nitrate windjammers'. In 1903, Laeisz commissioned the *Pommern*, the only 'P' Line ship to be built in Great Britain (in Glasgow) and the only four-masted windjammer still in its original state. She's now a museum ship at Mariehamn, the capital of the Åland Islands in the Baltic Sea.

The barque rig, of three or four square-rigged masts and a fore-and-aft-rigged 'jigger' mast at the stern, would become almost the standard rig for windjammers. The square-rigged masts provided the power with which to harness the global wind systems, and the manipulation of the smaller jigger mast sails, along with the headsails, gave the officer in charge the manoeuvrability needed to steer these giant vessels.

Before its experiments with five-masted ships, F. Laeisz & Co. built four four-masted barques. With their combination of power and manoeuvrability, they seemed to be the ideal rig for its purposes. Before *Potosi* and *Preussen II*, the company built *Pisagua* and *Placilla* in 1892, *Parma* in 1902, and *Ponape* and *Pommern* in 1903. After the big five-masters Laeisz built *Pamir* in 1905 and *Priwall* in 1917. Other 'P' Line ships were *Pera* (1890), *Pitlochry* (1894), *Preussen I* (1902), *Pellworm* (1902), *Pangani* (1913), and *Penang* (1905).

Laeisz lost his entire fleet to reparations after the First World War but, not to be discouraged, set about buying the best of them back during the post-war years. The *Ponape* was captured by Great Britain along with the *Pelikan* and went to the English shipping company J. Bell & Co. *Parma* and *Peiho* were allocated to the British government. The French government got *Potosi*, *Pinnas*, and *Passat*, while the Italian government got *Perim*, *Pamir*, *Peking*, and *Pirna*. The *Pommern* went to the Greek government and the *Penang* to the short-lived Free City of Danzig on Poland's Baltic Sea coast.

The recipients, for the most part, did not know what to do with the vessels and were happy to exchange them for German marks. *Peiho*, *Parma*, *Pamir*, *Passat*, *Pinnas*, and *Peking* returned to the old flag, and by 1922, the 'P' Line was back in business. By this time, it had been adequately demonstrated that the most economical form of sailing ship was the four-masted barque of about 3,000 tons. Post-war, Laeisz built the *Priwall* and its last sailing ship, the *Padua*, in 1926.

As a testimony to the durability of these ships in the very harsh environment of deep-ocean voyaging, *Pamir* operated for fifty-two years before sinking in the South Atlantic; *Ponape* for thirty-three years before being scrapped; *Priwall*, twenty-eight years; *Parma*, thirty-four years; *Pellworm*, forty-two years; and *Penang* was torpedoed after thirty-five years.

What is perhaps an even greater testament to their resilience is the fact that four of these ships still exist today, well over a century after they first slid down the ways. Three are museum ships: *Pommern* in Mariehamn, *Peking* in Hamburg, and *Passat* in Travemünde. Incredibly, the *Padua*, which was given to the USSR in 1946 as part of its war reparations, is still sailing today as the survey and training ship, *Kruzenshtern*, in the Russian Federation. In her heyday as *Padua*, she set, and still holds, the record for a sailing voyage between Hamburg, Australia, and Chile and back to Hamburg in eight months, twenty-three days.

France

The third-largest shipbuilder in the world at the time was France. The French government subsidies were highest on square-rigged sailing craft, no doubt at the behest of A. D. Bordes, which had much to gain. France built up a substantial fleet of vessels in the last decade of the nineteenth and the first of the twentieth centuries, and the rapid decline in sailing ship construction in Great Britain has been attributed to competition from across the channel.

Nevertheless, production in France remained subdued, although it did increase immediately before the First World War. Between 1892 and 1896, France averaged 87,000 gross tons. This rose to just over a quarter of a million gross tons in the five years before war broke out.

Antoine-Dominique Bordes began his career shipping coal to the Pacific ports of Chile and saltpetre (nitrate) and guano back to Great Britain and the French Atlantic ports in relatively small wooden ships that were mostly less than 1,000 gross tons. He subsequently bought three iron three-masted (fully rigged) ships from Glasgow builders, followed by another nine as the nitrate trade boomed following the Franco-German war of 1870. He made his three sons partners, creating Antoine-Dominique Bordes et Fils. In 1882, he bought his first iron-hulled four-master, the *Union*.

Antoine-Dominique Bordes (1815-1883)

Source: Wikimedia Commons

Antoine-Dominique Bordes died in 1883, but his sons, realising their superiority in the nitrate trade, continued to commission the construction of iron barques. In 1889 came the first steel four-master, *Nord*. In all, the company assembled a total of thirty-three four-masted barques, built either by Russell & Co. of Greenock, W. B. Thompson of Glasgow, or (after 1896) various French yards, assisted by subsidies from the French government.

In 1890 came a sensation, the five-masted 3,747-ton barque, *France*, built by D. W. Henderson of Glasgow. Equipped with her own steam-driven unloading cranes, she managed to unload 5,000 tons of coal in Iquique and load 5,500 tons of nitrate in just eleven days, a world record at the time.

The Giant Windjammer *France*

Source: State Library of Queensland

Until Frederic Laeisz launched the *Potosi*, the *France* was the largest sailing ship on the planet.

In 1870, the A. D. Bordes fleet consisted of fifteen wooden ships with a GRT of 16,830 tons. Most cargoes were at the behest of British nitrate interests. The Bordes brothers could see the potential of nitrate and began importing it into France on their own account. This enterprise was very successful, and by 1900, the fleet had grown to 119,560 GRT and forty-six ships. By 1914, the GRT of the fleet totalled 163,600 tons. In this last year, it employed 60 captains, 170 officers, and 1,400 seamen.

Half of Europe's nitrate imports were passing over A. D. Bordes's gunwales.

The Decline of the Nitrate Trade

Alas for A. D. Bordes, another new and 'creatively destructive' technology would soon compete with the nitrate and guano trades on which its expansion and prosperity had been built. The 'Haber–Bosch' method of producing nitrogenous fertiliser industrially would badly damage the Pacific nitrate trade. Also, the Panama Canal was opened in 1914, which freed up the trade to steamers.

Even so, by this time, other factors were affecting the viability of sailing ships.

For hundreds of years, ships had been manned on a two-watch system whereby the crews were divided into port and starboard watches. Except in the case of emergencies (when it was 'all hands on deck'), one watch ran the ship while the other rested. The introduction of steamships led to a three-watch system, which, if adopted by a sailing ship, would considerably increase its operating costs. As well, wages had to be increased to attract labour to what was a hard and, at times, dangerous occupation.

And then subsidies on sailing ship operations, at least in France, were withdrawn.

By 1926, A. D. Bordes was abandoning its fleet, and by 1935, it had closed down.

Laeisz survived this crisis by switching to steamships that were not nearly so specialised in their cargoes.

Looking back, it is difficult to understand why the proprietors of such a successful trading and shipping enterprise as Bordes did not foresee the future. The three Bordes brothers died in the 1940s.

Gustav Erikson

Unlike the Laeisz and Bordes families, who had strong backgrounds in commerce, Gustav Erikson was a sailor all his life and lived his seventy-five years at Mariehamn in the Åland Islands. Also, unlike the Laeisz and Bordes families, he never built a ship new.

Gustav Erikson (1872-1947)

Source: Wikimedia Commons

Erikson was at sea at the age of nine and by nineteen was in command of his own ship in the North Sea trade. After six years aboard deepwater square-riggers as a mate, he captained a number of them before getting to own one. His modus operandi was to buy old ships at almost breakers' yard prices, restore them, and put them back to work with minimum crews of mostly minimally paid youths.

Although he was not well-liked by his crews (probably because of his parsimony and the conditions under which his crews sailed), it was a successful strategy, and by the 1930s, he owned a significant share of the world windjammer fleet. He could not afford to insure his ships, but he did maintain them to 100-A-1 Lloyd Register (the internationally recognised minimum standard for insurance and charter).

During his career, Erikson fully owned sixty-six ships and had a share in another forty-seven. Of the fully owned vessels, twenty-five were steam or motor ships, but this was mainly late in his career when cargoes for windjammers were getting progressively harder to obtain. He certainly liked ships built in Great Britain. Of the forty-one sailing ships he owned, eighteen had been built in the United Kingdom, compared with seven in Germany (three of which were ex-'P' Line ships). This, however, may be attributed to Germany's later entry into windjammer construction—there were simply fewer German vessels around.

At one time or another, Erikson bought five ex-'P' Line ships (*Pommern, Penang, Ponape, Pamir,* and *Passat*) and owned a share in the *Parma.* Apart from the ex-'P' Line ships, many of the most famous windjammers passed through his hands, including *Åland,* a 3,300-ton iron barque built in 1887; *Grace Harwar,* a fully rigged ship of 2,950 tons; *Lawhill,* a four-masted steel barque of 4,600 tons; *Herzogin Cecilie,* a four-masted steel barque of 3,200 tons; *Archibald Russell,* a four-masted steel barque of 3,950 tons; *Olivebank,* a four-masted steel barque of 4,400 tons; *Hougomont,* a four-masted steel barque of 4,000 tons; *Winterhude,* a three-masted steel barque of 3,250 tons; *Melbourne,* a four-masted steel barque (ex *Gustav* and *Australia*) of 4,250 tons; *Viking,* a four-masted steel barque of 4,000 tons; *L'Avenir,* a four-masted steel barque of 3,650 tons; and perhaps the most famous of them all, *Moshulu,* a four-masted steel barque of 4,900 tons. Along with *Archibald Russell,* she was one of the two last great windjammers built in Great Britain: *Moshulu* was built in 1904 and *Archibald Russell* in 1905, both on the Clyde. *Moshulu* appears to have been one of the two largest four-masted barques ever built. (The other, marginally larger, was *Sedov,* built in 1921.)

Gustav Erikson died in 1947 when his sailing ship empire had all but collapsed. Before his death, he is reputed to have said, 'Living in a world without sailing ships makes no sense to me.'

The Twilight of the Windjammers

By the 1930s, the South Australian grain trade was one of the few left to the great windjammers. In 1939, *Moshulu,* along with twelve other ships, nine of which were Erikson vessels, raced back from South Australia in the last great grain race before the onset of the Second World War. These voyages stretched over 30,000 nautical miles, and the crew would perform at least four complete sail changes on each voyage, not to mention frequent taking in and setting of sails to suit the weather conditions—all this with less than thirty men.

In 1908, the proportion of sailing ships of the total number of metal vessels constructed in the United Kingdom was 24 per cent. In 1885, it had been 35 per cent. The absolute number of sailing vessels built had fallen from 186 in 1885 to 149 in 1908. By contrast, in the same period, the number of steamships had increased from 341 to 473.

Although the transition to steel had been slower in sailing vessels, these figures indicate the extent to which sail hung on. The Suez Canal, known as the 'dirty ditch' by sailing ship crews and commonly quoted as a prime factor in the decline in merchant sail, had been built almost four decades earlier, and there is no doubt that its opening had a significant impact on the clippers. Nevertheless, it would be the Panama Canal, opened in 1914, that contributed most to the decline of the windjammers, potentially depriving them of the guano and nitrate trades. But the fertiliser/explosive industries were becoming increasingly industrialised by that time anyway, with factory production taking over from the import of naturally occurring materials.

Improvements in the quality of steel provided windjammer hulls with their immense strength (compared to a wooden ship), and it was also the secret of another characteristic—their longevity. Despite regularly battling the fierce winds and mountainous seas of Cape Horn, many enjoyed half a century of useful life. Windjammers could survive sea conditions that would collapse smokestacks, douse steam boilers, and shear off propellers of steamships.

By contrast, the largest wooden sailing ship ever built, Donald McKay's *Great Republic*, lasted only nineteen years before her hull began to take water in a storm, and she was abandoned. Hard-driving and the inability of their wooden construction to withstand the enormous pressures generated by their giant rigs meant that clippers would invariably have to be cut down after five or so years. Also, their maintenance was extraordinarily high.

On the other hand, iron and steel construction of hulls, spars, and rigging resulted in a sturdy vessel. As well as lugging thousands of tons of cargo, a metal ship could withstand years of service with winds in the Great Southern Ocean (where they spent a considerable amount of their time), sometimes reaching 80 knots—almost 150 kilometres per hour.

Metal hulls may have been less appealing to the eye and cost less to maintain than wooden hulls, but they were no 'sluggards' through the water. Compared to the 465 nautical miles in twenty-four hours achieved by the clipper *Champion of the Seas* at better than 19 knots, the best twenty-four-hour run by the German windjammer *Potosi* was 378 miles at an average of 16 knots.

While they never reached the speed of the clippers at the height of their development, windjammers regularly clocked 18 knots over short distances. On one memorable occasion in smooth water and a gale-force wind in the Skagerrak Strait between Norway and Sweden, the *Herzogin Cecilie* ran a short distance between two lightships at 20 3/4 knots. Again, in 1927, when the ship was thirty-two years old, she outpaced a steamer that had drawn up alongside her. In a developing 35–40-knot gale, she outran the liner and was clocked at almost 18 knots.

Over very long distances, windjammers were also up there with the clippers. The British *Thermopylae* held the record for the London to Melbourne voyage, covering the distance in sixty days. Two German windjammer barques, *Padua* and *Priwall*, far more heavily laden, both managed to get from Hamburg to Port Lincoln, South Australia—a longer voyage—in sixty-five days.

The great windjammers drew on the accumulated knowledge of ages in how to best exploit the elements. But the secret of their success lay not only in their ability to cover vast distances without the need to refuel but in the toughness and durability of their steel construction. It was steel, too, that enabled steamship hulls to be built that could carry the weight of a massive propulsion system and fuel and withstand its incessant vibration.

The windjammers were a true product of the Industrial Revolution. In many ways, they were more efficient than the steamers, but winds don't blow to schedules, so they could not oblige the time and money imperative of the new age and stick to timetables.

Not only that, the world economy was growing faster than it ever had before.

Eventually, just as the volume of trade outpaced the smaller clippers, so it would outgrow the windjammers.

In the massive numbers in which they were built, the windjammers represented a crescendo in sailing ship construction—a twilight of the gods that had ruled the oceans of the world for centuries.

While they may have lacked the romance of the clippers and, in the age of steam, seemingly past their use-by date, six times as many of them were built.

Steel removed any size constraint on the steamers, although steam would shortly be superseded by more efficient means of propulsion: the diesel motor. Steel remains a timeless construction material, and the size of ships would continue to grow to the monsters that relentlessly plough the oceans of the world today.

In spite of steam and steel's 'victory', it would not be until 1949 that the famous windjammers *Pamir* and *Passat* would load their final cargoes of wheat in the St Vincent Gulf in South Australia. They were the last sailing ships to follow the famous clipper route home around Cape Horn.

The finale would come just eight years later, in 1957, when the *Pamir* was lost, and the *Passat* was laid up.

As author John Fowles put it, they were 'the last of the sailing ships, that splendid and sharply individualised zenith of five thousand years of hard-earned knowledge and aesthetic instinct'.

Non est finis—it was the end.

13
CHAPTER

The Future

Celebration

It is interesting to consider why big sailing ships are regarded with such awe and admiration today. No national celebration is complete, it seems, without the presence of a number of 'tall' ships dominating the scene, a gaggle of small craft churning up the water around them. Is it nostalgia for a bygone era, or is it that this concept—which played such a key role in driving civilisation along the path to modernity—has somehow become part of our DNA?

Big sailing ships are a constant source of wonder. They are man-made objects that are emblems of adventure, romance, and beauty. They celebrate the principle that form should follow function. With their soaring masts, great clouds of canvas, and quiet progress through the water, it is not surprising that the men who sailed them considered them to be alive, so beautifully did they adorn their salty environment, so at home were they upon the sea.

A Revival of Merchant Sail?

Will they ever grace the world's oceans again? The answer, surprisingly, is maybe, but it's unlikely we'll see the likes of a new clipper or windjammer any time soon.

A sailing ship is a highly efficient 'solar pump'. Simply put, the sun drives the global wind systems, and a sailing ship harnesses that solar energy. Unlike other attempts to harness solar power that are dependent on the sun shining, global wind systems blow day and night, endlessly. Thus, in an emissions-conscious world, there is good reason to examine using wind—and sail—as at least an auxiliary source of power.

The fuel crisis in the 1970s focused the world's attention on the issue. The chronically fuel-short Japanese were the most affected, and experiments were conducted in the early 1980s. A 26,000-ton sail-assisted bulk carrier was subsequently built, and Great Britain, the United States, and a number of European countries showed interest.

More recently, the incentive to innovate has been environmental as well as economic—reducing emissions caused from the burning of fossil fuels—and there's certainly been no shortage of promising activity.

The Wind Challenger Project, an initiative of the University of Tokyo in cooperation with Mitsui OSK Lines in Japan, is aiming to use sail to cut fuel consumption by 20 per cent. The concept features large multisectioned sails that can be raised and lowered and rotated according to wind strength and direction. They can be stowed during loading or when approaching bridges across waterways. The masts are independent of one another, and the number is optional. Scale-modelling has shown that an 80,000-ton Panamax bulk carrier with four masts operating between Yokohama and Seattle would achieve a 20% reduction in fuel consumption on a great-circle route and 30% on an optimised route. A Cape-sized 180,000-ton bulk carrier with nine masts has also been modelled with similar results. (Cape-sized ships are the largest dry cargo ships. They are too large to transit the Suez or the Panama canals and so have to pass either Cape Agulhas or Cape Horn to move between oceans.)

The Smart Green Shipping Alliance, which is responsible for the Wind Challenger Project, is looking at an even grander concept using wind driven generators on board a ship. These would generate electricity that would, in turn, be used to produce hydrogen, a clean fuel, to power the engines.

The sails are equipped with automatic sensors that raise or lower them and rotate the masts for maximum benefit from the wind. Peripheral technologies, such as strong compound materials and reliable controls systems, are also being developed to produce what is being presented as 'the ships of tomorrow'. An actual full-size ship has, however, yet to be built.

The Danish shipping company Maersk Tankers meanwhile has invented giant (100-foot) rotating cylinders which pull in the air around them, creating high pressure on one side of the cylinder and low pressure on the other. The differential pushes the ship forward, and it is known as the 'Magnus' effect. The concept was invented in 1924 by one Anton Flettner but failed to compete with diesel power. The company is testing the idea on one of its tankers and hopes to save 10 per cent in fuel costs. With fuel representing upwards of 70 per cent of a ship's operating costs, over an average life of twenty years, this amounts to a significant saving—not to mention a big reduction in emissions.

Norsepower Rotor Sails Fitted to the Tanker *Maersk Pelican*

Source: Wikipedia Commons

Sea transport, however, represents only around 3 per cent of global emissions, so it is likely to be economics, rather than the environment, that will drive these concepts.

The Norwegian company Lade AS's *Vindskip®* project features a hybrid gas-powered engine and a hull shaped like an aeroplane wing. It uses the pressure differential along the hull to move into the wind. In so doing, it claims to cut fuel consumption by up to 60 per cent and emissions by 80 per cent. However, in order to maximise wind assistance, the *VindSkip* sits very high out of the water, a characteristic that may have heavy-weather stability considerations and would preclude it from passing under many bridges across waterways and under existing loading gantries. It would also appear to be limited economically to carrying high-value roll-on, roll-off cargoes such as motor vehicles.

A Canadian project called SAILCARGO INC. is working on an emissions-free cargo ship called *Ceiba*. It is an attempt to demonstrate that with sails, underwater propellers, and a giant battery, it is possible to build a ship that can sail endlessly, constrained (as Columbus was) only by food and water to sustain the crew.

In a nod to one of the great operators of sailing ships, the design of the *Ceiba*—a three-masted topsail schooner—is based on a trading vessel originally built in the Åland Islands, Gustav Erikson's homeland. When completed, the *Ceiba* will carry the equivalent of nine containers and travel at a speed of 12 knots, operating between Costa Rica and Canada. By contrast, a modern container ship carries around *20,000 containers* and travels at between 16 and 22 knots.

The *Ceiba*—A Modern Approach to Traditional Merchant Sail

Source: SAIL CARGO INC Rendering Manta Marine Design

SAILCARGO INC. has recently announced the construction of a second vessel in the same design, the *Pitaya*, which will sail between Colombia and the United States.

It is an idealistic project, and its proponents are conscious of the fact that the return of sail as an economic means of ocean transport is (at least) dependent on the price of oil. Despite predictions of the 'end of oil', more and more is being found, and the price has stayed resolutely down. Until it increases decisively, there is little economic incentive to reduce its consumption. The incentive will come from global actions to reduce pollution.

With the exception of the *Ceiba*, almost all the attempts to use wind power relate to bulk carriers of one sort or another. This is largely because carrying large numbers of containers presents a big obstacle for the mounting of sails. These giant vessels that constantly circle the globe have containers stacked ten or twelve high above the deck. The *Vindskip*®, using the hull shape to harness the wind, is an attempt to overcome this problem, but it would be unable to load containers using existing facilities.

What Really Led to the Demise of Sail?

The business of merchant shipping is trade—the exchange of goods between parties in a way that benefits all. If countries specialise in what they are best at and trade those goods for those which they have no comparative advantage, or are not capable of producing, then both sides of the exchange are better off. As a result, after labour productivity, trade has been shown to be one of the most dependable drivers of economic growth.

In the last two centuries, since about the time the Western Ocean sailing packets began crossing the Atlantic, trade has transformed the global economy. Not all trade is waterborne, but it is significant that land-based trade had been happening for millennia with little growth. It has only been with the rapid increase in transoceanic trading that global trade has expanded so rapidly.

According to *Our World in Data*, in constant 1913 prices, international trade has grown by a multiple of *forty* in the last century or so. There were two distinct periods of growth. The first, and one in which sailing ships were vital participants, was from around 1800 to the beginning of the First World War. Growth then languished until after the Second World War, when it took off dramatically, contributing overwhelmingly to the forty times ratio referred to above.

Without sailing ships, growth during the first period would never have happened. However, sailing ship technology could not have coped with the second period of expansion. Had the world not developed steam and subsequent methods of driving vessels across oceans, that second period would not have been possible, and the world would be very much the poorer for it.

Moreover, we are now dependent on trade as a source of economic prosperity. It underpins our standard of living and (hopefully) increases international interdependence to the point where the future might be more peaceful than the past.

At the beginning of the First World War, trade as a percentage of global GDP was almost 14 per cent. By the end of the Second World War, that proportion had fallen to 4 per cent. This was the beginning of the second wave of growth, and by 2008, it had reached over 26 per cent—the highest it has ever been. The last observation available is 2014 where it sat at 24.5 per cent.

It's commonly thought that sail declined as a method of ocean transport because of its inability to stick to schedules. It's held that steam won out because it could provide a level of certainty. This may be partly true, but sail also declined because it could not cope with the second burst of forty times growth in international trade in the course of a century.

At the beginning of the windjammer era, in 1885, there were about 7 million tons of shipping capacity available. The world's population was then about 1.5 billion. There is now around 11 billion tons of shipping capacity globally—almost *160 times* the volume in 1885. By contrast, the world's population has only grown by a factor of five (to around 7.5 billion). The amount of cargo loaded was about the same amount as shipping capacity in 2018. We may mourn the passing of the great era of merchant sail, but had we been forced to stick with it, we'd be materially much worse off.

According to the BBC, global ocean transport emitted around a billion tonnes of greenhouse gases—equal to Germany's total emissions—in 2018. The International Maritime Organization (IMO) has a goal of reducing emissions by 50 per cent by 2050 on 2008 levels, but a recent study showed they had *increased* by 10 per cent between 2012 and 2018 and were on track to increase by *50 per cent* by 2050.

The IMO has recently introduced efficiency measures that will be voluntary until 2030 and will allow emissions to continue to increase over the next decade. That easing notwithstanding, the shipbuilding industry is beginning to respond to the need to achieve more environmentally acceptable ship performance in the next generation of ocean carriers.

One initiative is a joint venture between the Finnish very experienced heavy engineering and marine propulsion specialists, Wartsila, and expert bulk carrier shipbuilders, Oshima of Japan. Their project, the Ultramax 2030 65 DWT Bulk Carrier, intends to demonstrate that a vessel can be built that is compliant with the IMO's 2030 emission targets, affordable to build, and have operating expenses that will provide a payback period of twelve years. While the operation of the propulsion system (which uses natural gas) is complex, the vessel embodies other steps in an environmentally friendly direction. The hatch covers are covered with solar cells and, with a large battery, are intended to power the ship's 'hotel services'. Of more interest here is the fact that its design includes a large hard sail mounted on the bow that can be stowed as required. The vessel is equipped with a sixty-metre-high mast and a sail made of glass fibre-reinforced plastic (GRP).

The *Ultramax 2030* 65K DWT Bulk Carrier

Source: Courtesy Oshima Europe Oshima Shipbuilding Co Ltd

CONCLUSION

The technology embodied in the windjammers, indeed, the technology of windships since time immemorial, developed slowly and minimally. By contrast, the technology of the Industrial Revolution advanced in leaps and bounds—and continues to do so. Diesel internal combustion engines burning crude oil would eventually supersede coal-fired boilers raising high-pressure steam. The first diesel-fired engines were connected directly to the propellers. Now crude oil generates electricity, which drives electric motors connected to the propellers. This latter development provides enormous flexibility in driving the ship with multiple propellers capable of rotation to steer, as well as push the vessel forward or in reverse.

The application of technology to the recreational use of the wind, on the other hand, has seen a revival in recent times. When the famed twelve-metre 'winged keel' *Australia II* beat the American *Liberty* to take the 1983 America's Cup, the underlying technology embodied in the two craft was, in essence, the same as the big schooner windjammers of eighty years before and common for decades before that. The yachts featured 'displacement hulls' using fore-and-aft rigs with their maximum speed (about 12 knots) limited by their waterline length.

It was the same in dinghy sailing with the concession that one could overcome this physical limitation by getting a light hull to exceed the waterline length/speed nexus by planing across the surface, free of displacement restrictions. That development has now taken a great leap forward by lifting the entire hull and its crew out of the water on 'hydrofoils', overcoming the nexus of weight and water resistance using nothing but the power of the wind. Yachts employing this technology now race around the world single-handed and non-stop following the old clipper route.

Lifting the weight of a hull and the crew free of the physical constraints imposed by water is possible in a vessel made of incredibly light, enormously strong, and expensive materials. Alas, merchant marine activity relies on carrying cargo, and cargo that falls to shipping has enormous mass.

From the perspective of the first quarter of the twenty-first century, it is difficult to contemplate that these advances will ever be any more than recreational pursuits and symbols of national prestige. Moreover, just as the Americans turned away from the sea and towards their land frontier in the 1800s, so humankind would appear to be turning away from planet earth towards the challenges of the ultimate frontier—space! Nevertheless, the problem of moving immense and growing tonnage of heavy cargo around the earth in an increasingly environmental manner remains.

Realistically, the possibility of a return to merchant sail, other than in an auxiliary role, is remote. Rather than present arguments as to why it should be considered, the purpose of this book has been, hopefully, to make a small contribution to its story and the historical forces that drove its development. I also hope that it has served to keep alive the memory of a wonderful era in that grand narrative of human experience and endeavour.

SELECTED BIBLIOGRAPHY

Publication/Article	Author/Source
A Brief History of Shipbuilding in Recent Times & Databases	Tim Colton
A Cruise in an Opium Clipper	Lindsay Anderson
A Dictionary of Sea Quotations	Edward Duyker
A Global History of Gold Rushes	Benjamin Mountford & Stephen Tuffnel
A History of Portugal	Charles E Nowell
Along the Clipper Way	Francis Chichester
A Maritime History of Australia	John Bach
A Sea Trip in Clipper Ship Days	Mary Matthews Bray
American Sailing Ships	Howard I Chapelle
American Shipbuilders in the Heyday of Sail	Prof Larry J Sechrest
Blue Gum Clippers & Whale Ships	Will Lawson & Ship Lovers' Society of Tasmania
British Historical Statistics	B R Mitchell
British & American Clippers – A Comparison	David R MacGregor
Clipper Ship Owners Made Millions. Others Paid the Price	Simon Worrall
Clipper Ships	David R MacGregor
Clipper Ships and Captains	Jane D Lyon
Clipper Trades to California, Australia and the Far East	David R MacGregor
Cod	Mark Kurlansky
Deepwater Sail	Harold A Underhill
Economic Decline in Great Britain – The Shipbuilding Industry	Edward H Lorenz
Elizabethan Seadogs	Hugh Bicheno

Fast Sailing Ships – Their Design & Construction	David R MacGregor
Fontana Economic History of Europe	Mark M Coppola (Ed)
Foundations of the Portuguese Empire	B W Diffie & George D Winius
Globalisation & History	Kevin H O'Rourke & Jeffrey G Williamson
Greyhounds of the Sea	Carl C Cutler
Growth of English Shipping	A P Usher
Gustaf Erikson	Wikipedia
History of Ships	Bernard Ireland
Historic Ships	Norman J Brouwer
Historical Statistics of the United States	US Government
Jack Tar	Roy & Lesley Adkins
Jardine Matheson & Company History	Jardine Matheson
Merchant Sailing Ships 1815-1850	David R MacGregor
Ocean Freight Rates and Economic Development	Douglass North
Port Cities London	Port Cities website
Pictorial History of Ships	J H Martin & Geoffrey Bennett
Pride of Baltimore; The Story of the Baltimore Clippers: 1800-1900	Thomas C Gillmer
Report on Shipbuilding	USA 1880 Census Report (last six sections)
Rival Empires of Trade in the Orient	Holden Furber
Romance of the Clipper Ships	Basil Lubbock
Running Their Easting Down	W F Baker
Seamanship in the Age of Sail	John Howland
Ship	Brian Lavery
Ships	Hendrik Van Loon
Shipbuilding in the American Colonies	Wikipedia
Shipwreck	John Fowles & the Gibsons of Scilly
Slave Ships and Slaving	George Francis Dow

Social Dynamics and the Quantifying of Social Forces	Elliott W Montroll
Steam & Speed	Peter Stanford
Studies in Maritime Economics	R O Goss
Tall Ships - The Golden Age of Sail	John Noble
The Atlantic Crossing	The Seafarers Time Life
The Ascendancy of the Sailing Ship 1850 -1885	Gerald Graham
The Book of the *Pommern*	Jerker Orjans & Hakan Skogsjo
The British Shipbuilding Industry 1870-1914	Sidney Pollard & Paul Robertson
The China Clippers	Basil Lubbock
The Colonial Clippers	Basil Lubbock
The Command of the Sea	N A M Rodger
The Clipper Ships	The Seafarers Time Life
The Clipper Ship Era	Arthur H Clarke
The Dynamics of Victorian Business – The Shipbuilding Industry	A Slaven
The East Indiamen	Russell Miller Time Life
The Economics of Shipbuilding in the UK	J R Parkinson
The Era of the Clipper Ships	Donald Gunn Ross III
The Frigates	The Seafarers Time Life
The Golden Age of Sail	John Noble
The Great Chartered Companies	David Hannay
The History of Ships	Bernard Ireland
The History of Ships	Peter Kemp
The Maritime History Virtual Archives	Lars Bruzelius
The Nitrate Clippers	Basil Lubbock
The Opium Clippers	Basil Lubbock
The Opium Monopoly	Ellen N La Motte
The Opium Trade	Nathan Allen MD
The Origin & Chronology of Clipper Ships	Bernard Berenson
The *Peking* Battles Cape Horn	Irving Johnson
The Queen Who Never Reigned	C Bradford Mitchell
The Romance of the Clipper Ships	Basil Lubbock
The Search for Speed Under Sail	Howard I Chapelle
The Tall Ships Pass	W L A Derby
The Slave Ship	Marcus Ridker
The Tea Clippers	David R MacGregor

The Western Ocean Packets	Basil Lubbock
The Windjammers	The Seafarers Time Life
The Young Sea Officers Sheet Anchor	Darcy Lever
Tonnage Measurement of Ships	Steamship Mutual
Trading Places: The East India Company and Asia	Anthony Farrington
United States Trade & Census Data	US Government
Wikipedia	
Wikimedia	

INDEX

100-A-1 Lloyd Register 235

A

A. D. Bordes 214, 226-7, 230-1, 233-4
Aaron Manby 178
Aberdeen 175, 177, 193-4
Abraham Lincoln 173
Abrolhos Islands 96
Acapulco 73, 77
Achilles heel 143, 186
Admiralty 189
Adriatic 20
aeroplane 240
Afghanistan 91
Africa 3-4, 13, 20-1, 48, 51, 54-8, 60, 64, 66, 73-4, 88, 100, 102, 104-5, 109
Age of Discovery 13, 18-19, 21, 55
Age of Enlightenment 73, 100
the Age of Enlightenment 73, 100
Age of Exploitation 74
Aguas Blancas 212
Agulhas current 4, 57
Alabama 104, 111
Alabama fever 111
Alaska 72-3
Albany 137
Albenia Boole 158
Albion 73, 138
alcohol 32, 97, 127, 136, 146
Aleppo 83
Alexander Hall & Sons 175, 177
Alfonso V 55
algal blooms 174
Algarve 63
Algiers 39
Algoa Bay 57
alluvial gold 169
Altair 224
Amazon 60, 100

Ambon 95
American bottoms 200
American Eagle 200
American South 87, 105, 111
American War of Independence 29, 129, 154
Amerigo Vespucci 61, 70
Amity 132
ammunition 102, 105, 130
Andalusia 25, 79
Andaman and Nicobar Islands 84
Anglo-American 14, 37, 39, 43, 108, 115, 129-31, 151
Anglo-Dutch 29-30, 96
Anglo-French 170
Anjer-Lor 218
Ann McKim 148, 151, 153
Annandale 178
Annus Mirabilis 145
Antarctica xv, 68, 73, 133
anti-meridian 76
antifoulant 191
Antilles 69
Antoine-Dominique Bordes 231-2
Anton Flettner 239
Antwerp 52, 75, 136, 209
Arabs 20, 52, 64, 66, 102
Aragon 49, 57
Archibald Russell 220, 222, 227, 235
Archipelago 20, 68, 133
Argentina 230
argosies 113
Arica 213
arid 173
Ariel 180
arms 15, 56, 77, 102, 105, 116, 120
aromatic spice 87, 95, 97
Arrow 34
Arthur H Clarke 249
ash 14

Asian 14, 18, 30, 33, 50, 52, 57, 61, 64, 66, 70, 75, 93, 124, 169
Assam 179
Atacama 212
Australasia 138
Australia ii, xv-xvi, 36, 45, 73, 117, 146, 148, 155, 164-6, 168-9, 174, 221-3, 235-7, 247
Australia II 245
Australian 104, 162, 164-6, 192, 198, 229, 235
Austria 140, 229
Austrian 140, 186
Austrian Empire 140
Auxiliary steamers 176
Azores 24, 104, 223
Aztecs 99

B

B. R. Mitchell 195, 203, 206-7, 211
back-freight 138, 192
Bahamas 60
bald-header 214, 221
Baltic 29, 83, 94, 178, 224, 230-1
Baltimore 37, 43, 109, 115, 136, 151, 224, 248
Baltimore clippers 37, 43, 115, 151, 248
Bangkok 192
Bangladesh 84
Bank of England 92
banking system 52, 55, 95
Bantam 98
Bantu 102
Baquendano 212
Barbary 38-40, 83
barges 133, 137, 185, 202
Baring Brothers & Co 125
Barque xvii, 118, 218, 220
barque-rigged 182
Bartholomeu Dias 55-6, 63, 65
Basil Lubbock 109, 115, 121, 123, 171, 213, 248-50
Batavia 84, 95-8
battened down 141
Battle of Plessey 35
Battle of the Medway 95
baubles 102
BBC 242
becalmed 213
beech 14
Belfast 225
Belgium 189
Bell & Brown 148
Bengal 84, 90-2
Benguela current 4, 56-7, 88
Benzoin 76

Bermuda 129
Bessemer 193, 196-7
binnacle 179
biosynthesis 154
birch 14
Black Ball Line 131-3, 138, 143, 164-5, 176
Black Death 49, 52
Black Sea 170
Blackwall 32, 35-6, 90
Bloody Mary 77
Bloom & Voss 223
bluff-bowed 89, 134
Bohea 86
Bolivia 73, 230
Bombay 84, 91, 192
Bonaventure 78
boom 8, 19-20, 30, 132, 136, 146-7, 155, 165, 167, 169-70, 183, 195-6, 199, 201, 226
Bosnia 178
Boston 39, 136, 142, 146, 157-8, 162, 167, 199, 201, 209
Boulton & Watt 187
bounties 226
Bounty 68
Bow 43
bowline 110
Brazil 62, 65-6, 88, 99-100, 105, 107-8
breechblock 190
Bremerhaven 218, 220, 230
British bottoms 33, 130, 146
British-built 33, 143, 227, 229
British Empire 92, 108, 186, 229
British government 82, 85, 87, 92-3, 116, 119-21, 124, 127, 129, 142, 171, 231
British Isles 4, 33, 134, 224
British Register Tonnage 132
Bronze Age 196
Brookes 106
bubonic plague 62
Bulk Carrier 242
Bund 125
bunkering 194, 212-13
Burma 84, 94, 176
Burmeister & Wain 197
bust 37, 167, 192
butter 142
Byzantium 54

C

cacao 62
Cadiz 71, 78, 189
Cairngorm 178-9
Calais 79

Calcutta 91, 171

Calicut 64-6

California 135, 146-7, 155-7, 159, 161-2, 164-5, 167, 169, 176-7, 186, 214, 221, 247

Californian goldfields 147

Callao 213

Camellia sinensis 154

Canada 62, 147, 165, 172, 178, 219-20, 224, 240

Canadian Arctic 191

canal 17, 44-5, 71, 99, 107-8, 127, 136-7, 147, 154, 171, 181, 185, 187-8, 192, 235

Canary Islands 60, 104

Cane sugar 104

Canton 84, 86, 113, 120, 123-6, 152-3, 177

Cape Agulhas 57, 239

Cape Horn xv, 18, 34, 45, 48, 57, 68, 77, 84, 147, 165, 177, 212-14, 221-3, 236-7

Cape Horners 172

Cape of Good Hope 2-4, 14, 32, 34, 51, 56-7, 59, 63, 65, 73, 75, 84, 88, 96, 148

Cape of Storms 65

Cape Otway 176

Cape-sized 239

Cape Town 88

Cape Verde Islands 62, 64, 102

capital goods 204

capital investment 178, 211

capitalism 35, 55, 74, 95, 186

Caravela lateena 21

carbon fibre 149

cardamom 85

cargo space 17, 29, 32, 40, 42, 75, 85, 96, 129-30, 133, 144-5, 179, 188-9, 212

Caribbean 61-2, 71, 76, 100, 104-5, 107

Carl 43, 108, 166, 175, 183, 228, 248

Carl C. Cutler 43, 108, 166, 175, 183

Carnatic Wars 91

Carolinas 104

Carreira da India 24

Casa da India 28

cassava 62

Castile 49, 57-8, 60

Ceiba 240-1

Celestial 50, 85, 87, 120-1, 127

Cement 191

Central America 77, 99, 102, 107

centreboards 110

Ceuta 54

Ceylon 85, 87, 91, 95, 127, 184

Champagne Glass Stern 43

Champion of the Seas 42, 149, 165-6, 171, 174, 179, 236

Charles I 66-7, 83

Charles II 85, 104

Charles II of England 85

Charles Lamb 86

Charleston 136

Charlotte Dundas 187

Charts and Sailing Directions 161-2

Chemical fertilisers 174

Chesapeake Bay 84, 109, 115

chickens 132

Chile 153, 173, 209, 212-13, 216, 228, 230-1

Chin Chin 121

China 18, 32, 47-52, 56-9, 69-70, 76, 82-8, 90-3, 113, 116, 118-28, 152-4, 172-3, 176-8, 189

China packets 152

Chincha Islands 172, 212

Chinese 33, 49-51, 64, 70, 76, 84-6, 93, 113, 116, 118-20, 123-4, 126-7, 152, 172, 177

Christian 19, 48, 62, 100, 121

Christianity 68, 121

Cidade da Porto 222

cinnamon 85, 95

circular boilers 192

Civil War 44, 111, 143, 147, 162, 169, 174-5, 179, 199-200, 208, 211

clipper built 114

Clipper ship 43, 115, 158, 247, 249

close-hauled 123

close-winded 202

cloth 84, 87, 105, 110

cloves 73, 85

Clyde River 183

Coal 213

coast goods 105, 108

coastal trade 174, 200, 224

coasting vessels 110

coffin brigs 129

coke 218

Colloony 177

Colombia 70, 76, 240

Colonial 171, 249

colony 30, 36, 62, 70, 76, 84, 88, 90-4, 98, 100, 103-4, 154, 165, 171, 184

Columbus 2, 18, 23, 47-8, 57-61, 63-4, 70, 99, 102, 104, 110, 135, 240

Comanche 149

committed suicide 172

compass deviations 179

compass irregularities 179

composite 44, 160, 176, 178-82, 184, 189, 208

compound 192, 194, 239

condensation 173

Congress 37, 39, 67, 106, 108, 155

Congress of Vienna 37

Connecticut 14

conquistadors 63

Constantinople 54, 188

Constellation 39

Constitution 39, 104

continental shelf 20, 57, 213

Coolie 172

Copper 213

copper sheathing 13, 177, 179, 189

copper sulphate 191

Coriolis effect 2-3

Corn Laws 116, 142, 147, 154, 186

Cornelisz 97

Cornwall 86, 127, 221

Coromandel 95

corrode 179

Costa Rica 240

Cotton 110-12

Cotton packets 111-12

cotton wad 190

Country trade 33, 93

County Cork 138

Courier 131-2

Cowes 122

cowhouse 132

Crab Bay 230

crankshaft 197

Creative destruction 185-6

Cretans 17

Crete 17

Crimean War 170

crop rotation 172

cross-channel 7, 218, 230

crossover 207

Crown Prince Wilhelm 221

Crown Princess Duchess Cecilie of Mecklenburg-
        Schwerin 221

crystallised ginger 86

Cuba 61, 172

customs duties 113

cutter brig 114

cutter built 114

Cutty Sark 180-1

cylindrical shell casings 190

D

Danes 126

Danzig 231

Daoguang 120

Das Kapital 186

David Brown 148

David McGregor 149

DDT 108

Deadrise 42, 134

Deccan Plateau 91

Defiance 157, 164

Delaware River 178

Delhi 91

deliquescent 213

Denmark 29, 119, 220

Dent & Company 123

depression 44, 169, 176, 224

diesel 197, 237, 239, 245

diggers 146, 164

DIN 229

Dirk Hartog 96

Disease 98, 100

displacement hulls 245

distillation 104, 152, 173

DNA 1, 238

Donald McKay 41-2, 51, 142, 148, 150, 157-9, 162-6, 203,
        219, 236

donkey engines 201, 208, 210, 230

Douglas fir 202

Dover 230

Down Easters 183-4, 199

Dramatic Line 133-4, 152

Dreadnought 28

Driver 189

droghers 133, 151

Duarte 55

duchess 221

duke of Medina Sidonia 79

duke of Parma 78-9

Dumbarton 225

Dutch 5, 9, 26, 28-30, 32, 35, 52, 57, 74-5, 82-3, 85, 87, 91-8,
        100, 126

E

E. K. Collins 134

earnest money 108

earthquakes 213

East 24-6, 28, 30-6, 38, 48-55, 64, 74-7, 81-5, 87-90, 92-4,
        96-8, 100, 102, 123-4, 130

East India 14, 30, 32-3, 35, 76-7, 82-5, 87, 89, 92-4, 97, 110-
        11, 123-4, 130, 155, 178

East Indiamen 26, 28, 30-6, 38, 40, 85, 88-90, 96, 119, 128,
        130, 134, 155, 176, 249

East Indies 2, 24, 28, 30, 64, 74, 76-7, 81, 98, 100, 130

East Pakistan 94

East River 178

Eastern Monarch 177, 179

ebonite 191

economic cataclysm 173

economic credos 142

Edinburgh University 123
Egypt 17, 188
Egyptians 17, 64
EIC 30-6, 82-92, 94-6, 98, 116, 119-21, 130
Elcano 23, 68, 189
Eleanor A. Percy 200
Eleanor Creesy 162
Eleanor of Viseu 60
electricity 197, 239, 245
electrolysis 179
Eli Whitney 111
Elizabeth Bonaventure 78
Elizabeth I 26, 34, 77, 80, 83-4, 94
Elizabethan 71, 73, 104, 247
Emigration 140
emissions-conscious 238
Emperor 51, 73
Empire 26, 34, 48-50, 62, 65, 73, 77, 80, 83, 87, 91-2, 94,
    99-100, 108, 110
Enfield rifle 121
English 10, 24, 26-30, 32, 34-5, 38-40, 70-5, 77, 79-90, 93-
    6, 122-3, 146, 176-8, 186, 188-93
English Channel 7, 32, 38, 77, 89, 122, 180, 188, 218, 228
Englishman 72, 153, 165
Enlightenment 19, 73, 100, 110
Enoch Train 158
Erie Canal 136-7, 147, 154
Euro-Asian 18
Europe 25-6, 46-9, 52-4, 59-60, 62-3, 70, 74-7, 93, 95, 98-
    100, 103-5, 137-8, 140-2, 183-4, 211-14
explosive shells 15, 189
extreme clippers 43, 153

F

F. Laeisz & Co. 214, 216, 223, 231
Factories 119
factory ships 119, 128
Falls of Clyde 214, 220-1
Falmouth 129, 221
Famine 138
fast sailers 112
FDR 127
Feeder services 136
fennel 85
Ferdinand 18, 48, 58-9, 66-7, 107, 227-8
Ferdinand de Lesseps 107
Ferdinand Laeisz 228
Ferdinand Magellan 18, 48, 66-7
fertiliser 45, 88, 138, 173, 183, 212, 226, 233, 235
Fiery Cross 180
Fifteen Miles on the Erie Canal 137
Finland 222

fire hazard 142
Fire Island Light 157
fireships 79
first-class passengers 132
First World War xvi, 15, 44, 46, 194, 199-203, 206, 212,
    222-3, 227, 229-31, 235, 241
five-masted 46, 201, 210, 216, 218, 230-2
five-masters 216, 218, 225, 231
flat floors 43, 133, 144, 178
Flora 218, 230
Florence Nightingale 170
Flying Cloud 41, 159, 162-4, 179
fore-and-aft 1, 4, 6, 8-12, 20-1, 25, 29-31, 43, 46, 56, 109,
    114, 128-9, 184, 230
Foresight 28
Forth and Clyde Canal 187
forward buoyancy 145
Four-masted barque xvii, 220
four-master 200, 221, 232
France 10, 31, 34-5, 38-9, 49, 62, 73, 76, 84, 107-8, 111, 214,
    218, 223-7, 229-34
France I 218, 225
France II 216, 218, 226
Francisco de Almeida 66
Francisco Pelsaert 96
Franklin Roosevelt 127
free trade 116, 120, 154
free traders 130
fruit 83, 113, 129
Fujianese 86
fully-rigged 9, 216
furs 126

G

Gabriel Snodgrass 90
Gabrielle d-Ali 227
gaff 30, 114, 200
Galleasses 19
Galleon 25-7, 79
galvanic action 179, 190
gammon knees 128
Garrick 134
Garthpool 220-1
GDP 49, 241
geared turbines 194
generator 230
Genoa 58-9, 220, 229
Genoese 57, 70
geodesics 165
geology 212
Geopolitics 48
George Thompson & Co. Ltd 193

George W. Wells 200
Georgia 104
Gerald Graham 191, 249
German xvi, 46, 75-6, 186, 193, 212, 215, 218, 221-2, 225, 227, 229-32, 235-6
ginseng root 126
Glasgow xvi, 190, 194, 196, 218, 220, 224-6, 230, 232
glass fibre-reinforced plastic 242
Globalisation 248
go aloft 136
Gokstadskipet 22
Gold 70, 155, 164, 198, 212, 247
Golden Hind 27, 72, 81
Golden Lion 78
Gothenburg 223
Governor Ames 200
Grace Harwar 227, 235
grain xv, 142-3, 147, 154, 184, 186, 192, 199, 211, 221-4, 235
grain trade 223-4, 235
Grand Banks 14
Great American II 153
Great Britain 32-3, 37, 39-40, 93-4, 107-11, 115-16, 129-31, 145-7, 154, 175-8, 182-4, 195, 202-8, 224-7, 229-31
great circle xv, 3, 165
Great Circle 165
the Great Fire of London 145
Great Fish River 57, 64
Great Grain Races 221
Great Lakes 62, 136, 224
Great Republic 51, 159-60, 166, 170, 219, 236
Great South Land 48, 96, 214
Great Southern Ocean 162, 236
Great Western 132-3, 169
Great Western Plains 169
Greece 229
Greek Archipelago 20
greenhouse gases 242
Greenock 190, 225, 232
Greenwich 62, 67, 181
Greyhounds of the Sea 43, 248
greyhounds of the seas 166
GRP 242
Guanay cormorant 172
Guangzhou 84
Guano 172
Guinea 55-6, 64, 102-3
Gujarati 102
Gulf of Guinea 56
Gulf Stream 2, 4, 79, 135
Gum 247
gunwales 8, 132, 233
Gustaf Erikson xv, 248
gyroscopic spin 190

H

Hamburg xvi, 164, 189, 209, 220, 223, 229, 231, 236
Hamburg Port Museum 223
hand-to-hand 61, 88, 116
hand weavers 87
Hanseatic League 75, 83
hardwood 14, 177-9
Harlequin 122
Harvard 156
Havana 153, 172
Hawaii 214
Hebe 34
Hellenistic 47
Henry Eckford 148
Henry Hudson 83
Henry Moorsom 179
Henry VIII 13, 29, 63, 76, 80
hens 132
Hero 133
Herodotus 17
Herzogin Cecilie 215, 220-1, 235-6
hickory 14
hides 102
high-farming 172
high maintenance 145
high tensile 193
highly mineralised 212
Himalayas 87
Hindu 66, 91, 94
Hispaniola 60, 62, 102
Hittites 196
HMS Agamemnon 178
HMS Erebus 191
HMS Jackal 190
HMS Triton 190
Hogging 43
Holland 189, 229
Holy Roman Empire 26, 34, 49, 62, 73, 80, 87, 94
Hong Kong 120, 124-5, 154, 186, 209
Hong Kong & Shanghai Banking Corporation 125
Honolulu 164, 214, 221
Horn of Antarctica 68
horsepower 187, 194
Hougomont 235
Houqua 152
Howard Chapelle 35
Howland & Aspinwall 153-4
Howqua 126
Hudson River 137
Hugh Willoughby 83
Humboldt current 4
hydrofoils 245
hydrogen 239

I

Iberian Peninsula 12, 48, 53, 55
Immigrants 139
IMO 242
impact detonators 190
India 3-4, 13-14, 28-30, 32-3, 35, 47-9, 63-6, 82-90, 92-5,
    97-8, 110-11, 119, 122-4, 126-7, 176-9
Indian Mutiny 121, 170-1
Indian Ocean 4, 35, 51-2, 57, 64-6, 88, 102, 148
Indian opium 87, 116
Indians 70, 92, 102-3, 110, 116, 121, 156, 212
Indonesia 29, 32, 97-8
Indonesian archipelago 48, 95
Indus Basin 91
industrial entrepreneurs 211
Industrial Revolution 19, 45-6, 100, 135, 146, 154, 186, 188,
    196, 203, 236, 245
industrialisation 176, 195
industrialised shipbuilding 226
influenza 62
inhumanity 173
Initial Public Offering 84
intellectual property 28-9, 55, 74-5, 86
International Maritime Organization 242
iodine 212
Iquique 212-13, 232
Ireland 4, 58, 79, 115, 129, 138, 140-2, 146, 186, 248-9
Irish 135, 139, 188
iron-hulled 178, 194, 210-11, 221, 232
ironclads 157-8, 200
Isaac Webb 148, 153, 158
Isaac Wright 131
Isabella 49, 58-9
Isambard Kingdom Brunel 189
Islamic 47, 66
Italian 2, 20, 61, 70, 191, 231
Italy 20, 75, 140, 170, 191, 222, 229

J

J. Bell & Co 231
Jack Spurling 41, 149-51, 163
Jacob Bell 148
Jacques Cartier 62
James Baines 149-51, 164-5, 171, 174-5
James Cook 96
James I 81, 103
James Matheson 123-4
James Monroe 131-2, 143
James Roosevelt 127
James Watt 187
Jamesina 121
Jamestown 103

Jamsetjee Jejeebhoy 124
Japan 4, 48, 69-70, 73, 76, 229, 239, 242
Japanese 70, 98, 238
Jardine Matheson 121, 123-5, 178, 248
Jeremy Bentham 190
jibe 201
jiggermast 215
Joh C. Tecklenborg 230
John Company 30, 34
John Dryden 145
John Ena 220-1
John Fowles 183, 237, 248
John Prentiss 162
John W. Griffiths 148, 152, 157
Joseph Conrad 116, 192
Joseph H. Davis 200
Joseph Maudsley 188
Joseph Schumpeter 186
Joshua Patten 170
Josiah Creesy 162
Julius Caesar 17, 22
Jutepolis 220-1

K

Karl Marx 186
Kashmir 91
Kerala 64
kerosene 194, 214
Kevlar 149
Khozikode 64
kidnapped 114, 172
King George III 171
King Henry VII 59
King Philip II 73, 76-8
Kobenhavn 218
Kommodore Johnsen 224
Korea 4
Kruzenshtern 220, 224, 231
Kurt xvi, 220, 222

L

lacquerware 86
Lade AS 240
Lady Grant 177
Lake Superior 137
Lancashire 147
the land of the free 142, 186
Landlords 139
Lanrick 122-3
Lars Bruzelius 167, 182, 210, 219-20, 225, 249
Las Islas Filipinas 76
Lascars 33

The Last Grain Race xv, 222
later steel 15, 160, 208
Lawhill 220-1, 227, 235
Lawrence Hargrave 164
Le Havre 136
leguminous 172
length-to-beam ratio 23, 110, 114, 146, 153, 160, 162, 177
letters of marque 80-1, 84
Levant 82-4, 189
liberal revolutions 140
Liberty 194, 245
light airs 3, 6, 44, 56, 176-8
lighters 177, 214
Lightning 149-50, 165-6, 171, 174
Lin Zexu 120, 125
Lindbergh 131
Liner 37, 130
lingua franca 70, 76
Lisbon 4, 24, 28, 57-8, 65, 75, 104, 189, 222
Liverpool xv, 4, 42, 131-8, 141-3, 157, 164-6, 175, 191,
  209, 225
Lloyds of London 109, 209
Lloyds Register 154, 193, 229
logbooks 161
Lomas 213
lorchas 117, 123
Lord of the Isles 182
Louisiana 104
Low Countries 22
Luderitz 57
Lusitania 194

M

Macao 153
Macau 54, 70, 76
mace (clove petals) 85
Mactan 68
Madagascar 3, 35, 73
Madeline 226
Madras 91
Madre de Deus 84
Madre de Dios 24
Maersk Tankers 239
Magdalene Vinnen II 224
Magellan 18, 23-4, 48-9, 53, 66-70, 72, 77, 189
Magellanic Clouds 69
Magellanic penguin 69
Maine 14, 178, 183, 199-200, 220, 224
maize 62, 103
Makassar 95
malaria 62, 107
Malawi 102

Malay 68, 93, 117
Malindi 4, 64-5
Malta 188
Maluku Islands 67
Manchester 92
manifestly equipped 108
manila rope 208
Manuel I 57, 63-6, 94
maple 14
Mar Pacifico 68
Marco Polo 47, 149-50, 165
Marconi 131
Maria Rickmers 218, 225
Mariehamn 222, 230-1, 234
marine growth 179
marine historian 34, 229
Mariners 18, 187
maritime law 81
Mark Beaufoy 153
market failure 142
Martian 69
Martin Luther 76
Mary I 83
Mary Patten 170
Maryland 104
Massachusetts 14, 158
Matthew Fontaine Maury 161
matting 51, 116
Mauretania 194
Mauritius 35
Maya 99
Mayflower 131
McIness 191
mechanised weaving 87
Mediterranean 8, 17, 20, 38, 47-8, 52, 54, 60, 62, 83, 110,
  188-9
Medium 41
medium clippers 7, 43, 157, 160, 164, 170
Melbourne 42, 163-4, 166, 176, 194, 209, 235-6
mercantilism 186
mercantilist 86, 110, 116, 119, 130, 146-7, 186, 208
Merchant Adventurers 82-3
mercury 99
Mersey River 137
Metallurgists 185
metallurgy 192, 211
metalworking 211
metric 229
Mexican 44, 71, 147
Mexican-American War 44
Mexico 62, 99, 138, 156
Middle Ages 110
middle class 30, 55, 75, 95, 186

Middle East 51, 102, 170
Middle Kingdom 76
middle passage 105, 108, 112
Midwesterners 156
milk 132
millennia 1, 19, 52, 172, 186, 217, 241
millennium xvi, 17-18, 102
Mineral oil 194
minerals 173, 187, 213
Ming 49-50, 52, 55, 88, 91
Mississippi 42, 104, 112, 133, 136
Mitsui OSK Lines 239
Mneme 220, 222
Mobile 136
mobile warehouses 188
modus operandi 74, 158, 234
Mogul 91
Molasses 103, 107
Moluccas 66-7, 95
monarchical capitalist 64
Mongol 91
Monopoly 95, 249
Monsoon 3
Montevideo 108
Moors 58
Moorsom 13, 179, 183
Moravian 191
Morocco 54, 66
Moshulu xv-xvii, 220, 222, 227, 235
Mother of all Parliaments 92
mountain of silver 99
Mozambique 3-4, 51, 64, 88, 102
MS Combi Dock III 223
Mughal 91, 110
Mumbai 84
munitions 45, 173, 183
Muntz metal 191
Muscovy 82-4
Muslim 51-2, 66, 94, 110
Mutiny 121, 170-1

N

Namibia 57
Napoleon 34, 37, 142
Natchez 153
Nathan Allen 121-2, 249
Nathaniel Palmer 133-4, 148, 151-4, 160, 170
nautically decadent 175
naval blockades 113
Navigation Acts 14, 33, 40, 44, 116, 130, 147, 154, 174, 176-7, 181, 184, 186, 202, 206
navigational errors 179

Nawab 91
Ne Plus Ultra 143
Neath 218
Negroes 102-3
Nelson Chequer 32
Netherlands 29-30, 35, 55, 62, 73, 75-6, 78, 82, 84-5, 87, 94-5, 100, 120
New Amsterdam 154
New Caledonia 218
New Hampshire 14, 157
new measurement 179
New Orleans 42, 136
New South Wales 213
New World 53, 60, 62-3, 76-7, 81, 103, 105, 159, 184, 198
New York 43, 108, 115, 129, 131-3, 135-8, 143, 146, 148, 151, 156-8, 160, 164-6, 178, 199
New Zealand 169, 176
Newburyport 158
Newspapers 108
Nicolau Coelho 65
Nile 8, 17, 20
Nitrate 212-13, 233, 249
nitre 88
nitrogen-consuming 212
Nizam of Hyderabad 91
Nomex 149
Non est finis 237
Nord 232
North American 59, 99, 103, 107, 224
North Atlantic gyre 2, 4, 59, 135
north-east monsoon 4, 118, 153
North Equatorial Current 135
north-flowing current 3, 68, 213
North Pole 56
North Sea 75, 94, 188, 234
Northern Ireland 140
Northern Light 157
Northwest Passage 191
Nova Scotia 129, 158
Novel 103

O

Oak 13
obelisk xv, 214
Occident 184
ocean greyhounds 146
Ocean gyres 2-3
Ocean Monarch 142
Ohio Valley 224
Old China 86
old measure 153, 160, 226
Old World 38, 62, 146

Olivebank 220-1, 227, 235
Olmecs 99
Olympic 216
open hearth 197
Opium 113, 115-16, 118-25, 127, 186, 189, 247, 249
opium clippers 113, 115-16, 119, 123, 128, 249
Order of Santiago 63
Oresund 29
Orient 34, 37, 48, 59, 84, 92, 110, 171, 213, 248
Oriental 4, 34, 48, 93, 154, 174
Ormuz 75
Orthodox 48
Oshima 242
Ottoman 48, 54-5, 63, 65, 83
Our World in Data 241
overbuild 167, 169
oxygen 213

P

Pacific 4, 48, 59, 62, 68-9, 73, 76-7, 100, 132, 171, 200, 209, 214, 221, 231
Pacific Ocean gyre 4, 77
Pacific Railroad 171
packet rats 135-6, 164
paddle-wheel 185
paddlewheels 188
Padua 218, 220, 224, 231, 236
Pakistan 84, 92, 94, 176
Palmer Archipelago 133
Palmer Land 133
Palmyra 229
Pamir 220, 223, 231, 235, 237
Panama Canal 45, 233, 235
Panamax 239
Pangani 218, 231
Pantaloon 122
Parma 78-9, 227, 231, 235
Parsi 124
Passat 220, 223, 231, 235, 237
Patagonia 218, 230
patent winches 208
patents 180, 191
pau-brasil 62
Paul Jones 152
Pazhou Island 119
Pearl 119, 122, 125
Pearl River 119, 125
Peiho 227, 231
Peking 220, 223, 231, 249
Pelican 72, 239
Pelikan 231
Pellworm 231

Penang 231, 235
Peninsular and Oriental Steam Navigation Company 174
Pennsylvania 194
Pepper 76
Pera 231
Perim 227, 231
perishables 113
Persia 83
Peru 55, 73, 76, 99, 102-3, 172, 212-13
Philadelphia xvi, 136, 222, 224
Philippines 18, 26, 48, 67-8, 73, 76-7, 99-100, 103, 124
Phillip II 26
Phoenicians 17, 64
phosphorous 197
Pilgrim 184
pilot boats 43, 113
pilot cutters 110
Pinnas 227, 231
Pinta 60
Pirna 231
Pisagua 213, 221, 231
Pisco 213
piston 187-8, 197
Pitaya 240
Pitlochry 231
Placilla 231
planking 8, 13, 17, 22, 175-6
Plymouth 71
Point Spencer xv
Poland 231
Polymnia 220-1
Pommern 220, 222, 227, 229-31, 235, 249
Ponape 220, 222, 229, 231, 235
Pondicherry 84
Pope Alexander VI 62
Pope Julius II 4
Pope Sixtus V 73
poppy bowl 119
Porcelain 86
Port xv, 33, 57, 137, 223, 236, 248
Port Alfred 57
Port Lincoln xv, 236
Portsmouth, New Hampshire 157
Portugal 4, 13, 28-9, 35, 49, 52-8, 60-3, 66-7, 73-7, 81-2, 87, 94, 99-100, 105, 107-8
Portuguese 4, 12-13, 21, 23-6, 28-9, 55, 57-9, 62, 64-7, 69-70, 73-7, 84-5, 95, 100, 102-4
potassium 88, 172
potassium nitrate 88
potato blight 138
Potosi 216, 218, 227, 230-1, 233, 236
potteries 86
prahus 110, 116-17, 123

precious stones 86
preservative 88
President 39
pressed 32, 106, 114, 156
Prester John 48, 55, 66
Preussen 45, 216-18, 227-8, 230-1
Preussen II 45, 216-18, 227-8, 230-1
Prevailing westerlies 3
Prince de Neuchatel 115
Prince Henry the Navigator 21, 54-5
Princess Catherine 85
Priwall 231, 236
proa 117
propeller-driven 188-9
protectionism 186
Protestant 26, 29, 62, 71, 73, 76, 81-2, 87, 94
proto-triangular trade 102
Prussia 140, 221, 230
Pudel 228-9
pyramids 102

Q

Qing Dynasty 120
Qing emperor 120
quadruple-expansion 194
Queen Elizabeth 49, 72-3, 80, 94
Queen Victoria 93, 120, 171
Queensberry 178

R

R. C. Rickmers 216, 218, 227
Race-built 27
radiata pine 138
Rainbow 34, 78, 148, 153
Rangoon 192
Red Jacket 157, 166, 174
Red Rover 116
Red Sea 17, 20, 51
Red Star 133, 143
Red Swallow Tail Line 143
reef 89, 166, 172, 176, 218
Register of the Opium Fleet 115
Regulated Slave Trade 106
Renaissance 68, 77, 100, 110
Replica 24-5, 69, 79, 97, 115
Reunion 35
revenue cutters 113-14
revolution 19, 35, 37-8, 40, 45-6, 62, 100-1, 115, 131, 135,
    145-6, 154, 185-6, 196-7, 217
Rhode Island 14
Richard Chancellor 83
Richard Henry Dana Jr. 156

Richard Wagner 227
rifled barrel 15, 190
Rigging down 33
River Plate 68
riveted iron 173, 178
Roanoke Island 30, 84
Roaring Forties xv
Rob Roy 177
Robert Carter OAM xvii
Robert Clive 35, 84, 91-2
Robert Fortune 86
Robert Hilgendorf 230
Robert Waterman 148, 153
Roller reefing 181
Roman 26, 29, 34, 47, 49, 59, 61-2, 73, 76, 80, 82, 87, 94,
    100, 137
Roman Catholic Church 29
Romance of the Seas 179
Roscius 134
Royal African Company 104
Royal Institute of Naval Architects 192
Royal Navy 6, 35-40, 85, 90, 92, 96, 114, 116, 120-1, 130,
    153, 177-8
Royal Yacht Squadron 122
Rudolf Diesel 197
Rum 104
Runners 123
running their easting down 166, 248
Russell & Co 218, 220, 232
Russell & Company 115, 123, 125-7, 152, 154
Russia 83, 140, 170, 224
Russian Federation 231

S

Sacramento River 156
saffron 85
Sagres 55
Saigon 192, 218
SAILCARGO INC 240
sailing barges 133
Saint Lawrence River 62
Sal 137
salt cod 107
saltpetre 88, 231
Samuel H. Pook 148
Samuel Hall 157
Samuel Hartt Pook 156-7, 164, 166
Samuel Moore Pook 157
Samuel Russell 126, 156
San Felipe 82
San Francisco 155-7, 163-4, 169-71, 209, 221
San Francisco Shipping Co 221

San Pedro 221
Sandy Hook 157
Santa Maria 60, 76
Savannah 136
Scandinavia 22
scented wood 86
Schomberg 175-7
schooners 109, 114-15, 122, 151, 160, 200-2
Scientific Revolution 100
Scotland 175, 187, 190
Scottish Maid 177
screw-driven 178
sea time 177
Sea Witch 153, 156-7, 172
seal skins 126
seamanship xv, 61, 71, 77, 112, 118, 123, 148, 215, 248
search and seizure 108
Seattle 239
Sebastian Cabot 83
Second Opium War 120-1, 127
Sedov 220, 224, 235
Serampore 84
Serica 180
Setubal 63
Sevastopol 170
Seven United Provinces 94
Seville 61, 69
Sewall 178
Shakespearean 134
shallops 113
shallow draft 51, 96, 110, 136
shallow seas 14, 107, 113, 116, 118
Shanghai 125, 177, 209
shanghaiing 164
shark fins 126
Sheer 43
Sheerness 95
Sheridan 134
Shewan & Company 127
shipbuilding 13-14, 29-30, 32-3, 36-7, 44, 90, 94, 167-9, 174-6, 198-9, 202-4, 210-11, 224, 226-7, 247-9
Shipping interest 89
ships of the line 109, 154
Siddons 134
Sidney Pollard 227, 229, 249
Siemens 193, 196
Silk 47, 49, 54
Silk Road 47, 49, 54
Silver 93, 99
Sines 63
Singapore 218
Sir Francis Baring 125
Sir Francis Drake 26, 29, 49, 70-2, 104

Sir John Burroughs 24
Sir John Franklin 191
Sir John Hawkins 26, 28, 71, 103-4
Sir Lancelot 180
Sir Robert Peel 143
Sir Walter Raleigh 30, 62, 84, 103
Skagerrak Strait 236
Slave trade 37, 102, 106
slaver 39, 105, 108
Slavery 101
sloop 114, 133, 189
sluggards 236
small arms 105, 116
Smallpox 62
Smart Green Shipping Alliance 239
Smith and Dimon 153
smooth-bore 189
smugglers 110, 113, 119
Sobroam 180
soccer 215-16
Sofala 65
softwood 177-9
solar energy 16, 185, 238
South America xv, 2-4, 45, 58, 60, 62, 64, 68, 76, 99-100, 138, 161, 173, 189, 213
South Atlantic gyre 2, 4, 57, 64-5, 88
South Australia xv, 36, 222, 235-7
South East Trades xvii
South Orkney Islands 133
South Pass 156
South Street Museum 223
South Street Pier 136
Southampton 178
Southern Cross 70
Sovereign of the Seas 148-9, 164-6
Soviet Union 224
Spanish 12, 19-20, 23, 25-8, 30, 34, 48-9, 52, 58-60, 62, 66-7, 71-4, 76-81, 83-4, 99-100
spheroid 165
Spice Islands 4, 47-8, 66-8, 73, 76, 82, 84-5, 87, 95-6, 98
spinning jenny 110
Spitsbergen 83
spontaneous combustion 142, 192
squashed sphere 165
squatters 164
Sri Lanka 91
SS Aberdeen 193-4
SS Great Britain 178, 189
St Vincent Gulf 237
Stag Hound 159, 162
Standing rigging 11
state of war 81
state-sanctioned piracy 84

stateroom 147

Steam 17, 44, 143, 174, 183, 185, 187-8, 191, 193-5, 198, 204-5, 212, 249

steam engine 44-5, 187, 191-4, 196

steam power 7, 16, 101, 111, 185, 197, 226

steam tugs 169, 208

steam turbine 194

steamships 11, 13, 45, 64, 143, 166, 176, 178, 181, 184, 188, 202, 204-8, 210-12, 233-6

Steel 15, 44, 143, 177-9, 185, 189, 191, 195, 197, 202-4, 208, 218, 220, 224, 237

Stern 43

stock feed 107

Strait of Gibraltar 20, 83

Straits of Magellan 72

Straits of Malacca 61, 164

stranded 218, 221, 230

submarine 218

subsidies 184, 225-7, 231-2, 234

Suez 44-5, 107, 127, 162, 171, 174, 181, 183, 188, 192, 204, 210, 226, 235, 239

Suez Canal 44-5, 127, 162, 171, 181, 183, 188, 192, 204, 210, 226, 235

Sugar 103-4, 107

Sunda Strait 96

Sunderland 225

super barque 230

Superior 131, 137

Surprise 157

Swallowtail 133

Sweden xvi, 29, 119, 222-3, 236

sweet potatoes 62

sycee silver 116, 119

Sydney 149, 164

Sylph 118, 177

Symbiosis 195, 197

syphilis 62

Syria 83, 229

T

Tacking 6

Taiping Rebellion 120

Taitsing 180

tall ships xvi, 209, 249

The Tall Ships Pass 209, 249

Taltal 212

Tamil Nadu 84

Tanzania 102

Tar 191, 248

Tasmania 143, 247

Tate & Lyle 104

Tate Gallery 104

Tavistock 71

Tayleur 177

Tea 84, 154, 157, 176, 180, 249

Tea clippers 157, 176, 249

tea races 149

tea trade 84-5, 98, 154, 156, 164, 169, 174, 176-7, 181

telegraph 147

Tempest 179

Teremba Reef 218

Terra Australis Incognita 48

Texas 104, 194

Thames 30, 32, 90, 95, 181

Theaceae 154

Thermopylae 180, 236

Thirteen Factories 119

Thomas Newcomen 187

Thomas W. Lawson 201

three-decker 144

three-legged course 104

three-masted topsail schooner 240

time value of money 17, 101, 130

Times 154, 221, 247

Titania 180

Tobacco 103

Tomatoes 62

Tonnage 12, 132, 250

tooling 211

Topophilia 212

trade deficit 86, 118

Trade Winds 3

Train & Co 136

Transatlantic 147, 150

Transvaal 155

Treaty of Ghent 39, 115, 131

Treaty of Nanking 120

Treaty of Tordesillas 4, 55, 61, 63, 67, 73-4, 76, 84, 87, 94, 99-100, 105

treaty ports 120

triangular trade 102, 104-5

Trieste 191

Trinidad 23, 172

trinkets 105

triple expansion 193

Tripoli 39

tropical diseases 14, 98

tropical waters 61, 179, 190

Tsar Ivan IV 83

tsunamis 213

tubular boilers 191

Tudor 129

Tunis 39

Turkey 20, 83, 113, 126, 196

Turkey Company 83

turmeric 85
two-watch system 233
Two Years before the Mast 156
typhoon 123

U

Ultramax 242
Undersea cables 147
Union 224, 232
United Kingdom 4, 194, 206, 209, 222, 225-7, 235
United States 14, 36-40, 44, 99-100, 108, 110-11, 114-15, 121-2, 126, 129-31, 136-8, 140-2, 145-7, 171-2, 198-200
University of Tokyo 239
US Navy 114, 157-8
Uzbekistan 91

V

vanilla 62
Vasco Balboa 76
Vasco da Gama 13, 47, 60, 63, 65-6, 88
Venetian 48, 53-4, 75
Venice 47, 52, 54, 59, 65, 75, 83
Venus 69, 108
Vera Cruz 73
Vereenigde Oost Indische Compagnie 30
Vermont 14
Verrazzano 62
vibration 44-5, 184, 191, 202, 211, 228, 236
Viceroyalty of New Spain 99
Viceroyalty of Peru 99
Victoria 23-5, 68-9, 79, 93, 120, 164, 171, 176
Viking 22, 220, 223, 235
VindSkip 240
Virginia 103-4, 107
VOC 30, 35, 82, 84, 87, 94-8
vulcanising 191

W

W. B. Thompson 232
W. L. A. Derby 209
Wales 39, 213
Wanderer 109
Warley 33
Warren Delano 126-7
Wartsila 242
water xv, 1-4, 7-8, 16-20, 41-4, 67-8, 89-90, 101, 145, 177-8, 185, 187, 213, 236, 245
water frame 110
water mills 101
Waterline 42
waterlogged 177

watermills 185
watertight 33, 51, 90, 182, 224
Waterwitch 177
Wavertree 178, 221
Wearing 6
weather window 88-9
Weatherliness 5
went missing 142
West 2, 4, 14, 25, 38, 48-51, 54, 60, 62, 81, 91-2, 99-100, 102-5, 110-11, 130
West African 54, 64, 103
West Bengal 84, 91-2
West Cork 139
West Indies 2, 14, 25, 38, 48, 60, 62, 81, 99-100, 103, 110, 114, 130
Western frontier 14, 44, 129
Western ocean packets 4, 32, 37-8, 41, 110, 112, 128-9, 132, 134, 143, 178, 250
western plains 137, 154, 169
whale oil 164, 194, 214
Whampoa 86, 119
Wharf between two seas 75
wheat xv, 45, 168-9, 214, 220, 223, 237
wherries 113
White Diamond Line 142, 158
white oak 160, 202
white pine 14
White Star Line 166, 193
Whitehaven 225
whooping cough 62
William Bligh 68
William Dalrymple 92
William H. Webb 148, 224
William James 34
William Jardine 123-4
William L. White 200
William Low 152
Wind Challenger Project 239
Windjammer xvii, 16, 45, 209-10, 214, 220, 224-7, 233
Winterhude 235
wire 11, 182, 208
Wire 182
Woodrow Wilson xvi
Woods Hole 190
wool 45, 166, 168, 181, 192, 211, 214, 220
Workington 225
workshop of the world 154
Wreck Coast 176
wrought iron 90, 160, 211, 220
Wyoming 156, 200

Y

yachts 6, 113, 245
Yankee 200
Yellow fever 107
Yerba Buena 155
Yokohama 239

Yongle 49-52
Youth 192

Z

Zheng He 49-51, 53, 64
zinc 86, 190-1